Norman Foster
Buildings and Projects
of Foster Associates
1978–1985

About this book

This book and its sister volume took shape during a series of design sessions, involving Norman Foster, Otl Aicher and myself, that took place either at Otl Aicher's büro in Rotis, West Germany, or at a studio in Wiltshire. The first of these meetings – which also included the writer Chris Abel – took place in Rotis in February 1987. It lasted only two days but it was here, under Otl's clear guiding hand, that the concept for this series of volumes was established.

Our aim was to try and explain the full process of design; to show the inspiration, development and exploration of ideas that underlies each project using, wherever possible, only the original sketches, drawings and models by which their design was progressed. An open-ended series of volumes was proposed to allow each project the space it required. Our initial programme identified four volumes in which projects would be grouped to show how ideas and themes develop over a period of time. Unsurprisingly, this fell into a more or less chronological sequence, but liberties have been taken where 'family' ties were strong.

Like the architecture it explores, this book is the outcome of a more extended team effort than might first be apparent. A full list of those involved 'behind the scenes' is given with the credits at the back of this edition, but there are those whose efforts require special mention. My sincerest thanks must first be extended to Norman Foster for his untiring and sympathetic assistance during the preparation of this book, and for his generosity in making available his extensive collection of original material. Many members of Foster Associates, their consultants and clients, past and present, have given generously of their time and advice; Birkin Haward and Loren Butt, associates no longer with the office, have been especially helpful. Each of the contributors has added his or her own enthusiasms and interests. My thanks to Gordon Graham and Jack Zunz for their personal contributions, given, no doubt, when their time would have been better spent on more important matters.

Most importantly, and I know Norman will agree with me, my thanks to Otl Aicher. His generosity of spirit, his kindness, friendship and enthusiasm have been a constant stimulus and support. For once the old cliché has to hold true: without him these books would not have been possible.

Ian Lambot, Hong Kong, September 1988

Volume 1
Norman Foster
Buildings and Projects
of Foster Associates
1964-1971
Ernst & Sohn 1990

Volume 2
Norman Foster
Buildings and Projects
of Foster Associates
1971-1978
Ernst & Sohn 1989

Volume 3
Norman Foster
Buildings and Projects
of Foster Associates
1978-1985
Ernst & Sohn 1989

Volume 4
Norman Foster
Buildings and Projects
of Foster Associates
1982-1989
Ernst & Sohn 1990

Volume 3
1978–1985

Norman Foster

Buildings and Projects
of Foster Associates

with contributions by

Gordon Graham
Chris Abel
Penny Sparke
Jack Zunz
Tim Ostler
Otl Aicher
Norman Foster
Colin Davies
Hugh D. R. Baker
Patrick Hannay

edited by
Ian Lambot

Ernst & Sohn

Designed by Otl Aicher

First published in Hong Kong in 1989
by Watermark Publications

Copyright © 1989 Foster Associates, London

Copyright © 1989 Wilhelm Ernst & Sohn
Verlag für Architektur und technische
Wissenschaften, Berlin
(for the Federal Republic of Germany, Austria
and Switzerland)

All rights reserved. No part of this book may be reproduced in any form without written permission of the publisher.

'A Project Diary' by Patrick Hannay is reprinted from *The Architects' Journal* by courtesy of the author and The Architectural Press Ltd.

Typeset in Rotis 45 by Druckhaus Maack GmbH & Co. KG, Lüdenscheid
Colour separation by Evergreen Colour Separation (Scanning) Company Ltd, Hong Kong
Printed by Everbest Printing Company Ltd, Hong Kong

ISBN 3-433-02113-9

Contents

8	Gordon Graham	Foreword
10	Chris Abel	From Hard to Soft Machines
20		Great Portland Street Office
28–61	Penny Sparke	Architecture in Miniature
28		Furniture Systems: from Hille to Renault
42		The Tecno System
62	Jack Zunz	Architecture and Technology
68		Whitney Development
74	Otl Aicher	A Tree-house
76		Humana Competition
94	Norman Foster	Flight 347
98		Students' Union
102		Billingsgate Market
112–255		The New Headquarters for Hongkong Bank
128		Competition Scheme
148		Chevron Scheme
160	Hugh D. R. Baker	Fung Shui: Applied Ecology Chinese Style
162		Transition
174		Construction
188		Final Scheme
208	Patrick Hannay	A Project Diary
216		Structure
220		Cladding
226		Modules
232		Services
236		Interior Systems
240	Norman Foster	Handrails
242		Interiors
252	Colin Davies	Conclusion
256		Foster Associates 1978-1985
258		Project Profiles
262		Bibliography
264		Credits

Foreword
by Gordon Graham

Hong Kong, February 1981. As the architectural advisor to the Hongkong Bank, I was picking my way through the late afternoon traffic with Norman Foster to take leave of Michael Sandberg, the chairman. It was the end of one of the many intensive weeks of consultations and presentations which had become a regular feature since the appointment of Foster Associates as architects for the Bank's new headquarters just over a year before. The conceptual design phase of the project was as good as over; the Foster team were about to move up a gear in their effort to exploit the great opportunity with which they had been rightly presented at the end of the international competition late in 1979. As we were dodging across the stream of Hong Kong taxis, Norman asked me if I would consider giving up my engagement with the Bank to join him in heading the project. I said I would be prepared to consider it. Five minutes later over a drink in the chairman's office, I was amazed when Norman informed Sandberg that it was going to happen. After a joke or two about whether or not it would involve the Bank in extra professional fees, Sandberg readily supported Norman's idea and I flew out of Kai Tak Airport that evening with a new role in that fabulous project. I was already at an age when I might have been clearing my desk to concentrate on growing roses or improving a golf handicap, but I wasn't interested in either and the thought of working alongside Norman for a few years on the project of a lifetime was an infinitely more exciting alternative. And so it turned out. However, by the time the Bank building was finished, smack on schedule in November 1985, I was even more firmly engrossed in the

Norman Foster and
Gordon Graham in
conversation.

affairs of Foster Associates and I still enjoyably remain so as we embark on another project of a lifetime at King's Cross — the largest and most important urban regeneration project in Europe.

Two things about Norman come out of this episode. First, once he has made a judgement he wants to get on with the implementation of it. His announcement to Mike Sandberg had been preceded by a mere moment or two of conversation in a situation where the protection of life and limb was uppermost. It appeared to be impetuous at the time, but it proved to be right. He has a quite uncanny knack of proving to be right against all the initial odds. Perhaps it is his Mancunian persistence and refusal to take no for an answer — coupled with an almost cheeky ability to fly outrageous kites in circumstances which a management text-book might analyse as being the wrong set of circumstances — that lie behind a lot of his success.

Second, I am, at 68, living proof that day-to-day working contact with Foster — tensions and frustrations included — keeps one young, at least in spirit. My own pet name for him, which I have used to clients and colleagues alike, is the 'boy wonder'. I mean it. Like ordinary mortals, the members of the Foster office grow older year by year, but the spirit and ethos of the place remains one of youthful enthusiasm, of creative fun and enjoyment, where the immense privilege of not having to differentiate between work and pleasure is infectiously shared. It all spreads from the top downwards.

The very first time I shared a working experience with Norman was in 1978, 10 years ago. I was collaborating with Richard Rogers on the Coin Street project; a major public enquiry was not far away; a planning problem had been teasing us for days and nights; a brainstorming session with a fresh architectural mind seemed like a good idea; Richard invited Norman to join the two of us for an evening.

It was my first experience of the unbounded, infectious energy and enthusiasm for architectural problem-solving that personifies Foster. It was my introduction to the Foster talk-as-you-draw technique and, my goodness, he can talk, but equally he can draw — like the proverbial angel! Sometimes he is really talking aloud to himself as a mind-clearing exercise, before cutting through the welter of important, but secondary issues and getting to the real heart of the matter.

That evening was also an act of generosity. Although Foster and Rogers were old friends and ex-partners, they were, nevertheless, seriously competitive rivals. For both of them, their major opportunities were still to come. Such thoughts never entered Norman's head or diminished his effort to help crack the problem with which we were wrestling. It was the first of many kindnesses and acts of generosity I have known Norman to perform. I also know that for every one of which I am aware, there are many others that this basically shy man has kept to himself.

I am nearing the end of the space I was allotted to give a few insights into the make-up of a man of genius who is my friend and colleague. Some day, perhaps, I might write my own book about him — instead of growing roses or playing golf. Then I would be able to do justice to the biggest single influence on the man and his work; the person who stimulates and extends him in the way that he stimulates and extends those of us who are lucky enough to work with him — his architect wife Wendy. There are a few amusing stories I could tell about that relationship which would provide further insights into the life and work of two very remarkable people.

From Hard to Soft Machines
by Chris Abel

Chris Abel graduated from the Architectural Association in 1968 and has since taught architecture in the UK, Canada, the USA, Malaysia, Singapore and Saudi Arabia. He has published numerous papers on architectural education, theory and criticism, and writes regularly for *The Architectural Review* and other journals on architecture in both the developed and developing world. Since 1983, his permanent home has been in Malta. He is currently visiting professor at the Middle East Technical University in Ankara, Turkey.

1. Peter Collins, *Changing Ideals in Modern Architecture*, Faber & Faber, London, 1965.
2. Reyner Banham, *Theory and Design in the First Machine Age*, The Architectural Press, London, 1960.
3. Reyner Banham, ibid.
4. Robert Thorne, 'Paxton and Prefabrication', Derek Walker (ed.), *Great Engineers*, Academy Editions, London; St Martin's Press, New York, 1987.
5. John Heskett, *Industrial Design*, Oxford University Press, New York and Toronto, 1980.
6. Le Corbusier, *Towards a New Architecture*, The Architectural Press, London, 1927.
7. Philippe Boudon, *Lived-in Architecture*, The MIT Press, Cambridge, 1972.
8. J.F. Eden, 'Metrology and the Module', *Architectural Design*, March 1967.
9. John Heskett, op. cit.
10. Gilbert Herbert, *The Dream of the Factory-made House*, The MIT Press, Cambridge, 1984.

Transition

The First Machine Age meant many things to architects. From the nineteenth-century writer Horatio Greenough on, it meant drawing lessons from ocean-going liners and other mechanical and engineering achievements of the time, to point out how inefficient and otherwise outdated contemporary architecture was.[1] To Futurists like Antonio Sant'Elia, it implied that buildings and even whole cities should be designed to emphasise mechanical speed, both in streamlined architecture and exaggerated, criss-crossing movement systems. To Constructivists and others, it included more pragmatic considerations, like making the most of new lightweight materials and techniques of construction. To Bruno Taut and the members of the Glass Chain, it was synonymous with a transparent 'glass architecture', thinly framed in rolled steel and suffused with natural light. But above everything else it meant struggling — first like the Deutsche Werkbund and, later, like the teachers at the Bauhaus — to reconcile the art and craft of architecture with the new machinery of industrial production.[2]

The transition to the Second Machine Age was marked by equally spectacular advances in technology, dramatised in the 1960s by Russian Sputniks circling the earth and the answering American Apollo Space Programme that put man on the moon. As with the earlier change of gear, the social effects were profound. From providing mechanised benefits for the elite, modern industry has graduated to providing similar benefits for the masses. Automobiles, domestic appliances and communications are now available to most of the population of the industrialised world, and television, according to Reyner Banham, is the 'symbolic machine of the Second Machine Age', joining the older technology of mass production with the new technology of mass communication.[3]

For better or worse, TV has made its predicted impact, and created the 'global village'. But the true symbolic machine of the Second Machine Age turned out not to be the one-way, unresponsive TV, but the two-way computer, and especially the 'user-friendly' personal computer. And it is around the versatile microprocessor, rather than the inflexible mass-production line, that the emergent architecture of the Second Machine Age centres.

Background

It is against the background of this transition, and its meaning for architecture, that Norman Foster's achievements with the materials and tools of twentieth-century industry must be measured.

The contrast with the failures of earlier generations of architects to fulfil the promises of the First Machine Age makes those achievements all the more remarkable. For the plain fact is that the Foster team's mastery of the techniques and tools of machine production is a rare exception to the general professional record. As forecast, factories now turn out practically all parts of buildings by industrialised methods. But they do so without any significant participation by architects. Their role in building production is reduced to the job of assembly, selecting from catalogues components that have been designed and made by other people. To all intents and purposes, the profession remains just where it was when the first Modernists issued their rallying calls — detached from and ignorant of the means of production.

A Question of Standards

Something went badly wrong. But what? The commonly accepted version of Modern Movement history has it that the deciding battle for industrialised building was enjoined in the 1920s and '30s, and won in the '40s and '50s, with the general acceptance of Modern architecture. But not only was a vital part of that battle — gaining design expertise with the new tools of machine production — never even won, it was hardly ever properly begun.

The main obstruction was invariably ideological in kind. Joseph Paxton's prefabricated iron structure for the Crystal Palace created an enduring model for an architecture of the First Machine Age, built with the most advanced industrialised materials and techniques of the day.[4] But Paxton's use of a limited variety of structural and cladding elements based on a single glazing module grew amongst his later admirers from a practical concept of modular

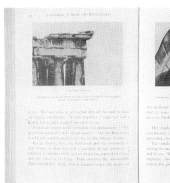

Two pages from *Vers une Architecture*. To Le Corbusier, the Parthenon and the Caproni hydroplane were comparable products of evolutionary selection 'applied to a standard'.

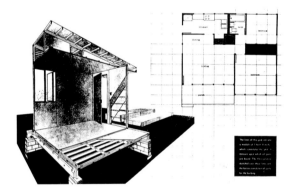

Despite an investment of US$ 6 000 000 and a decade's development work, Gropius and Wachsmann's standardised 'packaged house' project was a commercial disaster.

Raymond Loewy was one of the first designers to recognise the importance of 'mechanical efficiency as a factor of design'. This is his duplicating machine for the Gestetner Corporation.

construction, appropriate to a single large-scale industrialised building project, to an idealised concept of a universal architecture of standard forms.

The obsession with standardisation for ideological rather than industrial reasons runs like a common thread throughout much of the history of the industrialised building movement, shaping the main course of events and often negating the positive economic and social benefits that might otherwise have occurred. The general drift was already apparent in the nationalist Deutsche Werkbund's efforts to reconcile design with industry on the basis of a purely qualitative interpretation of standards, meant to confirm Germany's place in the modern world.[5] It reappeared to inspire Le Corbusier to compare the Parthenon with automobiles and aeroplanes as examples of the same evolutionary "product of selection applied to a standard",[6] as well as to shape all his early architecture. Le Corbusier's prefabricated dwellings at Pessac had little to do with either industrial or social realities,[7] but his Modulor geometric system of proportion had a profound influence on later efforts at modular co-ordination; a largely pointless exercise since it too demonstrated "little authentic contact with (production) engineering".[8] The same pattern of thinking seriously undermined Walter Gropius' well-meaning efforts at the Bauhaus to bring designers to work together with industry; the Bauhaus workshops remained essentially craft-based and few prototypes coming out of them ever went into industrial production.[9] And it doomed to consumer rejection countless later schemes, including the most promising, such as Gropius' later collaboration in the US with Konrad Wachsmann on the standardised 'Packaged House' project.[10]

For all their protestations of a new partnership with industry, most of the early Modernists only toyed with the idea. What was at stake was a general consensus on the 'new style' rather than any genuine understanding of industrial production methods;[11] even the 'machine aesthetic' was misunderstood and made to conform to preferred Platonic images.[12] In the end, they nearly all stuck to the same Olympian role of architect-as-artist that was most revered by the profession before the advent of Modernism. Only Mies van der Rohe, having spent much of his youth in his father's stone mason's yard, seemed able to find an effective working relationship with industry.[13]

Ditching most of the dogma that went with Modern architecture even before he moved across the Atlantic, Mies freely translated his early experiments with 'glass architecture' into an industrialised language for corporate America, an aspect which has often distracted European critics from the quality of his building technique.

It is no coincidence that industrial design emerged as a separate profession in the 1930s independently of any formal schools of art or architecture; and not even in Europe, where industrialisation was conceived, but in the US where fledgling designers had fewer academic or professional preconceptions to wrestle with. Significantly, the first designers willing to court industry also came from various commercial backgrounds, such as advertising, commercial art and even stage design, and had no misgivings about working in a competitive or industrial environment. The most successful of them, like Walter Dorwin Teague, Raymond Loewy and Henry Dreyfuss, also quickly grasped the importance of mechanical efficiency as a factor of good design. Working hand-in-hand with production engineers, they designed or redesigned everything from cameras and refrigerators to telephones that both looked and worked better than existing models.[14]

The notable exception to the familiar post-war catalogue of failures in this area was also American. Impressed by his studies of the British approach, at least with the theory if not with the practice, Ezra Ehrenkrantz spelt out much the same ideological message in *The Modular Number Pattern*:[15] standardisation, with a limited number of sizes carefully selected for their combinatorial value; and modular co-ordination, providing a numerical measure for determining those standard sizes. Ehrenkrantz nevertheless brought an American brand of realism to producing his factory-made Southern Californian Schools Development, or SCSD building system, even if it was to mark yet another professional retreat. Like the pragmatic American pioneers of industrial design, Ehrenkrantz understood the value of high performance in functional, structural and mechanical efficiency — factors which were eventually to account for most of the success of the SCSD project. But recognising that the weaknesses of the European building systems which he had studied were largely due to their architectural

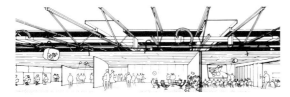

The flexible SCSD building type with its deep roof and services 'sandwich' (top) was a major influence on Foster's early work, as in the Newport Schools competition (bottom).

The glass wall of the IBM headquarters at Cosham, near Portsmouth.

designers' lack of industrial expertise, he handed over final responsibility for product design to the manufacturers themselves. The four major component sub-systems for the SCSD project were, accordingly, all designed by the manufacturers' own designers. What architects were assigned was the writing of performance specifications for each component and, as usual, the task of assembling the results.[16] In effect, the Ehrenkrantz formula completed the process of professional emasculation begun with the onset of the First Machine Age, and only further distanced architects from any direct contact with the means of production.

Discarding the Myths

Foster's entry into the field coincided with the same turbulent period of the 1960s in which Ehrenkrantz produced his SCSD system, and much of his early work was influenced by the SCSD model. As well as offering economic advantages and ease of prefabrication, the highly-flexible structural and planning concept suited Foster's functional and social aims of providing for changes of use and improving the workplace by pooling resources and encouraging conventionally separate classes of workers to share the same spaces and amenities.[17] The unitary building form with its regular open structure and roof-and-services 'sandwich' first appears in the Newport Schools competition, but was soon adapted as a general-purpose building type in the proposals for the Olsen Amenity Centre at Millwall Docks, in London, which brought dockyard workers and management together for the first time within the same building. Both projects were crucial in gaining the experience needed for the IBM Advance Head Office at Cosham, which was built as temporary accommodation — and for the same cost — but which pleased IBM sufficiently to make it their permanent regional headquarters. IBM Cosham was followed by the Factory Systems Studies of 1972, and the building of IBM Technical Park at Greenford in 1977, which included mezzanine floors, as opposed to the usual single-storey configuration. These are only the most obvious members of the same building type. If consistent elements such as the full-height glass walls are ignored, and attention concentrated on the deep-plan configuration, post-and-beam structure and roof-and-services 'sandwich', then it is possible to also include the Computer Technology Centre in Hertfordshire and the scheme for the VW-Audi headquarters at Milton Keynes.

But if his early architecture is influenced by the SCSD building type, Foster never accepted the implied defeatism in the Ehrenkrantz approach to product design, which left architects bereft of any direct design role. It is the Foster team's highly professional skills as both industrial designers and architects that separates their factory-made architecture from that of the industrialised building movement as a whole.

The same professionalism, involving increasingly close working relations with industry, had led Foster and his team to discard popular myths about the way buildings are made in factories. For all his refinement of similar building types and respect for qualitative standards, Foster never fell into the same trap as other designers in confusing such standards with those having to do with processes of industrial production. As Foster explains, when an architect orders a component from a catalogue, such as a window, he usually imagines that that component is lying around the factory somewhere all made up and ready to go. Not so. Most of the products taken out of a catalogue are not standard items at all, but are made up to order. What the factory actually has at hand is a range of industrialised materials and products in sheets or lengths which are cut up and assembled as required. Some factories might keep a limited stock of the most popular size ranges of assembled components, but even then the selection is dictated by customer preference. It has nothing whatsoever to do with economic or technological constraints of industrialised production, as modular mythology would lead architects to believe.[18] While flexibility of planning grids may require the use of fixed forms and size ranges within each building, manufacturers are not so constrained in the making of their products, and cannot be if they wish to reach the largest and most varied market. If a designer cares to take the trouble, therefore, as Foster proved, it is possible in many cases to get a manufacturer at little or no extra cost to the client, to modify his product to suit a particular job.

For this reason, comparisons between Foster's work and the use of 'off-the-shelf' components by other designers, exemplified in the house by Charles Eames,[19] can be misleading, and do little justice to Foster's greater

11 Chris Abel, 'Ditching the Dinosaur Sanctuary', *Architectural Design,* August 1969; and 'Meaning and Rationality in Design', G. Broadbent, R. Bunt, and T. Llovens (eds.) *Meaning and Behaviour in the Built Environment,* John Wiley & Sons, Chichester, 1980.

12 Reyner Banham, *Design by Choice,* Academy Editions, London, 1981.

13 David Spaeth, *Mies van der Rohe,* The Architectural Press, London, 1985.

14 John Heskett, op. cit.

15 Ezra D. Ehrenkrantz, *The Modular Number Pattern,* Alec Tiranti Ltd, London, 1956.

16 G.W. Cartmell, 'SCSD: Californian Schools Development Project', *RIBA Journal,* August 1965.

17 Chris Abel, 'Modern Architecture in the Second Machine Age: the Work of Norman Foster', *A+U,* May 1988.

18 Chris Abel (see 11 above).

19 Arthur Drexler, *Charles Eames,* The Museum of Modern Art, New York, 1973.

20 Chris Abel (see 17 above).

The curved wall of the Willis Faber & Dumas building still defines the state of the art in 'glass architecture'.

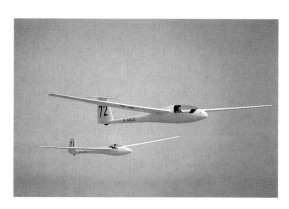

The lightweight glider symbolises Foster's design approach of doing 'more with less' materials and energy.

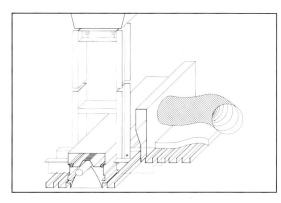

The aluminium reflectors in the suspended ceiling system in the Willis Faber & Dumas building were custom-made and integrate several different functions.

involvement with industry. Such practice, however, is rare, and Foster learnt early in his career that to get the most out of industry it was necessary, as he puts it, to "cheat the system and penetrate an organisation (in order to) get through to the shop floor". He recalls his experience with the Olsen Amenity Centre project, when, having learnt that no British manufacturer could supply a suitable glazed-wall system in the 11 month design-and-build period of the contract, he flew over to Pittsburgh in the USA to talk over the project with the PPG Company, whose glazing system seemed to fit the need. Met at the airport by a company representative, Foster was informed that he would be taken directly to meet the vice-president at the head office. Foster replied that he was not interested in meeting any vice-presidents, but would like to talk to the people involved in drawing up and detailing the components he wanted to use. Told that such operations were not carried out in Pittsburgh, but in another state at Dayton, Ohio, Foster demanded that either he was flown to Dayton forthwith or he would be on the next flight back to England. Soon enough, Foster was working round the clock with the workmen at Dayton and after a week returned to his own offices with the drawings he needed. The elegant glass skins of the Olsen Centre and IBM Cosham buildings were produced in just this fashion as an adaptation of an existing curtain-wall system, modified to work as a ground-supported, free-standing element with minimal connections to the structure, and thus minimal interruptions to the smooth, reflective qualities of the glass.

Design Development

From getting manufacturers to adapt their products to suit his particular requirements, Foster and his team soon became immersed in the full process of product design, development and manufacture, collaborating with industry to produce his own component designs. In practice, up until the collaboration with Tecno on furniture production, the Foster team had been mostly restricted to designing custom-made components for each building project as it came up, though they were frequently designed with the idea of some kind of 'spin-off' or wider use in industry in mind. The restriction could be viewed as a blessing in disguise, for it encouraged Foster to develop economic, high-performance components for small batch production, taking full advantage of the regular planning and constructional features of the unitary building type which characterises his work – a major factor in shaping his design approach and preparing the Foster team for the innovations in production technology that were eventually to come.

The key to Foster's approach to component design, just as it is with space planning and with the design of the overall enclosure,[20] is integrated design aimed at maximising performance. The approach, which Foster calls 'design development', is strongly influenced by Buckminster Fuller's philosophy of doing 'more with less' materials, weight or energy,[21] and is symbolised by the images of ultra-lightweight, man-powered aircraft, with which Foster invariably concludes presentations of his work, as well as by his own personal passion for flying gliders. It is also cogently summarised in the terse statement made by Jean Prouvé – another keen glider pilot and source of inspiration – in criticism of architects' obsessions with modular co-ordination: "Machines are seldom built with parts selected from various sources; they are aggregately designed".[22] What Prouvé expressed and what Foster discovered for himself is a basic principle of manufacture: if a product is to be designed for maximum efficiency, then its constituent parts must be integrated in the manner that most closely approximates to the desired performance specification for the whole. In sum, the approach substitutes high performance for high-volume production as the main criterion for good industrial design.

One way to achieve high performance is to get a single component to do what was previously done by many different ones. Among the first purpose-made component systems designed by the Foster team is the aluminium suspended ceiling for the Willis Faber & Dumas building. Though it has received less attention than the more striking glass wall, in some ways it demonstrates the Foster approach to industrial design even better. The parabolic reflectors in the ceiling, for example, do with a single, integrated component what is usually done with several separate systems, providing support for the ceiling, plus light, plus air distribution, plus sprinklers, and plus power distribution for the floor above. The ceiling itself is made up of simple, but non-standard, aluminium channels

'High-Tech' architecture? Foster argues that there have always been 'modern' architects who pushed at the boundaries of contemporary technology, as Brunelleschi once did with his dome for Florence Cathedral.

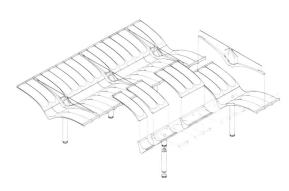

The concrete roof shell for the Televisa headquarters in Mexico City would have made the most of local building techniques.

spanning between the reflectors and, though it was the first of its kind to replace the conventional suspended panel system, development and production costs were covered by the number of channels produced within the one contract.

As for the glass wall, the near seamless curtain still defines the state of the art in 'glass architecture'. Mies would undoubtedly have applauded that gossamer skin, with its minimalist aesthetic, craftsmanlike detailing and reflected images of the old market town of Ipswich. But so also would have Camillo Sitte, whose 'artistic principles' of urban design[23] inspire much of Foster's sympathetic approach to dealing with problems of urban context.[24] The decision, for example, to make the perimeter of the building follow the existing pattern of streets led directly to the curved lines of the wall. To achieve this, the Foster team virtually created a new kind of glazing system. The patch plates and other components were already available, but they had never been used in this way before, to hang a glass curtain down from the top of a multi-storey building or to follow a curved perimeter. Much ingenuity and adjustment to parts was needed to take up differential movements between the glass skin and the reinforced-concrete structure. All of which involved pushing materials and technology — not to mention the manufacturers — to the limit of their performance.

Technology Transfers

For all its technological sophistication, much of Foster's work, as he readily points out himself, involves using conventional building materials in a new way — as with the glass wall at Willis Faber & Dumas. In the same fashion, he argues for factory-made buildings on the straightforward grounds that it is easier to ensure quality control and raise performance standards in a factory than on a building site. His work in the developing world is also marked by a notably conservative technological attitude. In their regional studies for the island of Gomera in the Canaries, the Foster team recommended labour-intensive industries, mud-brick housing and energy from windmills, while the structure for the Televisa headquarters in Mexico City is no more advanced than reinforced concrete, albeit used in an exceptionally graceful manner.

Where appropriate, however, Foster frequently steps outside the architect's normal compass of interest to borrow ideas, materials and techniques from other, technologically more advanced sources, like the aircraft and automobile industries. The stress here is on the word 'appropriate'. Foster sees nothing extraordinary in pushing at the boundaries of building technology, if that is what is needed to get the best job done. Architects have always done that, he insists, and rejects the 'High-Tech' label which has been foisted on his work. On a recent visit to Florence he wondered, for example, if Brunelleschi's contemporaries called him a 'High-Tech' architect for advancing building technology with his dome for Florence Cathedral.

Technology transfers from advanced industrial sectors, though already evident in early projects like the Computer Technology air-tent, nevertheless play an increasing part in Foster's work from the Sainsbury Centre onwards. As with the interchangeable cladding panels for the Sainsbury Centre, the choice of materials and techniques is usually made in order to achieve maximum performance whilst keeping any tooling costs down to a minimum — an essential consideration for the sort of limited production runs Foster was designing for — with research and development costs being generally borne by manufacturers eager to extend their product range and technical experience. The use of superplastic aluminium for the cladding panels was one of the first uses of the material in the construction industry, and was chosen for just these reasons. Developed for the aircraft industry, the lightweight composite material becomes highly malleable when heated, and can be stretch-formed this way into rigid shapes using compressed air presses and low-cost tools. The panels may look as though they were stamped out on expensive presses and mass-production lines in accordance with Modernist folklore — the raised surface pattern of the original design was inspired by the panels on the same Citroën 'deux chevaux' car model after which Le Corbusier named his Maison Citrohan project — but they were not. The neoprene jointing system running between the panels is equally ingenious and an archetypal product of Foster's integrated design approach, providing in one component a weatherproof connection between adjacent panels, a continuous gutter system for roof and walls, and an expansion joint. As with all Foster's component designs, the design development process involved the making and testing of full-size prototypes. In

21 James Meller (ed.), *The Buckminster Fuller Reader*, Cape, London, 1970.

22 Jean Prouvé, Address delivered at the UIA symposium held in Delft, 6-16 September, 1964, CIB (eds.), *Towards Industrialised Building — Proceedings of the Third CIB Congress, Copenhagen, 1965*, Elsevier, Oxford, 1966.

23 Camillo Sitte, *City Planning According to Artistic Principles*, translated by G.R. Collins and C.C. Collins, Random House, New York, 1965.

24 Chris Abel.

25 Quoted in Peter Collins, op. cit.

26 Chris Abel, 'A Building for the Pacific Century', *The Architectural Review*, April 1986.

27 Chris Abel, ibid.

28 Chris Abel, ibid.

29 Gordon Vincent and John Peacock, *The Automated Building*, The Architectural Press, London, 1985.

30 Nicholas Negroponte, *Soft Architecture Machines*, The MIT Press, Cambridge, 1975.

Hybrid structural forms and expressionism at the Renault Centre.

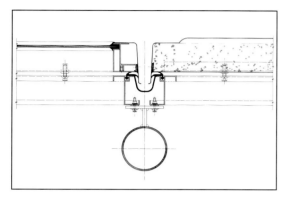

Jointing system of the cladding panels used on the Sainsbury Centre for Visual Arts.

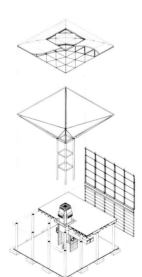

Structural and cladding components for the Stansted Airport terminal, with steel 'tree', dome and section of concrete undercroft.

one such test, a group of panels was bolted together on their aluminium subframe and subjected to a simulated 120 mile-per-hour rainstorm: the panels and jointing system held up splendidly, not leaking a drop, but the test rig was blown over.

Precision Engineering

The single span, hangar-like structure for the Sainsbury Centre was the first of a new series of advanced structural types, connecting Foster with those designers who believe, with Viollet-le-Duc, that "architecture can only equip itself with new forms if it seeks them in the rigorous application of new structure".[25] Large-span enclosures of advanced engineering sheltering structurally independent mini-buildings first appear in the Buckminster Fuller inspired Climatroffice project, then at the Sainsbury Centre, followed by the scheme for the International Energy Expo at Knoxville, USA, also done with Fuller, and most recently in the new terminal for Stansted Airport. Each structure took Foster and his team into new areas of precision engineering. For example, in order that the cladding panels for the Sainsbury Centre could be interchanged at any point on the exterior, the aluminium subframes had to be fixed to within tolerances of plus or minus 3mm over the full length and breadth of the 133- by 35-metres structure. Precision of this order is a form of technology transfer in itself and is found more often in mechanical rather than structural engineering.

The prismatic steel structure for the Sainsbury Centre was mostly concealed on the outside by the cladding panels and on the inside by automated, light-sensitive perforated louvres, and is only bared at each end to form impressive 'porticos'. The reticence did not last. In his more daring experiments, which place increasing emphasis on the structure's expressive qualities as well as on ever higher performance, Foster and his engineers combine new and old structural forms to produce original hybrid forms which sometimes defy conventional description. At the Renault Centre, steel trusses are part cantilevered, part suspended from slim 'mast' supports and steel cables, but also link together in two directions to act as interlocking, rigid portal frames. The design and manufacture of the structural components entailed a similar hybrid approach, involving both First and Second Machine Age technologies. The behaviour of the structure is so complex it could not have been designed without the help of computer analysis and simulation, while the spheroidal graphitic cast-iron fixings on the structural masts, that anchored the cable stays, were made with the kind of sand moulds used since the Industrial Revolution. Each structural component was carefully designed with the engineers at Ove Arup & Partners to look as though it is doing the task it was made for, as well as to perform in the required manner. The contrast with the smooth, unbroken skin of the Sainsbury Centre could not be greater, and marks the beginning of a new phase of structural expressionism in Foster's work, almost Gothic or Oriental in quality.

If the Renault Centre is Foster's first unequivocal work of structural expressionism, it also marks a high point in the technological shift, begun at Willis Faber & Dumas and continued at the Sainsbury Centre, from using ready-made to custom-made components from the factory. Almost all the major component systems at Renault were designed and manufactured for the job in hand. As in other projects, materials and techniques were also freely borrowed from outside the building industry: the flexible joint between walls and roof, necessitated by differential movements in the lively structure, is made from the same fabric used for the skirts of hovercraft; while the foam-filled, steel cladding panels with their unusually fine profile were made with existing tools used in the manufacture of wall panels for caravans. Despite being custom-made, the use of a small variety of repetitive units and low-cost tools helped keep total building costs down to the same as those for a standard industrial 'shed'.

Craftsmanship on a New Scale

All of Foster's previous achievements in factory-made building craft, advanced engineering and structural expressionism were eclipsed, however, by the Hongkong Bank. Foster's earlier tower projects for Whitney Museum and the Humana Corporation, in the USA, show simple, monolithic shapes with integrated skins and structures. The tower for Whitney Museum, especially, looks something like a vertical Sainsbury Centre, with similar cladding panels and rounded edges reinforcing the unitary appearance of finite form. The structural concept for the Bank, however, is closer in spirit to the

Indeterminism and megastructures were characteristic themes in the work of Japanese Metabolists, such as Kiyonori Kikutake. This is his Marine City of 1959, in which plug-in capsules are set into free-standing service shafts.

31 Chris Abel, 'Ditching the Dinosaur Sanctuary: Seventeen Years On', *CAD and Robotics in Architecture and Construction – Proceedings of an International Conference, Marseilles, 25–27 June, 1986*, Kogan Page, London, 1986. The same paper is reprinted under the title, 'Return to Craft Manufacture', *The Architects' Journal, Supplement on Information Technology*, 20 April, 1988.

32 Stafford Beer, 'Toward the Cybernetic Factory', H. Von Foerster and G.W. Zopf (eds.), *Principles of Self-Organisation*, Pergamon Press, New York, 1962.

33 Chris Abel (see 11 above). See also D.T.N. Williamson, 'New Wave in Manufacturing', *American Machinist*, 11 September 1967.

34 Quoted from *The Times Newsletter*, Council on Tall Buildings and Urban Habitat, Lehigh University, Bethlehem, December 1983.

35 Chris Abel (see 31 above).

36 Werner Blaser, *Furniture as Architecture*, Waser Verlag, Zurich, 1985.

37 Arthur Drexler, op. cit.

38 Stafford Beer, op. cit.

indeterminate 'megastructure' projects of Japanese Metabolists, and especially to the projects of Kiyonori Kikutake.[26] Foster even outdoes the Metabolists in flexible structures since, as actually built, their spaces are usually fixed for all time in concrete. The suspended floors of the Bank are also fixed, but the staggered gaps left in one side of the structure to meet daylight regulations can, if circumstances should ever permit, be actually filled in to produce another 30 per cent of usable space. The sturdy maintenance cranes atop each of the steel 'masts' add to the appearance of a structure still in the process of erection.

The urgency of the building programme as well as the restricted site and lack of suitable local industrial capacity necessitated a maximum level of prefabrication, involving manufacturers as far apart as Japan, Europe and the United States in the most complex exercise ever undertaken in factory-made building for a single structure. The making of the unique suspension structure alone set new standards of building craft on a hitherto unheard-of scale. The enormous stresses placed on the steel 'masts' for the eight structural towers, for example, necessitated technologies and welding techniques more in common with the offshore oil production industry – with which the Foster team had previous experience working on projects for prefabricated accommodation units – than with building construction. In appearance, they actually resemble the legs of a North Sea production platform. Similarly, the concentration of forces in the giant trusses requires very exact heavy engineering of a kind not normally associated with building construction at all, but with suspension bridges and with civil engineering projects with large moving parts, like the Thames Barrier. The spherical bearings used to connect the truss members together, for instance, have to cope with extremely high loads – 2000 tons at level 13 – pulling different ways on a very small area of steel. The manufacturing tolerances involved in the making of the bearings and the solid steel pins which they hold – 0.033mm between bearings and tongue plates and 0.25mm between pin and bearings – brought forth the sort of perfectionist attitudes and skills from Dorman Long, the British steel fabricators, that one thought belonged to another age. By all accounts, there was a remarkably high degree of personal commitment by the key men on the job: the father of one of the men who directed this job had been responsible for the steelwork of the Bank's 1935 headquarters, which were also fabricated by Dorman Long.

What was true of the making of the structure was also true of the building's other innovations. Almost all component systems set new standards of performance and industrialised technique, even where existing products were used. With the escalators and lifts made by Otis, for example, exposure of the support frames necessitated their complete redesign.

Most of the major sub-systems also involved technology transfers of one kind or another, with research and development costs being shared between the manufacturers and the Bank. The removable panels for the computer-type raised floor system for example – a development, like the escalators, from similar ideas used at Willis Faber & Dumas – are made from a lightweight but rigid aluminium honeycomb sandwich material used in the floor panels of Boeing aircraft. With their prominent edge trim, they strongly resemble the traditional Japanese *tatami* mat and dictate the planning grid in much the same manner, adding to the building's other Oriental qualities of delicate transparency contrasted with bold structure.[27]

The Foster team's earlier projects for the offshore oil industry also came in useful in the design of the factory-made service modules. The modules contain the air-handling plant and lavatories for each floor, and are built like shipping containers as rigid boxes, ready for transportation and hoisting into place either side of the main structure – the same aluminium-honeycomb material used for the floor panels is also used to clad the service modules. The arrangement not only frees up the internal spaces in the manner of Louis Kahn's separation of 'served' from 'servant' spaces in the Richards Medical Research Laboratories at Yale University,[28] but also enabled the 'plug-in' modules to be installed – ready for use – while the main structure was still going up. The contract was won by a Japanese consortium – not surprising since Japanese industry is the most advanced in the world in the field of prefabricated services. What impressed Foster most was the Japanese attitude toward quality control: he recalls that shoes were left outside the prototype, engineers entering only in stockinged feet: literally, a 'gloves and socks' operation.

Design of the environmental services also took the Foster team into the new but fast-growing field of 'smart buildings',[29] a technol-

'Served' and 'servant' spaces articulated as separate structures at the Richards Medical Research Laboratories, at Yale University, by Louis Kahn.

ogy with far-reaching consequences for the future of responsive forms of architecture. In *Soft Architecture Machines*,[30] Nicholas Negroponte extrapolates from experiments in artificial intelligence to forecast 'intelligent' environments able to comprehend and respond to users' needs on a fully interactive basis. Foster's architecture is firmly set in a similar direction and has been so for many years. Previous experiments with responsive environmental control systems include the 'tunable light box' for the Sainsbury Centre; and in the project for an office building at Vestby in Norway, Foster proposed both a light-sensitive skin and an external tracking-mirror system designed to bring as much of the low winter sun into the building as possible. This 'sun scoop' idea reappears at the Bank in built form, directing sunlight into the atrium at the heart of the building. The Bank also incorporates an 'intelligent' environment: its computerised building management system — overseeing everything to do with environmental control from the floor-based air-distribution network to maintenance schedules — is capable of monitoring the performance of the various systems it controls and improving their efficiency.

Toward the Cybernetic Factory

But the most important innovations were to come from the design and making of the cladding for the building. To understand their full significance for the future of industrialised building is to engage in a kind of 'gestalt switch' involving some of the most fundamental assumptions concerning the nature of craft versus machine production.

While generally drawing admiration for Foster's infinite care and attention to detail, the growing proportion of custom-made parts which go to make up Foster's buildings, even before the building of the Bank, has generated considerable confusion amongst architects who still associate industrialised building exclusively with mass production. The confusion is understandable, but it is erroneous.

In the earlier work described above, Foster demonstrated that by careful planning and design it is possible to adapt existing industrialised products, or even produce new ones, without getting involved with the expensive, fixed-purpose production lines and special tooling required for genuine mass production, such as in the automobile industry, for long the favourite model among industrialised building enthusiasts. The penalty is the reduction in variety which production runs for single building projects generally necessitate, resulting in a building with a highly uniform character. In effect, while Foster's design approach contradicts the still widespread assumption that the industrialisation of building necessitates standardisation among different building projects, it still implies standardisation within any single building project itself.

However, the innovations made in automated production machinery in the consumer industries mean that — planning grids and other constraints notwithstanding — architects may soon no longer need to accept even this limitation. Though special purpose mass-production lines still play an important part, their role in the manufacture of consumer goods, including automobiles, has been increasingly displaced over the last quarter century by more flexible production machinery, much of it now computer-controlled, able to keep up with ever-growing consumer demand for more variety and choice of product.[31]

The revolutionary consequences of this trend towards increasing variety and smaller batch production in industry were spelt out by Stafford Beer in his seminal paper on the 'cybernetic factory' of the future, written in 1962.[32] Based on cybernetic theory and advanced computer science and technology, Beer visualised a sensitive industrial 'organism' capable of responding to the fast-changing needs of a true market-orientated economy, turning out customised products as easily as standards on variable, computerised production machinery. By the mid-1960s there were already around 50 versatile industrial robots in use in the West and at least one adventurous concern by the name of Molins Machine Company, which has a highly variable product, was turning Beer's Second Machine Age vision of computerised production lines into reality.[33] Twenty years later the number of 'high-level' robots in use around the world had grown to nearly 23 000,[34] of which — as might unfortunately be expected from past performance — few belonged to the construction industry.[35]

Foster's architecture shows his unique grasp of these fundamental changes in industrialised technology. By refusing to accept conventional building practices, and by progressively increasing the level of his demands for high-performance, custom-made products, Foster and his team have led the way in encouraging a notoriously conservative building industry to catch up with other industries in confronting the new technological era and meeting individual consumer needs and values. What may have looked to some architects like craft technique imitating machine production is turning out to be more like machine production imitating craft technique.

Smart Tools of Production

If Joseph Paxton's standardised iron structure for the Crystal Palace with its minimal variety of cladding parts still epitomises the concept of factory-made building in the First Machine Age, then the first major building of the Second Machine Age is the Hongkong Bank, with its thousands of different cladding parts made with the help of robots and other 'smart' tools of production.

The exposed treatment of the suspension structure furthers the trend toward a richer structural expressionism in Foster's architecture, and the cladding was carefully designed so as not to interfere with that quality. The mast, trusses, suspension rods and cross-bracing all required layers of corrosion protection and fireproofing, which in turn needed some kind of maintenance-free cover. In order that the structure underneath all this should be still expressed as directly as possible, it was necessary that the finished aluminium cladding should follow the complex geometry of the structural members as closely as possible. Changes in the diameter of the columns, reflecting vertically decreasing structural loads, greatly multiplied the variations, necessitating the design and production of thousands of separate pieces of cladding, with almost as many variations in shape and size.

Problems such as these called for a major retooling by Cupples Products, the American firm selected for the job, including the purchase of state of the art computer-controlled production machinery. A computerised sheet-metal fabricator was used to cut the intricate and varied patterns for the customised panels, while forming of the complex shapes was carried out under microprocessor control on flexible hydraulic presses. Two Unimate industrial robots were also purchased and programmed to per-

Robotic welding in progress at General Motors' automobile production plant in Oshawa, Ontario.

A Unimate robot, at Cupples' factory in St Louis, welding aluminium truss mullions for curtain walling on the Hongkong Bank.

39 Chris Abel (see 11 above).

40 William Barrett, *The Illusion of Technique*, Anchor Press/Doubleday, New York, 1978.

41 B.F. Skinner, *Walden Two*, Macmillan, New York, 1948.

42 Asa Briggs (ed.), *William Morris*, Penguin Books, Harmondsworth, 1962.

43 David Watkin, *Morality and Architecture*, Clarendon Press, Oxford, 1977.

44 Colin Murray Turbayne, *The Myth of Metaphor*, University of South Carolina Press, Columbia, 1962.

45 Walter Gropius, 'Principles of Bauhaus Production', Ulrich Conrads (ed.), *Programs and Manifestos on Twentieth-Century Architecture*, The MIT Press, Cambridge, 1964.

46 Chris Abel (see 31 above).

47 Norman Foster, 'Hongkong Bank', *A+U*, June 1986.

form the high-quality, full-penetration welds required on the two-storey aluminium truss mullions supporting the curtain walling, which, like the main structure, have to withstand typhoon wind-loading conditions.

It is at this point that popular beliefs concerning the nature and cost of automated production lines break down. The high cost of conventional, fixed-purpose automated machinery of the sort still used to make engine blocks, for example, can only be justified by producing tens or even hundreds of thousands of identical engine blocks. The computerised machinery Cupples acquired also involved a sizable capital investment but, because of its inherent flexibility, it has almost unlimited capacity for use on other jobs requiring similar manufacturing operations. Initial purchase costs do not therefore have to be recouped by producing the maximum possible number of the same component, but can be amortised over a very wide range of different products.

Tecno's production line in Milan for the Nomos furniture range confirms the direction in which the furniture industry as well as the building industry is now headed. Aside from its reputation and experience as a furniture maker of the highest rank, the Tecno mode of operation, combining the use of modern materials with craft techniques and the most sophisticated computerised production machinery — as well as its highly flexible method of sub-contracting work out to a network of specialised firms as necessary — was ideally suited to Foster's need for an innovative manufacturer.

Based on his earlier experiments with furniture design, first for his own offices and then for the Renault Centre, the Nomos range is Foster's first product design aimed specifically at the open market and encapsulates much of his design approach. Foster himself describes furniture design as 'architecture in miniature', and the similarity between the furniture and the architecture — especially in the case of the Renault Centre — begs for comparison with the furniture of other distinguished architect designers working with industrialised materials.[36] Especially, there is also the same clear articulation of the different parts of each piece of furniture and a delight in solving the way they come together that is typical of the furniture by Charles Eames,[37] as well as the same professional attitude towards working with industry.

The name 'Nomos' also says much about his approach. Taken from the Greek word for law, it also means rhythm, or the beat and measure in music. It is difficult to think of a more appropriate name for the work of an architect who lays so much emphasis on structure and process in the making of things.

Early versions of the adjustable steel and aluminium worktop — the centre-piece of the range — were hand-crafted, involving 66 different welds. The Nomos version retains the same essential design, with its main support beam or 'spine' on to which legs and everything else are fixed, but it is made differently. Instead of welding parts together, Tecno devised a unique pressurised plug-in jointing system for the beam and a computerised production line on which to manufacture it. Consisting of four computer-controlled machines arranged in a circle, each machine performs a different operation on a steel tube which is fed in at the beginning of the line: the first cuts the tube to the required length; the second drills the fixing holes into the beam; the third expands each fixing hole so that it forms a raised edge ready to receive and cover its steel plug; and the fourth forces a plug into each hole at very high pressure. The plug itself has fixing holes into which other components of the table are screwed, so that the number of welds needed to put the table together is reduced to six. Each operation can be reprogrammed to provide as many variations as are needed, enabling Foster and Tecno to offer a considerable number of options within the basic range, making it one of the most versatile furniture systems on the market.

Like the machinery Cupples bought to produce the parts for the Hongkong Bank, the production line at Tecno was purchased initially for the Nomos range. But the machines can be used separately or together just as easily — and are already being so used — to help make other products, along with the industrial robot and other computerised machinery to be found elsewhere on the Tecno shop-floor.

Commenting on the contemporary industrial organisation of the 1960s, typified by the fixed-purpose mass-production line, Beer wrote that the only way such corporations could survive was by paying advertisers enormous sums "to make less mutable an environment to which the [industrial] organism cannot adapt. If the dinosaur can no longer live in the world, the world must be turned into a dinosaur sanctuary".[38] But as the computerised production

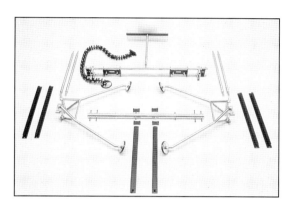

Aluminium, steel and plastic components for the desk system of the Nomos furniture range.

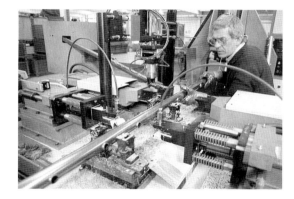

Computerised production of the steel support beams for Nomos furniture at Tecno's workshop near Milan. The man feeding the steel tube into the machine will eventually also be replaced by a computerised transfer line.

lines at Cupples and Tecno demonstrate, that need no longer be the case. Beer's cybernetic factory has come to stay. Instead of tuning the consumer to the machine, it is now possible to tune the machine to the consumer.[39]

Changing Definition of Machine

In *The Illusion of Technique*,[40] William Barrett defines a machine as "an embodied decision procedure. By going through a finite and unvarying number of steps it arrives invariably, so long as it is not defective, at a definite result." Barrett warns of the danger of applying the same kind of restricted operational logic to complex human issues, and points to the totalitarian society described in B.F. Skinner's novel *Walden Two*[41] as an ominous example of deterministic ways of thinking.

Similar warnings have been regularly sounded by architectural writers, from William Morris' nostalgic rejection of industrialised society as a whole[42] down to David Watkin's critique of historical determinism in architecture.[43]

History justifies the warnings, but they are founded on a definition of 'machine' which has hardly changed since those two arch "metaphysicians of mechanism", René Descartes and Isaac Newton, used the machine model to try to explain the workings of the universe.[44] That definition is now outdated, and if mechanical metaphors have shaped much of human thought in the past it is also becoming increasingly clear that the word 'machine' in the Second Machine Age no longer means what it used to. It is therefore reasonable to expect corresponding adjustments in language and thought, no less in architecture than in other spheres of human endeavour.

Understandably, William Morris and his followers in the Arts and Crafts Movement saw nothing in industrialisation but 'hard' machines, rigid mass-production lines, human alienation and a block to artistic expression. What they could not see was that industrialisation would not always have to mean such things. Neither is it necessary to subscribe to any mystical Zeitgeist, or 'spirit of the times', in order to recognise the impact of technological change on society, or to want to get the most out of the available materials and tools of modern industry, as Foster does. Failure to do so would mean a tragic loss of opportunity to take advantage of the new technology to create a more responsive architecture. Unlike the machine models of the First Machine Age but like the computers which are increasingly used in their design, manufacture and day-to-day operation, Foster's architectural 'machines' are designed for interactive use. They might also be called 'soft machines', not just for their adaptability or 'smart' environmental control systems, but because they exhibit a responsive character in the way they are made. Anything but the stamped-out replicas of early Modernist ambition, they look like the finely crafted, custom-made machines they are. As such they resolve some long-standing architectural conflicts of aims. The Bauhaus failed to deliver the "new kind of collaborator for industry and the crafts" promised by Gropius,[45] because neither he nor any of his colleagues could cross the gulf between the creative and craftsmanlike attitudes and skills taught in the Bauhaus workshops, and the technological and commercial realities of industrial production. Foster's work demonstrates that the gap between the art and craft of architecture and the machinery of industry can be bridged after all, but only by dispensing with orthodox Modernist dogma on standardisation. And that goes for even conventional production machinery. With the general introduction into the building industry of Beer's cybernetic factory, the gap promises to be reduced still further, to the point where it may become meaningless.[46] As Foster puts it: "The concept of a new era of craftsmanship — 'hand made by robots' — opens up an exciting prospect in which technology can design out standardisation and produce richly customised 'one-offs'."[47]

There was always more than a touch of hypocrisy in the way the early Modernists approached the industries they held up as the future providers of homes for the common man. It was all right to symbolise the machine in stucco, but actually getting down to the factory to work with the people who really knew what machines were all about was another matter. For all Foster's achievements in improving the quality of the workplace in his buildings, breaking down his own professional and class barriers between the architect's studio and the factory shop-floor to bring architecture into the Second Machine Age may turn out to be his most significant social accomplishment.

1981 **Great Portland Street Office**
Londres
England

"The Foster style cannot be ignored. It is immediately apparent at the practice's new office, the ground floor of an old central London block. Between structural masonry, glass; no name or other distinguishing symbol visible to the street; only one bay, its glass set back, is not blanked by perforated full-height metal louvres. On approach, the glazing vanishes automatically, inviting one to step up on to the deck inside the cavernous white and grey space.

Islands of grouped white plan chests are plinths to models; deeper inside, at vast drawing-boards and under red Anglepoises, sit the designers. The firm grey suspended floor hides servicing, allowing un-interrupted tall space. In the bays, marked by a rhythm of old columns and deep cornices, are slightly dropped acoustic ceilings. Background noise is low; telephones and typewriters do not distract. Large low white tables are rock solid on their Foster-designed minimal structures. Plain walls contrast with three large glossy photographs: a sailplane, a view out through the Eiffel Tower, and a microchip blown up and multiplied to look like ordered city squares – three key icons for Foster."

John McKean, *Architects' Journal*, March 1983

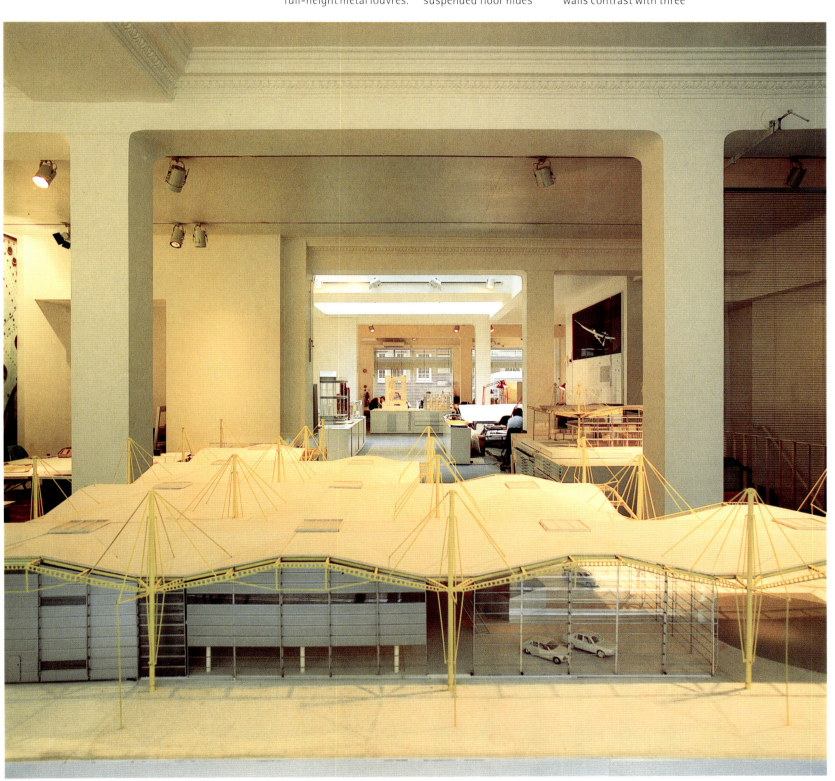

"The moment I entered his airy white office... the spacious interior, peppered with scarlet Anglepoise lamps over distant drawing-boards, instantly communicated a message about Foster's attitude to architecture and life – space, time, order and relaxation."

Stephen Gardiner, *The Listener*, February 1983

"There is a lot of interaction in this office: it operates as a very strong and close-knit team, with a high degree of commitment and enthusiasm right across the office. There is a very high threshold of responsibility – even students on their year out make real contributions to the schemes they're working on. I suppose because the office has an open mood about design – no idea is too crazy to put forward."

Norman Foster, *Building*, May 1982

1

1 Gordon Graham
2 Chubby Chhabra
3 David Nelson
4 Chris Seddon
5 Graham Phillips
6 Ken Shuttleworth
7 Norman Foster
8 Spencer de Grey

"The Eiffel Tower is Foster's icon for 'the economy, the elegance and that unerring eye for proportion'; to him 'it does more with less'. His anecdote that the vertical column of air over its base to the top weighs more than the steel of the tower itself is startling indeed; a comment worthy of his other friend and mentor, Bucky Fuller."

John McKean, *Architects' Journal*, March 1983

"What fascinates Foster is the language of assembly: the grading of components, the pared down junction, the smooth immaculate fit. His office walls are adorned with blown-up details of key images of heliostats and airstream caravans, for he belongs to the last generation of students to be weaned on the seductive imagery of *Vers une Architecture*. It is hardly surprising that a book which twins the Parthenon with the cockpit of a Caproni sailplane on a double page spread should have left an indelible mark."

Alastair Best, *Architectural Review*, April 1986

"If you were to walk around our office at any moment during the day and peered over everybody's shoulder, you'd find an incredible richness and diversity of activities. Some people would be working with computers, some working with calculators, some drawing with 2B pencils, some modelling in plastic or card, and some itemising a full-size mock-up."

Norman Foster, *Building*, May 1982

"The office on London's Great Portland Street is a step, if not into the future, at least aside from the usual trappings of architecture."

Hugh Aldersey-Williams, *Metropolis*, December 1987

"Like all the architects who believe seriously in technology, I think Foster proposed – quite seriously, quite honestly – to advance from a serious, rational consideration of the client's needs and problems to a rational solution; to the good servicing of those needs and problems. But the man is an architect, not an engineer. The visuals will never go away. They are always in the head. They are always in the back of the eye. Ask an architect a question and he will draw you a picture.

If Foster had simply been an engineer, if he had simply been a functionalist, goodness knows what he would have delivered. But being a man with an eye full of imagery – of which the Yellow Bicycle stands simply as one example – he could not help converting that rational, functional solution to the client's demands into a piece of sheer visual magic, which is the best kind of magic because you can see how the trick is done. Good architecture, in a sense, is transparent to the mind if not to the eye. This reflective to the eye, transparent to the mind is about as good as you can get, I think, given the sort of proposition on which Foster's architecture is placed."

Reyner Banham, the Yellow Bicycle lecture at UEA, June 1985

7

8

Mock-ups serve as a tool for discussion, both among the design team and with the client. With the Hongkong Bank project, Foster foresaw that such large-scale elements would be invaluable and, in 1981, warehouse premises close to the main office were leased as a new permanent home for the model-shop. Mock-ups of part of a typical office floor from the Hongkong Bank and one of that project's lift-cars can be seen in the background to this picture. The warehouse continues in use today but the model-shop has since returned to the main office, as it was felt an element of direct interaction had been lost with it in a separate location.

Cardboard mock-ups of some of the structural elements for a recent project. Norman Foster has involved model-makers as permanent members of the design team since the early 1970s, preparing study pieces such as these as well as more detailed presentation models.

"First of all the office. An open, flexible space; a range of activities; changeable; a test-bed in some respects...; lighting that changes; colours that change; internal layouts that change and reflect the groups of people, the way that they are interacting and that whole sort of team dynamic. A belief in the way that disparate skills can come together on an active, and not a passive basis; the idea of architects, engineers, economists coming together in a dynamic relationship, changing hats and changing roles in a shared endeavour."

Norman Foster, lecture at Hong Kong University, February 1980

This wood and plastic mock-up of one of the Hongkong Bank's lift-cars was prepared as a means of communicating with the manufacturer the intentions of the design. Later the manufacturer would prepare his own working prototype as a development of this process, before production began.

An overview of the model-shop when it was located in the warehouse.

The presentation models for the BBC Radio headquarters competition were also made in the warehouse.

More recently, the warehouse has witnessed much of the development work carried out on the Tecno furniture system.

A mock-up of the underfloor services at the Hongkong Bank was set up and proved a very useful tool in analysing the complicated layering and tolerance calculations that had to be resolved before prefabrication could proceed.

A working prototype of the glazed plaza panels Foster Associates proposed for the Hongkong Bank.

1978–1982 Architecture in Miniature
by Penny Sparke

Furniture systems: from Hille to Renault

Penny Sparke is a senior tutor in the Department of Cultural History at the Royal College of Art in London where she teaches the History of Design, specialising in the areas of twentieth-century furniture and products. She has published a number of articles and books in this subject area – among them *An Introduction to Design and Culture in the Twentieth Century* (Allen and Unwin), *Twentieth Century Furniture* (Bell and Hyman), *Japanese Design* (Michael Joseph), and *Ettore Sottsass* (Design Council). Her latest book *Italian Design: 1870 to the Present* has recently been published by Thames and Hudson.

Like all successful and long-lasting designs, Norman Foster's office furniture has grown out of need rather than whimsy. Back in the 1860s William Morris had discovered that the only way of acquiring the furniture items that he needed for his own domestic environment was to design them himself. Similarly, Norman Foster realised that the demands that he made of his own office furniture were such that the only way of fulfilling them was to set about designing an entirely new system. There the similarity ends, however: Morris' designs were intended to meet his needs and his alone, whereas Foster's new office system was envisaged as leading, with further development, to possible mass production and the market-place. From its inception in 1978 to its near completion in 1987, the project has proved to be a much more thoroughgoing and revolutionary proposal than was originally imagined and it has extended the Foster oeuvre into radically new directions.

The idea of an architect designing furniture is, of course, not a new one. In this century the work of, among others, Le Corbusier, Marcel Breuer, Mies van der Rohe, Gerrit Rietveld and Mart Stam demonstrated the important link between the Modern building and its 'equipment'. If the house was a 'machine for living in' then the furniture items within it were the cogs and wheels of that machine. Within these early Modern projects, the distinction between the concepts of internal and external space was eroded, as, indeed, was the division between furniture for domestic and commercial ends.

A cardboard mock-up of the Hille storage system was set up in Norman Foster's house in Hampstead. The use of large-scale prototypes has always been an important element of Foster's working method.

In spite of a general commitment to the 'age of the machine', the relationship of modern furniture from the early years of this century to mass production was more metaphorical than literal. While the widespread use of geometric forms and new materials – tubular steel, laminated plywood and so on – evoked the abstract idea of machines and industrial processes, they were, in practice, a long way from them: the tubular-steel chairs, designed by Mies and Breuer, for example, were fabricated by labour-intensive, craft techniques. While Le Corbusier discussed, at length, the principles of standardisation and rationalisation within mass production, and cited the examples of cars and aeroplanes as the poetic inspiration behind his architectural and design projects, the only mass-produced furniture he actually included in his buildings were the simple bentwood pieces manufactured by the Thonet company.

It wasn't until the post Second World War years, with the work of the American Charles Eames, that a resolution to the problems of mechanised, mass production of furniture was finally combined with an imagery that suited it. Even then Eames' pieces were not manufactured in vast numbers but remained within the restricted world of the 'avant-garde'. While

Scale models – in vacuum-formed plastic – were prepared of the system of storage furniture designed by Foster Associates for manufacture by Hille. The project was conceived as consisting of a set of standardised components, which would be able to perform a number of different functions.

Though only in cardboard, the mock-ups allowed ideas and variations to be explored in considerable detail.

Norman Foster is clearly indebted to the ideas of the early Modern masters, it is the work of Eames, a favourite of his, that stands firmly in the shadows of his own foray into furniture.

Eames stood at the end of what the architectural historian Reyner Banham called 'the first machine age' – the era of mechanisation and standardised mass production that was epitomised by the activity of Henry Ford in his Highland Park and River Rouge factories. Foster belongs, however, to the later period, described by Daniel Bell and others as 'the post-industrial age' and characterised by the use of electronics in production and the growing pluralism of mass society. As we shall see, Nomos – the office furniture system that Foster designed in the mid-'80s – clearly belongs to this later era and is defined entirely by its parameters. In spite of the fact that it retains some features of the visual language of the early Modern period,

The models were used to demonstrate possible, high-level configurations of the various components available in the system. The individual standardised units, which offered a range of different functions, were intended to be made of lightweight pressed metal panels attached to a metal frame.

by taking on board the practical requirements of the new electronic office, the new, flexible forms of manufacturing and the demands of the market-place, Foster has been able to evolve a furniture system which is philosophically in tune with a much more complex age.

An awareness of the need to develop a range of office furniture which took the problems of manufacture not only as a means to an end but as its very raison d'être dawned gradually rather than suddenly however. The first proposals for a range of office furniture, made by the Foster team, headed by David Nelson, were destined to be manufactured by the British furniture company Hille – best known for its production of a highly-successful polypropylene chair designed by Robin Day back in the

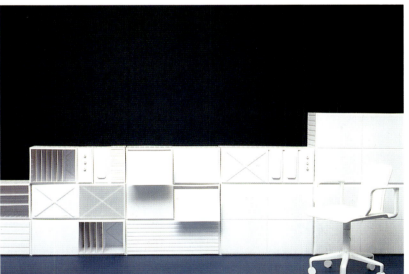

Low-level assemblies of the units were also possible with the models, which were detailed enough to show some elements with open access storage and others with drawers. For proper ergonomic studies, however, the cardboard mock-ups proved invaluable.

A table was also conceived as an adjunct to the Hille system. Although little more than an afterthought at this stage, it included features – among them a tubular steel frame and an inclining surface – which were to reappear during the project's next stage of development.

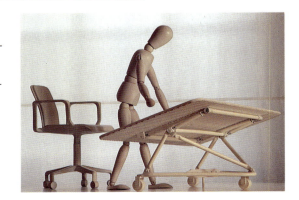

Norman Foster's earliest sketches of a desk system for the new Great Portland Street office show the concept of a tubular spine supported on angled legs. Here a reception desk is shown, including an extra shelf and 'vanity' panel.

"We could not find anything that would work as a drawing-board to our satisfaction. They were either too heavy, too clumsy, too expensive, we did not like the way they looked or you could not move them around. Our response was a series of components – not made by the traditional furniture industry at all – which could produce a table for use as a conference table, as drafting stand or to hold a model at a particular height."

Norman Foster, lecture at the Metropolitan Museum, New York, November 1982

The traditional office desk with its fixed table-top and heavy pedestals, both features which Foster wanted to avoid in his own system.

early 1960s. (After several years working on the Hongkong Bank, Nelson returned to the furniture project during the development of the Nomos system.)

The wall system that was evolved for Hille concentrated more on the possibilities of assembly of the components involved, than on the manufacturing process to be employed in its fabrication. In keeping with the methods used in the Foster office in the process of architectural design, scale models and full-size cardboard mock-ups were used from the outset as a means of working with something which resembled, as nearly as possible, the final version. The idea of a set of standardised and individual components which could be arranged flexibly, and which could fulfil as many varied needs as were required, emerged fairly rapidly as work on the proposal progressed. Hille's involvement with the Foster office as a possible manufacturer of the system made this a real, rather than a fantasy project and encouraged a great deal of development work at the prototyping stage. What failed to emerge, however, was a close liaison between the Foster office and the manufacturer concerning the way in which the mass production of the design might necessitate a commitment to new tooling on the part of Hille. Inevitably this would have proved an expensive exercise. By this time, Foster had evolved a highly rigorous approach towards architectural design which accepted, when appropriate, the special production of components which

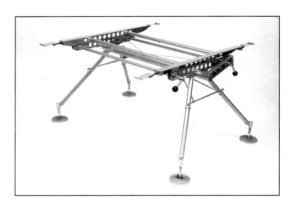

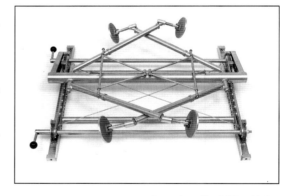

Complete flexibility. Not only would the basic base unit accept a variety of work-tops and allow them to be positioned over a wide range of heights and angles, the legs were designed to fold down so that the unit could be easily transported.

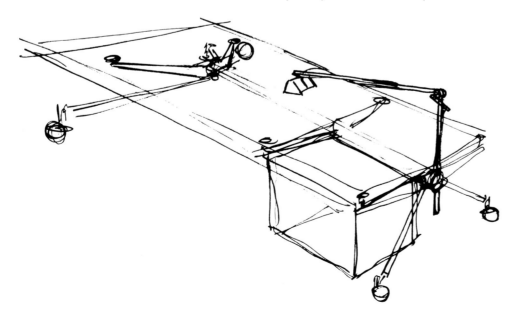

For fixed table-tops, brackets could be attached to the central spine, which might then also be used to support under-desk storage units.

Foster set about designing his own desk for the Great Portland Street office because existing models proved unsatisfactory. The brief was very specific – it had to be light in weight and appearance and very flexible. The proposal that evolved contained a mechanism which enabled the top to rise and incline in a variety of ways, thereby allowing it to perform multiple functions – among them those of drafting table, projection screen, flip-chart and exhibition stand. The desks were made for the office's use alone, with hand-welding on a 'batch', rather than mass production basis, by a small company called Presentation Systems.

"It takes you beyond mere necessity into the world of expressive necessity. You could design a lighter table; you could design a cheaper table. You couldn't design a table which is quite so much fun. You have to admire it. And the thing is, there will always be that kicker in the admiration that you know it's also like that for perfectly good reasons."

Reyner Banham, the Yellow Bicycle lecture at UEA, June 1985

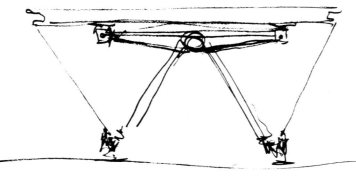

For added stability when using a fixed table-top, one sketch by Norman Foster suggests tension wires stretched between the top's edge and the feet.

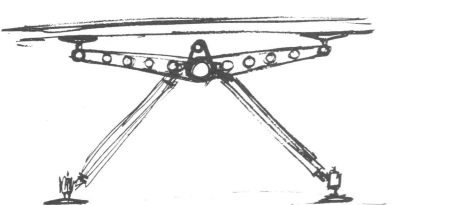

could not be made by existing machines. Usually this meant 'inventing' a tool to fabricate the required item. This uncompromising approach has become one of the hallmarks of Foster's design philosophy, reaching maturity in the work for the Hongkong Bank, a scheme which coincided, chronologically, with the furniture project. As Hille lacked commitment to this thoroughgoing approach to fabrication, Foster felt that the alliance with them was unlikely to prove fruitful and withdrew from it.

The Hille project had been concerned, primarily, with the idea of storage but it had also included a desk — almost an afterthought at this stage — supported by a flexible, tubular-steel base, which could double as a drawing table. With the dismissal of Hille, the furniture project became a much more private undertaking. New impetus was provided, in 1980, by the office's planned move to new premises in Great Portland Street, in 1981, and the desperate need for new drawing tables with which to furnish it. In spite of the fact that both time and financial resources were in short supply, the problems that were found to exist in all the available 'off-the-shelf' models — they were either too heavy, expensive, inflexible, or

A fixed-top table was developed in parallel with the more flexible desk unit and for both Foster proposed holes drilled in certain elements. This not only reduced their weight but also helped articulate the structural differences between various components.

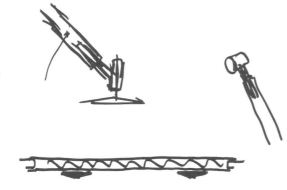

Much attention was given to the way in which the leg met the foot. In addition, a lightweight honeycomb-cored top, with an aluminium extruded edge trim, was proposed as a clip-on surface for the desk.

A height adjustment detail was envisaged for the foot of the desk from the outset. This would enable it to adapt with ease to individual preference and, at a more pragmatic level, to differences in floor levels. Much attention was paid to the way in which the foot junctions might be articulated.

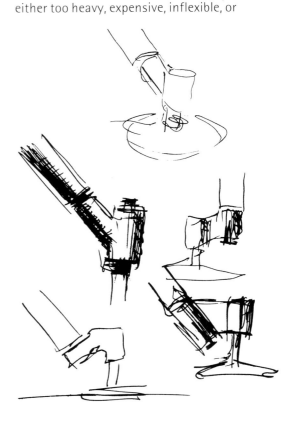

An alternative use of tension wires. Here they stretch from the end of the brackets to hold the table-top in place.

A sketch by Norman Foster showing a possible frame for the office table. In this proposal the splayed legs and circular feet are mirrored by the tubular steel structure and rubber discs which support the top. Although this concept was rejected, the steel spine which holds the whole structure together became a fundamental element of the final design. Equally, the visual character of the splayed members remained a strong feature of the office table which Foster was to develop several years later for the Italian manufacturer, Tecno.

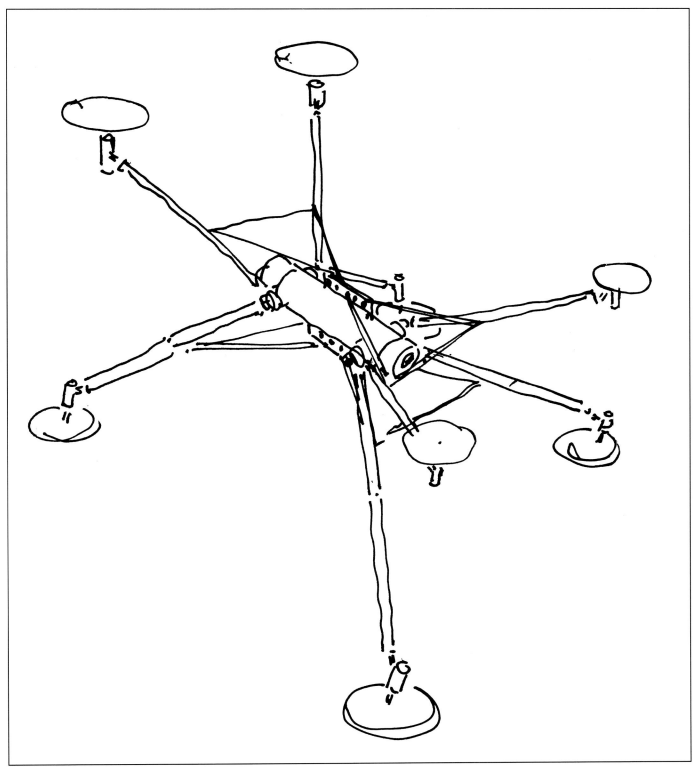

A sketch developing the idea of the desk top being supported only by the end details of the frame, thereby eliminating the central spine. The mechanism, which was integrated into the metal frame of the desk, allowed the desk top to move from a horizontal to a vertical plane.

"Now one thing an architect's drawing desk must do is stand secure. For one thing the architect will lean on it for much of his life and it would not be life enhancing if it kept falling over on him or whatever. Furthermore, his lines should not wobble and things like that. It must stand secure. This device, but this is the point, makes a big scene of standing secure."

Reyner Banham, the Yellow Bicycle lecture at UEA, June 1985

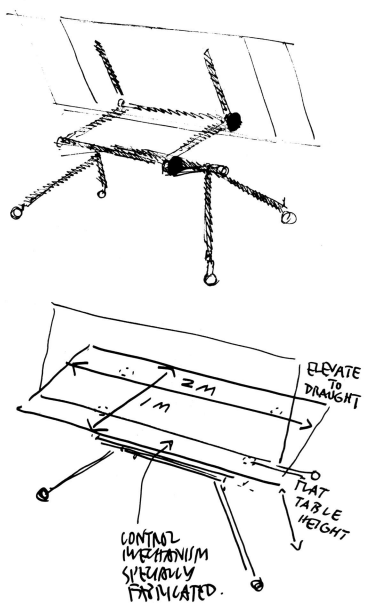

The question of optimum dimensions for the desk top was discussed at length in order to allow for the greatest possible flexibility of use.

required a long delivery time — meant that the office had to undertake the enormous task of designing and making its own tables.

The brief for the desks for Great Portland Street was very specific: they had to be light, flexible, collapsible, adjustable in height and angle, affordable, and good to look at. It was also anticipated that future variations on the initial theme might well include storage units under the desk top. The design that emerged responded ingeniously to these requirements through the use of a tubular-steel subframe and a special mechanism which allowed the desk to perform multiple functions. It was the invention of the honeycomb-cored table top, however, that was the real key to the desk's success. Drawing on recent technology from the aerospace industry, the design team was able to manufacture — from aluminium honeycomb only 25mm thick laminated on both sides with plastic laminate — an impressively light but perfectly flat desk top, two-metres wide and one-metre deep.

While the drawing tables themselves provided the initial point of departure, they were seen, from the very early stages of the project, as just one element within a larger system. Based on the concept of a tubular-steel spine, which served to link together disparate elements in a number of alternative configurations, the system enabled a flat desk, for instance, to be connected to low-level storage, which in turn could be linked to a tilting table. The possibility of creating a 'Y' joint in the spine permitted arrangements which deviated from the principle of the straight line.

The philosophy of the office system as a whole, and the rationale behind its detailing, therefore were fixed, broadly speaking, right from the beginning of the project. From the first, Foster envisaged a system which responded sympathetically to the increasingly flexible requirements of the contemporary office. The desk, which doubled as a drawing-table, projection screen, exhibition stand or flip-chart, was a mark of such flexibility, while the system as a whole offered the possibility of a number of 'clip-on' accessories, among them below-level storage and — proposed in sketch form only at this stage — eye-level storage and uplighting.

Two prototype models for the Great Portland Street desk were developed. The first (top) was quite basic, being intended only to show the concept. Tubular steel arms were attached to the mechanism which enabled the incline of the desk surface, with each arm, in this instance, being operated independently. In the second prototype (centre), the mechanism has become more compact and the arms are made — from top to bottom — of an angled piece of steel, a flat piece of sheet steel, and a piece of box section steel. They are all pierced to maximise lightness while retaining strength. The lowest photograph shows this version of the mechanism in operation.

Without springs, adjustment of the desk top requires some care — especially with a heavier work-top in place — and is not quite child's play. Within the confines of the office, however, this arrangement has proved more than adequate.

The double pivot arrangement of the supporting arms allows an impressive range of movement which the widely splayed legs securely support.

The dentist's chair. Norman Foster was fascinated by the concept of clip-on components being added to a basic service spine as required. Were there lessons to be learnt here that could be applied to the design of office furniture?

By positioning the tubular spine at a fixed height, and attaching everything to it, the system became a 'kit-of-parts' which could be adapted to a number of different uses. The idea of an 'inventory' – a term used recently by Foster to describe the Nomos system – was already present in the project, therefore, back in the early 1980s.

In 1980 and '81 development work was undertaken through a process of sketching all the individual components, working on full-size mock-ups and finally providing a prototype which was presented to the manufacturer – at this stage a company, based in Norfolk, called Presentation Systems. The desks for Great Portland Street were essentially 'batch production' objects: they were manufactured in small numbers with hand processes by a 'cottage industry'. Wherever one piece of steel met another piece hand-welding was utilised, the complexity of the design of the subframe meaning that over 60 such welds were actually needed. As the desk was intended for use by the Foster office alone, however, this small-scale production proved adequate and the Great Portland Street office was quickly supplied with enough desks to enable it to operate efficiently.

Aesthetically, the Great Portland Street desk clearly belonged to the same family of 'High-Tech' forms for which Foster had already become well-known through his architectural projects, although it is a label with which he is less than happy. Its imagery derived its symbolic impetus from a number of loose associations – none of them either specifically, or self-consciously, injected into the design – with existing engineered structures; among them the triangular frame of the bicycle, the Eiffel Tower and the splayed legs of a space landing-craft, images of which were to be displayed on the walls of the new Great Portland Street office. A few highly distinctive features – among them the particularly innovative foot detail which consisted of a short vertical tube attached to a round disc – were proposed at this time and were to remain characteristics of the project right up to the emergence of Nomos in 1986.

The need to furnish the interior of the Renault building, an architectural project which was in the office when early thoughts about the office system were being articulated, provided

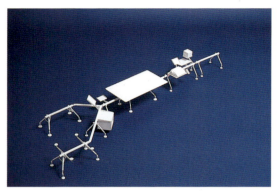

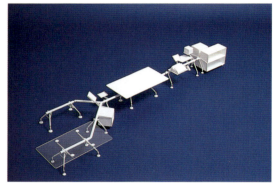

Using models, this sequence of photographs demonstrates the way in which the concept of the simple desk, designed for the Great Portland Street office, could be extended to create a highly flexible office system to suit a multitude of needs.

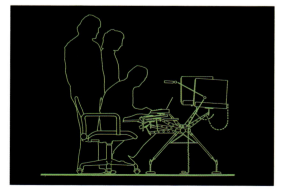

A series of diagrams was prepared to illustrate the way in which the central spine could allow any variety of components to be added, creating different types of work station suitable for the modern electronic office. The starting point for all this complexity, however, remains a simple table.

Colin Chapman's classic design for the chassis of the Lotus Elan. Norman Foster used the analogy of such a chassis to develop the idea that a single frame, with different components attached to it, could provide the foundation for a number of different models.

In its final form, the model sequence shows the full range of possibilities offered by the new furniture system. Tables, with tops shown at a variety of angles, are interspersed with different clip-on components ranging from video monitor or typewriter stands – adjustable to height – to suspended storage units. A 'Y' joint in the spine allows the system to expand in more complex organisational forms. Fixed storage units, similar to the Hille proposals, are also shown as a necessary back-up to the spine-based furniture options and, for the first time, a free-standing glass-topped table appears.

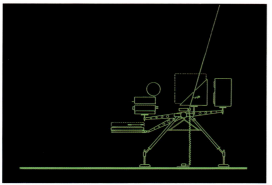
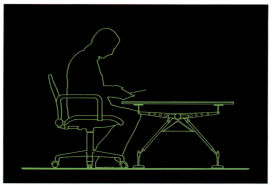

In a similar analogy to the dentist's chair, Foster put forward the modern racing bike, on to whose fixed frame any combination of components might be added.

"The table that Foster designed for use in his own office was a deliberate attempt to produce a design that would overcome his principal objection to the Action Office, that is, its tendency toward breaking up interiors with a cellular maze of partition walls."

Deyan Sudjic, *Blueprint*, February 1987

Flexible joints were proposed as a means of creating work stations which would not be restricted by the need to assemble sets of components in straight lines.

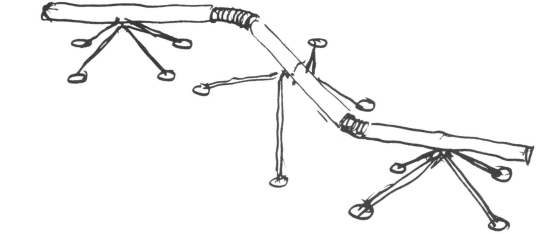

An extension of the Great Portland Street desk. Foster's sketch proposes a system which turns a corner, support at the point of pivot being provided by a pair of straight, rather than splayed, legs.

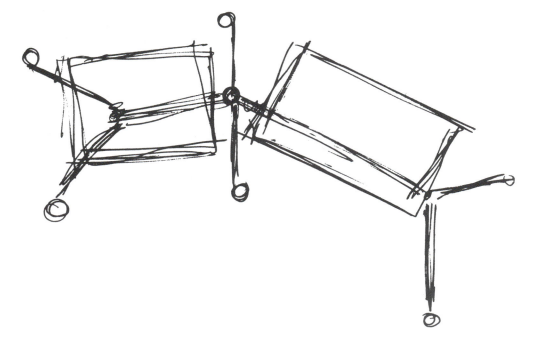

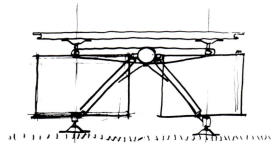

The idea of under-surface storage which could be cantilevered off the central spine was developed through a number of sketches.

yet another opportunity for Foster and his furniture team — at this time Arek Wozniak, assisted by Ralph Ball and Paul Heritage among others — to further their designs. Whereas the furniture specification for the earlier Sainsbury Centre had resulted in the inclusion of 'ready-made' furniture by Charles Eames, Hans Coray and Yrjo Kukkapuro, all highly appropriate items for that particular interior, the Renault building provided an occasion for developing a range of simple office furniture which would blend, both conceptually and visually, with the building itself. This was the first opportunity of its kind which had been presented to the Foster office, and it came at an opportune moment inasmuch as it allowed the furniture designs, still in a state of gestation in many ways, to undergo the test of functioning in an environment other than the rarefied atmosphere of Foster's own office.

From the outset of the project, Foster was keen to provide new furniture for the Renault building but only limited funds would be made available from the French company to cover this part of the work. The Renault director responsible for the project, Pierre Jocou, suggested that Foster and his team might use what limited funds were available to develop what he described as

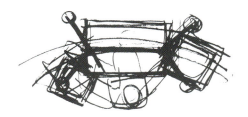

A rough sketch by Norman Foster showing how the original desk could be adapted into an intensive work station through the addition of two wings on either side.

The 'kebab' principle – the idea that many different elements could be 'threaded' on to a central spine – was proposed as one possible method of assembly. In this sketch, steel supports are threaded on the steel tube at the centre of the system, with under-surface storage then attached to these through its sides.

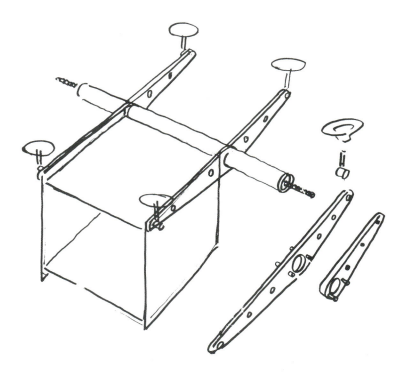

Foster was keen not to dispense with any of the multiple functions performed by the original desking system and he produced sketches to show that the inclined desk could incorporate under-surface storage as easily as the flat one. Placed next to an inclined drafting surface, a flat desk top could be used by a designer as layout space.

'the spirit' of their own table into a range of furniture suitable for the office areas, restaurant and reception of the new building.

It proved an exhausting exercise as the Foster office became necessarily involved not only in designing a new range of office furniture for Renault – based on its own table system – but also in the process of subcontracting its manufacture, transporting it to the site and assembling it. The initial design team had to expand considerably to execute these last two tasks. It was an enormous undertaking which stretched the skills of those involved to their limits, but its eventual success meant that the traditional, commercial practices involved in specifying furniture were bypassed completely. It is in this sense that Foster uses the term 'architecture in miniature' to describe his experiences with furniture. So pleased was Jocou with the furniture that he requested a table for his own dining-room in Detroit.

What came, later, to be called the father table – characterised by its splayed legs and diagonal steel supports for the top – was developed in the form of glass-topped dining-tables for the Renault building. It accompanied a simple desking system, which was specifically

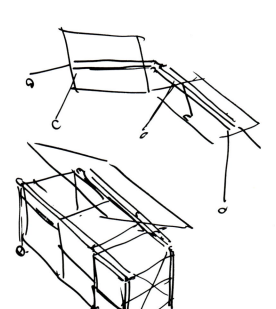

Cantilevered from one side of a central spine, large storage units needed a solid fixing to avoid sagging. A reinforced spine was proposed with 'ridges' added to top and bottom, against which the support brackets could be adequately braced.

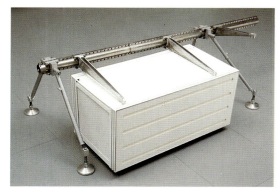

Designed at the same time as the furniture system, though by a different team, this view of the Renault Centre clearly demonstrates the similarities between furniture and architecture. It was with this likeness in mind that Pierre Jocou, a Renault director, suggested that Foster might like to develop the furniture used at Great Portland Street for use in the Renault Centre – an opportunity that was to give the Foster office a chance to extend its achievements so far into a new environment.

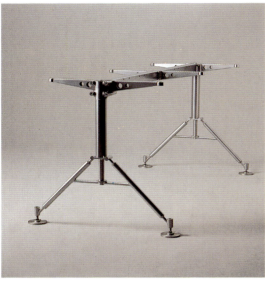

A variety of work-tops could be attached to the basic frame. Because the project was for a limited number of items, few advances were made in the manufacturing process. Construction was still achieved primarily through welding and little effort was devoted to reducing the number of joints required.

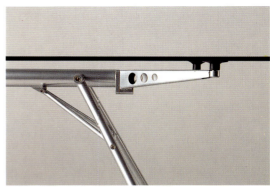

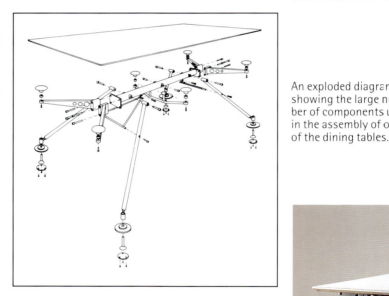

An exploded diagram showing the large number of components used in the assembly of one of the dining tables.

A detail of the dining table showing the brace, which strengthened the intersection between the tubular steel spine – retained in this model – and the legs.

The desks for Renault were supported by a rectangular section steel spine on to which the legs and top supports were attached. A quite new arrangement for the legs was used which was more compatible with independent 'roll-boy' storage units.

One of the variations on a theme was a round-topped table designed specifically for the Renault building.

An alternative leg unit was created for desks requiring a narrower work-top.

The glass top of the dining table was a logical choice, allowing the considered and well-crafted details of the table's frame to be clearly seen and appreciated.

"Within the tightest technical and, indeed, economic disciplines, Eames showed how much freedom for the designer there was. And the lessons I think have not been lost on the Foster office."

Reyner Banham, the Yellow Bicycle lecture at UEA, June 1985

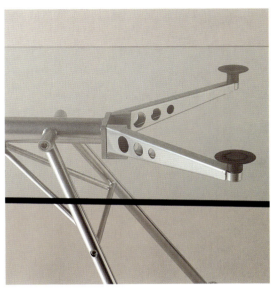

developed from earlier proposals for this context, and a round-topped glass table. The main change, where the system was concerned, was the substitution of the original steel-tube spine by a square-section steel backbone to which support brackets were fitted at right angles. The main manufacturing process was still the time-consuming welding, although one simple casting was included at the junction of the spine and the vertical tube section of the leg. Turned aluminium was used for the feet. Presentation Systems were the fabricators once again, although they subcontracted out the work on the table-tops.

By 1983 ideas formulated four years earlier had reached a maturity equal to the level of their conceptualisation, their aesthetic and their use. Adequate means of manufacture for supplying a limited number of items had been developed and a unity had been achieved, for the first time in the public's eyes, between Foster's architectural work and his forays into furniture design. An already fairly lengthy gestation period meant that the ideas which sustained the furniture were now fully developed and allowed for variation on a simple theme to transform a set of basic alternatives into a more ambitious project.

The reception desk designed for the Renault building. By interchanging and adding to the basic components — a modesty panel is included here, for example — the 'kit-of-parts' allowed many different configurations.

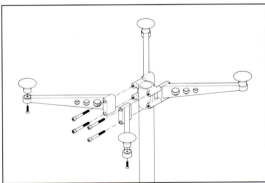

An exploded drawing showing the connection of the top casting for the circular table.

A central top support for the glass-topped dining table.

This could not be realised, however, on the modest scale that had so far determined the production of the furniture in question. It required the involvement of a manufacturing company which was not only sympathetic to the project but which also had enough maturity, experience and flexibility of its own to be able to act as a catalyst in turning an idea with potential into a radically new proposal for office furniture.

The dining table, shown here complete with Eames' chairs, represented an important consolidation of a series of design developments which had been taking place over a couple of years. It was also to be the springboard for the next stage in the evolution of Norman Foster's furniture project.

1985–1987 Architecture in Miniature
by Penny Sparke

The Tecno System

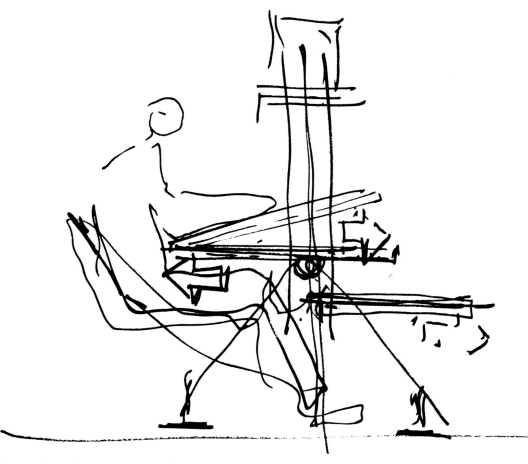

Norman Foster's concept sketch for Nomos, the office system that was to be developed in association with Tecno. This early visualisation contains many of the important characteristics of the system which were to feature in the final version – among them high-level storage supported by a superstructure attached to the central spine, and adjustable work surfaces. From the outset the system was seen as serving the needs of the modern electronic office.

Ever since the aborted Hille project Foster had been looking for a manufacturer who would be able both to develop and mass-produce the pieces that he had been working on since the late 1970s. The main requirements were that the company concerned would be willing to invest in new tooling and that it would have sufficient expertise and experience in working in the particular materials in question. A strong sympathy for the idea of 'quality' – both of materials and of general workmanship – was also essential in the appearance of the new pieces, as well as in the efficiency of their functional flexibility which would depend entirely upon a rigorous approach towards the details of the manufacturing process.

In many ways it was utterly predictable that the only really feasible approach was made, not by an English manufacturer, but by an Italian one. By the '80s, Italy had achieved a reputation not only for fine, high-quality furniture with a strong design profile, but also for a very special kind of furniture industry which relied upon the concept of 'flexible specialisation'. What this entailed, in brief, was an industry which depended upon a great deal of subcontraction to small specialised firms which, in turn, combined the use of advanced numerically-controlled machines with artisan traditions.

This special formula permitted a highly flexible approach to furniture production: it made innovation easier than within a more centralised mass-production system and it encouraged a high level of craftsmanship. Most importantly, for the Foster project, it meant that an Italian company could, with great facility, develop a system which combined a degree of standardisation with a high level of object variation – a concept which lay at the philosophical core of Foster's designs.

The development of the principle of 'flexible specialisation' had grown, in Italy, out of two distinct historical moments within the post-war period. The first was the Communist scourges of the '50s, during which a number of skilled workers had left the large companies – Fiat primarily – to set up small, highly-skilled workshops of their own. Later, during the strike waves of the latter half of the '60s, many of the large companies sought ways of bypassing the problems associated with the union activities which were disrupting their production lines and causing wages to rise. They introduced a new approach to mass manufacturing which focused on the principle of decentralisation: instead of raising wages within the factory, they turned to the smaller workshops to manufacture their components for them. As many of the smaller firms functioned within the 'submerged economy' and were therefore able to operate cheaply, this proved a profitable strategy. Also they were often family concerns thereby managing to keep their overheads as low as possible.

Throughout the '70s, more skilled workers left the large factories and moved into the smaller ones, most of which were established outside the traditional 'industrial triangle'. What developed as a result has been described as a 'High-Tech cottage industry' combining skilled labour with a highly flexible approach to advanced technology. Multi-purpose machinery was frequently introduced and design played a vital role as the firms aimed their products at a sophisticated, international market. This

"Of course the Foster name would be just as bankable should he choose to append it to a fountain pen, a range of luggage, or a mineral water bottle – all options that would certainly be open to him should he choose to take them up. But the fact that he has done none of these things does not protect him from a sneaking suspicion among the more world-weary of commentators that Nomos is just such a project. The very fact that Foster had designed a piece of furniture tended to obscure any serious discussion of what he had come up with."

Deyan Sudjic, *Blueprint*, February 1987

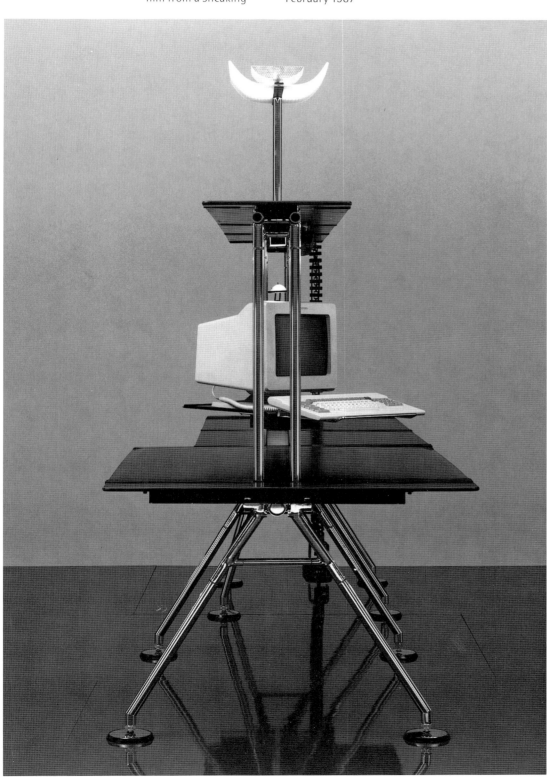

A photograph of an early prototype of Foster's desking system taken for the Compasso d'Oro, the highly prestigious Italian design prize which was awarded to the Nomos system. It shows a number of components added to the original structure – uplighting and a wiring spine among them.

An early sketch by Norman Foster shows the path of the wiring spine, an independent element that would move up from the floor, past the work surface to the top of the superstructure.

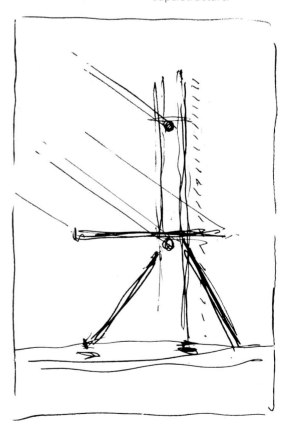

A variety of images was employed by Norman Foster, during his early discussions with Tecno, as a means of conveying the underlying spirit of the furniture system. The grasshopper's slender legs offer stability in the way they are widely spread.

"Foster's approach to architecture invariably involves dispensing with preconceptions as to how buildings should look, and Nomos follows a similar pattern. The elements of the system have little in common with traditional ideas of what furniture is like."

Deyan Sudjic, *Blueprint*, February 1987

tendency coincided, in fact, with the period of expansion and diversification of world markets. As it made the production of more varied and customised goods increasingly easy it came into its own in this new context.

The Italian furniture industry provides one of the best examples of this model of manufacturing. Unlike the large automotive and steel manufacturers it had, due to the nature of its product, never expanded beyond a certain size: also, from the early post-war days onwards, it had depended largely upon subcontraction. Tecno, the company which was to work with Foster in developing his furniture, is an interesting company in this particular respect. Set up in 1954, on the basis of a much older furniture workshop established by the Borsanis, a family of furniture craftsmen skilled in woodworking, it expanded rapidly through the '50s and '60s, mass-producing a number of furniture items, primary among them Osvaldo Borsani's famous P40 lounge chair of 1954. It also worked, simultaneously, on individual interior installations. During this period the company built up relationships with local suppliers of materials — marble, glass and so on — which it needed in small amounts for its one-off projects.

A sketch, by Norman Foster, establishing the height of the work surface and high-level storage from the floor.

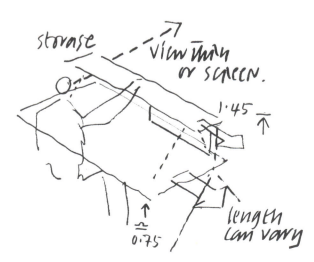

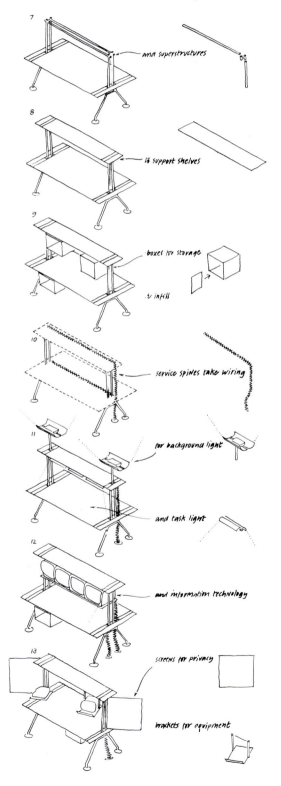

A series of sketches was prepared by Norman Foster to demonstrate clearly how, on the basis of a simple tubular spine, a variety of alternative work stations could be devised, ranging from a simple drafting table to a station which includes high-level storage, uplighting and facilities to cater for electronic equipment. Individual work stations could then be joined together to provide desking systems in ever more complex configurations, simply by adding components and varying the shapes of the elements which link the desks together. Depending on the size and shape of the office for which it is destined and end-user requirements, Nomos can be modified in a seemingly endless number of ways.

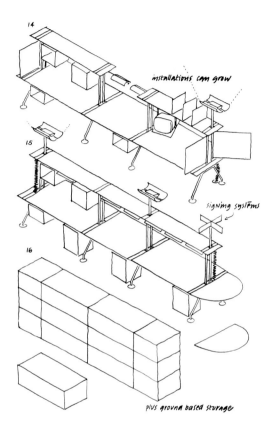

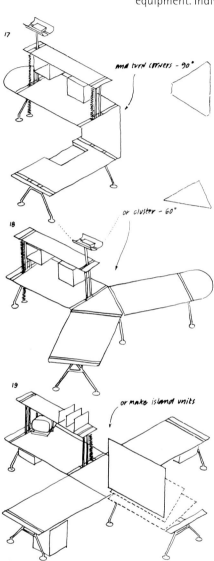

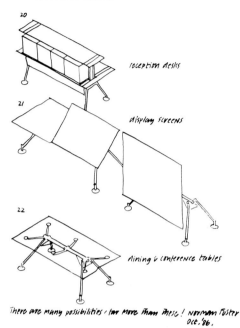

45

Early full-size mock-ups show the development of design for the Nomos desking system, including the way in which the superstructure was introduced. In its initial form (left), a family resemblance to many of the components of Foster's earlier table is retained, particularly in relation to the legs and feet. To promote discussion, an alternative solution was prepared (right), based on a radically different arrangement for its basic support. Both options were developed in parallel for some time.

A view of Foster Associates' model-shop. Mock-ups became an essential part of the design process and were used extensively to promote discussion and simplify communication, as well as to allow the more detailed study of various methods of assembly.

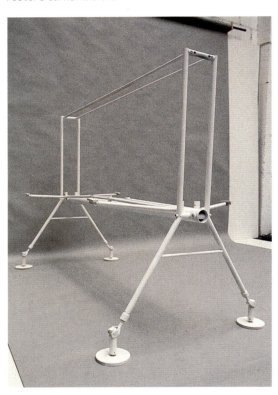

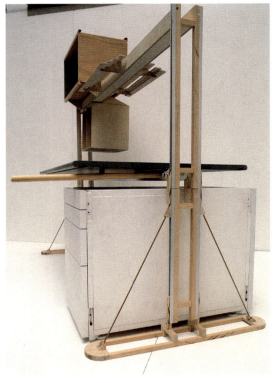

At the Milan Triennale of 1968, Tecno launched a new office system called Graphis, which made an enormous impact on both the domestic and international markets until well into the '80s. It introduced clean, white, standardised office furniture into an environment which had hitherto been dominated by murky colours. A decade after its introduction the company began to look around for a new design which would provide the same impact in the '90s as Graphis had in the '70s and '80s.

Foster had already been approached by a number of manufacturers, all wanting to produce furniture designed by him. Alias, in Italy, and Knoll, in the US, had already made overtures to him when he came into contact with Tecno, at first through the agency of Robert Timoschi, the firm's representative at the London showroom which had opened in 1982. Foster was cautious about committing himself to an alliance with a manufacturer because he felt that all the conditions had to be ideal before he ventured into such an important new direction. On meeting the Borsani family and Marco Fantoni, a director of Tecno and their chief in-house designer, Foster felt, however, that the 'chemistry' was right, that the firm was capable of producing his designs in an appropriate manner and that he was ready to agree to work with them on the design of a furniture system to replace Graphis. Once the formal arrangements had been carried out, work proceeded very rapidly and the prototypes of the new system were on show at the Milan Furniture Fair of 1986.

Although elements of that office system — the boardroom desks, the flexible drawing table, the flat desk with its overhead storage and so on — bear a striking family resemblance to Foster's sketches of six years earlier, and to the systems evolved both for Great Portland Street and the Renault building, they are, in many ways, quite new products which have grown from scratch out of a collaboration between the Foster office and Tecno.

An important modification to the earlier design resulted from the fact that the numerous welds on the Renault desk prevented it from moving, economically, into larger-scale production. The 'gestalt' thinking that was required to transform it characterised the thoroughgoing inventiveness of Tecno and the Foster office in the way they went about developing and ex-

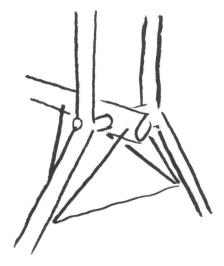

The junction between legs and spine is the single most important joint in the whole system. Sketches, models and working mock-ups explored a multitude of options.

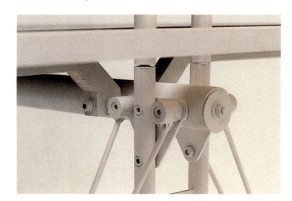

The cockpit of a modern passenger jet. In aircraft, controls are not restricted to 'table-top' levels, but are grouped in easy reach of the crew when seated. Could the same principles be applied to furniture?

An alternative mock-up, made in plastic and wood, showing a double work station complete with superstructure and a wide range of storage components both above and below the work-top. The lower desk was for use as a typing surface.

The mock-ups were developed and used as a means of studying the ergonomic implications of various storage configurations. This side of the research was undertaken rigorously throughout the development of the system.

tending the system. The problem of reducing the number of welds used in the manufacture of the metal substructure, for instance, was solved by creating a number of cast-aluminium pieces which act as joints linking one piece of steel to another. The use of a fixed group of castings means that only the steel tubes which are attached to them need be cut to varied lengths to increase the flexibility of the system. Much of the work undertaken during the latter part of 1985 and the early part of 1986 was dedicated to perfecting these castings which were vital to the production feasibility of the subframes of both the office system and the 'father' table.

Tecno is in an advantageous position where the manufacture of aluminium castings is concerned. For over 25 years the company has worked with a small foundry which processes non-ferrous metals. Based just outside Brescia, the Cervati family firm, the Fonderie Cervati, is

These sketches by Norman Foster propose the introduction of an asymmetric leg to move the high-level storage away from the user.

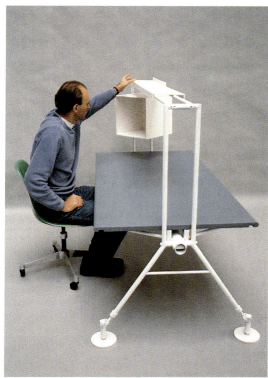

Because of its complexity, the junction between leg and central spine underwent a number of developments. The sketches (left and far right) show some of the early stages.

The aluminium casting which joins the leg to the central spine is shown here, in its final form and with half of its mould.

"...but technology is simply the making of things and the making of things can't by its own nature be ugly or there would be no possibility for beauty in the arts, which also include the making of things. Actually, a root word of technology, 'technikos', originally meant 'art'. The ancient Greeks never separated art from manufacture in their minds, and so never developed separate words for them."

Robert Pirsig, *Zen and the Art of Motorcycle Maintenance*, Bodley Head, 1974

Just one of a series of full-size prototypes developed by Tecno to test the viability of joining the leg to the central spine by means of an aluminium casting.

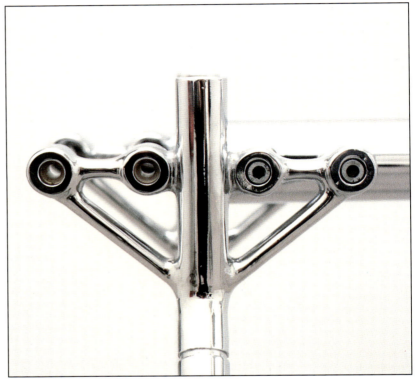

Any number of variations on how the leg-joint casting might be achieved were sketched and discussed before the best options were taken up by Tecno and produced in prototype form. Two options are shown in these sketches. The first (left) explores the possibility of freeing holes in the central spine so that they could be used for securing other components. For the sake of stability, however, all four fixing points had to be used (far right). The direct connection between superstructure support and leg proved unnecessary and was removed in the final version.

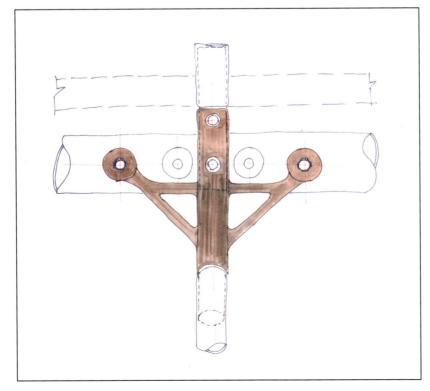

a prime example of the kind of subcontractor discussed earlier which runs its workshop according to the principle of 'flexible specialisation'. With only about 140 employees it works, none the less, with a number of international clients and in fact devotes much of its energy to supplying the Caterpillar company with specialised engine parts.

Tecno has a policy, where its subcontractors are concerned, of not working with firms which have contacts with other furniture companies. Thus a degree of 'specialness' is maintained while it benefits from the specialised skills offered by these small firms. Communication is both easy and direct due to the long-term nature of their relationship and to the fact that Cervati's engineers frequently visit the Tecno plant in Varedo for discussions with the design team based there.

The complicated high-pressure die-castings that are required to make the furniture items more economical to produce in large numbers necessitated the special design and manufacture of tools. While Tecno funded this exercise and provided drawings, the new tools were made by

Tecno had years of experience with prototypes, which meant that the system could be rigorously tested before a final solution was reached. Franco Rizzato is shown here fixing the final version of the leg-joint casting to the tubular spine.

"I think the respect and the esteem for people who make things and service things, is at a pretty low ebb and has been for a long time. I find that very difficult to believe because the creation, the making of anything, seems to me one of the noblest professions and if we have achieved anything as architects, it is because of a genuine humility and respect for people who make things."

Norman Foster, Eric Lyons Memorial lecture, November 1986

Cervati engineers. They represent a very high financial investment on the part of Tecno, particularly the ones which have the added complication of moving parts.

The process of inventing tools in order to create components which are necessary parts of a design was not new to Foster. As we have seen, it represents a fundamental facet of his design philosophy. As Marco Fantoni has pointed out: "It is better to spend an extra pound on the machinery than an extra penny on each component produced." Foster was confronting the exigencies of mass production head-on and thereby confirming his commitment to a Neo-Modern design philosophy which requires that there is a direct relationship between the nature of the production process and the final product. In this case the use of flexible, electronically-controlled manufacturing systems means that the requirements of the consumer, and of use, determine the degree of variation present in the products. "No longer is the consumer a slave to the production line", as he was in the early days of mass production, claims Foster.

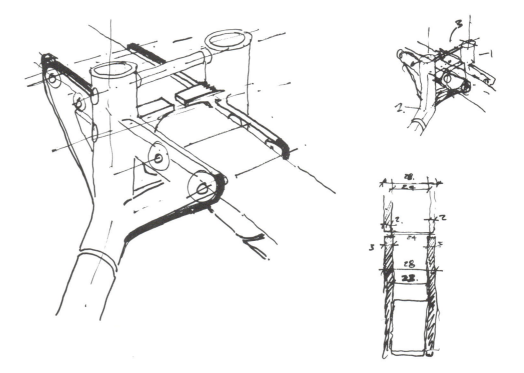

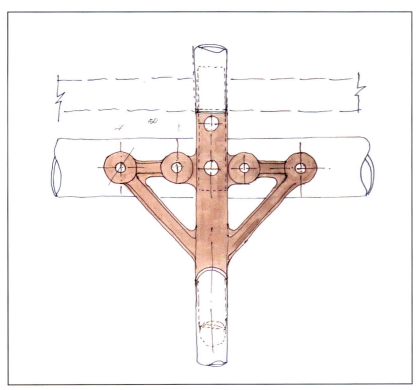

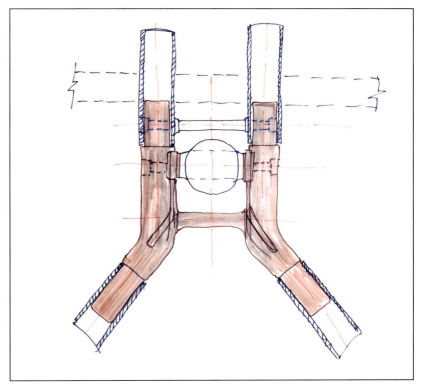

Through its long-standing use of sub-contractors, Tecno was able to produce the components for Nomos extremely efficiently and with a high level of skill and craftsmanship. The Cervati metal-casting company had worked with Tecno for a number of years on a wide range of projects. It is now being used again to produce the aluminium castings which are such an important aspect of the way in which Nomos is manufactured. The close collaboration between Tecno's engineers and Cervati's craftsmen resulted in the production of a set of components which eliminated the need for the large number of welds used in the manufacture of the Renault desks and tables. This use of highly specialised subcontractors is widespread in Italy and is an important factor in the success of its manufacturing industries. Shown here are some of the stages of collaboration that took place between Tecno, Cervati and Foster Associates.

The Nomos team: from left to right, Norman Foster, John Small and Martin Francis of Foster Associates, and Angelo Figus, Kugo Toru, Franco Rizzato, Pierluigi Zabotto and Marco Fantoni of Tecno.

The production of prototypes during the later stages of development took place in Tecno's engineering shop. Skilled and experienced engineers constructed a wide range of full-size models which were vital to the development of detailing of the structure, the inclusion of the high-level storage and the addition of the wiring spine.

These photographs illustrate work undertaken at Tecno on these important developments, as well as many of the team members involved in the project.

Early on in the development of Nomos it was decided that the foot should include a degree of flexibility and allow for the attachment of a number of different components. An important modification was the introduction of height and angle adjustment on the table feet to allow for different floor levels. Also suggested was the idea of a wheel as a substitute for the static disc foot as well as a range of different shapes for the disc itself. Tecno's solution, shown below in prototype form, could hardly be simpler.

"Nomos is Greek for 'pasture', and the 'nomad' is a clan elder who presides over the allocation of pastures. Nomos thus came to mean 'law', 'fair distribution', 'that which is allotted by custom' – and so the basis of all Western law."

Bruce Chatwin, *The Songlines*, Jonathan Cape, 1987

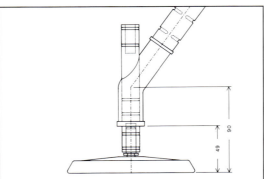
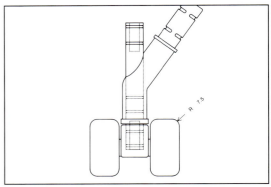

The principle of industrial design that was achieved by the Foster/Tecno alliance, therefore, was one which was in keeping with both parties' approaches. While the castings provided one of the most dramatic transformations, other highly-inventive changes were also made. One remarkable innovation, on the part of Tecno, related to the steel backbone itself. Research was undertaken into finding a way of replacing the system of passing the smaller-diameter steel component through holes in the larger-diameter tube and welding the joints. Tecno invented a process which removed the necessity for welding. The robot-controlled machine invented to make this possible was patented by Tecno and installed in late 1987 specifically to facilitate the production of the Foster furniture system, or Nomos as it was christened in 1986.

Although radical changes were being made to Foster's designs, they in no way damaged the original 'feel' of the early concept. Fantoni has said, in fact, that as soon as he saw Foster's designs he could easily envisage the final

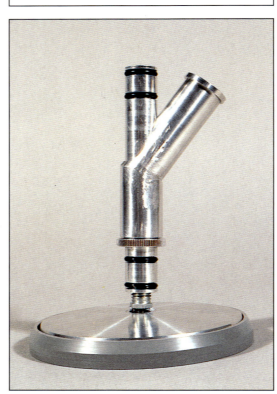

product, adapted to mass production but still encapsulating the spirit of the original proposals in its entirety.

In addition to the metal firms which Tecno uses as subcontractors, other companies are used either to fabricate components or to supply parts. All the sheet metal comes from a firm with whom Tecno has had a rapport for 20 years and whose main activity is making steel beds for hospitals. A small plastics company manufactures the vertebrae used to house the cabling, while marble, glass, chipboard and melamine are all provided by concerns which have supplied Tecno with materials for many years. This mature system of subcontraction and collaboration allows Tecno itself to concentrate on wood and assembly-work. The highly organised, yet eminently flexible, system that Tecno has developed has proved ideal for the manufacture of Nomos, depending as it does upon a variety of both standardised and individual components which can be assembled in a number of different ways.

The story of the vertebrae demonstrates yet another instance of the high level of innovation – both conceptual and otherwise – in the

"They have scoured the factories of northern Italy for spin-off technologies to minimise costs – storage panniers on the system may be made using techniques of forming pioneered by refrigerator companies, for example."

Deyan Sudjic, *Blueprint*, February 1987

For Martin Francis, the main inspiration for the concept of a wiring spine was the human backbone and its interlocking vertebrae. The challenge was how to provide the same amount of flexibility with simply manufactured components.

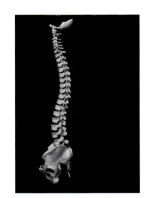

Sketches showing the development of the cable spine. It is produced from a series of plastic pieces connected in such a way as to maximise flexibility. Spaces offset in alternate components allow cables to be threaded into or out of the spine simply and at any point.

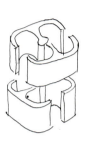

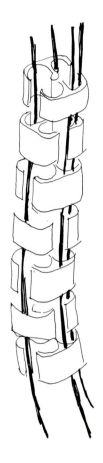

The completed desk with its wiring in place. As an independent element, the spine can be readily positioned – or even omitted – to match user requirements exactly.

Foster furniture system. The decision to eliminate any 'built-in' capacity for wire-management in the system, to allow it to function independently of its structure, means that the customer can buy exactly the amount that he needs for his particular installation. While existing systems inevitably offer either too much or too little wire-management and allow no flexibility, Nomos presents a more open and much more practical approach to the problem. The vertebrae come in two sizes to accommodate different types and amounts of wiring and are simply clipped on to the system.

The idea of providing a knuckle-jointed plastic system for housing the cables was developed and refined by Martin Francis, who modelled it on the human spine. Foster has since pointed out that its roots, however, also lie in the principle of the old-fashioned 'wiring loom', a principle with which Foster had become familiar during his national service days while working with radar. He has also referred to the analogy of the highly flexible wiring systems used in warships which have to respond to a number of very different requirements very

As with the earlier leg-joint casting, for the manufacture of the wiring spine Tecno once again decided on a subcontractor as the best way of obtaining its components. Cavi, a small plastics manufacturing company, produce, in two standard sizes, the plastic pieces which form the basis of the spine. By using a specialised subcontractor, Tecno is able to use the most suitable material for this element without having to move into plastics manufacture itself. Meanwhile, the expertise and small-scale nature of Cavi allows high-quality components to be produced in a very short time.

In preparation for an exhibition of the Nomos furniture system at Centrodomus in Milan, it was decided to collect all the elements that had been developed for the system. These were then displayed chronologically within the exhibition to demonstrate the developmental stages of the project. These photographs of the exhibit — as it was being set up — show how the system gradually evolved through a series of modifications, refinements and additions.

"I actually believe in the use of design to achieve improvement. If we want higher standards when we work, rest and play, then everybody has to actively pull in that direction. I include all those who use, inspire, guide, select, finance, entrepreneur, design, criticise, legislate, approve, cost, engineer, provide and build. When all the parties care enough, the end results show it: if there's a will, there's usually enough motivation to overcome the obstacles — even though at times it seems that most of the world is busy erecting barriers to prove that it all has to be mediocre."

Norman Foster, *RIBA Journal*, October 1976

For fixing points in the central spine, Tecno has developed a new drilling bit that not only makes the hole but also gives it a protruding flange which provides localised stiffness. The whole procedure, including insertion of a fixing rod, is carried out in a continuous operation on a specially-created rig.

A computer-generated drawing of the Nomos desk system, with all its components displayed in the form of an exploded isometric. Colour is used to differentiate between materials: red for aluminium castings or extrusions, blue for steel elements, and green for plastic components.

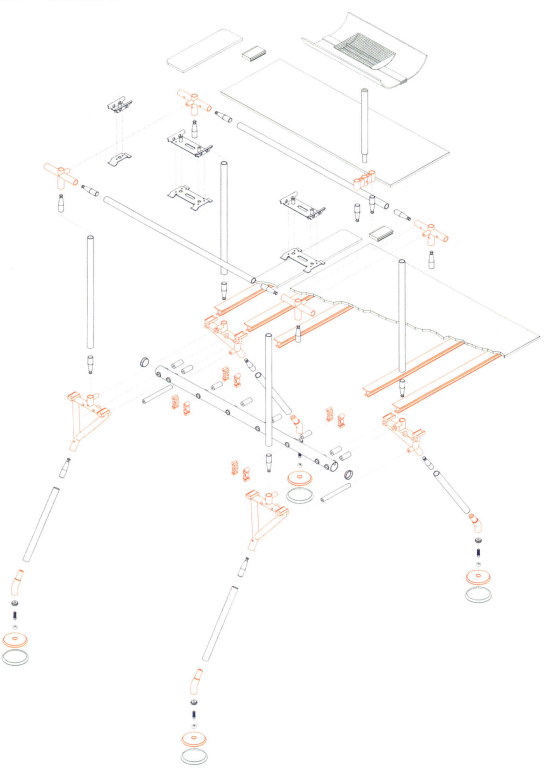

quickly. The use of these related but distant precedents is characteristic of his rigorously logical approach to design.

A number of other details concerning the design and manufacture of the final system were also consolidated in the 1985/6 period. One concerned the feet which had been the subject of numerous modifications through the project's lifetime. Tecno discovered that the adhesive, used to stick the foot to the leg, changed during the heating process which was used to apply a coat of paint to the product. To counteract this result the original adhesive was exchanged for an aeronautical variety — in keeping with Foster's constant reference to the aeroplane as a technological model — and gluing and fixing were then undertaken after the paint had been applied. This open-minded approach to change, and to the borrowing of technology from areas quite outside furniture manufacture per se, is yet another characteristic of both Tecno's and Foster's working methods which facilitated the rapid development of Nomos. Foster frequently talks about the idea of 'appropriate technology', a concept which underpins the whole furniture exercise.

Other additions from this period included Foster's refinement of the second level or overhead storage, which makes use of a space which had previously been largely ignored, and the addition of uplighting. Although the germ of these last ideas had been present, in sketch form, several years earlier, it wasn't until now, with the pressure of production deadlines pending, that decisions became more vital and conclusions were reached. A task light already available on the market was selected to accompany the system, interestingly identified by both Foster Associates and Tecno simultaneously. No such alternative for an uplighter was available, however, so one has been developed especially for the project to a design by Foster.

In spite of the geographical separation of Foster Associates' office from the Tecno plant, the working process on the research and development of Nomos proved to be very efficient. The meetings between Foster and the Tecno team in Milan and London were highly intensive sessions at which much progress was made. Foster and his team — Martin Francis,

A sketch by Norman Foster explores the possibility of using continuous uplighting in conjunction with the Nomos desks. From the outset, lighting was always considered an integral part of the system.

David Nelson, Rodney Uren, John Small, Tony Smith and Clifford Denn – presented sketches, and the Tecno team – Marco Fantoni, Kugo Toru, Pierluigi Zabotto, Angelo Figus and Franco Rizzato – made prototypes which were inspected by all concerned at regular intervals. Mock-ups were made in Foster's London workshops, particularly in connection with the refinement of specific components. Lessons were being learnt on both sides. While the rigour of Foster's approach to design encouraged Tecno to push the limits of its production capabilities, Tecno's manufacturing skills and experience showed the Foster office how to achieve the desired end through modified and, where mass production was concerned, improved means. It was a fertile relationship which made progress towards the shared destination extremely rapid.

For the Foster team the Tecno experience meant working within the context of an industrial culture which is unknown in Britain. The same degree of 'confidence in the product' is unusual on British soil and the willingness to invest in the invention of new tooling extremely rare. Even rarer is the special combination of skilled work and advanced technology which is found, not only on the Tecno shop-

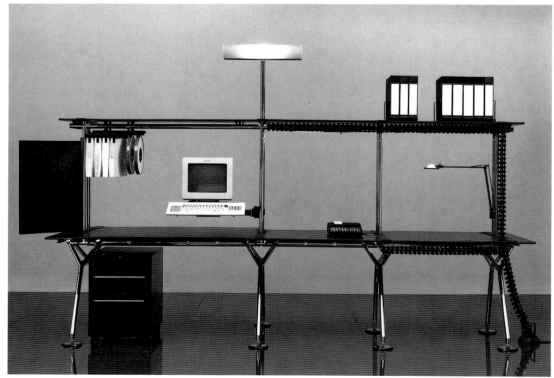

floor, where one-off pieces are still made by hand alongside numerically-controlled machines for mass-production purposes, but in the workshops of its subcontractors as well.

Tecno's role does not end, however, with production. Its in-house design team, headed before his recent untimely death by Roberto Davoli, is responsible not only for some of the development work on Nomos but also for its packaging and its publicity material.

A particularly innovatory approach has been used in the way Nomos is packed. The steel spine provides the support not only for the tables and desks themselves but also for the packing system which is, as a result, extremely light and compact. Tecno also provides a service in designing office layouts for the customers of Nomos. The company offers them a book with suggestions of possible configurations and works with its clients to design a particular layout to suit their special needs. This is in keeping with the kind of work that Tecno has undertaken in the past and carries the project to a logical and satisfactory conclusion.

"It's the first office system to be designed with the dealing room era in mind, in which the office has been transformed from a white-collar, status-conscious environment into a semi-industrial arena in which the workforce no longer sit at desks all day but work standing up much of the time, in which paper has been all but abolished, in which anybody without a keyboard is fast turning into an economic irrelevance."

Deyan Sudjic, *Blueprint*, February 1987

The prototype shown below and, from a different angle, on the opposite page is from the later stages of development. Including many components from this phase of the system's evolution – high-level storage, wiring spine, side screen, an elevated computer terminal support and task lighting among them – it was in this form that Nomos was submitted for the Compasso d'Oro award.

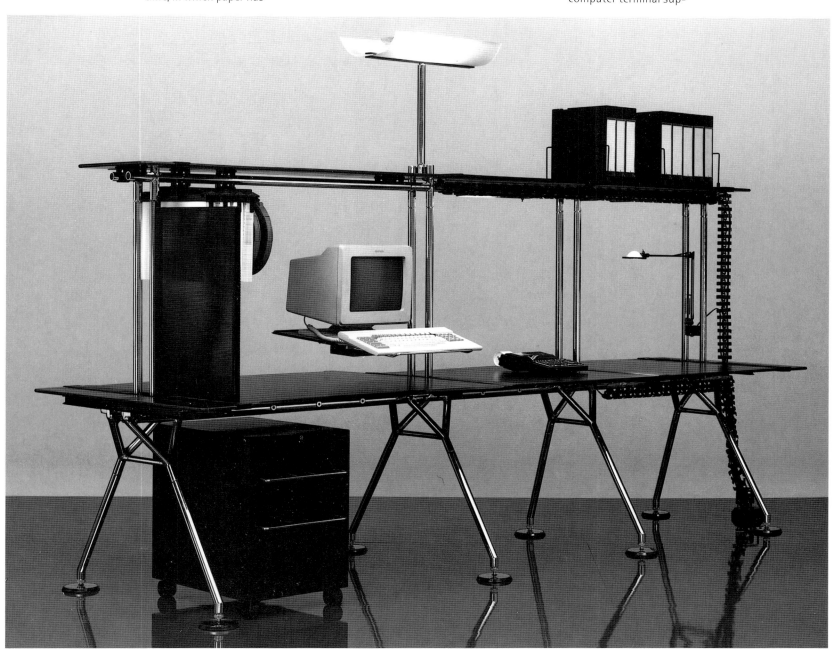

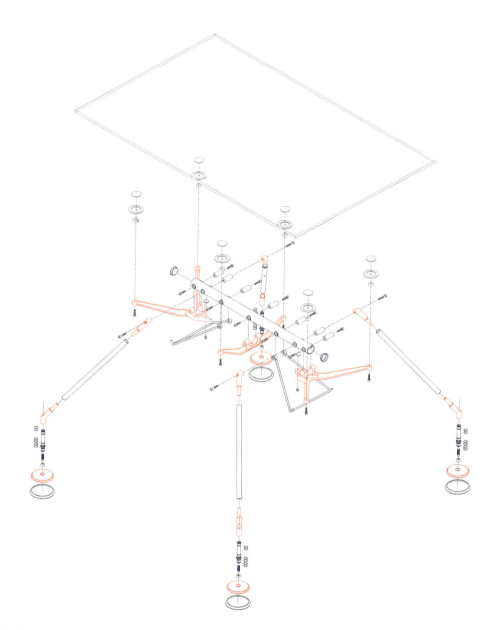

The philosophy of Nomos was consolidated during 1985 and '86. It became increasingly clear to Foster during that period that he was dealing with a 'family of objects' which fell into two distinct groups — those associated with the table, which had splayed legs, and those associated with the desk, which had straight legs. Both depended on similar components to a large degree, but they tended to move in two divergent directions. Foster feels now that the distinction between the two groups could be clarified by calling the flexible desking system 'Nomos' and finding a new name for the more finite table.

Increasingly, as the almost infinitely extendable elements of the 'inventory' began to clarify themselves, the multiplicity of ways in which they would function in an office environment also began to suggest themselves. The system embraces the principle that work in the office of the present and the future is a much more mobile activity than ever before. The advent of the personal computer has brought a new freedom into the contemporary office which means that neither surfaces nor storage spaces can be seen as such fixed identities any more. People move increasingly from desk to desk, using the available hardware as and when they need it.

Foster is also very clear in his mind about the notion of design catering for a plurality of life styles: the desks, for instance, can function either as work stations or as dealer desks, while the tables can be found either in the boardroom

Similar to the computer-generated drawing of the desk unit, this exploded isometric shows all the components used in the manufacture of the Nomos table.

The complete 'kit-of-parts' for a simple Nomos table. Once the problem of manufacture had been resolved by Tecno, it turned to the important question of how the system was to be packaged. This required a highly creative approach to which Tecno's graphic designers responded by using the tubular-steel spine to provide both the main structural element and carrying point.

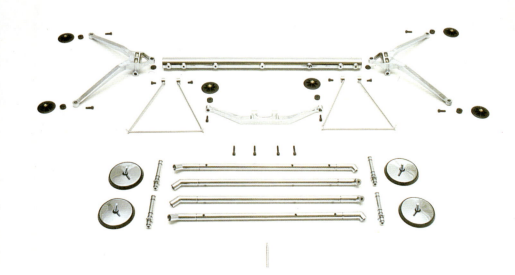

"The minimalism and lack of concession to office cosiness, generally present somehow in modern systems, are extraordinary in a product intended for the mass market."

Penny McGuire, *Architectural Review*, February 1987

A prototype jig was produced to explore the best way in which the components of the table might be assembled.

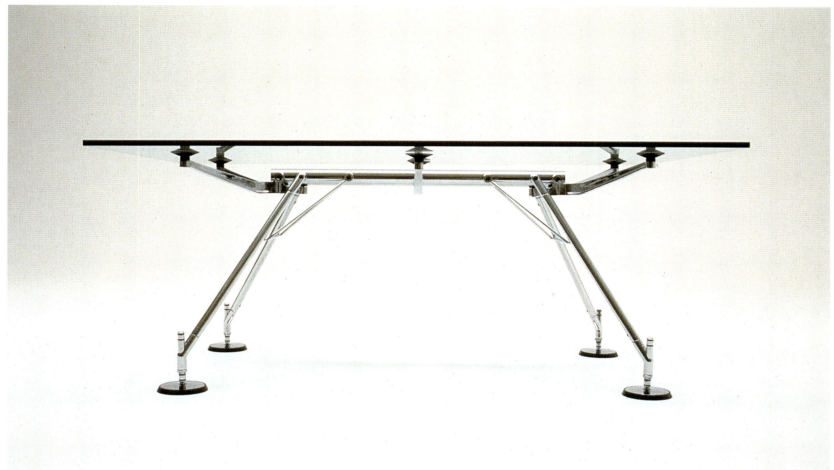

or the dining-room, functioning in the latter context as either dinner or coffee tables. The linguistic open-endedness of the system is such that additions can be made to it continually. This kind of renewal is in keeping with the philosophy of Foster's original design which saw the system as an ever-expanding family: it resembles a meccano set which is put to ever new uses but for which the basic concept and components remain fixed.

The choice of the name 'Nomos' for the furniture system was made as a result of much deliberation. It describes the essence of the project very succinctly. The Tecno catalogue published in 1986 explains the spirit of the term, which means, literally, 'the law', as "man controlling the chaos of the environment, proposing a supra-rational programme of behaviour". This points to the fact that while, from both a functional and from a manufacturing perspective, Nomos is an ultimately flexible system, it is, none the less, highly deterministic culturally. The choice of the unambiguous, industrial materials – steel, aluminium, glass; the choice of finishes – black, chrome and gun-metal; and the overtly technological aesthetic which has allowed the project to retain its unique personality throughout its development, combine to create a highly univalent product, although the possibility of including the traditional materials – marble and wood – on the tops does introduce a softer feel into the system. On the whole, though, it is the visual expression of a Neo-Modern philosophy which exalts in those aspects of the near future which are just visible in the present.

Foster has, however, successfully extended the ethos of the Modern Movement into a new climate in which a renewed social and technological context makes different demands on the

Through the use of sophisticated robot production and some high-pressure die-cast aluminium components, many of the welds present in earlier versions of the table have been eliminated. In spite of the advances made in its manufacture, Tecno's 'father' table bears a strong family resemblance to the earlier furniture projects of Foster Associates.

These sketches were executed by Norman Foster for a presentation to Tecno which took place at a fairly early stage in the development of Nomos. They envisaged a wide range of uses for the desking system, among them dealer desks which could cope with a variety of electronic equipment, work stations which incorporated a number of storage options, a drawing table for a design studio, platforms for technical equipment, mobile trolleys, and a projection stand.

architectural project or mass-produced artefact. Like Le Corbusier before him, Foster uses the automobile as testimony to a new age of mass production, but while Ford, with his theories of product standardisation, was right for Le Corbusier it is the General Motors principle of 'flexible mass production' and product variation which is more appropriate in the context of Foster's oeuvre. Foster himself uses the more contemporary analogy of the VW Golf, sold either as a basic model, the GL, or as a more up-market version with additional features, the GTI. His idealist universe, in which technological progress rules the day, is not very far away from that of Le Corbusier but the context has changed and the rules, now, are both different and more complicated.

The Nomos project directly echoed ideas that had been developed in the architectural projects that coincided with it chronologically — in particular the Hongkong Bank. The principle of 'special production' was as fundamental to the design of the Bank as it was to the furniture system. In the latter context the relationship between Foster Associates and the manufacturer has been a two-way process in which the expertise of the producer has made possible developments which, in furniture production, were unlikely to have occurred outside Italy.

In the end, however, the fundamental determining factor behind the philosophy of Nomos, and of the manufacturing systems which have made its production possible, is the growing differentiation of markets and the need for increased product variation. The Italian system of 'flexible specialisation', an important facet of the more general concept of 'diffused industrialisation' which has developed in that country since the late '60s, exists principally in relation to this social phenomenon.

While, in the early days of mass production, Taylorism and rationalism were the determining concepts behind the standardised manufacture of products such as cars and office furniture; with the fragmentation of the consumer society and the advent of electronic machinery, the idea of batch production for differentiated markets has become increasingly commonplace. Nomos belongs to this new world: it has responded to 'the spirit of the age' by defining for itself a new set of rules which allow changing life styles and new manufacturing patterns to set the pace.

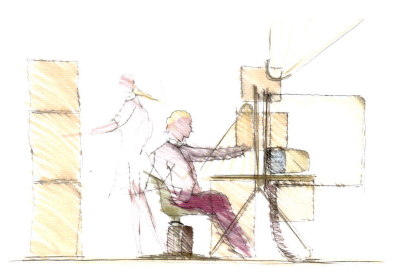

from the complex - storage & machine intensive

Drawing office Design Studio

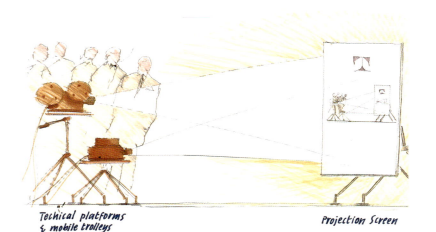

Technical platforms & mobile trolleys *Projection Screen*

"Nomos could turn out to be the most significant development in office furniture since Herman Miller launched the Action Office. And remarkably, it has come from a company which has not, so far at least, been at the centre of the stage in office furniture."

Deyan Sudjic, *Blueprint*, February 1987

The table — which was designed to accompany the Nomos system and which was fabricated from components developed for it — was also seen as incorporating a multitude of functions. In his sketches, Norman Foster envisaged it being used for conferences and dining and even as a low coffee table.

Conference Tables

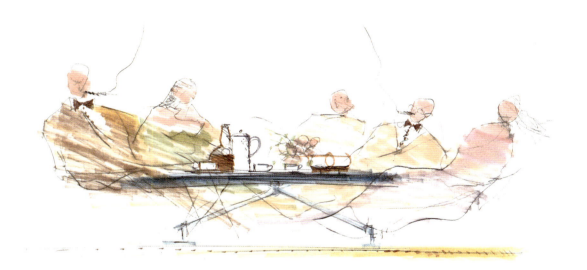

Dining Tables .... candlelight champagne ...

Architecture and Technology
by Jack Zunz

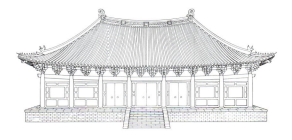

A 'Grade 2' building of the tenth-century Sung Dynasty in China. Already architectural expression is rigidly formalised.

Jack Zunz joined Ove Arup in 1950. He became a senior partner in 1965, chairman of Ove Arup & Partners Consulting Engineers in 1977 and co-chairman of the Arup Group, the Ove Arup Partnership, in 1984. Although the Arup Group operates in many diverse fields, Jack Zunz as a practising structural engineer has retained an active interest in the technology of buildings.

He has worked with many architects in the UK and elsewhere and has been associated with a number of notable buildings, including leading the team which constructed the superstructure of Sydney Opera House. He has worked closely with Norman Foster on a number of his projects. He is the author or co-author of a number of technical papers.

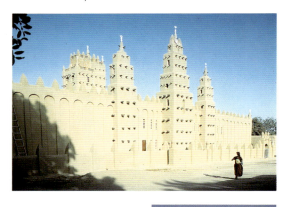

Architecture without architects — the Great Mosque at Niono, Mali, is built entirely of mud and requires maintenance after each rainy season.

A detail of the village mosque at N'Tongoroko, Mali. The bunches of palm sticks projecting from the walls form a permanent scaffolding for the regular resurfacing work that has to be carried out.

The often self-conscious examination of the role of engineering in architecture is a comparatively recent phenomenon. Creating good architecture has never been an easy business, but the notion that it has become more difficult — with increasing specialisation, increasingly complex sociological criteria and planning restrictions beyond the comprehension of early builders — though arguable, is probably correct.

In earlier times, there were only two — or very occasionally three — parties to the building process: the architect, either as designer or in the combined role of designer/builder/craftsman, and the proprietor, more often than not an authoritarian body who commissioned the project. It was possible, therefore, for Vitruvius to describe succinctly the requirements in the education of the architect by saying that, "...the architect should be equipped with knowledge of many branches of study and varied kinds of learning, for it is by his judgment that all work done by the other arts is put to the test." He then went on to prescribe that it was also necessary for an architect to acquire manual skills as well as scholarship — a prescription which, in more recent times, has unfortunately fallen into disuse. But the essential point is that the much-admired Classical architecture of Vitruvius' day could be concisely described in a relatively small volume, which not only detailed the educational requirements for an aspiring architect, but dealt with construction methods, materials, the servicing of buildings and even threw in some astrology for good measure.

While little has changed since the days of Vitruvius in principle, the sheer volume of knowledge, on almost every conceivable topic raised in Vitruvius' Ten Books, has multiplied to the nth degree, to a stage where specialisation is the order of the day. A building project in the latter part of the twentieth century requires the special expertise of not only the architect, but also of engineers of many different kinds, acousticians, cost consultants, not to mention the multitude of accountants and lawyers which all such enterprise brings in its van — and in its wake. The halcyon days of the all-omniscient architect of Vitruvius' time, and indeed of most of the following centuries, have gone — unless of course the computer with its expert systems brings the need for the specialist to an end. In the meantime, however, the architect of the day faces the awesome task, not only of extracting from increasingly diffuse clients briefs heavily circumscribed by layered planning regulations — which in themselves are fair game to exploit and circumvent whenever possible — but also of ingesting, co-ordinating, absorbing and above all harnessing efficiently the technology of the day. This process usually comes in the form of engineering advisors, collaborators or, at worst, sterile information. Of the multiplicity of specialist advice which abounds, that of the structural/civil engineer and that of the mechanical and electrical engineer will have the most impact on the way the building is assembled. In the latter part of the twentieth century, real architecture can only come from teamwork.

Much has been said and written about this necessary multi-disciplinary collaboration between all the professions in the building industry. It is easy to pontificate, to state the imperative or necessary ingredients; it is much more difficult to achieve harmonious, let alone creative collaboration. In addition to the very normal tensions existing in any human relationship, there are other inhibiting factors resulting from diverging educational and social backgrounds which play their part. But the climate is changing and the problems are at least understood, so there is hope for improvement.

Generalisations are always dangerous but it is probably fair to say that in purely aesthetic terms — in terms of using technology to create distinctive architectural forms — the structure is the most important tool. That is not to say that some architects are not able to exploit the forms of space and the hardware required for mechanical and electrical installations in unique, interesting and often controversial ways,

In the centuries following their standardisation, functional structure and precise colour-coding deteriorated into purely decorative elements. Is there here a metaphor for Post-Modernism?

The Stave church at Kaupanger, Norway, one of the oldest surviving wooden structures in the world.

but that is the exception rather than the rule. The often self-conscious expression of structure in architecture has led to endless debate. Much has been published on what is, of course, very difficult to articulate, because we are talking about art. Architecture is an art – some say the mother of arts. Engineering is a science as well as an art. Nevertheless many people, even amongst the architectural fraternity, still think of the engineer as a purveyor of an exact science, although nothing could be further from the truth. The engineer has, of course, to deal with the laws of nature – gravity and all that – but the manipulation of the data is an art which was traditionally manipulated by that 'Vitruvian' architect.

Today good, even outstanding, engineering does not always result in good architecture. Conversely, good, even great architecture can be created, even though the engineering is indifferent – clearly the structure must be stable but it can lack elegance and creativity. Similarly, the services can be functional without necessarily being particularly innovative, resourceful or economic. However, when engineering, or to be more accurate the technology of the day, is harnessed deliberately in the service of architecture, the frontiers become blurred. Engineering and architecture become an integrated whole, but unlike the days of Vitruvius or, indeed, succeeding centuries, creative architecture today is a team effort and all teams need a captain or a leader.

Norman Foster's architecture is an interesting touchstone in what Walter Gropius has described as his "disgust at the havoc wreaked by critics on the work of creative people by buttressing various theories without comprehending the background." Foster's architecture has been variously labelled. Few if any of these labels grasp the essential issue, which is simply that Foster is doing what builders, architects, designers – call them what you will – have been doing since time immemorial; that is using the technology of the day to create spaces, images and architectural delight.

There is nothing new in this. It is only in recent times that we have become rather self-conscious about actually using our technology and being seen to be using it. Bernard Rudofsky's books are full of examples of the natural creative expression of often so-called primitive communities the world over who build the artefacts they need at the limit of the skills and materials they possess.

Some examples might be instructive. Unbaked earth has been used for thousands of years, not only in rural housing and churches

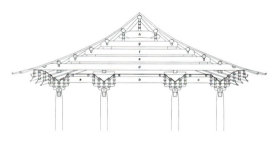

where it is still widely used, but also for large monuments such as the Tower of Babel and the Great Wall of China.

In contemporary Mali, stone is rare and timber too scarce to fuel brick kilns, so construction using sun-baked brick finished with mud plaster is common. Islamic tradition and construction in mud have combined to produce a unique and striking mosque architecture of which the Great Mosque at Djenné is typical. The rainy season requires these mud structures to be annually repaired and maintained. Carefully spaced bundles of palm sticks project from the walls and form a permanent scaffolding to provide access to the exterior surfaces for re-plastering of the walls. While the scaffolding fulfils its basic functional requirement, however, it also provides an essential ingredient of the architectural quality of these buildings.

Another example is one of the earliest-recorded building standards, those of the first Sung Dynasty (tenth to twelfth century). These standards had been in the making for some 20 years when Emperor Che Tsung, in 1097, ordered them to be completed. The task was carried out by one Li Chieh and the resulting document, consisting of some 1078 pages, was presented in 1100. It is the oldest standardised building manual known, and a fine example of how the technology of the day was harnessed to create fine structures which were not only functional and well designed to resist severe wind and seismic forces, but also had a very strong aesthetic appeal.

Some of the buildings survive to this day: they were built of white cedar which has very good structural qualities. The roofs, though three to four times heavier than modern Western tiled roofs, were able to withstand wind forces easily. The many joints in the timber, as

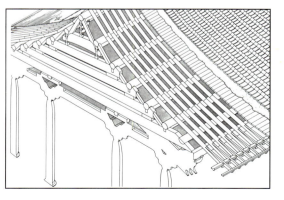

The traditional roof structure of the Sung Dynasty as specified in Li Chieh's 'manual' presented in 1100. Six tiers of beams are supported by four bracket-arm sets, which in turn support purlins carefully positioned to define the curve of the roof.

A sectional perspective of the church at Kaupanger. Joints were detailed to protect the end grain of the wood, producing a technology so successful that many buildings have survived for over 1000 years without renovation. Only the roof at Kaupanger has been replaced.

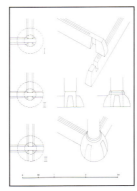

A detail of a joint in the foundation sill showing how 'bowls' of wood were used to lock and seal the joint at the same time. The main structural columns, the staves of the church, are single tree trunks rising the full height of the building.

well as the symmetry of the structures, enabled them to withstand the seismic forces to which they were subjected. The roofs were supported on a series of wooden columns. Long overhanging eaves shielded the structure from summer sunlight but let in the rays of the low winter sun.

Poised between each roof beam and column head were elaborate sets of blocks and corbelled bracket arms in a variety of standardised shapes and sizes which were fitted together in mortice and tenon fashion. Commodity, firmness and delight — how better can one describe this effective expression of the expertise of the day?

An interesting postscript in the context of the late twentieth century's penchant for change: the florid decoration of an identical bracket arm set makes use of numerous colours actually specified in Li Chieh's code. In the following centuries the bracket sets supporting the eaves lost their shape and became elements of decoration — are there here interesting metaphors with Post-Modernism?

Another example of expressing technology is found in the 'Stave' churches of Norway. These churches date back to the tenth century and their ancient Norwegian builders have

Ten years before the Great Exhibition of 1851, Joseph Paxton completed this, the Great Conservatory at Chatsworth. Here, only the main columns were in cast iron; the great curved ribs were, in fact, formed in laminated wood.

In this rare photograph of the Great Conservatory under construction, the workmen bring scale to this immense structure which, when completed, was to cover over three-quarters of an acre.

shown that, with sound design and maintenance, wood buildings can be permanent — an exception to the norm. Virtually all large structures which have survived from antiquity, or even from mediaeval times, are built of stone. They are an illustration of the intelligent application of timber technology. The staves of these churches are no more than stout wooden columns. They were built in large numbers from the eleventh to the fourteenth century. Their design has a primitive grandeur, the exterior is exotic and the interior serene: the builders combined Christian as well as pagan motifs in expressing the structure of these churches. It is intriguing that these structures have survived for more than 800 years. There are three good reasons for this: extraordinary care was taken in the preparation of the wood; the overall design is excellent, well suited to the exposed sites; and significant structural innovations have served to protect the wood from deterioration.

But it was left to the Victorians, an era which produced so many remarkable men, to produce a personality, Joseph Paxton, who probably more than anyone in the recent past celebrated in the most exuberant manner possible, the flair, inventiveness and creativity of his age. This original self-taught, self-made personality — gardener, railway speculator, architect, engineer — pointed the way to so much that is now accepted as part of twentieth-century building idiom. Of all his works, and the list is extensively impressive, none was more seminal than the Great Conservatory at Chatsworth. It was 277ft long, 123ft wide and 67ft high, covered an acre and was substantially completed in 1841, 10 years before the Great Exhibition. Conceived as a wooden structure, iron was substituted for the columns: the final building provided the foundation from which so much else followed.

In this tradition, Foster's architecture can be seen as no more than a natural part of historical progression. That it is conceived and built at a time when the traditional architect/designer/builder is no longer able to function — in the context of the explosion of knowledge and expertise — makes his quest for excellence much more difficult and, of course, that much more interesting. Not that all his buildings and projects depend for their aesthetic imagery on structural forms or expression alone: some do

The gentle arch of the Frankfurt athletics stadium was based on a segment of a circle, a structural form that allowed simplicity of prefabrication.

and some don't, but all, in one way or another, attempt to exploit to the full the most recent technology.

Probably one of the finest examples of the total integration of engineering and architecture, to the extent that they become an indivisible whole, is the competition-winning project for the athletics stadium in Frankfurt. The scheme has undergone the unfortunate trials of fiscal stop/go/stop policies and will, unfortunately, probably not be built, but, in its concept and subsequent detailed development, it illustrates the wholeness of a concept which evolved out

of the sensitivity of a wooded site, resulting in the desire to create an unobtrusive low-key elegant envelope. This was achieved with a vault based on the segment of a circle, with the arena and abutments set below grade. The shallow protrusion of the roof kept the site edges free for circulation, and maintained a separation from flanking buildings, while preserving views through the end glass walls on to the two wooded aspects of the site.

Technically, the vault gave a low surface to internal volume ratio, which helped the heating. The merging of roof and walls allowed more uniform daylighting on the arena, and the buried abutments could call on stiff reactions from the dense sand subsoil, so that the usual tie at arena slab level could be left out. The abutments also offered rotational fixity at the roof springing points, and this led to shallower, lighter roof trussing. The choice of a circular roof profile combined the usual structural advantages of reduced bending with ease of prefabrication. So the response to the site occurred at many levels simultaneously.

With roof shape chosen, the question arose of structural framework geometry. A triangular plan grid took the arching forces on a longer route than the more usual orthogonal grid, but it provided more frequent braced points, and the resulting reduction in compression member lengths allowed them to work more efficiently: the longer route could be offset by savings in the weight of steel. The cellular pattern of the triangular grid also offered good opportunities for prefabrication of both structure and cladding. The grid had no lines running perpendicular to the visually dominant long axis of the vault. This was an important ingredient in the aesthetic treatment of the vault surface, and was applied to all non-structural components in the roof as well, such as ducts, pipes, electrics, cladding and attachments.

The triangular grid was refined by offsetting its longitudinal lines by half a cycle, to create a pattern of hexagons and triangles. This doubled the number of braced points, to further structural advantage, while also providing larger apertures in the pattern to receive radiant

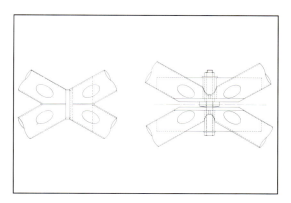

Joints for the individual structural elements combined welded and bolted connections to form a quickly erected but rigid frame.

The triangular plan grid offset the longer route of arching forces with the provision of more frequent braced points. The structure was to be manufactured as a series of identical prefabricated truss units in the form of individual diamonds.

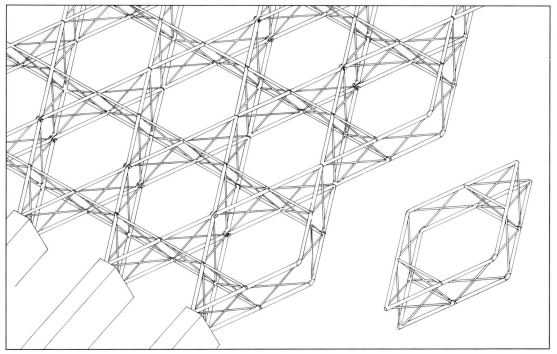

65

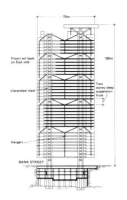

An east-west section through the centre bay of the Hongkong Bank, showing the main structural elements.

The steel superstructure of the first phase of the Stansted Airport terminal nearing completion in September 1987.

A detailed elevation of one of the double-height structural suspension zones of the Hongkong Bank. With the top compression boom in place a rigid truss is formed.

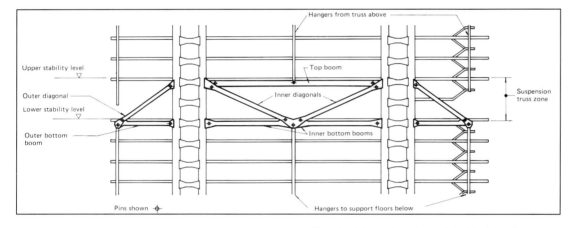

Analytical computer models, prepared by Ove Arup & Partners, demonstrate deflection profiles to the main steel structure under wind loading.

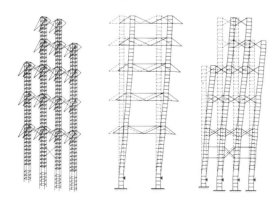

panels, roof-lights and vents. These apertures were set at the largest dimension for pressing and transporting prefabricated panels. The choice of webbing, connecting the top and bottom chords of the truss, was designed to allow the necessary passage for the parallel grid of ventilation ducts. The choice of a slender and efficient structural frame was therefore quite indivisible from the choice of servicing, cladding, construction or aesthetic preference.

The visible relationships between form and function, as well as the purity of expression of the materials used in construction, have been endlessly debated and provided fodder for theorists and critics. The trouble is that after all the analytical studies of the designer — whether these studies embrace urban design, space planning, environmental impact studies, engineering analysis or any of the many other financial and technical problems associated with the design of a modern building — it is as much his subjective hand that will determine whether the result is real architecture or just another artefact more or less fit for its purpose but of no value in lifting the human spirit. So the form/function relationship, much to the consternation of some idealists, cannot be simply based on factual or scientific data but is ultimately at the mercy of the architect or engineer, whoever is the final arbiter of what is to be built.

There are few recent buildings where this relationship and its resulting imagery are more significantly expressed than in the new headquarters building for the Hongkong Bank. The decision to dedicate the plaza to public use implied a large column-free area. The main banking hall was raised 12 metres above plaza level, yet obvious and easy access was necessary to ensure that the Bank's customers would not be deterred by having to move up from street level to conduct their business. A transfer structure at the banking-hall level, transferring the very large forces of a 50-storey building over a long span, would have resulted in impossible planning problems, so the concept of a suspended or hanging structure with large unobstructed floor-spaces was the only functional solution. Early schemes used exposed 'Warren' trusses from which to hang steel members, which in turn supported the floor system. Subsequent schemes included one where 'chevrons' were attached to several floors providing a very distinctive overall image, yet retaining the essential functional needs. The form which finally evolved is one which not only minimises interference with space planning, both at the support and lower banking-hall levels, but also results in a distinctive architecture with an artistic touch at its very root — which after all is what architecture is, or should be, all about.

The structure of the Hongkong Bank project stretched contemporary technology to its limits. Its expression underlines the meaninglessness of the assumption that whatever functions best is right. Functional needs are never precise and even when they have some definition the resulting forms are to a large extent arbitrary. Architectural design cannot be mathematically controlled. Providing equilibrium to the forces to which the building is subjected is a necessary requirement, but after that other considerations play their part. What are the requirements for its maintenance and durability? How will the structure affect movement of people and services between spaces? What are the financial constraints in the context of the total building budget? Is the building stiff enough to avoid the occupants feeling uncomfortable when the wind gets up? The synthesis of all such factors is a process which requires infinite adjustment, and ultimate unity can only be achieved by sure intuitive judgment. While this ultimate 'Solomon'-type judgment is normally in the hands of the architect, it is, or at least should be, the result of uninhibited team-

A computer-generated image of the central node that gathers the tensional loads created by the splayed branches of the individual structural trees.

A single structural tree complete with its roof module in place.

work in which all participants play significant roles. In exercising this final judgment as to the overall merit of a particular solution, some architects, albeit all too few, exercise a confident hand. Foster is one of the very few who inspires confidence in exploring unusual architectural forms while retaining a balance between often divergent issues. Amongst these surely the Hongkong Bank must stand as a most significant landmark.

The structure for the new terminal building at Stansted Airport is of quite a different genre and its planning marks a radical change from the perceived wisdom. The building is fundamentally a simple two-storey affair with baggage handling, mechanical plant and other services at one level while arriving and departing passengers are all at the second. The objective here was to create a large, calm space where clarity of function and convenience of use were the primary requirements. The space had to be as free of columns as was compatible with reasonable economy.

The solution lay in a grid of sufficient dimension to satisfy the checking-in and baggage-handling requirements of a modern airport. In the final scheme, tubular steel 'trees' are uniformly spaced at 36-metre intervals. This structural grid is well within the capability of modern engineering and results in a relatively generous column-free space. But a roof which spans only half this distance is more economic, so early on it was decided to splay the trees in such a way as to enclose an 18-metre square, reducing the structural span to a similar 18-metre square area. The trees were proportioned to include service 'pods' which draw the various services — air, water and power — from the level below, as well as providing the source from which information is distributed. The expansion of the trees into four-legged structures was a direct consequence of the servicing of the building.

Above the 'tree trunks', the canopy is formed by the 'branches' splaying out to support the roof. The cross-bracing is required to resist out-of-balance forces and to stiffen the canopy. It is pre-stressed to reduce its bulk and look less obtrusive. It was important for the structure to play its part in creating a calm atmosphere. The 'trunks' also were originally cross-braced. However, as this restricted the passage of air-ducts, this was removed. An interesting by-product of the removal of the bracing was that it made the elimination of structural breaks in the roof possible. This in turn facilitated the waterproofing of the roof.

The structure was then subjected to a rigorous process of detailing, where every joint, every connection was examined in minute detail, because at Stansted the structure is tactile, it is all around you and visible as you cross the concourse. This rigorous, sometimes ruthless attention to detail, whether of structure or any other aspect of the building, is one of the hallmarks of Foster's work.

George Bernard Shaw in a foreword to an exhibition by the MARS Group, in 1938, spoke about the unprejudiced search for new beauties of form in architecture. With typical Shavian wit he went on, "...for the seekers after what Dickens' blacksmith happily called the Architectooralooral always find themselves back again at Lancaster Gate or the Tate Gallery. And we have had enough of that..." In this context, he could not have foreseen just how many were to "find their way back" to those and numerous other historical references.

Wishful thinking will not turn back the clock. The present and the future are a challenge which demands a positive response. Foster's architecture is a bold and robust response to those who claim that anything that is designed and built today is but a poor shadow of what was created yesteryear. His relentless analytical approach to architectural problems leads him inexorably towards solutions in which he harnesses appropriate technology, a kind of fusion of architect and engineer. His unprejudiced and unfettered approach to urban design and architectural problems is refreshing, thought-provoking and, at its best, simply brilliant.

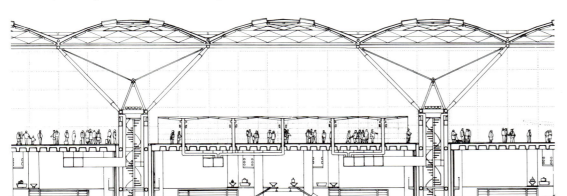

A presentation section through the Stansted terminal. The structural steel trees are set out on a 36-metre grid but utilise splayed branches to reduce main spans to only half that, to support identical 18-metre square roof modules.

The 18-metre square roof modules were pre-fabricated for on-site assembly at ground level. Once completed they were lifted into place in one operation.

1978 **Whitney Development**
New York
USA

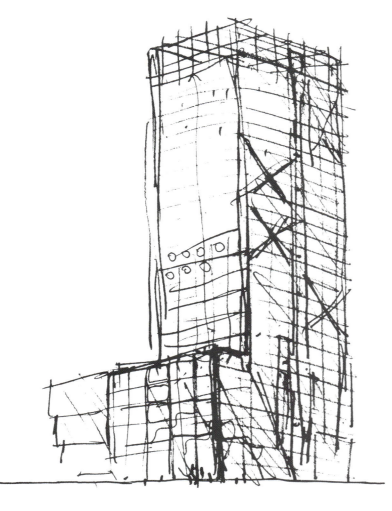

Norman Foster's earliest sketches introduce a podium atrium that responds to the existing Whitney Museum, expressed cross-bracing and a roof-top 'winter garden'; all elements that were to be retained through to the final proposals.

The Whitney development project began in 1978 when Norman Foster and Derek Walker were asked by Italian developers Sviluppo Tecnica and SGI/Sogene to prepare proposals for a mixed-use tower for a site on Madison Avenue. Designed jointly with Derek Walker Associates and the engineer Frank Newby, the project was to be Foster Associates' first skyscraper. The new building would also have an unusually powerful neighbour, Marcel Breuer's quintessentially Brutalist building of 1966, the Whitney Museum of Art.

The site on which Foster and Walker would be working was owned by the Whitney, on whose behalf, two years previously, consultants in New York had already prepared a variety of development possibilities. Sviluppo Tecnica and SGI/Sogene's involvement derived from a 90-day option which they had been awarded for the purpose of preparing proposals for a condominium tower. Included in the new development however, at the developers' request, was an additional 50 000 square feet of gallery space for the neighbouring Museum which, if carried out, would have had the effect of doubling its existing display areas.

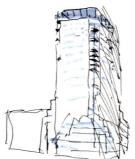

A means of comparison. Sketches appear that follow quite different principles as a way of testing the preferred solution.

In direct contrast to Breuer's earlier building, Foster wanted the new galleries to be openly exposed with a full-height glazed atrium giving on to Madison Avenue.

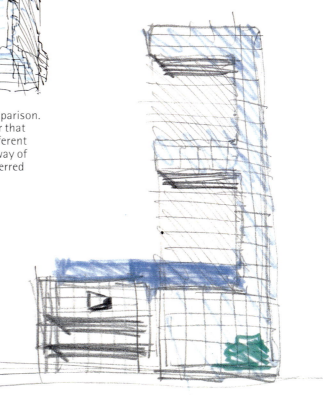

"A scheme of high architectural quality was called for, both to live up to the original museum, designed by Marcel Breuer in the 1960s, and to ease the project through the maze of New York building restrictions and active tenants' groups."

Deyan Sudjic, *Building Design*, July 1979

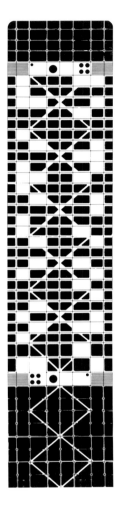 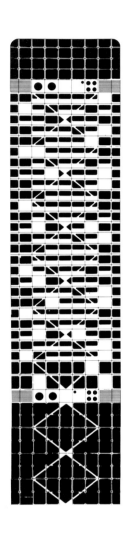

The first line drawings of the elevations. The relationship to the Sainsbury Centre is clear, though here the panels are more informally grouped and include special elements that express the cross-bracing of the bearing wall structure. The same structural system continues to ground level, creating a formal straight-sided tower.

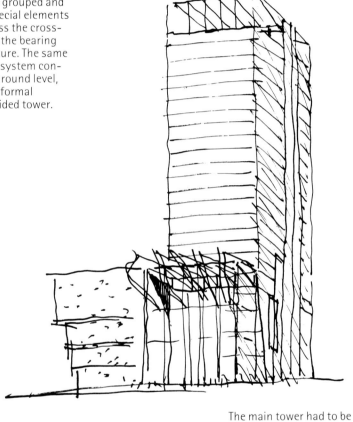

The main tower had to be set back from Madison Avenue. In contrast to the line elevations, Foster's sketches show the podium stepping forward to the correct street frontage.

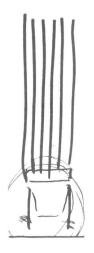  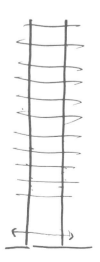 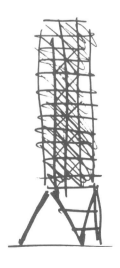

As at the Hammersmith Centre, Foster preferred to clearly identify the structural differences between the large-span zones of gallery levels in the podium and the smaller scale of the tower above. Sketches explore the options.

"While the Breuer design, with its inverted ziggurat form, polished masonry skin, minimum of windows, and bridged moat suggests a fortress, the new design would see a massive use of glass to make the interior clearly visible from the street. The old Whitney is reticent and discreet. The new one would flaunt its A-frame structure."

Deyan Sudjic, *Building Design*, July 1979

The visual excitement of the all-glazed galleries is captured in this detail from Helmut Jacoby's elegant perspective drawing. Drawn as though looking north along Madison Avenue, the historic Carlisle Hotel – which the Whitney redevelopment was intended to complement – is seen a few blocks along the street.

Marcel Breuer's late work for the Whitney could hardly be further away in character from the lightness of touch characteristic of Foster Associates. Norman Foster's own description of the building was a "fortress-like tomb for art". For the new hanging areas, Foster and Walker were looking to create a very different kind of space: one which would not intimidate passers-by but, instead, act more as a shop-window to excite their curiosity.

As at Hammersmith, the challenge was to find an economical way of providing varying spaces at different levels of the building: clear spans at top and bottom – for the roof-top garden and gallery/foyer respectively – and cellular accommodation in between. Some early sketches by Norman Foster show a clear break, both structurally and elevationally, between the glazed five-storey foyer/galleries linked to the existing Museum, and the tower above. Others display more abstract elevations with large areas of glass. But the team were anxious to avoid the conventional tower and podium solution, as they felt the formal problems presented by this approach would be almost insuperable. They eventually settled on a remarkable giant

At the top of the building, a double-height area encloses a residents' club. An internal mezzanine contains a circular swimming pool.

The lower level of the residents' club contains restaurant facilities, bar areas and informal seating. The entire club is situated within the all-glazed 'winter garden' allowing spectacular views of the city.

Residential floors could contain up to four generously proportioned apartments, neatly planned to fan out from the offset lift lobby.

Lower levels were set aside for office accommodation. Open-plan office floors are shown with storage units used to break up the area.

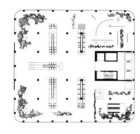

Office floors could also be readily compartmented, either for a single user – as shown here – or for quite separate tenancies.

The final elevations. The A-frame podium structure is clearly revealed through the all-glazed walls of the podium, now supporting a storey-deep truss that acts as a structural transfer zone. Above this, the tower is similar to the earlier drawings and shows the cladding grid, diagonal wind-bracing and random variations of window panels all expressed within the elevational plane. Regulated by two bands of wider panels on the north and south elevations, this interplay is one of the project's most noticeable external features.

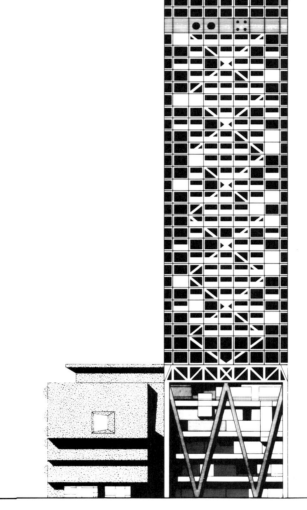

triangulated structure that acted as a rigid base for the tower rising above. This was not unlike Foster's early sketches for Hammersmith from the previous year.

In order to allow greater planning freedom at the lower levels, the scheme – presented to the Whitney trustees in October 1978 – contained a lift and service core located to one side of the building. This had the added advantage that the lifts, if clad in glass, could enjoy spectacular views over Manhattan. The tower allowed occupancy of totally mixed use, from open plan to compartmented office or to apartments, all handled with equal ease. With its off-set service core, planning the apartments presented an interesting geometric problem, but the site's relatively small area allowed this to be resolved in a particularly satisfying way; each apartment's main living area fanning out from the entrance in an orderly sequence of spaces.

The Whitney development came not long after the Sainsbury Centre and, from the experience gained there, Foster again proposed a cladding system of interchangeable metal and glass panels. Instead of a simple table-cloth effect folding over three planes, however, here the

"Like all Foster Associates' schemes, this design pays close attention to commercial value judgements – floor area ratios, zoning heights, borrowing rates, building costs, rents, site costs and the space to be given over to the museum – yet manages to extend these purely commercial constraints to encompass good design and public amenity."

Haig Beck, *International Architect,* No. 2 1979

system would clad the building on all five planes, rising to form a squared-off glazed 'bubble' over the roof-top residents' club. The double-height 'winter garden' thus created – with its internal mezzanine restaurant and swimming pool – would therefore have been able to enjoy an unprecedented view of city and sky.

There is an undeniable appeal in placing the structure and/or services on the outside of a building, as it provides a very powerful means of articulation. But it also creates a whole set of possible problem areas when dealing with damp penetration or heat loss. In a world of rain, cold and dust, it generally makes more sense to follow the standard practice and place a smooth cladding on the outside. Unfortunately, the result is too often a kind of anonymous sheath that conceals the structural reality within.

Both alternatives imply a relatively loose bond between cladding, structure and services. In the Whitney development, Foster Associates were to pioneer a closer relationship between structure and cladding with a bearing wall structure – that is, the wind-bracing and a major part of the primary structure were contained within the external wall zone. Unlike the Sainsbury Centre, where the structure is exclusively con-

Glazing of the winter garden was 'wrapped' over to form a clear glazed roof to the residents' club and its top-floor mezzanine swimming pool.

Photographed at sunset, the model captures the changing moods possible with the silver cladding panels.

This diagrammatic section clearly indicates the areas of architectural excitement contrasted with the grey floors of commercial reality, available either for residential or office use. A two-storey basement contains car parking.

A day-lit view of the model. Blue and green tubes within the model indicate the position of vertical services and lift-shafts. Glazed sides to the lift-cars were intended so that changing views of Manhattan could be enjoyed by those within.

With internal walls omitted, the model is seen in a far more transparent form than reality would allow. However, this sunset view did produce a dramatic image with which to impress the client.

An alternative view of the roof-top glazing, sketched by Norman Foster as a possible option for the model.

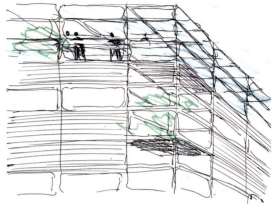

tained within the external wall, the openings in the cladding of the new building would go to rather greater lengths to reflect the arrangement of the frame within.

At the lower levels of the building, the structural scale increased dramatically and the cladding diverged into two parts — solid panels wrapping around the columns with large expanses of clear glazing spanning between. At street level the building now became completely transparent, a dynamically changing shop-window linking inside and outside. The gallery levels rose to the height of the existing Museum, overlooking a tall triangular-sectioned atrium filled with sculpture and greenery. It was Foster's intention that this 'podium' — terminated by the trusses at the base of the tower — should relate directly to the prevailing scale of the surrounding streetscape, while the height and massing of the whole building also held affinities with the nearby Carlisle Hotel, a historic landmark only a few blocks along Madison Avenue.

The project evolved following meetings between members of the Whitney Board, the developers and their architects. In the event, however, the development option was not taken up by the Whitney, who pursued instead an expansion plan which would have involved the demolition of the Breuer building, a decision which became a 'cause célèbre' in New York.

Interestingly, the concept of a mixed-use tower built over and funding new galleries was to be taken up a few years later by the Museum of Modern Art, also in New York and only a few blocks away from the Whitney site.

Tim Ostler

1982 A Tree-house
by Otl Aicher

The most architectonic works of nature are trees: their structure — how they hold out their leaves towards the sun — is still unsurpassed by technology. No technical form has arms that, in relation to the material outlay, stretch as far as those of beech trees — like those of the Savernake forest in Wiltshire say — large, spreading monoliths with the disposition of autonomous individuals. No work of technology can compare with them: stretching upward from one point and supported on a single column, the trunk, they develop a volume large enough to achieve the maximum surface-area required for the assimilating function of the leaves.

Norman Foster lives on the edge of a park in Wiltshire; his boys played there before they left home and went to university.

A building without a tree is like a lost child. Building and tree complement each other, whether the ornamental tree on the boulevards

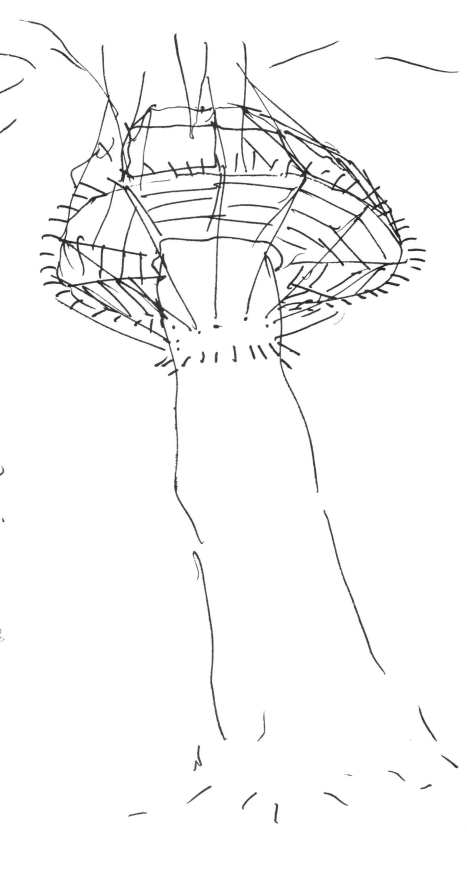

of Paris or the protective tree that watches over a farm. The solitary building without a tree is exposed, defenceless against the weather. Tree and building complement each other without surrendering themselves or their sovereignty. But they have common laws. Both have an evolved, constructive character. They contain and envelop the light that is appropriate to man, the light that falls through trees, not the relentless flood of light in a desert. If the imagined world of the architect has no trees, it is impoverished, empty.

Perhaps this has to do with the fact that man, seen in the light of historical development, comes from the trees. From our understanding of ontogenesis, we know that every individual works through the developmental history of his species in shortened form. For a time the human embryo even begins to grow gills. Life originally came from the water.

But perhaps we live through the stages of our developmental history not only in terms of nature, but also in terms of culture.

All children build huts, houses, camps; and they all dream of a house in the trees, of a house in the uncovered heights, beneath which lies the world. Here one can be entirely sovereign, independent, unburdened, removed from the bustle. One can be oneself.

Another device of this kind is a wall; the wall around a monastery, around a yard, around a house. It protects and also delineates, creating its own territory. But the house in the trees needs no wall. The whole world is there at one's feet. One lives with the birds, with the sun, with the clouds, with the wind, and with the land beneath. One just needs a rope-ladder that can be drawn up.

The tree-house is more than a child's dream. The architect may have designed it for his children; but it can also be a space for a way of life, for man as he would most deeply like to be. We do not dream only of a freedom in which everyone has equal rights, we dream also of a freedom that consists in living just for oneself – without claim, without obstacles, without pressures. A house in the trees would suffice for that.

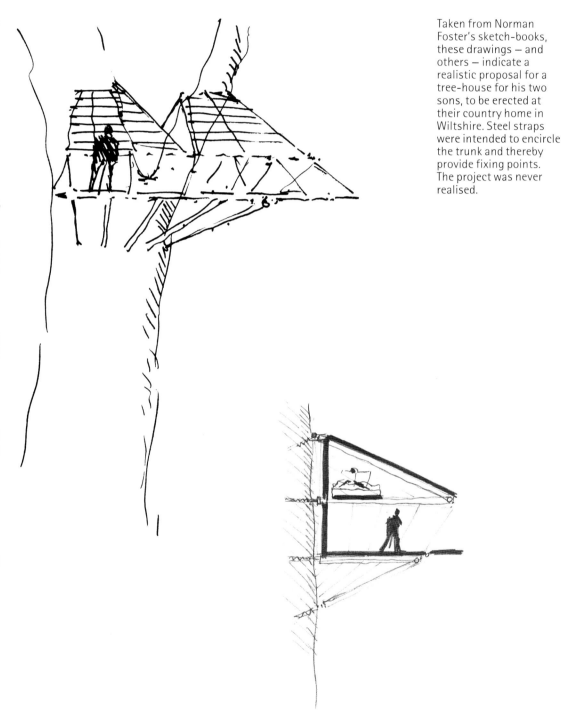

Taken from Norman Foster's sketch-books, these drawings – and others – indicate a realistic proposal for a tree-house for his two sons, to be erected at their country home in Wiltshire. Steel straps were intended to encircle the trunk and thereby provide fixing points. The project was never realised.

1982　**Humana Competition**
Louisville
USA

Norman Foster's earliest sketches concentrate on the 'landmark' aspect of the brief and take on an almost rocket-like form showing a circular plan developed around a central core. While the latter was to disappear, features like the entrance plaza/atrium, mid-point interchange zone and exaggerated radio mast were to provide a sound basis for development.

In January 1982 Foster Associates were one of six practices invited to take part in a limited competition to design a new headquarters for Humana Inc. The client, based in Louisville, Kentucky, was one of the world's largest private hospital and medical insurance corporations. At the time, it was housed in four separate buildings across the city. It was looking for a "landmark building of architectural importance".

Louisville lies on a flat, featureless plain by the Ohio River. At the turn of the century it was a river port serving America's farming heartland and, as such, played a major part in the expansion of agricultural wealth in the Mid-West. Correspondingly, the city was to suffer severely during the Depression and, following the war, became increasingly dominated by industrial and service companies.

The site for the new building, on the north-east corner of Fifth and Main Streets, was close to the waterfront and hard by a pre-existing tall office slab. Immediately to the west was a gaggle of low-rise nineteenth-century commercial buildings subject to a preservation order, while across the street lay a two-storey bank by Mies van der Rohe.

Humana was looking for a building with some 350 000 square feet of office space. Of this just under 200 000 square feet was to be

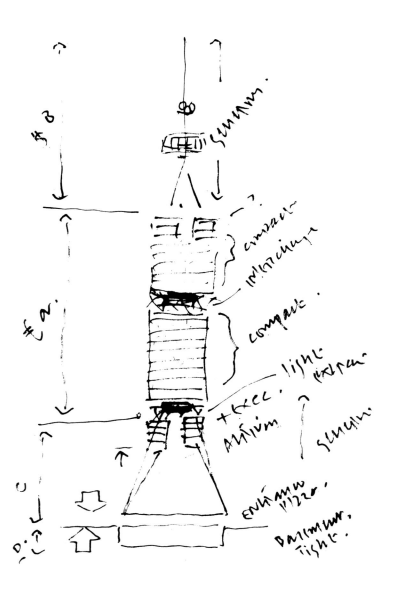

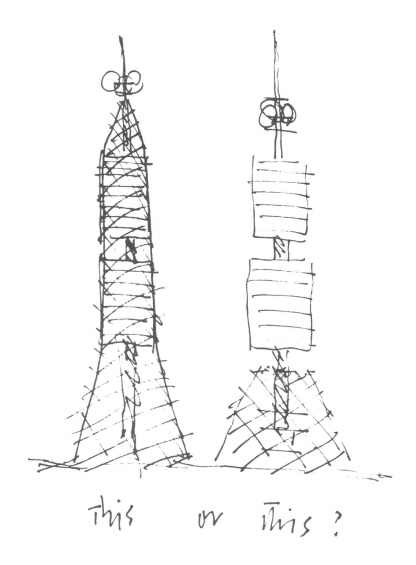

"It is our notion that creativity can be kindled by example. This building, by achieving a recognisable national significance, will spark and encourage innovation and quality architectural design in Louisville. To satisfy this objective it must be a good building. It must solve the practical and functional requirements of the client. It must be built within the financial resources of the client. It must, in the end, create excitement and capture the imagination of the public."

Competition briefing document, January 1982

"We had a number of invitations at the time and we said, 'What shall we do – the National Gallery or this one?'"

Norman Foster

occupied by Humana itself; the rest was to be let to tenants and kept in reserve for future company expansion.

Foster Associates realised immediately that cost would be a major factor in Humana's assessment of their work. The conventional American approach would have been to put up the structure quickly and economically, then spend a relatively large part of the budget on a high level of finish and an expensive cladding system. A more thoroughly integrated solution on the European model, although probably more economical over the life of the building, could be expected to work out more expensive in terms of immediate capital expenditure. Keeping the design philosophy simple would offset this and give their submission the best possible chance of success.

The competition briefing was to be held at Humana's offices in Louisville. Norman Foster was unable to attend; instead, Birkin Haward and Richard Horden represented the office. Their trip turned into something of an adventure when, due to a freak snowstorm, they and the other competitors (among them Helmut Jahn, Richard Meier and Michael Graves) found themselves stranded in a hotel together.

Humana is not only the world's largest medical corporation, it has also one of the most buoyant stocks on Wall Street. Under its founders David Jones and Wendell Cherry, it had, by 1982, grown to encompass a network of 94 hospitals in the US and around the world. It was confidently expected that this international dimension would become even more important – there was even a possibility that Humana might launch its own communications satellite.

The new building would be the nerve-centre of this global network. For this reason, Foster's early sketches reflect the idea of communication as a theme for the design as well as the building's role as a landmark.

From these early sketches the building also took on a cylindrical form. In architectural terms the shape had a number of advantages: it turned the corner elegantly; its form complemented the communications equipment at high level; and it contrasted with the office slab across the road. The imagery was rationalised further as the drawings developed: in Norman Foster's earliest sketches it appears in almost rocket-like form emphasising its landmark qualities and responding to the skyscraper tradition of the 1930s including the Empire State and Chrysler buildings, influences of which Foster was to acknowledge in the final report. From the nature of the selected competitors Foster was aware that the competition was to be as much a styling exercise as a quest for architectural quality. These early sketches are almost a pastiche in response. But the basic form, and the resonances it produced, did have their merits. What was required was a rational form that tied these resonances into an architectural solution worthy of Foster Associates.

By developing a 'bearing wall' concept similar to the Whitney redevelopment, the structural core could be eliminated. As with the Hongkong Bank, the design of which was well advanced at this time, Norman Foster's sketches now begin to indicate service risers drawn to the edges of the building.

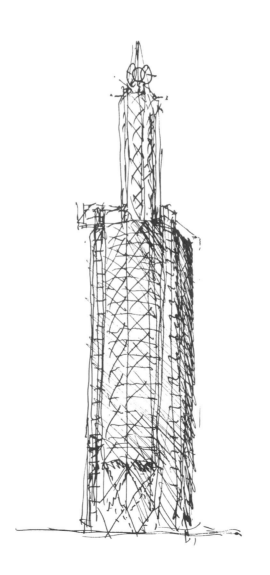
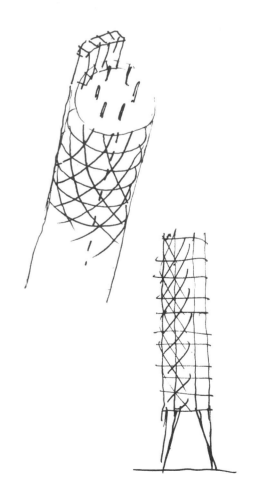

As part of the competition submission a group of reference images was gathered on one panel to illustrate the various stimulae that helped inform the design process. Radio antennae and satellite communications are combined with alternative examples of stressed-skin structures and monocoque construction, as well as more architectural material such as earlier landmark buildings and inspirational spaces.

"Competitions are very stimulating. I think the ideal is a balance where you are realising designs in physical construction while also carrying out competition entries in parallel."

Norman Foster, *Building*, May 1982

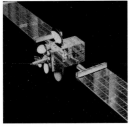   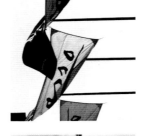

Any design problem offers a number of paths to a solution. Which of them is explored depends as much on personal enthusiasm as on architectural judgment. Norman Foster's personal reaction to the American tradition had appeared in his first sketches for Humana. But to find a more refined means of expression, these preliminary responses needed the stimulus of good consultants. As the design team was assembled a clearer philosophy began to coalesce, centred on Ove Arup & Partners' structural proposals.

Arup's structure was founded on industrial precedent and source material alluded to in the images contained in Foster's final competition submission. These included Buckminster Fuller's geodesic structures, a cooling tower by Frei Otto, and Barnes Wallis' stressed skin for the Wellington bomber, along with references to landmarks, space-age communications and simpler statements on urban spaces. Separate pictures of nets and basket weaves were used to illustrate the principles behind the proposed triangulated wall structure.

The combined result of these influences was a cylindrical tower design, the shape and texture of which would be unique in its setting. This was entirely appropriate. Humana was Louisville's most successful company and had funded the development of the entire downtown area. It could therefore be said to have earned the right to a headquarters with the status of a local landmark — Louisville's equivalent of the Empire State Building. Sited where it was, Norman Foster felt strongly that it should form a pivotal role in the city. The American skyscraper tradition was obsessed with height, both in absolute terms and when compared to other competing buildings in the same city. In these terms Humana's spire, unusually tall as a proportion of the building's overall height, would have had the effect of bringing the height of the tower above all others in the city.

However, it was the structural implications that were to provide the greatest benefits in the building's development. Most tower blocks are built around spines, rather like kebabs on a skewer. The effect is to limit planning options above ground — and totally destroy the foyer space at ground level. Foster, at this time, was involved in the planning options for another high-rise building with his work on the Hongkong Bank project. That building had successfully adopted an open plan for the floors by

Images of woven cane and nets were used in the final presentation to convey the natural benefits of such solutions; immense strength being achieved with relatively little material.

Following early discussions with Foster Associates as to the form of building that might be developed, Ove Arup & Partners proposed a triangulated perimeter structure that would require only the minimum of internal columns to carry floor loads, thereby leaving the central area completely free. Independent service towers could be propped against the rigid perimeter structure for stability. Prepared by Arup's, this early computer diagram was used to explain the principles of the structural system to the design team at Foster Associates who were immediately enthusiastic to develop the scheme further.

removing the structure and all services — including lift-shafts — to the sides. Arup's structural skin solution for Humana allowed the same planning freedom for a circular tower, removing the need for a heavy structural core.

In this way Humana put into practice Foster's constant desire to maximise interior space and flexibility. On the Whitney redevelopment project, Foster Associates' earlier tower project, this had been achieved by moving the core to the side of the plan but retaining it within the main envelope. The Bank project had taken the concept considerably further. At Humana it was to be taken one step further again, as the structural integrity of the skin would allow various parts of floors to be removed, and double- or even triple-height spaces created at any level of the building.

The simpler form of spire that was eventually chosen to provide a fitting pinnacle to the building. At its base, an electrographic sign could display local information as well as the Humana name.

Humana's spire played an essential role in cultivating its image as a landmark. It was also a convenient solution to the problem of how to end a tower building.

There was an understandable impulse to reduce its weight to a minimum, and a number of options were explored involving trussed and tensile structures. One sketch includes a skysign; others pick up on Buckminster Fuller's geodesic forms. Eventually, however, Foster came to feel that too complex a mast structure would compete visually with the perimeter lattice of the offices below and, for the final scheme, an option was selected that was simpler in appearance rather than structurally the lightest.

Mounted on it were to be a local microwave link, two-way televisual links to all Humana hospitals, an earth-station antenna, laser displays and electrographic signs intended to communicate local information and advertise Humana's name.

Satellite dishes require exceptional stability to work at their best, and in this respect the ideal location for them would have been at the base of the building. Unfortunately this would

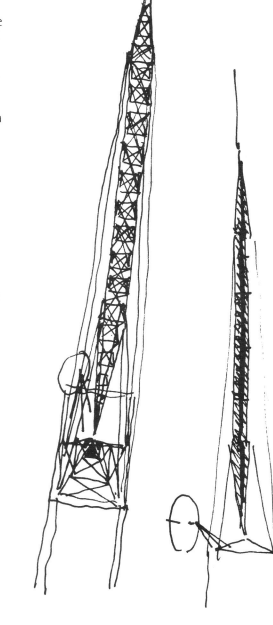

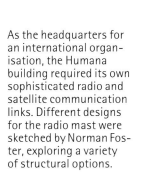

As the headquarters for an international organisation, the Humana building required its own sophisticated radio and satellite communication links. Different designs for the radio mast were sketched by Norman Foster, exploring a variety of structural options.

Seen in relation to the building as a whole, Norman Foster moved away from complex mast structures, preferring a solution that would not compete visually with the lattice structure of the main tower.

have led to their line of sight being obstructed by surrounding buildings; instead, they were mounted at the base of the mast.

In form and texture the building as a whole — the effect Foster Associates were seeking was "light, silvery, glowing and rounded" — was deliberately in contrast to the 40-storey "dark box-like slab" opposite, where the prime evocation was one of muteness and alienation. But despite its technological appearance, Humana is rooted in established precedent. Although its counter-helical, self-bracing external steel frame is a novel application of the technique, the concept of a bearing-wall structure is based on principles used for many of the tallest buildings in the US. Even the use of a circular tower to celebrate and turn a corner is a traditional device dating back to the Renaissance.

In his early days at Yale, Foster had been greatly impressed by Louis Kahn and had designed buildings with external service towers akin to those at Kahn's own Richards Medical Research Building. It was a building that had clearly influenced early developmental work on the Hongkong Bank, where the service and

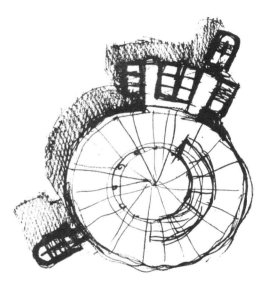

Various groupings for the vertical service and circulation towers were explored, initially following a fairly random distribution.

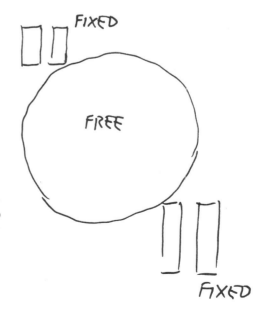

Shown here in diagrammatic form, the final arrangement of the service towers was formalised to create a grouping appropriate to the building's corner site in a city organised on a simple grid street-plan. The service towers would be fixed items, but capable of serving any variety of main spaces.

"Louisville is a river city with a low profile and a long waterfront. The site occupies a prominent position on the waterfront, overlooking the Ohio River. This enables the building to be seen in its totality, providing a distinct opportunity for the designer. Adjacent to the site are a variety of buildings which create a rich and varied context: nineteenth-century cast-iron front warehouse buildings, several examples of the International Style (including one by Mies van der Rohe), and the Kentucky Center for the Arts."

David Jones and Wendell Cherry, *Humana Competition Final Report*, July 1982

circulation towers were located on each side of the building. The placement of Humana's towers followed this precedent and for the same reasons. The plan was freed for total flexibility, while services which required maintenance were removed from the inconvenient core and located where they were easily accessible.

Early studies looked at the effect of orientating the towers radially around the building. But aligning them with the street pattern freed up the tower itself and provided fixed 'anchoring points', thus a relationship with adjacent street frontages could be created. There was one major and one minor tower, the larger containing the lifts but both of them providing distribution of servicing and escape stairs. Together they took on the appearance of the gantries for a rocket.

Humana, as Foster Associates saw it, was to be a social condenser, buzzing with activity. The idea of communication was interpreted in physical as well as in electronic terms, and included a roof-top helipad which would allow non-stop flights of up to 400 miles to be undertaken, as well as fast connections to the local airport. Beneath this was a roof garden and running track. A double-height sky-lobby at the halfway point would accommodate a communication centre, audio-visual facilities, an auditorium, club and restaurant – again an idea gained from experience on the Hongkong Bank. At Humana, the impressive space could also provide a reception area for the upper part of the building while it was still let to tenants.

Humana's eventful composition of cylinder and service towers reinforced a trend within the Foster office towards a greater articulation of form that had been evident since the time of Hammersmith and the Hongkong Bank. Although services and circulation were kept relatively compact within their own towers, Humana went further than either of these projects in the extent to which they were removed beyond the main bulk of the building.

In principle it promised to ease maintenance and subsequent upgrading of those parts of the building with greater potential obsolescence. But the real gains were architectural. Humana, like Hammersmith and the Hongkong Bank, was designed for an urban and not a green-field site, and the two service towers played an essential part in bonding the building to its surroundings. Placed at the south-east and north-west corners, they served to connect the tower to the neighbouring street facades on Fifth and Main Streets.

Humana's internal spaces were designed to provide both maximum flexibility and excellent outward views. The brief called for a certain number of fixed offices, and these were designed to be located on the perimeter around a central area of open-plan offices. For these purposes the circular plan offered a net to gross usable floor area of better than 80 per cent – a considerable improvement on the more usual figure for a standard office block of nearer 70 per cent.

The building's innovatory structural cladding system enabled the circular perimeter wall to work as a continuous triangulated framework, transmitting both floor loads and wind loads economically downwards to the foundations. Foster Associates put forward a series of options for cladding panels in various combinations of stainless or colour-coated steel.

At the ground-floor foyer level, a five-storey independent truss system would support glazing independently from the main

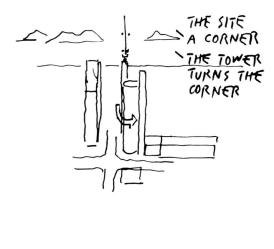

Norman Foster's 'storyboard' diagrams identify the design's most important qualities in a comprehensible form.

With slight amendments (see page 87), these simple diagrams were retained as the best way of communicating with a lay client.

This three-dimensional drawing was prepared for integration into an aerial photograph of downtown Louisville, to create a realistic impression of the building in its true setting.

structure. Service and circulation towers would be clad in clear and translucent glass. Further up the elevation, as at the Hammersmith Centre or the Whitney redevelopment, the change of use from public to private was reflected in the change in scale of the structure.

Ten medium-speed passenger lifts were provided in banks of four and six, as required by the brief; but design studies suggested that the efficiency of circulation could be improved by means of double-decker lifts, higher speeds, or a combination of lifts and escalators.

As at Hammersmith, heating would be effected by means of decentralised but interconnected heat pumps, which would transfer heat from interior to perimeter zones in winter. In theory, the optimal cladding surface to plan area ratio promised excellent energy efficiency; this would, however, have been offset by the articulated nature of the plan as a whole.

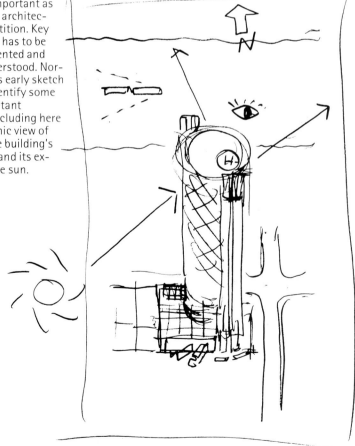

Communication is almost as important as design in an architectural competition. Key information has to be clearly presented and quickly understood. Norman Foster's early sketch begins to identify some of the important elements, including here the panoramic view of the river, the building's orientation and its exposure to the sun.

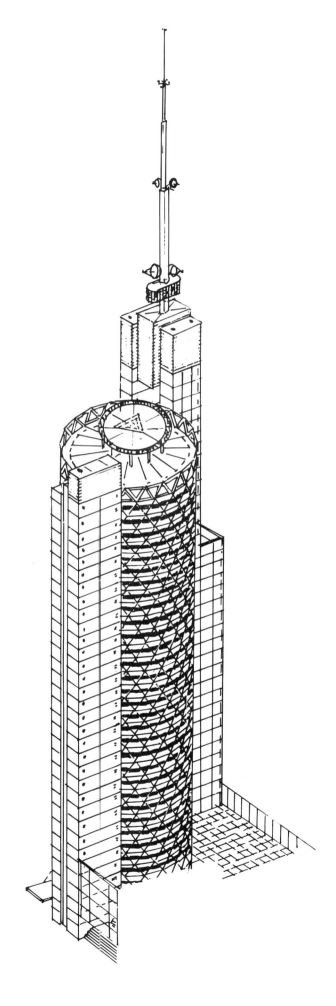

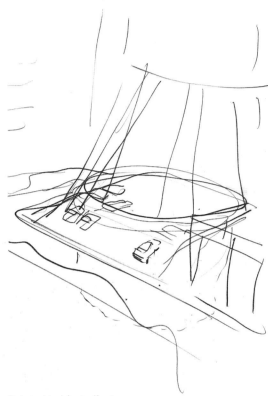

Related to his earliest sketches of the scheme, this simple drawing by Norman Foster continues to express his desire for a dramatic base to the tower, with the walls dissolving to reveal an almost structureless interior.

Competitions have almost as much to do with clear and concise communication as with the ideas themselves. Most, after all, allow only a minimum of time for the judges to consider the ideas contained in the entries. Foster Associates were aware of this, and placed heavy emphasis on getting across clearly the main principles behind their scheme.

The ground rules implicit in a competition are distinctly different from those operating in a conventional commission. In the case of Humana, although the concept of the office floors was based on strict rationality of use, the overall concept was seductive and individual enough to provide areas of excitement to tempt the judges.

For example, the height of the spire compared with that of the rest of the building imparted the feel of a radio mast at the same time as creating a skyscraper truly worthy of the name. But one similarity that apparently was purely coincidental was the building's resemblance to a syringe. Richard Horden confesses that he did worry a little about this, as he thought it might have appeared that Foster Associates had glibly based their design on a visual pun derived from the nature of their client's business. As it happened such fears were to prove unfounded.

It was at the base of the tower that the most focused area of excitement was needed. The foyer was at once a dramatic entrance of varying height, appropriate to a major corporation, and a public place, with ease of access and of use. As at Whitney, clear glass and openness transmitted a message of accessibility. This impression was reinforced by the public gallery spaces and sculpture garden that grew out to enclose the space between the building and the nineteenth-century offices next door.

The sculpture garden would have been enclosed by greenery and translucent walls. It was a homage to New York's Paley Park of 1967 – landscape architects Zion & Breen, consultant architect Albert Preston Moore – a text-book example of how a small space can create a sense of rest that is disproportionate to its size. It is one of Norman Foster's favourite references, and at the time of Humana he produced a number of sketches and study models examining the extent to which its principles could be applied to Humana.

The brief had called for the executive areas to be not more than 100 feet above ground level. Foster Associates felt this requirement reflected Humana's 'hands-on' management style and entered fully into its spirit, locating the executive suite towards the upper part of the ground-level atrium. The public spaces below would link up with the recently-completed Performing Arts Center across Main Street.

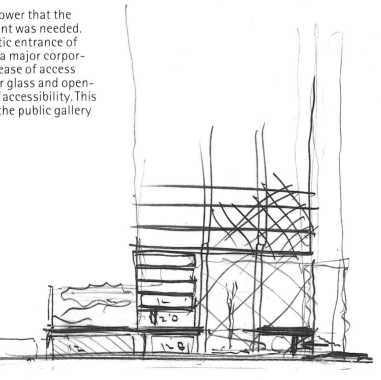

Sketches show the main entrance raised to first floor level to allow uninhibited vehicular access to the site, beneath the main pedestrian level and associated sculpture garden. Above this level, partial mezzanine floors overlook the main atrium which has a fountain as its centre-piece.

"An architectural competition, though rather traditional in Europe, is quite new in America. Given our objective to attain a landmark building of architectural importance, it was a necessity that we have a competition. A competition creates the requisite tension and deliberate objectivity necessary for good work and good decisions on the part of all involved. In this case, we believe it served us well."

David Jones and Wendell Cherry, *Humana Competition Final Report*, July 1982

A spirited and free drawing — a distinct departure from Norman Foster's normally more controlled technique — begins to explore the possibilities offered by an entrance atrium opening out to the street.

"The matching of architect and client is surely the most uncertain step in the entire process of creating a building; it requires from both parties a leap of faith beside which the anguish of actual design can often seem far less risky. Not the least of the attractions of an architectural competition is that it provides a neat route around all of this guesswork — instead of viewing each other as participants in a blind date, architect and client can evaluate each other on the basis of tangible evidence of their needs."

Paul Goldberger,
Humana Competition Final Report, July 1982

At the base of the main tower, a six-storey high atrium was proposed. As with the Hammersmith Centre and Whitney redevelopment proposals before it, the change of use from public to private was reflected in an impressive change of scale in the main structure, which also emphasised the building's minimal support. Supported by its own structure, clear glazing rose the full height of the atrium on the street elevations, to create an entrance suitable for a public corporation so closely linked with the city. Housing public exhibitions and performances, the space could also be linked to the Kentucky Center for the Arts across the street.

A high water-table precluded deep basements but some underground parking would be possible beneath the main tower.

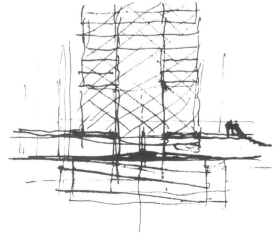

"I think that we try very consciously to understand the nature of the client, whether it's an individual, a small group of individuals or a very large entity – and these are all quite different. And we try to respond to the nature of that organisation with a way of structuring the project, of communicating and exploring ideas that is appropriate to both the users of the building and the owner, who frequently are not the same people."

Norman Foster, *Building*, May 1982

Planning efficiency and flexibility were emphasised, with the tower's structurally open plan offering excellent usable area statistics.

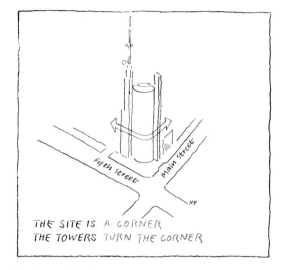

A series of simple drawings was prepared by Norman Foster to form part of the competition submission. Key information is given in simple note form directly on the drawings.

A screen protecting the sculpture garden relates the tower to the far smaller scale of Louisville's Main Street.

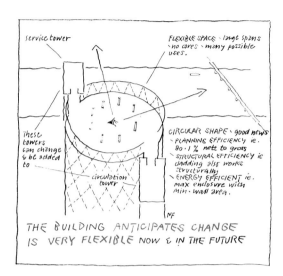

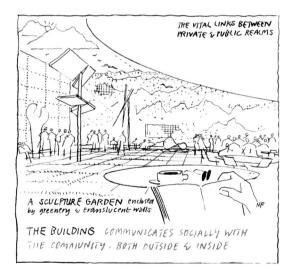

At ground level, the internal corner of the site could be given over to public use in the form of a quiet sculpture garden.

The entrance level atrium could be developed as an exciting space, opening up the building to the local community.

It is important to note that the drawn scheme is only a first option. Foster emphasised that a realistic design could develop only in collaboration with the client.

87

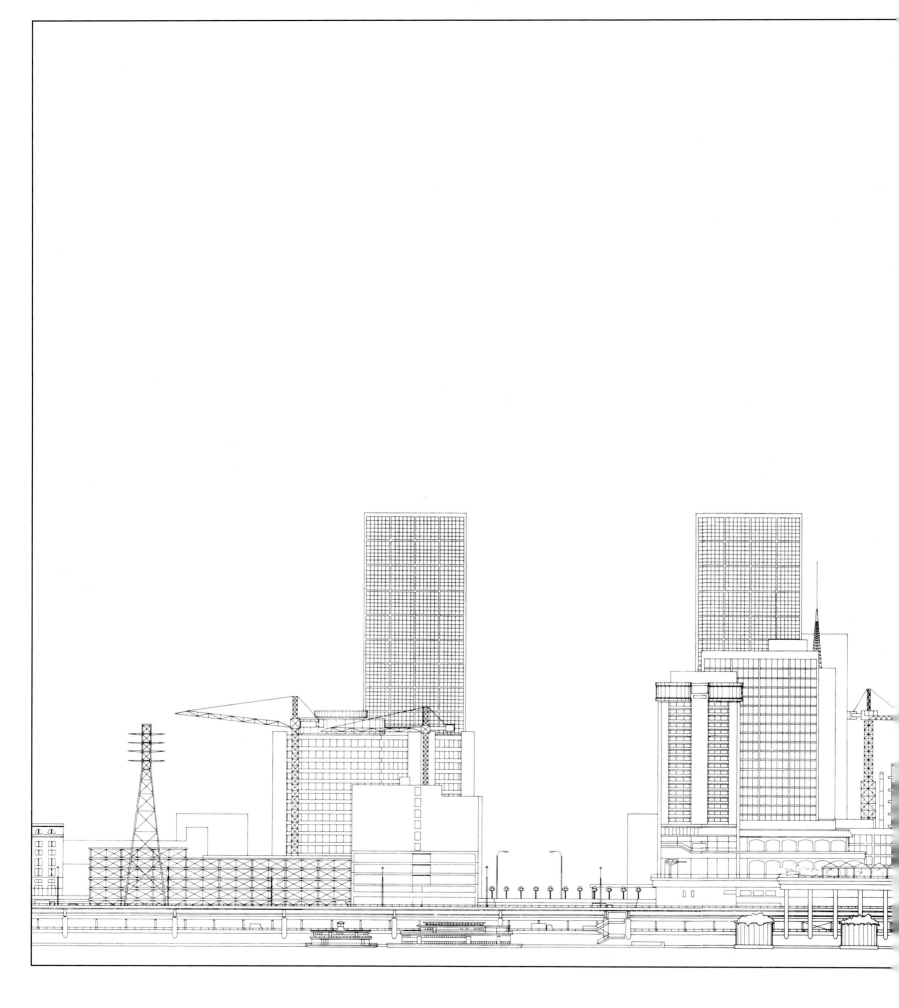

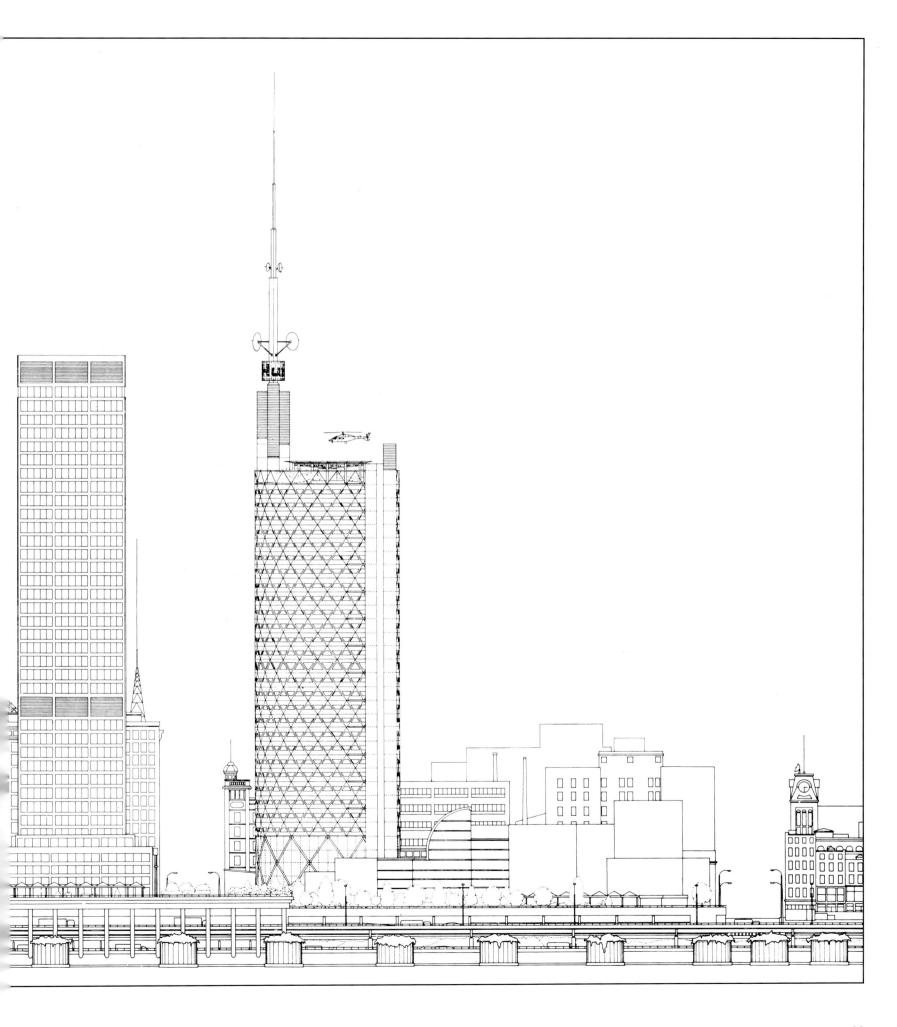

Previous page: Taken from the set of presentation drawings prepared for the competition submission, the north elevation of the building is seen in the context of the rest of Louisville as if from across the Ohio River.

Circular buildings are generally regarded as difficult to divide satisfactorily. Foster Associates, consistent believers in the free plan, could have been expected to go to considerable lengths to overcome this reputation.

Humana's exceptional planning flexibility compared with other buildings of its shape owed much to the absence of a central core. As these plans demonstrate, the plan could be divided in any one of a number of possible geometric divisions of the circle. This logic was observed in almost all respects: the services distribution was annular and the structural grid radial. Some activities not falling within the pattern were also accommodated: one floor (not shown here) incorporated rectangular squash courts fanning around a central space.

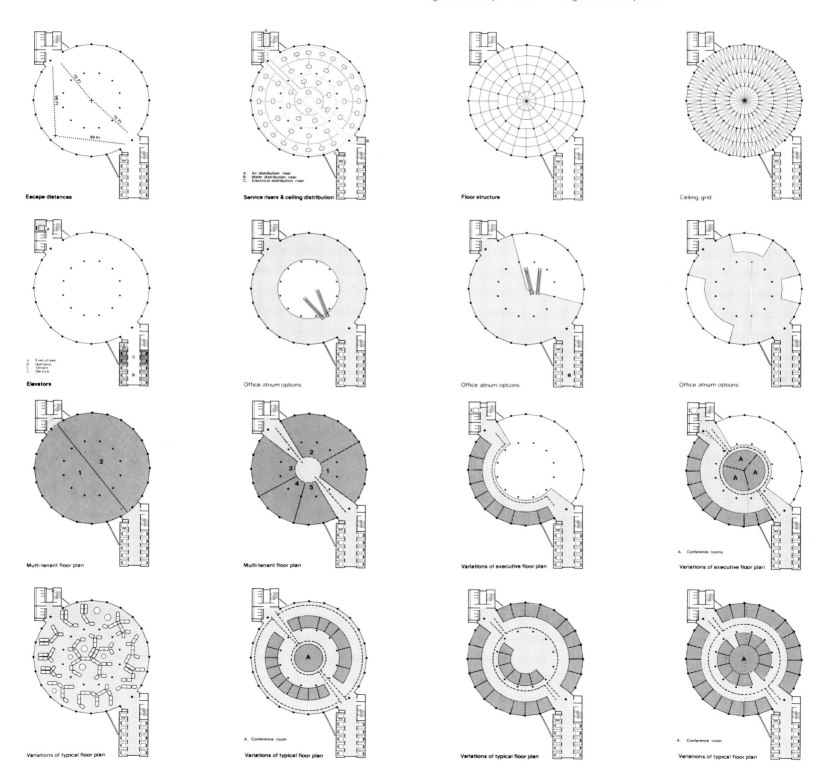

90

There were no height restrictions on the site, so the decision was made to maximise the height of the building by planning the tower to cover only a modest portion of the site. A diameter of 37.5 metres was established which created individual floors with a usable area of approximately 1100 square metres. Two service towers align with their respective street frontages. The smaller, adjacent to Main Street, houses only washrooms and an escape stair, with a secondary lift serving only the podium levels. The larger, on Fifth Avenue, is given over entirely to one service and 10 passenger lifts, and a second escape stair.

The main entrance plaza of the Kentucky Center for the Arts.

Main Street. The site for the Humana building lies at the intersection with Fifth Avenue.

A flight of steps rises from Main Street to give access to the public sculpture garden.

A small restaurant serves both the public garden and atrium.

The sculpture garden.

Vehicular and delivery access.

Undeveloped plot used for off-street parking.

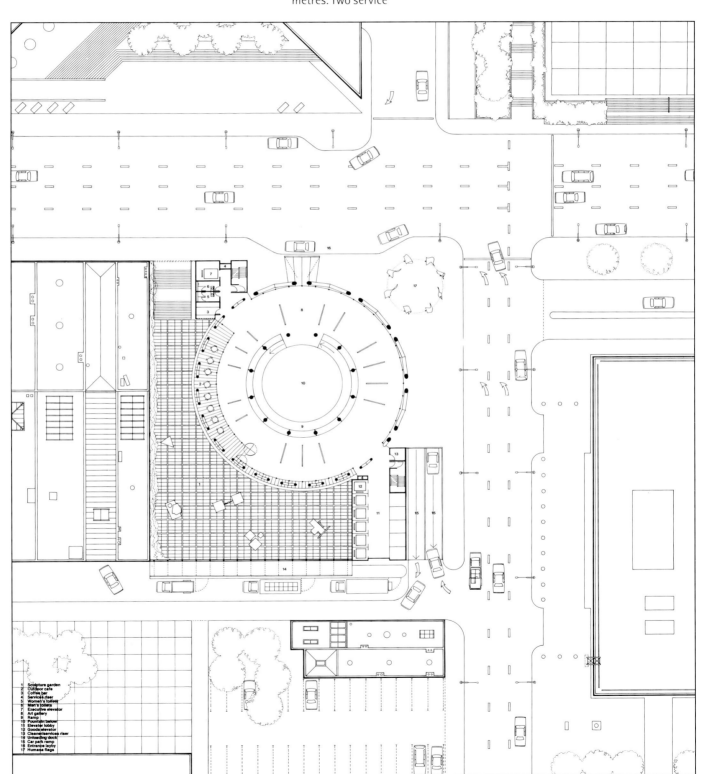

1 Sculpture garden
2 Outdoor cafe
3 Coffee bar
4 Services riser
5 Women's toilets
6 Men's toilets
7 Executive elevator
8 Art gallery
9 Ramp
10 Fountain below
11 Elevator lobby
12 Goods elevator
13 Cleaner/services riser
14 Unloading dock
15 Car park ramp
16 Entrance layby
17 Humana flags

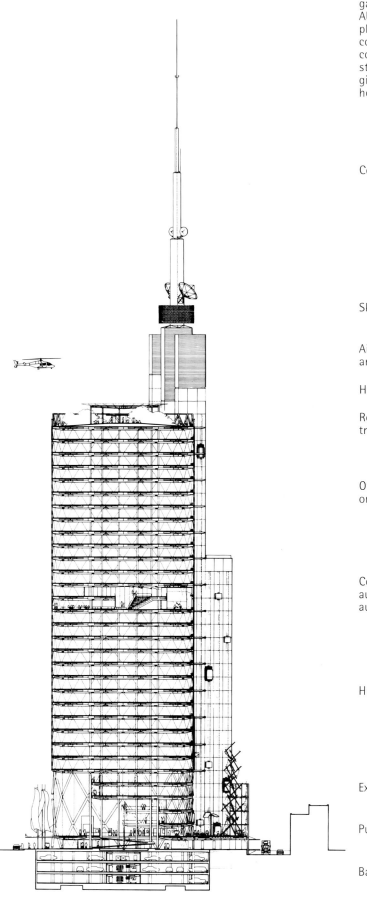

The main tower rises 32 storeys to a roof-top garden and helipad. Above these, high-level plant-rooms and the communications tower continue for a further 30 storeys effectively, to give the building a total height of 230 metres.

Communications tower.

Sky-sign.

Air-conditioning plant and lift-motor rooms.

Helipad.

Roof garden and running track.

Offices for tenants and/ or future expansion.

Communications centre, auditorium and restaurant facilities.

Humana offices.

Executive floors.

Public atrium.

Basement car park.

Competitions tend to encourage a particular kind of design response from participants, with competitors more often inclined towards a longer view, taking the opportunity to develop ideas about the kind of work they would like to do more of in the future. Briefs are often non-specific enough to allow the exploration of individual preoccupations. As a result the designs generated may be very different from those created by a normal commission.

Clients, too, act differently during competitions. In the case of Humana the disparate range of architects invited to take part lent some weight to the impression that the competition was to be as much a styling exercise as a search for the right architectural approach. The fact that Foster Associates were the only foreign architects invited to take part gave added urgency to the effort required.

Under the circumstances Foster Associates decided to present a very clear statement of their philosophy. Thanks to their experience of teamwork and its application to competition submissions, a great deal of thinking and research was able to be undertaken and brought together over a short space of time, resulting in drawings of great richness and power. Assessment by independent quantity surveyors also evaluated the cost effectiveness of the final design highly. Recognising the difficulty of coming to a practical solution in isolation from the client, however, the final page of their presentation stressed that their proposals were only a range of options, not a fixed and final proposal. Nevertheless the competition was won by Michael Graves, with a design that could not have been further from the Foster philosophy.

In retrospect, Graves' success was perhaps not so surprising. Questions of massing and historical reference are easier to put across in an architectural presentation – especially to a lay client – than an architecture that concentrates on matters of detailing and usage. Possibly even more to the point, Foster Associates belong to a European tradition that aspires to satisfy philosophical as well as functional criteria. The structural and engineering determinism that informed their design for Humana would probably have proved more popular in Europe than in the United States, where structural elegance alone is not often thought palatable. There, as in car or product design, the idea of styling remains firmly entrenched.

Tim Ostler

In Norman Foster's presentation sketch, and in the similar model photograph, the form and finish of the Humana scheme is shown to stand out from the earlier rectangular towers that make up Louisville's skyline. The cladding panels could be either stainless steel or colour-coated aluminium.

Flight 347
by Norman Foster

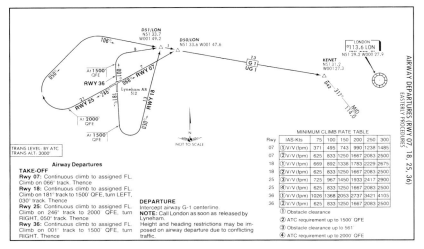

All the information required to fly across Europe is contained in airway manuals such as the Jeppesen, four thick volumes which contain the necessary data to arrive or depart from any listed airport. This data – which is constantly updated – is contained in a series of diagrams, one diagram for each clearly defined manoeuvre. The example shown here describes the standard instrument departure procedures for aircraft leaving Lyneham from runway 25 to join airway Green One on an easterly heading. During the procedure, information is confirmed by radio with Lyneham's control tower who liaise with the main air traffic control for that sector to ensure individual aircraft join the airway at the correct time and altitude.

The flight of a modern aeroplane can be seen as a metaphor for design; the design of a book, a building or a piece of furniture. Both flight and design involve unseen forces, obey certain rules and for their realisation depend totally on communication.

The flight described here brought together three people whose personal interaction was to help realise this book. Otl Aicher, in Germany, is the architect of the book and his involvement is an act of friendship. Ian Lambot, from Hong Kong, is the book's publisher and editor; if it were a building project then he would be both client and contractor.

Otl has the concept for a series of documents that will communicate at several levels; a hierarchy of information in which the reader can scan a visual story or delve deeper through the medium of the written word. Otl is also concerned to reveal the processes behind the work; to show the relationship of drawings, models and prototypes to the final product. He is interested in the comparison between informal sketches, as ideas made visible, and the more formal language of communication that evolves as responsibilities transfer from the private to the public realm.

The book, like the buildings it portrays, is a team effort, initially orchestrated by Otl, then later by Ian in his role as editor. Activities alternate between a studio in Rotis, southern Germany, where Otl lives and works and a studio in Wiltshire, the West Country of England. Joint working sessions might last a week or merely a single intensive day. Spaces are 'wallpapered' with mock-ups of page layouts so the book can be viewed as a continuous sequence or examined a single page at a time. The disciplines which Otl sets as a designer seem initially quite rigid, but as the work proceeds it becomes evident that they provide an overall order within which there is almost infinite scope for choice and variation. Otl's selective eye always seems to be guided by a strong inner philosophy.

The book as a project appears suspended in space and time. At Rotis, Otl, who has a passion for history, provides insights into the past culture of Schwabia and its strong Celtic traditions, which also happen to permeate the West Country of England. The intensity of design activity in Wiltshire is interspersed by long

The main commercial air-routes over Europe are defined by a comprehensive set of radio beacons which act as 'traffic roundabouts' between which the routes themselves connect. Flights along these 'air corridors' are carefully monitored by air traffic control centres responsible for their own clearly defined sectors, who set the height and spacing of aircraft travelling the same route. Once assigned a position within the air corridor, electronic 'auto-pilot' equipment within the aircraft can be set to the appropriate beacon's frequency, allowing the plane to calculate its own true heading while maintaining an even airspeed and height. Permission from air traffic control has to be received before each subsequent section of the route can be joined. The chart below contains all airways information for the flight from Lyneham to Leutkirch.

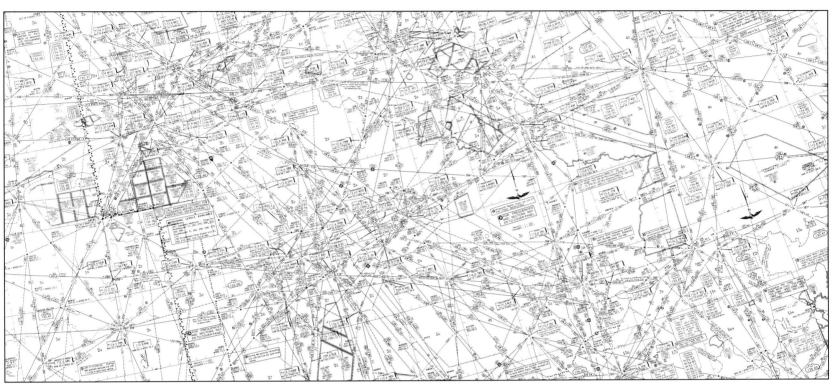

walks to view the prehistoric Ridgeway and Silbury Hill, and the White Horse at Uffington. We speculate that the ancient fortifications of the Ridgeway were part of a defensive system protecting a latter-day Silicon Valley, for here was the high technology of the day, a source of flint for tools and armaments.

This flight connects these two locations in England and Germany. Ian and I leave Lyneham, a military airbase in Wiltshire, to spend the day with Otl. Although it is a private flight in a small aircraft, it will share the same airspace and operate within the same instrument flight rules as the big jets flying scheduled services. After take-off at dawn the aircraft, still climbing, passes 7000 feet to join controlled airspace: a world in which rules, procedures and instrumentation follow internationally agreed standards. The climb to its requested flight level is stepped to fit into the early morning rush-hour traffic which is now building up around Heathrow and Gatwick. The aircraft, more than any building so far conceived, is environmentally self-sufficient. At 37 000 feet, with the capacity to climb higher, its occupants shuffle papers and go through the ritual of morning coffee while contemplating the incredible beauty of bright sun and limitless blue sky. This is the poetic and understated component of its performance. The aircraft is now a vessel pressurised to simulate conditions close to those at sea level. With its own sealed air supply, it is comfortably warm despite an outside air temperature more than 60 degrees below freezing.

Safe passage and compatability with other traffic on this three-dimensional aerial highway, called Upper Green One, is assured by a language of communication which transcends political and cultural barriers. The en route charts with their related arrival and departure procedures are models of graphic clarity designed for rapid and unambiguous access by the crew and their ground-based counterparts. As the flight proceeds control is handed over from British to Dutch and, eventually, German centres; the combination of radar, radio and the flight plan, which was filed some hours earlier, ensures that this event is part of an invisible global network. Just over an hour from departure the aircraft descends through cloud, passing 5000 feet, to leave the relative protection of controlled airspace and, as visual contact is established with the ground, the flight enters the domain of visual flight rules. Here the onus to avoid conflicting traffic passes from the ground controller back to the pilot, on the basis of seeing and being seen. Navigation, which has so far been by electronic aids, is now by eye as ground features are interpreted on a topographical chart showing roads, railways, water and the like to scale; quite different from the graphic abstractions associated with instrument flight rules.

Leutkirch, the destination airfield, comes into view as a single short runway set in rolling green countryside: its identity is confirmed from

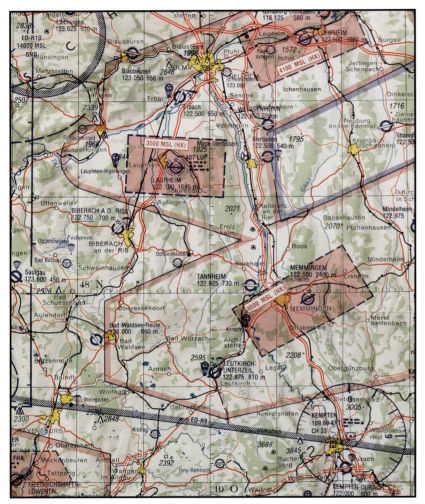
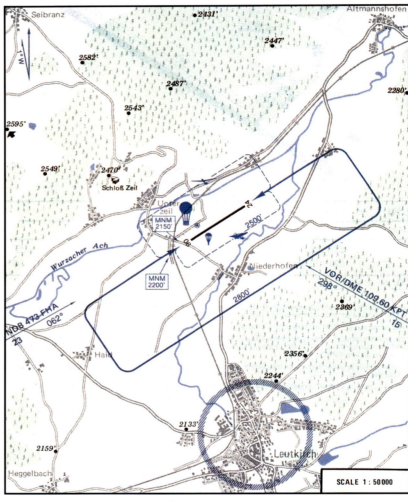

For aircraft flying on instruments alone, or on the air-routes at high altitude, diagrams give all the relevant information regardless of the geography of the land beneath. For visual flying, large-scale Ordnance Survey-type charts are available from the national aviation authorities which combine the most important aspects of this information with a standard map identifying the areas' main geographical features. Airports are clearly marked together with their call-up radio frequency and length of runway. For the flight to Leutkirch – shown in this section of chart positioned centrally in the lower one-third – the final approach, after leaving the main airway, was 'vectored' by military radar to the vicinity of the airfield, close enough for visual recognition to be established.

The Bottlang manual is available for flying by visual references, again with the relevant information for each airport clearly laid out in a diagram, now recognisable as a simple map. Approach heights and routes are clearly marked, as are the most important surrounding features. Possible hazards at the airport and headings from the nearest radio beacons are also given, while the hatched blue circle around the village of Leutkirch indicates an area not to be overflown. More specific information – runway type, length, height and so on – is given on the reverse of the sheet.

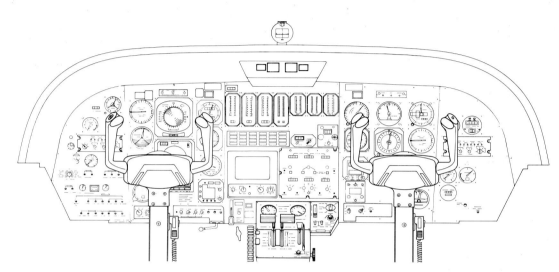

The cockpit arrangement of a typical long-range small aircraft is a complex arrangement of guages, switches and indicators. The pilot sits on the left, with a certain amount of instrument duplication allowing the plane to also be flown by the co-pilot on the right. This drawing is based on a Cessna Citation 1.

the charts by the relationship of roads and the nearby town. After throttling back and negotiating a visual circuit of the field, the aircraft touches down to complete the flight. Unlike the standard international airport everything here is simple, direct and friendly — Otl can be seen waiting by his car almost as soon as the aircraft turns off the runway. The arrival formalities are minimal and the group is soon on its short journey to Rotis.

It is worth comparing the simplicity of the very first airfields with the complexity which we now take for granted in large international airports. Is it merely size that turns airports into those anonymous mazes which are so hostile to the users, or can a fresh design strategy recapture the friendly immediacy and orientation of a place like Leutkirch? It seems necessary to keep going back to first principles to question such preconceptions, and historical models are often a valuable inspiration.

However, the lessons from aviation for architecture are not confined to those buildings that host the aircraft and their users. They are operational, concerned with how people work together, as much as technological. An air traffic system has a relatively simple objective which is the safe passage of an aircraft from one place to another. Despite the diversity of professions and interests that are involved — nations, airlines, manufacturers, controllers, pilots, unions and so on — the existence of a shared language of communication with the agreed procedures ensures the achievement of that safe passage.

Similarly, the design process involves many disparate interests and disciplines — clients, architects and surveyors, structural, civil, mechanical and electrical engineers — as well as a host of political and regulatory bodies. Each of these is likely to have its own technical and cultural aspirations and is lacking in any shared language of communication. Even the single line schematics of one of the engineering professions will be incomprehensible to an engineer from a different background. Certainly the education of each skill will have paid scant, if any, respect to the existence of others involved in the total process. Given this state of affairs, one of the earliest tasks on a project is to design operating structures and evolve methods of communication which will unite the separate interests in commonly shared objectives. Only then can the creative process be unleashed.

When all the interests involved are not united in their endeavours then weaknesses become apparent; whether in air traffic networks or the design of buildings. As traffic densities increase, newer technologies emerge to cope with the increased flows, but junctions with earlier systems threaten the total network. Europe, for example, has at this time sophisticated computer-managed systems, but each extends only within the limits of its own national boundaries. It is not uncommon for the linkage between systems to be dependent still on an outdated telephone system. The result is a wasteful and inefficient redundancy of overlapping capabilities rather than a totally optimised single system. The same dilemmas can appear in the design of a complex building where the weak links are junctions between old and new technologies. These can be the outcome of the many specialists involved, each with his own area of expertise. In the absence of a shared vision, the result will be a complexity of individual systems each superimposed on the other. The opportunity for a single system of more elegant simplicity will have been lost.

The barriers to a single European traffic network are the politics of national pride. Similarly, the barriers to creating the best design for a building are likely to be the pride of one profession competing for its share of the total, rather than combining its skills in the more worthwhile search for a philosophy of integration. Perhaps this is at the heart of the difference between truly creative teamwork and design by committee.

Both air traffic networks and buildings, like any other human endeavour, have their share of failures; arguably these are inevitable as techniques evolve over time to cope with the stress of seemingly rapid growth and change. It is virtually taken for granted that the way forward to higher levels of safety in air traffic control will eventually be achieved by the reasoned application of newer technologies. The same tendencies are apparent in the hardware of flight itself as quieter, more energy-efficient craft become available. There is undoubted potential for the same pattern of progress in architecture, and the world of aviation has much to offer in technology transfer. In these circumstances, there is a certain irony in the proposition that failures in architecture could be redeemed by harking back in time to a falsely nostalgic vision of the past. That would be akin to suggesting that the difficulties of patrolling the skies by radar should lead back to navigation by road maps. Both propositions are equally absurd.

1980

Students' Union
University College London

As shown here in this study model, the first scheme for University College's new Students' Union building was kept as low as possible on the main street elevation. To create the total amount of usable space requested in the brief, however, this approach required a low-level extension at the rear of the building, which would have eaten into a large section of one of the University's existing quadrangles. To maximise the usable area of the new building rooftop tennis courts were proposed.

In 1980 University College London set out to build a new Students' Union, to be funded by a public appeal commemorating the College's recent 150th anniversary.

The new building was to rise on a site in Gordon Street, Bloomsbury between the College theatre block – designed in the 1960s by James Cubitt & Partners – and a Georgian terrace that formed the western border of Gordon Square. Foster Associates were asked to develop proposals up to a level suitable for outline planning permission. As with an earlier project for Open House, a commission to carry the design further would depend on the success of the fundraising appeal.

The brief, developed in collaboration with College and student representatives, included provision for a café and shop, entertainment areas containing lounges and bars, a theatre workshop and a sports hall with seating for 250 spectators. The new building would be linked to the existing theatre block, which had already been partially converted to include squash courts and associated changing rooms above the main theatre.

Early models studied the volumetric consequences of accommodating this brief on the site while keeping the height of the building to the parapet line of the Georgian terrace next door. At ground level, easily accessible from other parts of the College, was the entrance concourse and entertainment area. Above it was the triple-height sports hall.

This occupied the bulk of the building's volume; and because space was so tight it was important to reduce wasted space to a minimum. The roof above the sports hall was therefore used to accommodate three open-air tennis courts, enclosed on all sides by mesh fences. This idea may have been inspired, to some extent, by the site visits of members of Foster Associates working on the Hongkong Bank project: due to pressure of space it is standard practice for schools in Hong Kong to make use of flat roofs in this way.

Still, despite such prudent husbandry of space, at ground floor level the building volume was forced to extend to the rear, taking up a large part of an area – currently occupied by

The view along Gordon Street, in model form. The new building had to form a link between a four-storey Georgian terrace and the University's 1960s theatre block.

The first scheme respected and matched the height of the adjacent Georgian terrace, with only the supports for netting around the tennis courts extending above the parapet line. A service/stair tower connected the new building to the theatre block, but was set back to create a visual break.

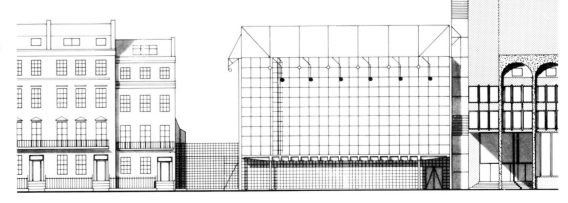

In the revised scheme, the gap between the new building and the theatre block was widened to form a new concourse. Glazed at its roof and at either end, this natural link connected the street and the main college buildings beyond the quadrangle, now retained by raising the height of the new building. A ramp (also shown in the drawing on the opposite page) leads down from the street-level entrance to the quadrangle. A high-level bridge links the sports hall with changing rooms installed in the upper levels of the theatre block.

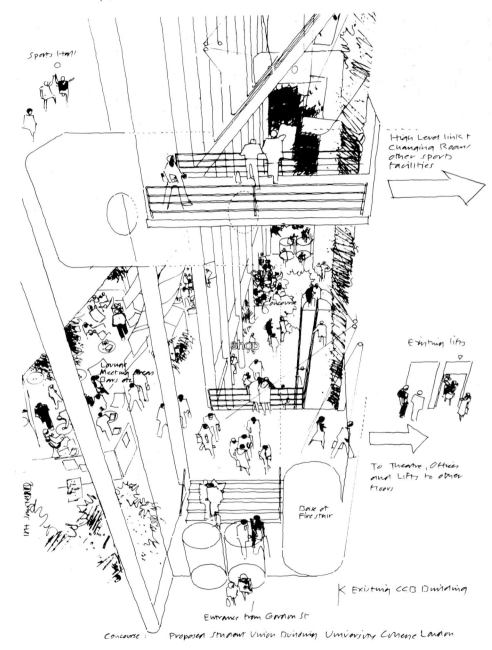

Concourse: Proposed Student Union Building University College London

huts – which had the potential to develop into a pleasant collegiate quadrangle. Although the flat roof of the extension could be made available for sitting out, its siting over the bar would have precluded a close relationship with the social and entertainment areas below. Also, maximising the width required for the building had reduced the space between it and the theatre block, resulting in an uncomfortably cramped junction between the two buildings.

It became clear that the benefits of keeping to the Georgian terrace's parapet line were outweighed by the disadvantages at ground level. An alternative proposal was therefore prepared that placed more emphasis on a clearer planning concept. As Foster Associates were also concerned to demonstrate the way in which the new external spaces would now conform to the spirit of the existing University College complex as a whole, the plans for this second scheme were presented in the context of the overall College layout.

The revised design placed a priority on maintaining the quadrangle at the rear and articulating the break between old and new. This junction with the theatre block prefigured that later adopted for Billingsgate. Instead of clashing with the existing structure, the new Union building was pulled away from it and a combined entrance concourse created in the cleft formed between the two buildings. At roof level and on its two elevations this space was glazed, creating a visual separation while maintaining physical and practical connections. Again, as at Billingsgate – and also at Open House – this concourse doubled as a through route. The building became not only an end in itself but also a path to other things, in this case, via a ramp, to the quadrangle beyond and on to the main collegiate building.

For concerts or dances the social areas, now double-height, could be partitioned off from the entrance. For very grand occasions they could be linked directly with the theatre foyer to form a flexible open plan, through which space flowed both horizontally and, above the entrance, vertically. Dominated by ambitious vertical planting up one wall and

"The essence of Foster's approach is pragmatic. His designs spring from a simple concern with what a building is expected to do, and how it will be built. He does not go in for the arcane ramblings of those who set out to turn architecture into an abstruse branch of philosophy."

Deyan Sudjic, *The Sunday Times*, June 1983

by bridges spanning across at second and third floor levels, the combined concourse promised to be a dramatic space.

A series of trusses on the second floor supported the sports hall floor. Catwalks gave access to the lighting and other services located within this zone. Above this, the multi-purpose hall allowed level access via a bridge from changing rooms in the theatre block next door. A large space-frame structure spanned the full width of the building to maintain a column-free space for the main sports hall itself. As with a number of other details the nature of this structure was never studied in full: the primary purpose of the design was to do no more than act as the subject of an appeal. In these circumstances, Foster Associates prepared a scheme that, although only taken up to concept stage, provided a sound framework that was realistic enough both to accommodate future detail

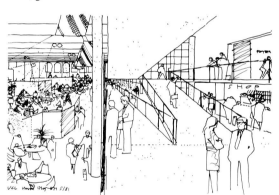

design without major alteration and – most importantly – provided a basis for sound economic assessment.

In this instance, response to the appeal did not match early expectations and, in the light of increasing cutbacks in university funding, the scheme did not proceed further.

Tim Ostler

Lower ground level: the new Students' Union bar opens out on to the recreated quadrangle while movable partitions allow the semi-basement areas to be organised into a variety of spaces suitable for meetings, dances or other events.

Upper ground level: the main street entrance links the theatre block on one side with the main lounge areas of the new building on the other.

Sports hall level: the sports hall establishes a clear span across the building large enough for a single basketball or netball court, leaving sufficient space on one side for the storage of apparatus or temporary spectator seating.

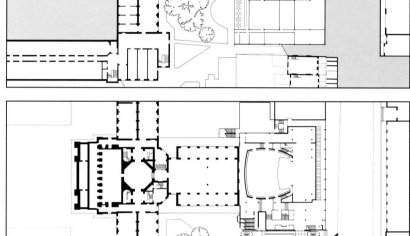

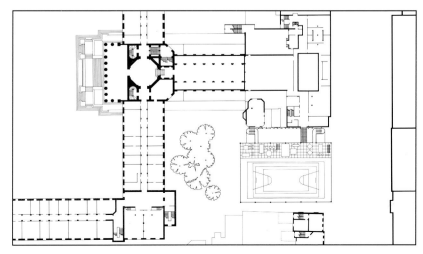

1981 Billingsgate Market
London
England

The redevelopment of Billingsgate fish-market presented Foster Associates with the challenge of reconciling the demands of speculative offices with the need to reflect and enhance several layers of London's history. Following the demise of the Hammersmith Centre, the project also offered them another chance to construct a building in London – something Norman Foster was keen to achieve.

The client, Furness Withy, was owned by a Hong Kong-based Chinese family who were looking to establish a major presence in central London. Billingsgate, the subject of a developers' competition, seemed a suitable path to this goal. The commission was an indirect result of Foster's work for Willis Faber & Dumas.

Billingsgate Market, as it is known today, is the result of Sir Horace Jones' extensive enlargement and remodelling, into the French Renaissance style, of a much earlier building.

Furness Withy occupied the offices Willis Faber had vacated when they moved into their new headquarters in Ipswich, and had heard about Foster Associates from their predecessors. Working once again in collaboration with letting agents Jones Lang Wootton, the design team at Foster Associates was able to profit from the experience of speculative office design accumulated during the Hammersmith saga.

Billingsgate lies on an inlet in the riverbank, long since obscured by development. Fish had been sold on the site since the Middle Ages, and throughout this period it had offered a convenient harbour for fishermen. But by the time Foster Associates were approached in 1981, it had begun to suffer from extreme congestion. In this respect it was like other markets in central London: with the decision to relocate Billingsgate's market activities to a new site on the Isle of Dogs, only Smithfield meat market remained operating from its original site.

An existing lorry park beside the Market provided the site for a new commercial development. The task remained, however, of finding a new use for the existing Market building that would not compromise its historic status. Designed, in 1875, in the French Renaissance style by the City Architect Sir Horace Jones – who went on to design the markets at Leadenhall and Smithfield – it was a listed building of some elegance and importance to this part of the Thames waterfront.

This was by no means the only sensitive aspect of the project. A few hundred yards to the west stood the Monument commemorating the Great Fire of London. Foster Associates' design options were circumscribed by the need to preserve the view from the top of the Monument towards Tower Bridge and the view back from the bridge towards the dome of St Paul's Cathedral. In addition, beneath part of the lorry park, important archaeological remains had been found which had to be protected and retained in the new scheme.

Their initial strategy was influenced by the ambiguous symmetry of the existing building. The two main facades were symmetrical, but of different lengths; as a result the plan itself was asymmetrical. Although Foster Associates wished to preserve the Market itself in its totality, it was felt that a block of shops on the west side – adjacent to the lorry park and itself an addition to the original Market building – was of dubious value and therefore dispensable. As at University College, the use of a glass arcade between old

To be built on a site immediately adjacent to Billingsgate Market, massing of the new development required sensitive handling so as not to overpower the existing building. A stepped form appears in the earliest sketches.

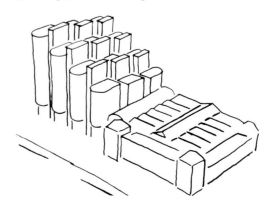

"Britannia of Billingsgate looking down from the pediment might wonder what is to become of her; my own fear is that she will live to preside over a place of phoney 'events', where almost everything is rootless, pointless, tourist haunted, uncongenial to intelligence – where you can buy ice-cream and souvenirs, watch craftsmen at work and clowns on stilts, as at Covent Garden."

Geoffrey Fletcher, *Daily Telegraph*, August 1980 – just one of several gloomy predictions, published following announcement of the Billingsgate redevelopment, which Foster Associates were determined to avoid.

and new buildings would physically connect the two while maintaining a visual separation. At the same time it would provide a suitable entrance and through route, in this case between the street approach and the riverside walkway.

Norman Foster's early sketches show a desire to break up the scale of the building in plan and elevation existed from the very start of the project. Paradoxically, this scale also had to be sufficient to shield the Market building from the excessively overbearing bulk of St Magnus House alongside, while respecting the proportions of both the Market building and the old Customs House immediately to the east.

The stepped section that emerged offered a number of advantages. The low eastern end was of a scale in sympathy with the existing Market; while at its western end the building was more than large enough to confront St Magnus House. It also allowed a large part of

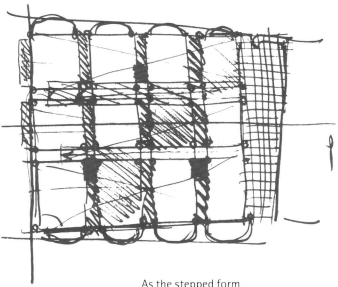

As the stepped form developed so did proposals for a 'tartan' planning grid: independent modules of open floor are separated by narrow strips of services, circulation or void. Between new and old buildings, a glazed arcade appears linking the two but maintaining a visual separation.

Situated next to the site of old London Bridge – for over 1000 years the only bridge across the Thames – Billingsgate lies at the heart of the ancient city of London.

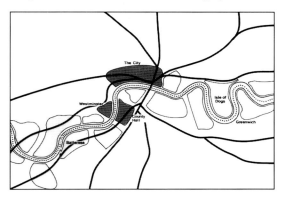

the offices to be provided with direct access to 'gardens in the sky' on the terraced platforms, with views out towards the south-east along the river. Finally, it promised to minimise obstruction of the important views from the Monument and back to St Paul's, retaining a view of the roof profile of the Market building silhouetted against the water.

The new building, with its priceless river frontage, would lie on the important tourist route between the Monument and the Tower of London. It offered the prospect of involving the new building with important archaeological remains in rich and exciting ways.

Old Billingsgate Market lay at the centre of the mediaeval city that grew up on the north shore of the Thames between the Tower of London and old London Bridge. The remains of the wharves on which it began, on an inlet in the river-bank, were to be preserved in the new building.

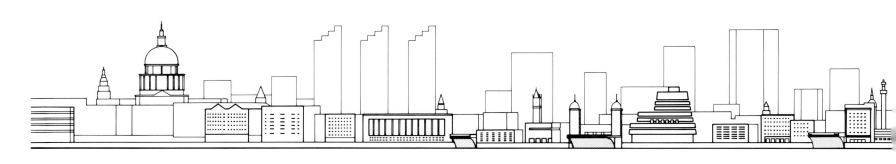

Just one incident along a river frontage that has not always been well treated in recent years. In this 'city' elevation from the river, the new Billingsgate development is overshadowed by London's tallest building, the National Westminster Tower.

"For too long London has turned its back on its great river. Its enormous potential as a visual component of the capital's urban texture and as an opportunity for public enjoyment has been virtually ignored. Hopefully, attitudes are changing and every instance of riverside development must make positive contributions towards the reinstatement of London's unique river artery. Billingsgate is not only no exception, but is a special opportunity to return an important sector of river heritage back to the people."

Foster Associates' design report, August 1981

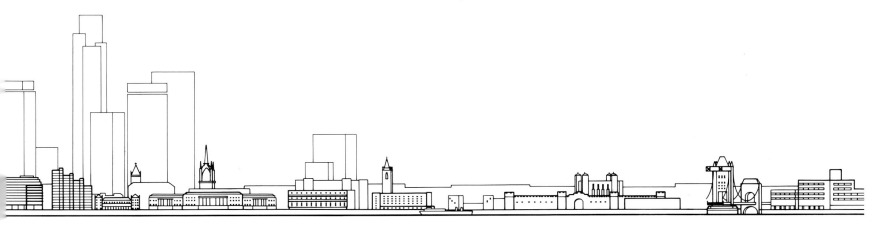

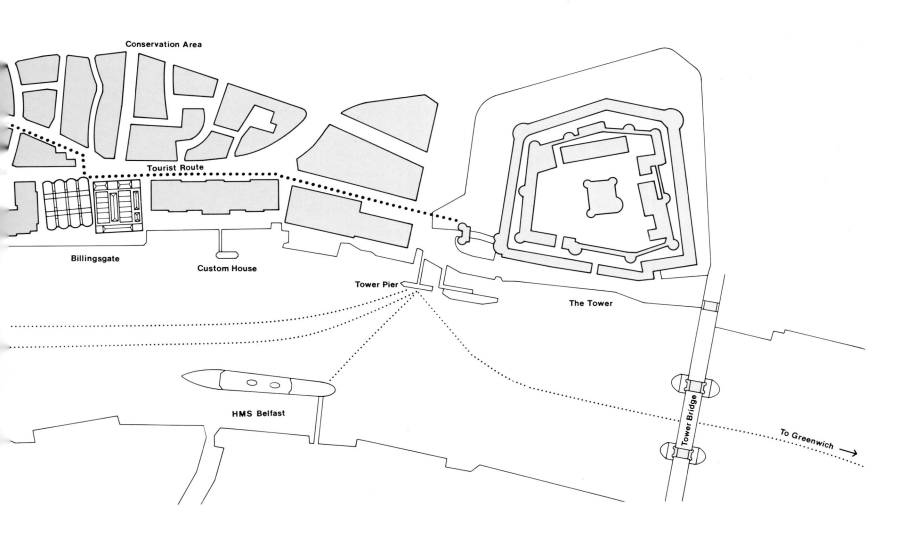

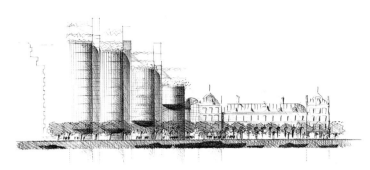

Norman Foster's sketch shows the scheme well developed. Efforts to keep the profile of the building as low as possible were compromised by the developer's need for maximum space and the final study model shows the building slightly higher.

Recent developments on the river, with their monotonous facades, were seen to be quite out of scale with the older buildings. By articulating the frontage of the new development, Foster hoped to create a texture which better respected the proportions and rich incident of the old Market.

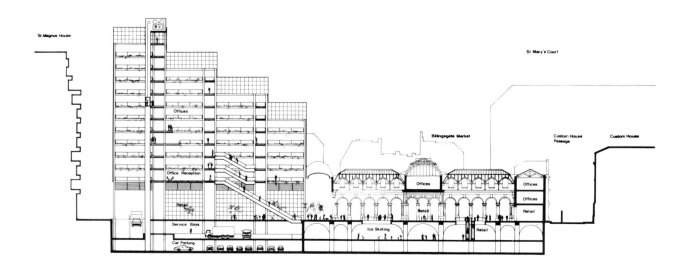

At ground floor level and below, the new and old parts of the scheme were closely integrated, both being given over to retail units and public amenities. The new offices were clearly separated with double-height escalators leading up from the entrance arcade to a main office reception at the upper levels.

"Unlike ordinary big shopping centres, Rouse's festival marketplaces have no department stores. Their pulling power depends on an intricate blend of light-hearted good taste and restrained but canny design that makes visiting them fun whether the visitor goes to dine, drink, shop or just enjoy the scene. They recapture the timeless delights to be found in the marketplace, the historic reason for cities."

Quotation from *Fortune*, July 1981 – used as a positive example in Foster Associates' design report.

It was a condition of any planning permission obtained for commercial development that a cultural or tourist use be found for the old Market building. Precisely what form this might take was a subject on which Foster Associates held strong views.

They pointed to the public response to the Draft City Development Plan, which showed a desire not only for development, but also for the conservation and enhancement of existing amenities. Foster felt that the best modern equivalents of this type of scheme could be found across the Atlantic, for example in Boston's Faneuil Hall – also known as Quincy Market – or in other similar projects such as South Street Seaport in New York City which was also based on a former fish-market.

Both of these developments had been carried out by a US firm, the Rouse Company, which had become widely recognised as leaders in the field. In each case the sale of food had proved to be a key factor behind the financial and social success of the development. As an activity that lends itself to night trading, it was likely to be an important factor at Billingsgate, where the St Katharine Dock marina and the Tower Hotel were only a few hundred yards to the east. At both Faneuil Hall and South Street Seaport nearly two-thirds of retail units were food shops or restaurants. Much closer to home, the original Covent Garden market building had recently been developed, also along the lines of the American experience, and was showing the benefits of such a policy.

These examples did not depend on big department stores to draw custom, but instead drew on the nostalgic appeal of the traditional market-place. Following visits to Boston and New York, members of the design team met representatives of the Rouse Company, who expressed an interest in collaboration on Billingsgate should Foster Associates' proposals be accepted.

From a commercial point of view, Billingsgate possessed one enormous advantage: a site beside the Thames. Like many other commentators, Foster Associates felt that London had for too long turned its back on the river. Although there was no walk immediately on either side of the site with which to connect, it was the City of London's policy gradually to construct a riverside path as and when it became possible.

Accordingly, Foster Associates suggested that, in addition to a walkway in front of Billingsgate, a pedestrian link should be built to

The roof-level terraces, created by the stepped form of the building, would enjoy magnificent views along the river towards Tower Bridge and beyond.

To the east of Tower Bridge lies St Katharine Dock, a complex of refurbished warehouses already popular with tourists and locals alike.

Foster Associates proposed a new river connection linking with the new development.

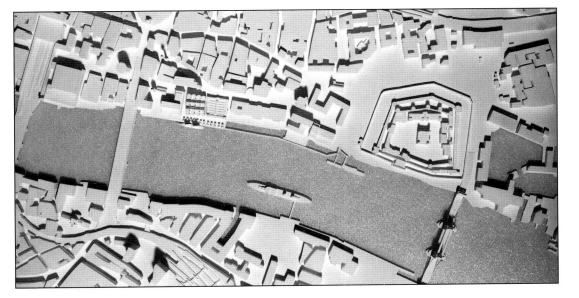

"The riverside itself must be a place to enjoy – to sit and stare, to eat and drink, vitality, colour, trees, sunshine and shade."

Foster Associates' design report, August 1981

Drawing on the experience of Covent Garden and that project's progenitors in the USA, Foster Associates intended to capitalise on the drawing power of nostalgia for the old building by introducing a rich mix of uses to create a social magnet for city workers and residents, Londoners in general and for tourists who already visited that part of London in large numbers. The attraction of the river was to be enhanced with the introduction of a generous tree-lined plaza fronting the development, which, it was hoped, would eventually form part of a future riverside walkway from the Tower of London.

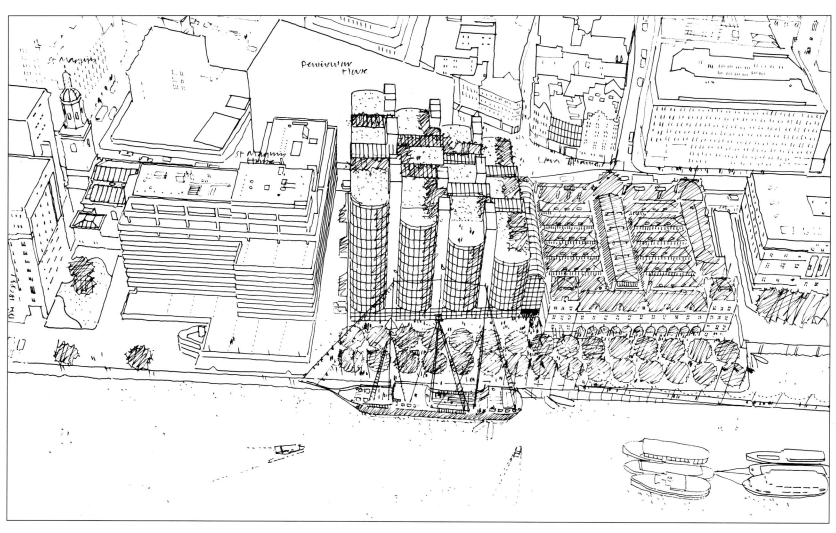

pass in front of the Customs House and connect with Tower Pier, giving access to the Tower of London, Tower Bridge and St Katharine Dock beyond. The site could be used to provide a terminal for a new river-transport system; while discussions with the National Maritime Museum confirmed that there was no lack of historic boats available to exploit the valuable riverside frontage that would be created.

The volume of the new office development, although substantial, was effectively broken down by the decision to articulate it into four vertical 'slices'. The aerial perspective of the final scheme demonstrates the success of this planning device as a visual buffer protecting the small-scale linear bays of the existing Market building from the uncouth bulk of St Magnus House. The bands of the resulting tartan grid accommodated goods lifts, lavatories, staircases and services. In this way two problems were effectively solved at once: namely, how to introduce a human scale, and how to provide a means of dividing a commercial office building into separately-serviced individual tenancies of varying size, each with the option of a river view and/or roof garden.

Foster Associates felt the views along the river to be even more important than those directly across it. Bearing this in mind, the building's curved bays were intended to allow views to the west towards London Bridge and the South Bank complex near Waterloo, and to the east towards HMS Belfast, Tower Bridge and the Upper Pool of London's old dockland area.

The building's modular organisation clearly prefigures the later scheme for the BBC and, to a lesser extent, one of the transitional proposals for the Hongkong Bank project. Whereas these buildings were for a single occupier, however, there was the distinct possibility that the Billingsgate building would be split into separate tenancies. The grid, clearly defining circulation routes and multiple core areas, allowed this to be achieved without difficulty.

The upper gallery levels of the existing Market building overlooked the river and were set aside for small office and residential units separate from the new development. Meanwhile

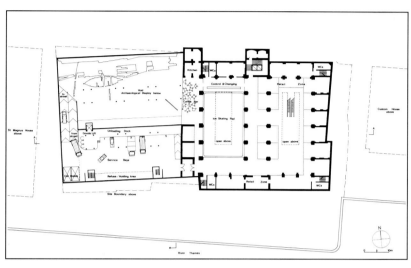

Lower ground floor. The remains of the mediaeval wharves had to be retained under the new development. Proposing that these should form part of a popular display on the history of the area, Foster Associates included a viewing gallery and a cafeteria overlooking the most impressive sections. A small ice-skating rink was also proposed as an alternative attraction.

the ground floors of both buildings would be visually unified, by co-ordinating floor levels and finishes.

At ground and basement levels both the old Market and the new building were to be given over to retail and leisure activities. Here Foster Associates expanded the set brief in order to encourage a broader pattern of public use by proposing a small recreational ice-rink for the first basement of the existing Market building, overlooked from the ground floor. The intention was for the rich mix of uses at ground and basement levels to spill out on to the riverside terraces and bind the new development into its surroundings. In this way the building would form a new social magnet for the area.

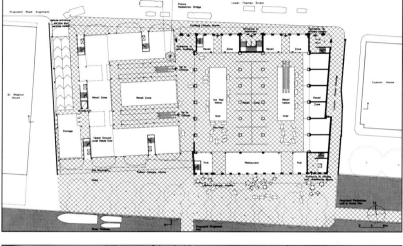

Ground floor. The entire ground floor area of both new and old buildings was given over to retail purposes. To integrate the new development with the existing Market, the floor level and floor finish were uniform throughout, including the riverside plaza. The ceiling height of the new development also matched that of the Market, while two openings in the ground floor provided access and daylight to the basement areas below.

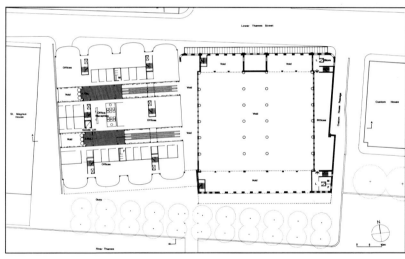

First floor. The upper areas of the existing Market were left open so that the retail areas might enjoy the daylight filtering through the magnificent roof. Existing mezzanine areas were given over to self-contained offices. In the new development, the first floor marked the lowest floor of the office areas and included their main reception.

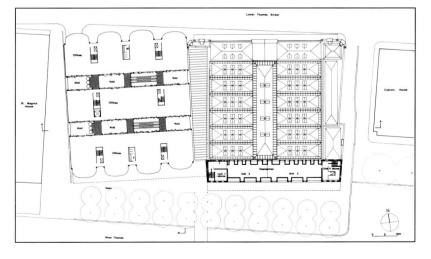

Third floor. To allow for greater flexibility, three blocks of office floor space were created, separated by two full-height atria which brought daylight into the heart of the building. These atria also formed the lift and escalator circulation zones while services and escape stairs occupied the alternative north-south strips of the building's tartan grid.

The riverside elevation; one of the presentation drawings prepared for the final report which, unfortunately, was never to be submitted. The stepped form has survived from the earliest sketches, though the service zones of the tartan grid are now more strongly defined. The roof-top terraces are shown landscaped but otherwise the surface treatment of the building itself is left deliberately vague, maintaining the option for future refinement and development should the scheme have gone ahead.

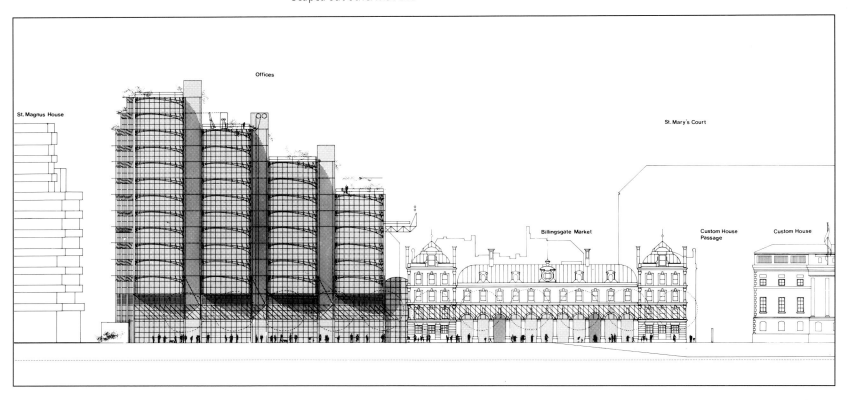

The extensive basement of the existing Market formed the obvious location for a display area. A restaurant takes up the extra space while, under the new development, a small car park was created, access being by hoist only.

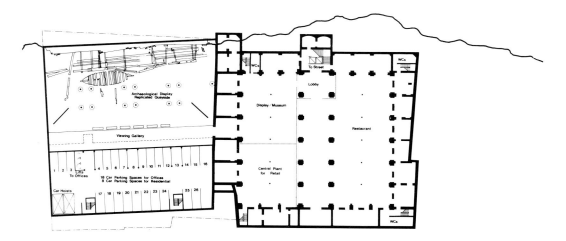

The section and elevation forming part of the final presentation drawings illustrate the way in which Foster Associates expected the roof terraces to be used for extensive landscaping. They also show the relationship of the building to the Monument on one side and a new riverside plaza on the other. With the possibility of restaurants spilling out of the new building and with a fine old ship moored alongside, the tree-lined plaza made the most of the development's setting.

Once again Foster Associates were aiming to establish the building as a popular public right of way and thus create a flow of casual visitors passing through — here towards the various new attractions on the river-bank. A bridge link above Lower Thames Street was suggested in order to improve the new building's pedestrian connections with the City.

Visitors to the offices would be carried on dual escalators from the retail level, up through the lowest part of the two 'atrium slots' dividing the building, to a reception foyer on the first floor. The 'slots' continued upwards through the building as far as roof level, bringing light to the central parts of the office floors. According to the pattern of letting, they could be bridged as necessary to allow communication between different zones on the same level. The size of the modules was designed to allow either open-plan or cellular offices.

The new building would lie on the main tourist route from the Monument to the Tower of London. The Museum of London, asked to advise on the archaeological aspects of the design, pointed out that the general public seems to have an insatiable appetite for archaeology and, in its prominent position, the new development was well placed to exploit the tourist potential of the remains of the mediaeval wharves that had been found on the lorry park site. Rather than preserving the remains, as required, only to seal them from view – the solution adopted in the scheme eventually built – Foster Associates proposed making a feature of them, at the same time taking the opportunity of linking them to new exhibition areas in the basement of the existing Market.

The structure of the new building was designed to minimise disruption of the remains. But what was to be on display, overlooked by a viewing gallery and coffee bar at mezzanine level, was not the original quayside but an in-situ replica. The Museum of London agreed with Foster Associates that although the original material was of national, or even international, importance, it did not seem promising as a subject for public display. Provided it was sensitively carried out, with the true remains adequately protected, a replica would be both archaeologically acceptable and more appealing to tourists. Around it could be formed a display illustrating the history of the Port of London from 50 AD onwards; there was also the possibility of a link to the remains of the Roman Baths which had been similarly preserved beneath another recent development nearby, on the other side of Lower Thames Street.

Billingsgate was among the first of Foster's buildings to be so strongly articulated. There is even a hint of the theories of Herman Hertzberger in its division into convivial small-scale units. Its end, when it came, was particularly unfortunate, the extraordinary result of a sudden family crisis within the Chinese family who controlled the client company. Just as the scheme was coming to the end of its development, the 91-year-old mother of the Chinese family died. For the project, the effect was catastrophic. In a state of shock, the mourning family withdrew from a number of their ventures around the world and the scheme was never submitted.

Tim Ostler

Below: A section through the new development shows the building's relationship with the Monument, the commemorative tower close to the site where the Great Fire of London started. The stepped form of the building was, in part, intended as a way of reducing the new development's impact on views from the Monument. Discussions with the National Maritime Museum had revealed that several historic craft were available, one of which might be moored off the riverside plaza as a further attraction.

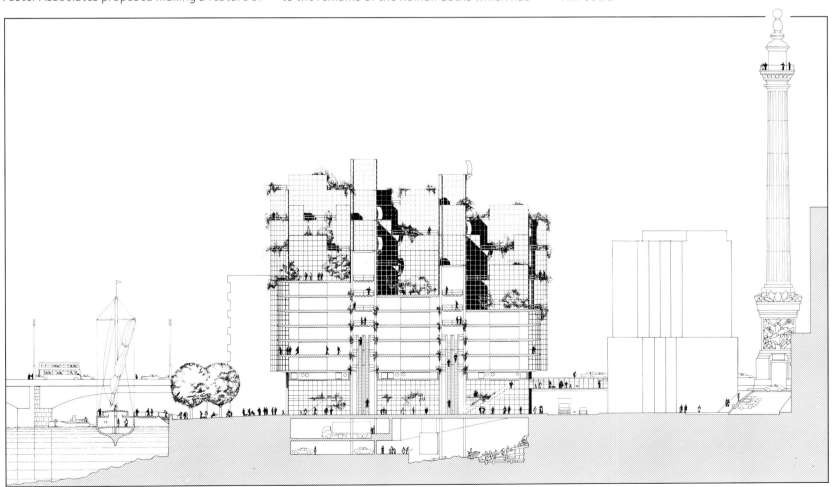

1979–1986 The New Headquarters for Hongkong Bank
1 Queen's Road Central
Hong Kong

October 1978 Feasibility studies commissioned to consider options for redevelopment of 1 Queen's Road Central.
June 1979 Skidmore Owings & Merrill, Harry Seidler Associates, Yuncken Freeman, Yorke Rosenberg & Mardell, Palmer & Turner, Hugh Stubbins and Foster Associates invited to submit proposals for a new headquarters for The Hongkong and Shanghai Banking Corporation.
July–September 1979 Foster Associates prepare proposals in response to competition brief – submitted early October.
October 1979 Norman Foster invited to make personal presentation.
November 1979 Foster Associates appointed as architects under interim agreement.
February 1980 Foster Associates formally appointed as architects for the new headquarters; Ove Arup & Partners appointed as civil and structural engineering consultants; J. Roger Preston & Partners appointed as consultant mechanical and electrical engineers; and Levett & Bailey in association with Northcroft Neighbour & Nicholson appointed as consultant quantity surveyors.
March–September 1980 Design development proceeds. Considerable research into new materials and techniques undertaken and companies with appropriate expertise identified.
January 1981 Presentation of preliminary design to Hongkong Bank board.
March 1981 University of Western Ontario commissioned to undertake comprehensive wind-tunnel testing of proposed structure and location.
May 1981 Interim agreement signed with Cupples Products to progress design of aluminium cladding system.
6 July 1981 China Swiss Engineers Ltd commences demolition of 1935 building.
21 July 1981 John Lok/Wimpey Joint Venture officially appointed as management contractor.
22 September 1981 Formal contract for production and erection of cladding and curtain walling system signed with Cupples Products.
19 October 1981 Structural steelwork contract awarded to British Steel Corporation/Dorman Long Joint Venture.
23 November 1981 Bachy Soletanche starts preparatory work for diaphragm wall construction on site.

2 December 1981 Dynamic testing of prototype cladding commences at Cupples Products' main plant in St Louis, USA.
24 December 1981 Structural service modules contract awarded to HMT Consort (HK) Ltd.
2 February 1982 Presentation of Final scheme to Hongkong Bank board.
8 February 1982 Production of cladding commences in St Louis.
April 1982 Fabrication of structural steelwork commences in the Glasgow, Manchester and Teesside regions, UK. Production of glass for curtain walling commences in North Carolina, USA.
3 June 1982 Bachy Soletanche commences construction of main access shaft to proposed 'sea water tunnel' at Star Ferry.
20 July 1982 Diaphragm wall at main site completed. Testing of prototype service module at Mitsubishi Electric Corporation's production facility at Ako, Japan.
27 July 1982 Dragages et Travaux Publics commences site preparation for basement and caisson foundation work.
September 1982 Work on main access and secondary foundation caissons starts.
November 1982 R. J. Mead & Company appointed project co-ordinator.
30 December 1982 Caisson foundations and site working platform completed.
3 January 1983 Preparatory work for structural steelwork starts on site – erection of cranes and positioning of structural baseplates starts immediately.
16 January 1983 First steelwork arrives in Hong Kong. Held at Junk Bay for post-production work and preparation.
6 February 1983 Aoki Corporation starts work on main sea water tunnel.
9 February 1983 First structural steel positioned in access caissons by Argos Engineering.
23 April 1983 Structural steelwork emerges from main access caissons.
26 April 1983 Basement level B1, structural slab complete.
July 1983 Basement level B2m, slab complete.
August 1983 Production of escalators starts at Flohr Otis works in Stadthagen, West Germany.
1 September 1983 First level of suspension trusses at level 11/12 complete.
9 September 1983 Typhoon Ellen.
15 September 1983 On-site application of corrosion protection commences.
10 October 1983 Erection of 'cathedral wall' trusses commences.

17 October 1983 Erection of steel escape stairs commences.
24 October 1983 Basement level B2, slab complete.
12 November 1983 First HMT Consort service module lifted into position.
16 November 1983 VSL Engineers commences site fixing of basement rock anchors.
21 November 1983 Morceau (Fire Protection) HK Ltd commences site application of fire protection to structural steelwork.
18 December 1983 Second level of suspension trusses at level 20/21 complete.
23 January 1984 Cupples Products lifts first cladding panel into position.
27 January 1984 Breakthrough of shaft from basement into sea water tunnel completes underground link to harbour.
6 February 1984 Ryoden Mitsubishi commences preparatory work for sub-floor services.
20 February 1984 Drake & Scull (HK) Ltd takes possession of basement levels B2m and B2 and commences preparatory work for installation of central services.
25 February 1984 Third level of suspension trusses at level 28/29 complete.
27 February 1984 Otis Elevator (HK) Ltd lifts first escalator into building.
12 March 1984 Installation of main refrigeration equipment commences in basement.
20 March 1984 Basement level B3, slab complete.
9 April 1984 H. H. Robertson (HK) Ltd starts erection of raised floor system on site. Getz Corporation commences installation of fixed fire partitions.
25 April 1984 Fourth level suspension trusses at level 35/36 complete.
30 April 1984 Dragages et Travaux Publics commence structural work for ground floor plaza.
6 June 1984 Last level of suspension trusses at level 40/41 complete.
8 June 1984 Production of lift-cars starts in Liverpool, UK.
15 June 1984 Highest escalators installed between levels 34 and 35.
18 June 1984 GIG/Listo JV starts erection of glazed 'underbelly' to atrium.
21 August 1984 Naka/C. Itoh JV commences installation of suspended ceiling system.
6/7 September 1984 Atrium escalators lifted into place.

"The 1935 headquarters aroused much excitement and controversy in its time. Its main tower, 220 feet high, made it the tallest building between Cairo and San Francisco. But it was the technological innovations that made the building truly unique in the region. High-tensile steel, not previously used outside North America, was used in the stone clad frame; it had high-speed lifts and air-conditioning, both rare in Asia then; and it had provision on the roof for a landing pad for autogiros."

Chris Abel, *Architectural Review*, April 1986

"Many of the buildings I like best are true vernacular. For example, the tremendous richness and variety of the streets of Hong Kong; a patina of sun-shades, signs, balconies, voids and planting, reflecting the individual nature of its occupants as parts of an immense serviced framework."

Norman Foster, *Building Design*, October 1979

Over the years, many of the older buildings have accreted their own ad hoc additions, bringing an extraordinary richness to their otherwise shabby facades.

The love of colour and vitality — neon signs along one of Hong Kong's main streets.

Fighting for dominance, suspended steel signs stretch almost to the middle of some streets.

Buildings and balconies — at every scale the elements of the environment are densely packed.

Even the shops make the most of every corner and surface for display.

14 September 1984 Last service module lifted into position.
17/18 September 1984 Main plaza escalators lifted into place.
18 October 1984 Practical completion of structural steelwork.
19 November 1984 Johnson Controls (HK) Ltd commences installation of computerised management systems.
17 December 1984 Last escalator installed between plaza and level B1.
18 December 1984 Schindler Lifts (HK) Ltd commences installation of electro-hydraulic vehicular lifts — Bank Street to level B3.
31 December 1984 Naka/C. Itoh commences installation of internal cladding panels.
28 January 1985 GIG/Listo JV commences installation of internal sun scoop at level 11/12 over atrium. Installation of luminaires begins.
1 March 1985 Sea water tunnel completed.
18 March 1985 Otis Elevator (HK) Ltd installs first passenger lift-car.
24 April 1985 Internal sun scoop completed.
2 May 1985 First furniture arrives on site.
20 May 1985 Topping out ceremony to celebrate practical completion of cladding and curtain walling.
1 June 1985 Lions moved from Statue Square back to 1 Queen's Road Central. Unveiling ceremony on 8 June 1985.
30 June 1985 Last passenger lift-car installed.
1 July 1985 Hongkong Bank takes possession of first phase, including main banking halls and offices surrounding atrium, and plant-halls, safe-deposit vaults and public reception areas in the basements.
30 July 1985 Public banking halls open for business.
12 October 1985 Metallbau GmbH commences erection of external sun scoop structure on plaza.
27 October 1985 External sun scoop lifted into position.
18 November 1985 Private ceremony at level 41 celebrates official handover of completed building to Hongkong Bank.
7 April 1986 New headquarters of The Hongkong and Shanghai Banking Corporation officially opened by His Excellency the Governor, Sir Edward Youde.

"Hong Kong is built along the lines of a Brobdingnagian bed of nails where even the most modest building mimics its skyscraper neighbours in the vertical emphasis of its proportions. The partially reclaimed strip of land along the northern coast of Hong Kong island, squeezed between Victoria Harbour and a high ridge, is bristling with towers. As if to balance the enormous vitality at street level, with its picturesque confusion of signs, shops, restaurants, stalls, pedestrians, and vehicles, nearly everything built above a certain height is sterile and devoid of imagination. These towers provide the sharpest possible contrast to the new headquarters of The Hongkong and Shanghai Banking Corporation."

Hiroshi Watanabe, *Architecture*, September 1985

"It's certainly the most exciting place I've ever been. I've never known a place which could make Manhattan look like a kind of quiet Sunday afternoon."

Norman Foster, Frontiers of Design lecture, September 1979

"Is this Hong Kong building a return to the idea of the skyscraper as a city in itself? The plaza that sweeps under the building has angled escalators reaching down to lure the customers inside but, banking apart, it is in no sense a public building. It is a city in the sense that it is self-contained and has all the spaces and energy it needs to be self-sufficient. By Western standards this is a major new design, the fact that it is being built as an ambassador for British architects in the East is a cause for rejoicing. London and New York had better look to their laurels."

Colin Amery, *The Financial Times*, February 1981

"Instead of having a solid skin pierced by tittering openings like its neighbours, the Hongkong Bank luminously opens itself to the world: in one of the best Modern Movement traditions, inside and outside are a continuum (which... works from inside to out as well). The effect is grand: languorous, large, ample, awesome, generous. You are compelled to believe that the people working in such noble spaces are doing more than just pushing bits of paper around."

Peter Davey, *Architectural Review*, April 1986

"The structure of our building is quite different from the usual office tower in Hong Kong. It is steel, which is one-fifteenth the bulk of concrete; it has a wide span and achieves an unusually high percentage of usable space, along with a number of other benefits."

Norman Foster, lecture at Centre Pompidou, February 1981

"The skyscraper, the architectural form of the twentieth century, is a product of modern economics as much as of modern technology. Its status and worth are judged mainly by its height and exterior form. From the tall office buildings of Chicago, built around the turn of the century, to the curtain-walled glass boxes of Ludwig Mies van der Rohe and his many imitators, to today's slick corporate monoliths sporting the latest haphazardly historic Post-Modern divots and curves, the search for a skyscraper form has been reduced to a variation of surface, a question of superficial image-making.

The Hongkong Bank, on the other hand, is an integrated whole, with the exterior once again

120

in conversation with the interior. The entire structure is meticulously planned. Its design and details display an old-fashioned attention to the craft of building. The scale of the structure is once again human, directed towards the individuals who work within and around it. The futuristic look, coupled with early twentieth-century attention to craftsmanship, has produced a structure that is as much a part of skyscraper history as it is a part of the future."

Maya Lin, *The New Republic*, December 1985

"I have never felt before to quite the same extent the inadequacy of trying to reduce three-dimensional sensual reality to two-dimensional images on a page and the drawn-out one dimension of narrative. To really experience the Bank, you have to stand on the beautifully gradated gently-sloping floor of the plaza and feel the sunlight reflected first from the giant sun scoop, then from the top of the atrium. Your shadow is cast by sun on the granite – but you are in the middle of an enormous building."

Peter Davey, *Architectural Review*, April 1986

"The texture and the colour of the Barrystone is really quite important. Very important in terms of its friendly feel under the plaza, the fact that it reflects light and has a sparkle about it."

Norman Foster, client presentation, March 1984

"The sight of parasols being used to ward off the heat of the sun brought home the realisation that there was a real lack of shady outdoor spaces in which to relax away from the noise and bustle. Paley Place in New York is a small garden oasis in the middle of downtown Manhattan, a cul-de-sac as opposed to the grander nineteenth-century arcades such as the Galleria in Milan which opens up as a generous short-cut to the main cathedral square. Both examples were cited to the Bank to communicate some of the intentions behind the new building and the kind of outdoor space that might be created at the base of the building."

Norman Foster, Flexibility in Design lecture, Brighton, April 1981

"Would that more Western architects could submit themselves to directives of the Chinese geomancer's compass, for in the Bank the angled approach into the rectilinear great hall is oddly reassuring: everything is not totally rational."

Peter Davey, *Architectural Review*, April 1986

"Travelling up these skeletal escalators, one has the feeling of being carried into the belly of a spaceship. As you pass through the hatchway, the noise of the street fades yet the constant bustle of the street is visible through the glass. The world below is oddly silent, and the brave new world above beckons."

Maya Lin, *The New Republic*, December 1985

"It is characteristic of Norman Foster's architecture that with each new building something new is learned about the nature of materials and techniques. His work advances the craft of architecture. In this building the unrelenting externalisation of detail particularises every surface. The resulting gradations of scale are virtually without parallel in anything but the Gothic, or perhaps the nineteenth-century iron-and-glass architecture that Foster admires. Some of this detail may be considered excessive, but its ultimate purpose is to make the technologies of our era familiar, beautiful, and exhilarating."

Arthur Drexler, *Three New Skyscrapers*, MOMA exhibition catalogue, January 1983

"There is a lot more that is Gothic than Classical in all this structural and spatial magic, contrary statements about Foster's work notwithstanding. If the 'mediaeval' service towers, 'flying braces' and 'incomplete' appearance of the building had not already prompted the idea, then the soaring proportions of the atrium (read nave) and the great translucent eastern window, easily justify the building's popular description as a 'cathedral of commerce'."

Chris Abel, *Architectural Review*, April 1986

"Towards the top of the building, where the floor bays draw further back to reveal the full assemblage of masts, trusses and now 'flying' crossbraces, the structure takes over completely in an unabashed display of naked brute strength. The impression that the building is incomplete at these levels is reinforced by the sight of sturdy maintenance cranes perched atop some of the masts, looking much like the construction cranes which had been placed in similar positions in the process of boot-strapping the structure up into place.

Up here it is all pure megastructure, overwhelming in its unabashed delight in what advanced engineering can do for architecture, and taking for granted that visual excitement is more than enough compensation for the loss of human scale. But in the same way that the bared structure of the Eiffel Tower — another favourite source image of Foster's — relates to the scale of Paris and not to the people in the restaurant enjoying the view, so does this Godzilla-strength structure relate, if not to the inhabitants of the building itself at these heights, then to the population of Hong Kong looking down on the roof-space of the Bank from the skyscraper apartments of the Peak rising up behind."

Chris Abel, *Architectural Review*, April 1986

1979 Hongkong Bank
Competition Scheme

The Hongkong Bank is a powerful presence in Hong Kong even appearing on the Colony's bank-notes. The 1935 headquarters is seen here on a $500 note issued at the time of that building's completion. New notes would be issued in 1986 depicting its replacement.

The Hongkong and Shanghai Banking Corporation is almost as old as the colony itself. It first set up shop in 1864 in a rented office building known as Wardley House on a waterfront site near the centre of town. The address was 1 Queen's Road Central and the Bank's headquarters have been there ever since. Colony and Bank have grown up together. Hong Kong has become one of the most important financial and trading centres in the Far East and the Bank has become one of the biggest and most powerful in the world. For the people of Hong Kong, the Hongkong Bank has become the symbol of their community and the barometer of its fortunes. There is an economic, but also a superstitious link. The bronze lions, made to guard the entrance to the 1935 headquarters and still doing faithful service, are touched by passers-by in the belief that they bring good luck. It is said that if the lions should disappear then Hong Kong will suffer. The Bank is also looked to for signs of confidence in the future, and what clearer sign of confidence could there be than a new headquarters building?

The Bank's first new, purpose-built headquarters was designed by Clement Palmer, a 24-year-old architect from Lancashire, and completed in 1886. It was a time of rapid commercial

The scale is inaccurate but the sense that office floors should make the most of the spectacular views is clearly apparent in this early sketch.

Norman Foster spent nearly three weeks in Hong Kong discussing and observing. In sketches, he recorded a wide range of incidental detail: this is one of the paths on the tree-covered slope that rises behind the site.

expansion after the depression of the 1870s, and the ornate Classical replacement for Wardley House was symbolic of Hong Kong's growing importance in the world economy. After the Wall Street crash of 1929 it was time for a new boost of confidence and a new headquarters building. Sir Vandaleur Grayburn, the Bank's chief manager, commissioned Clement Palmer's now well-established Hong Kong practice, Palmer & Turner, to design "the best bank in the world". The result, completed in 1935, was a handsome building with a 220ft high tower – in its day the tallest in the Eastern hemisphere – and a number of technical innovations, such as air-conditioning, a high-tensile steel frame and high-speed electric lifts. Continuing the tradition begun in 1886, the Bank proudly placed a picture of the new building on all its new bank-notes.

By the late 1970s the Palmer & Turner building had become outdated, both in the practical and the symbolic sense. It was too small for an organisation which now had nearly 200 branches in Hong Kong alone – with 300 projected for 1980 – and it could not easily accommodate new banking technology. Hong Kong

Only one month after his first visit to Hong Kong for the Bank's briefing session, sketches in Norman Foster's notebooks show the building close to the form submitted for the competition entry. With only three months between briefing and final presentation, decisions had to be made quickly. What is surprising is how many of the basic concepts were to survive through to the final design.

"Since we want and love skyscrapers, and spend so much time in them, their design ought to involve other issues besides external styling."

Arthur Drexler, *Three New Skyscrapers*, MOMA exhibition catalogue, January 1983

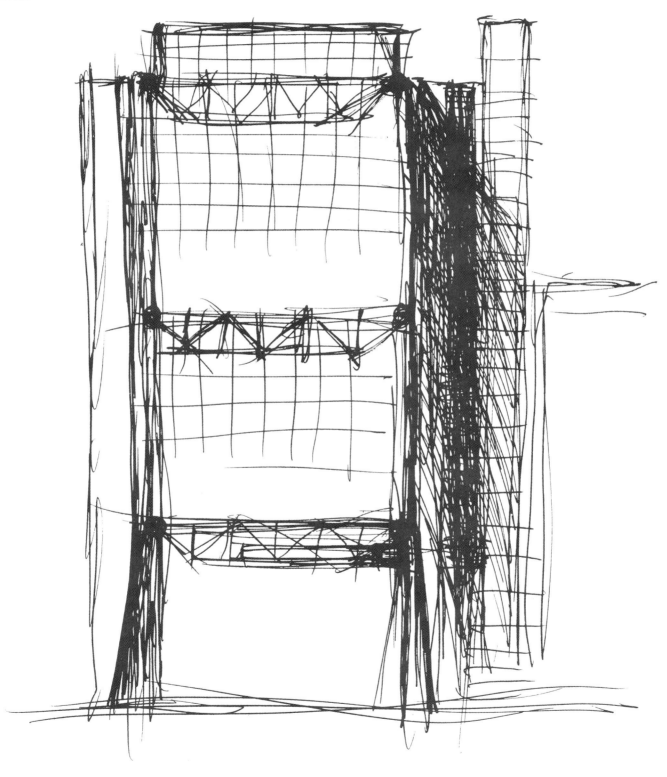

Another of Norman Foster's sketches made on that first visit to Hong Kong. This is the Courts of Justice, one of the colonial buildings that was to inform the design of the new headquarters.

"The new buildings in Hong Kong seem to ignore completely both climate and context, unlike the earlier Victorian colonial buildings with lots of shade and arcades, and some of the more anonymous buildings in Hong Kong that accumulate, quite naturally, gardens, shades and signs. We tried to learn some lessons from the past in protest against the banality, the repetition, the poor performance and the miserable appearance of office towers the world over."

Norman Foster, *Building*, June 1983

Until the construction of the Mass Transit Railway line under the harbour, the Star Ferry was the main pedestrian link between Kowloon and Hong Kong. It is still in constant use.

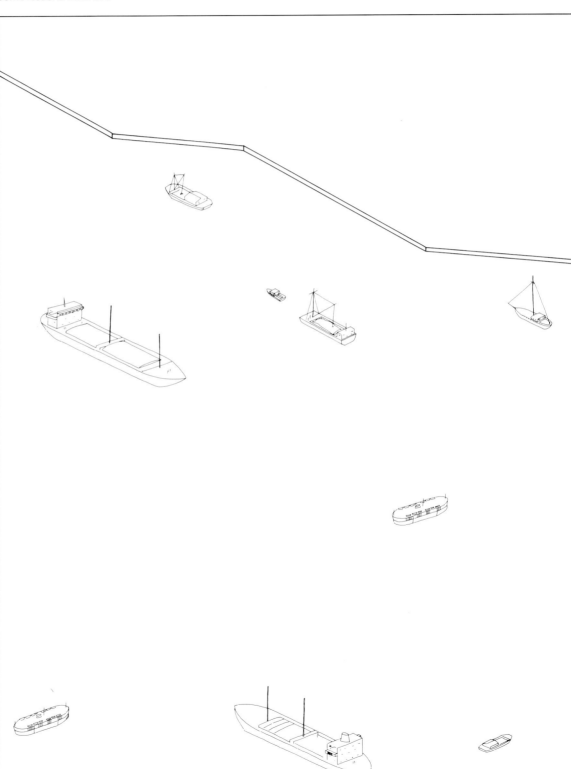

was now a skyscraper city in which the old building was dwarfed. One of the most valuable pieces of real estate in the city was being underused. Besides, difficult times lay ahead for Hong Kong. The end of British sovereignty was in sight and it was time for another demonstration of confidence.

In June 1979 the Bank, having carried out a detailed feasibility study, invited seven international architectural practices, including Foster Associates, to submit proposals for a new building. In the Foster Associates office, the huge Hammersmith project had just fallen through. Here was an opportunity to compensate for this disappointment and to keep a talented design team together. Norman Foster went to Hong Kong determined to win the job. Most of the other competitors left soon after the initial briefing session, but Norman and Wendy Foster and Spencer de Grey stayed on for nearly three weeks, studying how the Bank worked, interviewing department heads, sketching, measuring and photographing the site, and generally absorbing the unique urban phenomenon that is Hong Kong.

The importance of the 1 Queen's Road Central site in its urban context is shown in this isometric drawing. The Bank building dominates Statue Square and closes off the long vista from the Star Ferry terminal and the harbour. Overlooked by the old Courts of Justice building, Statue Square is the historical and commercial heart of Hong Kong and, as one of the very few urban open spaces, is always thronged with people.

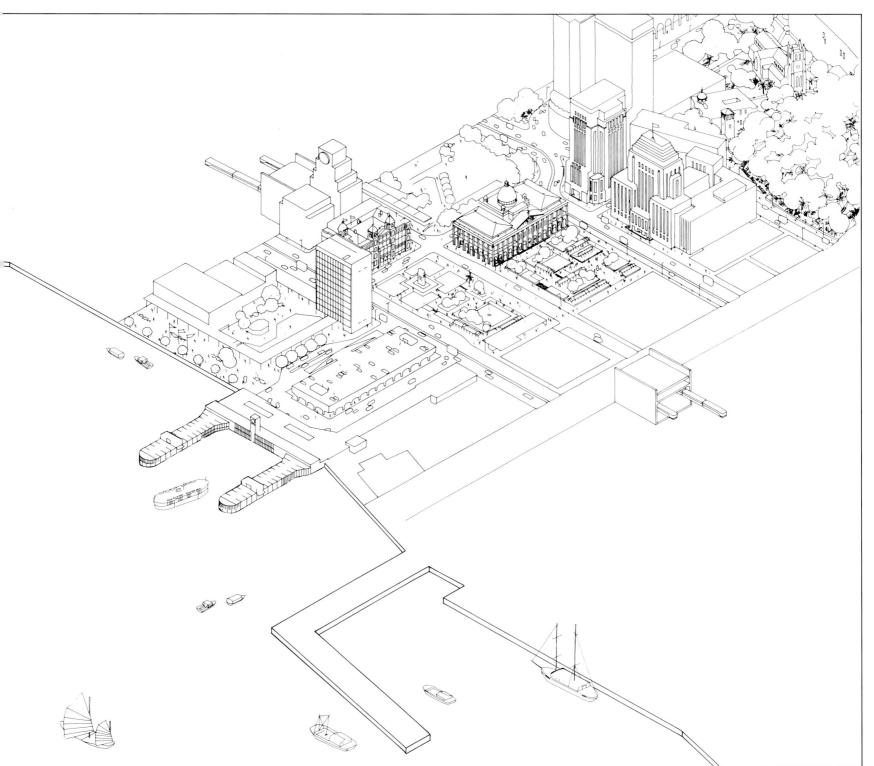

The key issue, it seemed to Foster, was the integration of new generation banking activities within the urban context of Hong Kong. That context leaves a vivid impression on every visitor, but for Foster there were specific lessons to be learnt from it. He was about to design his first high-rise building and there were plenty of precedents here to study. He was, however, much less impressed by the post-war skyscrapers than by the older colonial buildings, which seemed to have a dignity, urbanity and responsiveness to climate which was entirely lacking in the office blocks built in the 1950s and '60s.

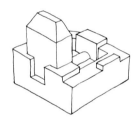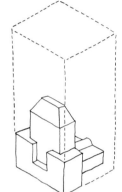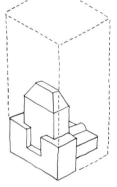

His imagination was stimulated too by the extraordinary battered hulks of the pre-war multi-storey buildings with their accretions of ad hoc balconies, awnings, shop-fronts and signs. What they lacked in conventional architectural virtue they made up for in raw vitality. These multi-functional buildings, accommodating offices, shops, workshops and restaurants, as well as apartments, seemed so much more alive than the sterile, zone-planned ghettos of conventional bureaucratic Modernism. These lessons – responsiveness to climate together with functional and social richness – were to become important themes in the design of the new Bank building.

But first it was necessary to tackle the more immediate practical problems presented by the brief and the site: what to do with the existing building; how to cope with Hong Kong's complicated planning regulations, which set strict limits on the bulk of the building in relation to the surrounding streets; and, most important, how to provide the kind of flexibility that Foster knew from his previous experience would be necessary if the building was to satisfy

This sequence of sketches clearly illustrates the concept of 'phased regeneration'. Initially, a simplified representation of the 1935 building and its various extensions. A distinction is then made between the heart of the existing building – the banking hall and North Tower – and the extensions to the south and west which are to be demolished to make way for the first stages of the new building.

The problem is clearly stated: how to create the maximum building volume, indicated by the dotted lines, while retaining the existing banking hall and tower.

The North Tower and banking hall remain while the first bays of the new bridge-like building are built. Development could stop here; the building is 'complete' at every stage.

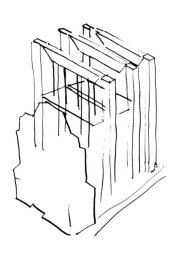

If more space is required then the new building advances bay by bay to replace the old North Tower. The banking hall might still be retained.

The Bank has always occupied 1 Queen's Road Central and there was a superstition that should it ever leave the site then its fortunes, and those of the colony, would suffer. The problem, therefore, was to find a way to maintain occupation of the site during construction of the new building. Foster's early sketches, many of them made on the first visit to Hong Kong, explore various versions of the new building as a bridge over the old.

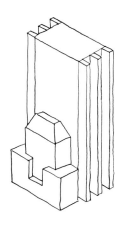 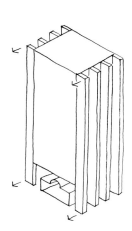 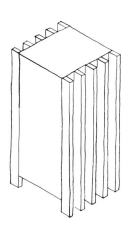 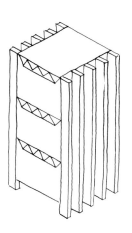

The new bays would interconnect with the remaining parts of the old building to allow the best utilisation of available space.

At the final stage the building has four bays and a bridge-like suspension structure. In essence, this form is very similar to that of the building as built, except that the number of bays was to be reduced to three, each rising to a different height.

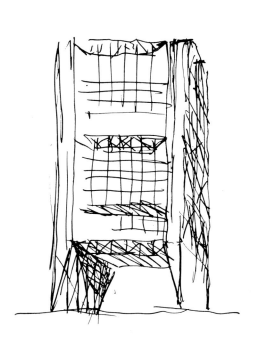

The early sketches never ignore practical problems. The structural requirement for north/south cross-bracing between the towers is shown, in this case at the very edge of the building in front of set-backs to the floors. The need for set-backs allowed a greater articulation of the bays.

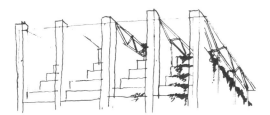

Overshadowing regulations demanded set-backs at the top of the building on the east side.

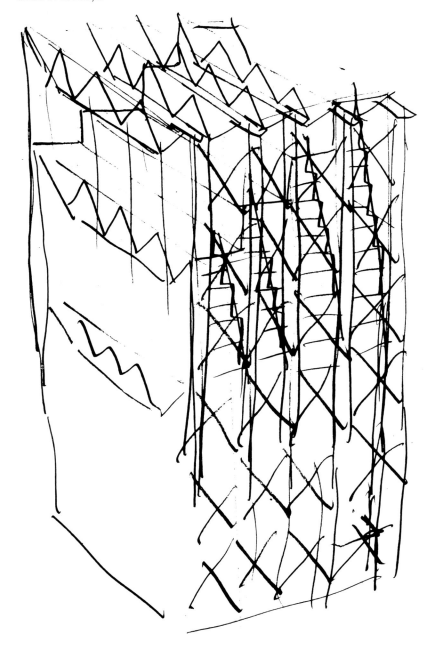

the needs of the Bank over several decades of rapid technological and organisational change. Already, in the very earliest sketches, these problems are being tackled head-on. A clear strategy seems to have emerged very quickly and, characteristically, it was based on a complete reappraisal of the Bank's requirements as set out in the briefing documents.

In drawing up the brief for the seven competing architects, the Bank had identified two possible general approaches. The first was to demolish the south-west part of the existing building and build a new, slim tower beside the existing banking hall. The second was to redevelop the site completely in phases so as to maintain a banking operation on the site throughout the construction period. Both implied a building operation that would work towards a single, predetermined solution. Foster's alternative was to present an open-ended plan that might lead to one of several possible final buildings. It would leave the client room to manoeuvre, both in the short term, in what Foster calls the 'dialogue stage', and in the long term within the 'finished' building. This alternative strategy was called 'phased regeneration'.

The basic idea, as shown in the early sketches, was to build a tower which would bridge over the existing banking hall. This tower could then, if required, be extended northwards to replace the 1935 tower and/or downwards to replace the banking hall. The concept of phased regeneration thus gave rise to the basic idea of

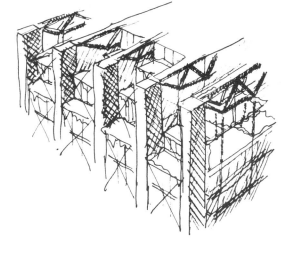

Norman Foster explored the options in a series of sketches that clearly enjoy the sculptural possibilities where elements of long-span structure, cross-bracing and set-backs were combined.

"So the building was designed around banking, designed around people; it was a protest, socially, against the kind of anonymous inhuman buildings. It was an attempt to provide these clusters of accommodation one on top of the other. It was also designed from the outset with an awareness of the way it would be built, aware of the pressures of the programme."

Norman Foster, lecture to Sainsbury's Executive Club, March 1984

"Not just book ends", says the note. A simple structural outline frames a complex form within: floors are set back or omitted altogether to form atria and open terraces. In this way the box-like form is broken down.

the tower as a multi-storey extendable bridge. But the early sketches show much more than this. Indeed they incorporate most of the main architectural ideas that were to be realised in the final building. There is the characteristic 'laminated' plan, here with four structural bays later to be reduced to three. The floors are shown suspended from large trusses set at intervals in the height of the building, and the services and vertical circulation are pushed to the east and west sides so as to leave the floors completely unobstructed. It is even possible to see how the

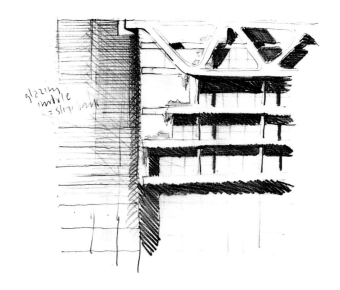

"Glazing module = step back." Sketches show a concern for detail and dimensional co-ordination, even at the earliest stages. Note the carefully drawn gaps which indicate that the floors are suspended from the truss, not supported directly by the tower.

floors might be set back at the upper levels between the structural towers thus conforming to the planning regulations.

These ideas did not, of course, arise solely from consideration of the problems posed by this particular brief and this particular site. They had already appeared in different forms in many of Foster's buildings. Take, for example, the pattern of distribution of services. If the original banking hall was to be retained in the centre of the plan, then clearly vertical services and circulation would have to be pushed to the edges. But this suited Foster's design philosophy perfectly. The division of the accommodation into two main categories, 'served' and 'servant' spaces, is an idea which can be traced back to the buildings of Louis Kahn, whose work had a profound influence on Foster in his student days at Yale.

Kahn's Richards Laboratories building is the best known application of the principle. Vertical services and circulation are accommodated in brick-clad servant towers which are clearly differentiated from glass-clad blocks containing the served laboratory space. This space is thus completely free of vertical obstructions and can be planned and replanned with great flexibility.

In the early sketches for the Hongkong Bank, there is a similar rationalisation of the plan. Instead of a series of servant towers there is a servant strip, containing lavatories, vertical ducts, lifts, lobbies and escape stairs, along the

AN EXPLORATORY SEQUENCE FOR DISCUSSION
— TARGET PRACTICE

A favourite image used to convey to the client the nature of the option testing procedure. The process of trial and error will continue until the target is hit.

west side of the building, leaving a large expanse of uninterrupted working space. Later the servant spaces were to be distributed roughly equally on east and west sides of the building. The plan of the Sainsbury Centre at the University of East Anglia clearly demonstrates the application of this principle to a single-storey building: here the service spaces form continuous strips on either side of the main gallery space. Indeed it is not too fanciful to see the Hongkong Bank design as a multi-storey version of the Sainsbury Centre plan. In appearance these buildings are very different, but conceptually there are strong similarities.

The served/servant principle is more than just a planning method. It has important technical implications. The Richards Laboratories' design was a positive architectural response to a basically technical problem: how to cope with the masses of pipework, ductwork and cabling

From the earliest sketches, the structural towers on each side of the building were seen as also containing the building's services, leaving the large-span floors free from obstruction. In this alternative, the service areas were entirely separated from the floors and pulled away to one side of the building.

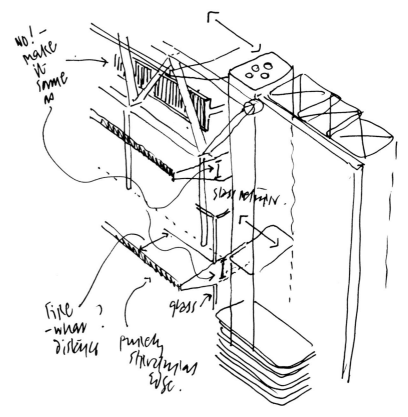

The integration of structure, services, lifts and facade was explored in a variety of sketches. Projecting fins in this drawing separate floors as a means of providing fire protection. Not required for this purpose, the idea persisted in the form of sunshades.

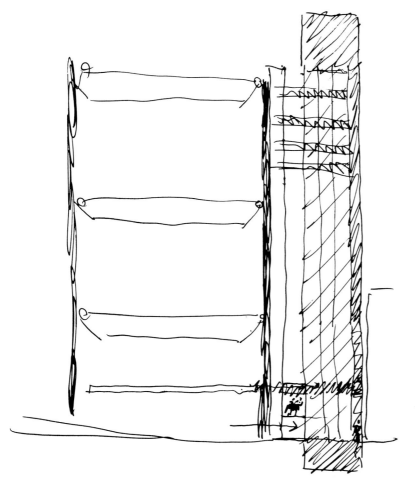

required by a modern research laboratory and at the same time allow maximum flexibility in the arrangement and rearrangement of partitions, benches and equipment. In the 1980s even ordinary office blocks require a similar level of mechanical, electrical and, increasingly, electronic servicing.

The problem has a temporal as well as a spatial dimension. The main structure of a modern office block can be expected to last for 50 years or more, but the mechanical equipment necessary to make it usable has a life span of only 10 to 15 years. Modern electronic services might last only a year or two before increased demand and new developments in information technology call for extensive alterations. This is one of the reasons why Foster placed the services at the perimeter of the building where they are easily accessible and can be altered or replaced with the minimum of disruption.

There are other reasons. The basic plan of the Bank is a rejection of the conventional office-tower form, or what Foster calls the 'kebab' solution. Most office towers have a central concrete service core piercing a stack of

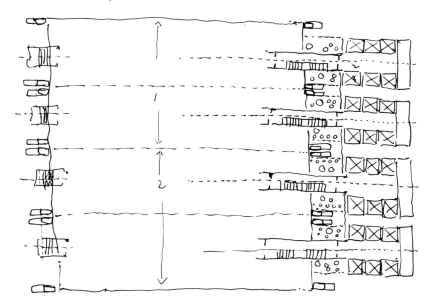

"From the outset both the Bank and ourselves placed a high priority on flexibility for rapid internal changes – an essential feature if the new building was to be an efficient 'tool', able to respond to dynamic commercial change."

Norman Foster, *L'Architecture d'Aujourd'hui*, February 1986

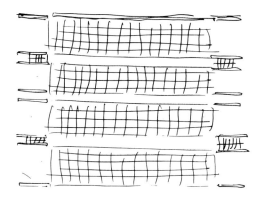

The structural form at its simplest. Independent structural fins support each line of trusses, with escape stairs inserted between certain 'paired' fins separating the individual floor bays.

The full range of options was explored in sketch form. Here service zones, escape stairs and liftshafts are all clearly defined elements quite separate from the structure supporting the floors – which is still shown in four bays and clearly marked for two phases.

identical floors like a skewer. This not only puts the services where they are least accessible, but also drastically reduces the planning options. The working area itself becomes literally peripheral while at the centre of the building there is nothing more spatially exciting than escape stairs and lavatories. By moving the 'core' to the sides of the building Foster frees the plan, increases the planning options and opens up the whole of the working area to panoramic views of the harbour to the north and the Peak to the south. The internal space becomes, effectively, a continuation of the landscape.

As the design progressed these characteristics were to be further developed with the introduction of raised floors for the horizontal distribution of services and the invention of a unique system of circulation by a combination of lift and escalator. But the first important decision was to group the main services and movement systems at the edge of the building. We can see from the sketches that this decision was taken almost immediately, and that the possible retention of the existing banking hall was only one of the underlying reasons.

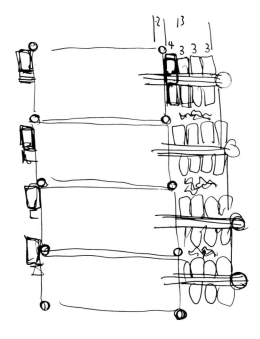

The 'one-sided' variation was not to last but, even in this simple diagram, dimensions are already being considered.

A regular planning grid is essential to co-ordinate a building of this complexity and it is Norman Foster's method to get to grips with the detailed co-ordination as soon as possible. The building is already conceived as an assemblage of components fitted together in precise dimensional relationships. This sketch represents a detailed exploration of the implications of a basic three-metre grid, with 500mm 'tartans' inserted for the main structural elements.

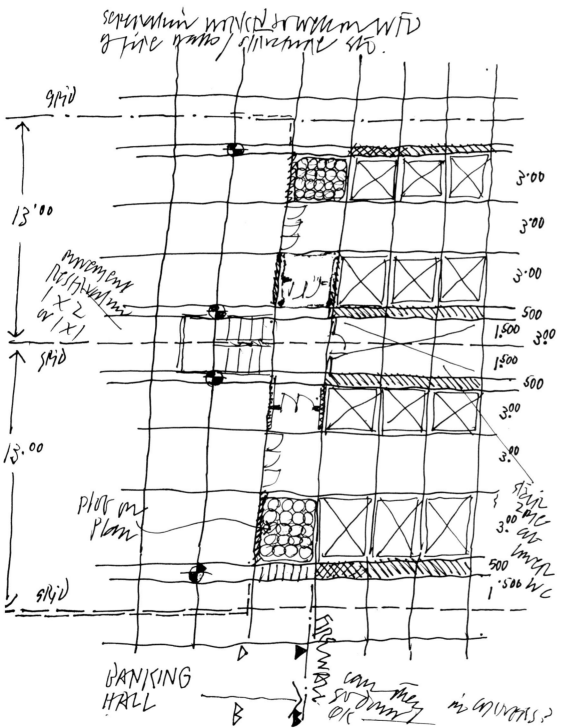

The assumption that the design of a building is a relatively straightforward two-stage process is not without foundation. Vague concept sketches drawn by the chief designer with a soft pencil are passed to a team of technical draftsmen who work them up into fully-dimensioned and annotated production drawings. First comes the architecture, and only then the building construction. Although widely practised, this approach has few advocates; certainly Foster is not one of them. For him the earliest concepts are always as much technical as spatial and formal. There is no demarcation line between the aesthetic and technical aspects of architecture, between design and production, form and structure. Right from the start every architectural idea includes the technical means by which it might be realised.

This, of course, has a profound effect on the finished buildings. In many modern — and ancient — buildings architecture and construction are only loosely related. Facades apparently constructed of stone are supported by hidden steel frames; a seemingly solid ceiling turns out to be a thin skin concealing a mass of trunking; the wall that looks like marble proves to be merely artfully painted plaster. There are no such deceptions in a Foster building: the architecture is always a clear and direct expression of the technology employed in its production. The steel frame will usually be clearly visible, a suspended ceiling will always look like a suspended ceiling, and no material will ever pretend to be some other.

Thus in the early sketches for the Bank there are very detailed explorations of the technical as well as the visual implications of design decisions. The building is already conceived as an assemblage of components fitted together in precise dimensional relationships. Though the sketches are free-hand and not to scale, they are nevertheless gridded and dimensioned. Plans show the position of fire walls, estimated sizes for service ducts and precise locations for structural elements. Sections show the exact relationship between, for example, the massive double-bridge girders, the floors suspended from them, the hangers, the external cladding and the horizontal service voids.

These sketches demonstrate the importance that Foster gives to the production process and its architectural consequences. They are abstract, technical experiments rather than pictorial representations, but they nevertheless clearly indicate the visual character of the

"At any stage of its evolution it was also, quite literally, shaped by its 'buildability' — the technology of its production. The appearance of the Bank both inside and out, its internal organisation and the spatial experience that it offered were all defined, ordered and modulated by the structure which supported it and the walls which enclosed it."

Norman Foster, *Process Architecture*, March 1986

As dimensional analysis progressed, the effect on the appearance of the building was also continually checked. Here, a more articulated service tower is introduced.

building. It is already obvious that it is to be a building assembled from components made in factories and workshops and that this aspect of its production will be clearly visible in the finished product. There will be no deception; every element will have its own expression and every junction will be elegantly resolved.

This is not to say that the larger formal and spatial issues of building are being neglected. Accompanying the many technical sketches are

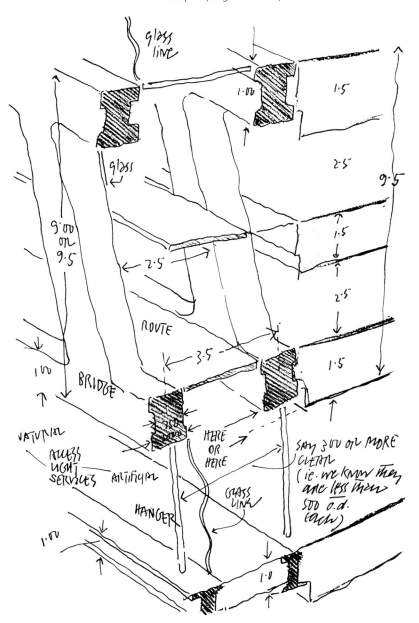

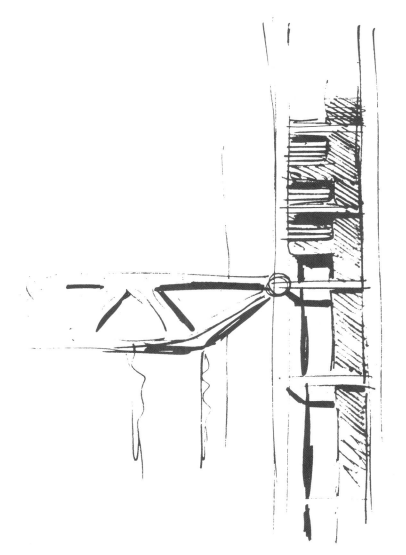

Zones have to be defined and dimensioned in section as well as on plan. This careful isometric sketch explores the relationship between the storey height and the depth of the large trusses. Access to services, external cladding line and sizes of structural members are also considered. The floor-to-floor dimension and the depth allowed for services distribution correspond almost exactly to the final design.

For every sketch that studies construction, another explores the visual and spatial results. The building is nearing the form in which it was submitted. Trusses at three levels support suspended floors, creating an open plaza beneath the building and double-height spaces at each truss level.

Already, at this very early stage, the 'sun scoop' makes an appearance: mirrors reflecting sunshine deep into the heart of the building and down into a large central atrium.

This early sketch might be a section through the building as built, with a basement, an open plaza at ground level and a multi-storey banking hall reached via escalators. Very early on, the decision was made that there would be no roof-mounted services, meaning that large plant would have to be accommodated in a basement. This sketch also anticipates the requirement for a secondary banking hall, below ground level, serving the security vaults.

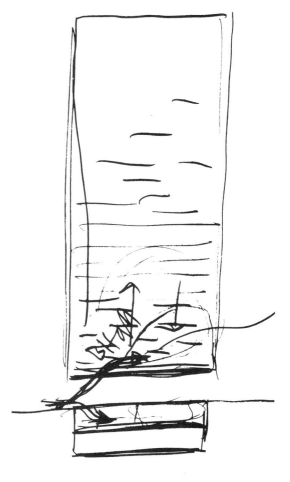

sketches of a more pictorial kind exploring the visual quality of the whole building, inside and out, in relation to its site. What until now has seemed a dry, machine-like object now takes on light and shade, scale and context. Two issues predominate: the relationship between the building and Statue Square – almost the only urban public open space in Hong Kong – and the idea of the banking hall as an atrium approached by escalator from the street below. Both were to be fully explored in later phases of the design, though with different degrees of success. The atrium banking hall was triumphantly realised in the final building, but the various schemes by Foster Associates for the development of Statue Square were to come to nothing.

Though the site of 1 Queen's Road Central was originally at the water's edge, successive campaigns of land reclamation over a period of 100 years have left it three whole city blocks distant from the harbour. However, agreements between the Bank and the Government have ensured that the land in front of the Bank has remained undeveloped except for a two-storey car-park building and the Star Ferry terminal, both built in 1958. Foster has always perceived his real site as the whole strip, from Bank to ferry terminal, and here in the early sketches the formal relationship between the building and its foreground – Statue Square, the ferry terminal and the harbour itself – is explored in carefully constructed free-hand perspectives.

Equal scrutiny is given to the quality of the internal spaces and to the views from the building of the harbour to the north and the Peak to the south. It now becomes clear that the simple served/servant diagram and the 'laminated' plan have a rich spatial potential. By omitting floor slabs from one or more of the structural bays, atrium spaces in a variety of shapes and sizes can be created anywhere in the building. The most obvious application of this device is in the eventual replacement of the 1935 banking hall. Already one of the most exciting spaces in the building as built has been considered and sketched – including the idea of a system of mirrors to reflect sunlight deep into the building.

Note that in all of these sketches the building is shown in its final form. Nothing remains of the old building, despite the fact that it was the possible retention of parts of the old building that gave rise to the design concept. However, as already indicated, many aspects of this concept – the service zone, the open floors, the tension structure, the atrium with escalators – are identifiable in earlier Foster buildings and projects. They are part of an established vocabulary. 'Phased regeneration' was the justification or trigger for the deployment of these devices, but that does not mean that they would not have been used anyway. In the event, the strategy of phased regeneration was abandoned, but the design concept remained and was realised in the final building.

"We have developed the idea of a 'sun scoop' where, by the use of mirrors which have been developed with an awareness of feedback from the space programmes and so on, sunlight is pulled into the heart of the building and right down through to the plaza. In this way, the plaza below does not become a drab, shaded area: it becomes diffused with sunlight."

Norman Foster, lecture to Sainsbury's Executive Club, March 1984

Inside/outside space. The interior of the building is seen as a continuation of the surrounding landscape. Though this is a pictorial sketch, designed to show the spatial effect, the various structural elements are faithfully reproduced.

Models are an essential design tool for Foster Associates, whether to explore technical details or, as in this case, to assess the scale and presence of the building in context. At this stage it was assumed that east/west cross-bracing would be necessary, though only on the south side of the building.

A study model shows the view from the harbour, with the North Tower retained. This is one of a sequence of views to explain the phased regeneration concept.

In October 1979, three months after the first visit to Hong Kong, the scheme was ready to be presented to the client. The presentation took the form of a comprehensive set of drawings, a report illustrated by extremely clear diagrams, and a model showing the building in context — including the whole site down to the ferry terminal. The model very nearly didn't make it. Almost completely demolished in transit, it had to be rebuilt overnight — a clear sign to Foster and his colleagues that if they were to have any future in Hong Kong then they must not underestimate the practical problems of operating at long range.

The brief had required that the client's two options — the construction of a south tower and complete redevelopment — be considered. These were duly considered and duly rejected. In a 127-page report by Foster Associates, they warranted only 14 pages. "Designing a building without the benefit of a working relationship with the client", says the report, "is rather like a game of blindman's-buff." What was needed at this stage was not a scheme for a final building but an open-ended strategy capable of offering a number of different options. 'Options' is one of Norman Foster's favourite words and it crops up again and again in the report. Indeed it could be said to sum up his design method: to keep every possible option open for as long as possible, both during the design and construction phase and after the building has been completed.

The bulk of the presentation was therefore devoted to an explanation of the concept of phased regeneration and an exploration of the various options that this offered. For convenience the project was presented in two phases, each phase being divided into a number of 'sequences'. Thus phase one involved the demolition of the east and west wings and the annexe of the existing building, and the construction of a two-bay tower bridging over the existing banking hall and standing behind the existing North Tower. Phase two began with the demolition of the North Tower, the addition of two more bays to the new building and, finally, the replacement of the old banking hall.

It is important to realise, however, that the building presented in these drawings and diagrams can never be said to have reached a complete and final state; or, to put it another way, it can be said to be complete at any stage in its construction. The existing North Tower and the new phase-one tower can co-exist quite happily as a stable architectural composition. And even if the North Tower has to go, there is no reason why the old banking hall, with its spectacular Italian mosaic ceiling, should not form a permanent part of the new building.

The tower-as-extendable-bridge concept is actually far more flexible than this simplified two-phase suggestion implies. A chart of options which accompanied the presentation shows how the building might have bridged over the North Tower as well as the banking hall, how the heights of the different structural bays could be varied to suit the shadow regulations, how it would be possible simply to omit several floors and leave a hole through the building to accommodate a large garden terrace, or how a single huge top-lit atrium, higher than any cathedral, might be created.

Even within the relatively sober, box-like form of the building as presented, the flexibility offered is of a new order. In the design of office buildings flexibility has usually meant little more than a degree of choice in the placing of partitions — flexibility in plan only. In industrial buildings the concept has sometimes been extended to the configuration of external walls.

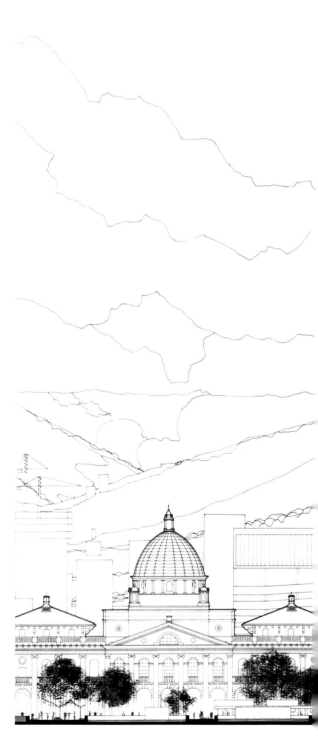

142

"...an indefinite number of offices piled tier upon tier, one tier just like another, one office just like the other offices — an office being similar to a cell in a honeycomb, merely a compartment, nothing more."

Louis Sullivan, *The Tall Office Building Artistically Considered*, first published in 1896

This detailed north/south section is one of many impressive presentation drawings prepared for the competition submission. It shows the half-way point in the phased regeneration sequence. Statue Square is still dominated by the North Tower standing in front of the new building, which bridges over the existing banking hall. The structural form permits double- or even triple-height spaces to be introduced anywhere in the building, for the first time allowing flexibility in section as well as plan in a clear break with Louis Sullivan's famous 80-year-old definition of the skyscraper.

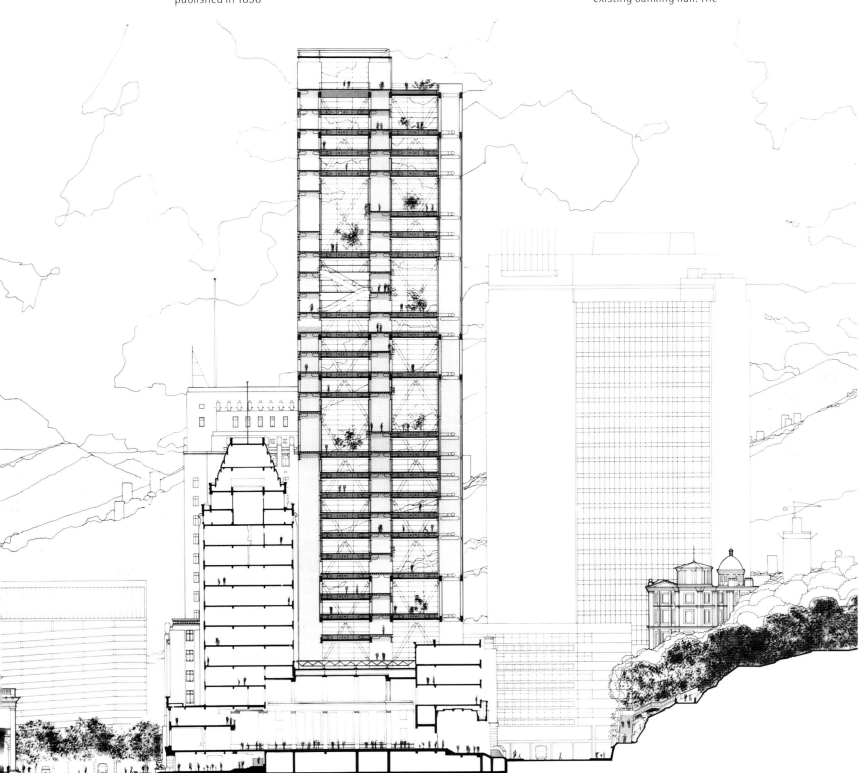

An east/west section looking north, showing double- and triple-height atria, and the set-backs between the concrete towers on the east side to comply with the over-shadowing regulations. With the old banking hall removed, a new generous atrium is created, with escalators cascading through the six-storey high space. An upper-level walkway on the west side of the building spans major roads that run either side of the site, linking a popular route down the hill behind the building to a well-established walkway system between other nearby buildings.

Part of the phased re-generation sequence, showing the model with the North Tower now removed.

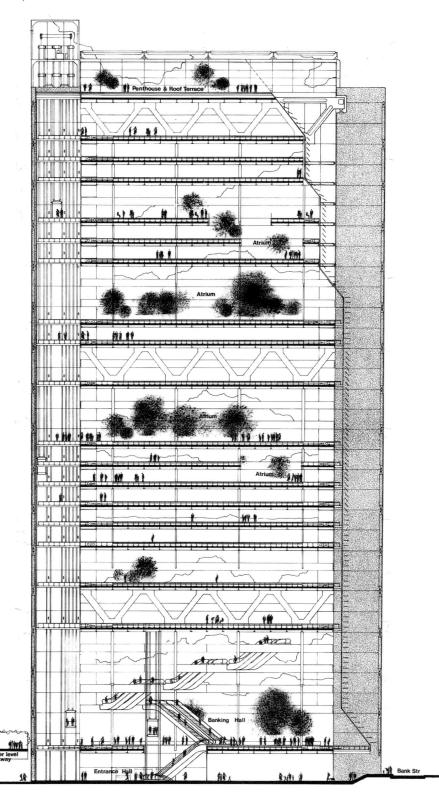

Over the last 20 years or so curtain-walling systems have been developed which permit panels of different types — solid, glazed, insulated, louvred and so on — to be arranged in any pattern within a grid. This might be described as flexibility in elevation.

This scheme, however, offers something new: flexibility in section. It is the section drawings that illustrate best the exciting spatial potential of the concept. It is not seriously suggested that whole floors will actually be moved about in the finished building — though this idea is latent in the design — but that, at the dialogue stage, the client is offered a vastly greater range of three-dimensional spatial options without affecting the basic design. In this respect the Competition entry is more adventurous and more complex than the building as built.

Nevertheless there are great similarities. This scheme is unmistakably the prototype of the final building, more similar to it, in fact, than the so-called Chevron and Organ-pipe schemes that were to follow. The main features of the final building are all evident in the Competition scheme. Some, like the 'flexibility in section', were to be compromised as the dialogue with the client progressed; others, like the idea of an open, column-free plaza beneath the building were to be clarified and emphasised. In the Competition scheme the plaza takes up only half of the ground floor, the other half forming a conventional, if very large, entrance lobby giving direct access to the lifts on the west side and enclosing the public escalators leading to the banking hall above. Over the banking hall the main atrium rises to a height of six floors with galleries and more escalators. It would, no doubt, have been a very dramatic space, but it lacks the clarity and monumental quality of the plaza, atrium, banking hall arrangement in the final building.

Structurally, too, the building was to become more rather than less adventurous. The vertical structural elements of the Competition scheme are of ordinary slip-formed concrete, a technique that would have been familiar to the client's technical advisors and therefore unlikely to cause any unnecessary anxiety. In the final building, however, these concrete towers were to be replaced by massive, composite steel masts emphasising the bridge-like nature of the

The Bank's geomancer, Koo Pak Ling, was consulted on the favourable aspects of the site in terms of its *fung shui*. His sketch identified the corner from which entry to the new building would be most propitious, a direction reflected in the angle of the main entrance escalators.

"Hong Kong is a city of skyscrapers with more of them, I'm told, than anywhere else in the world. It was the very nature of such buildings that we attempted to challenge: their boring inhumanity and anonymity, in which the only apparent difference between the good, bad and indifferent was skin deep, and in which every floor was a dreary repetition of the other."

Norman Foster, Royal Gold Medal Speech at the RIBA, June 1983

The ground floor plan of the final Competition scheme. A grand entrance lobby with water features occupies half of this level, with escalators taking customers up to the banking hall atrium or down to a secondary banking hall in the basement. The remainder of the space beneath the building is an open, public plaza referred to as 'Bank Square'.

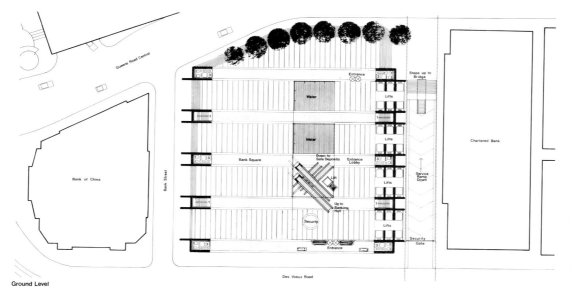

Ground Level

A 'typical' full-width floor, showing five alternative furniture arrangements. Vertical circulation is conventional, with lift lobbies at every floor on the west side of the building.

The new banking hall occupies most of the first floor and is shown here with a continuous counter 213 metres long, weaving in a very free form around the space.

The roof-top penthouse enjoys open terraces on its north and south sides. Set-backs between the structural towers on the east side are angled to the vertical, their sloping glazed walls protected by louvres.

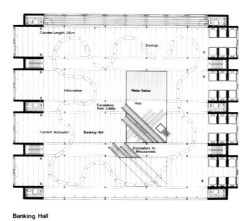

Banking Hall

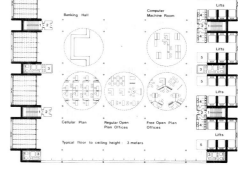

Full width Floor

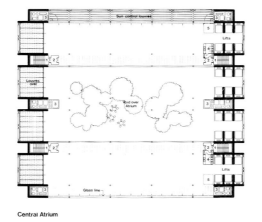

Roof Level

Central Atrium

The central atrium recurs throughout the development of the project — here as an option for use anywhere in the building's height. Rationalised to form the main public banking hall at the lower levels, the idea is triumphantly realised in the final building.

The presentation drawings were all laid out in the Foster office for a final view prior to being packed and sent out to Hong Kong.

"To explain our thinking to the Bank we showed a series of drawings which demonstrated the possibility of retaining pieces of the existing fabric. The new building could bridge over the banking hall and keep the original 1930s facade to Statue Square. This approach offered a gentler range of possibilities for developing the site, rather than just bulldozing the whole thing. It also kept open the option of extending over the site in such a way that the new building could later grow and eventually replace the original pieces."

Norman Foster, lecture at Centre Pompidou, February 1981

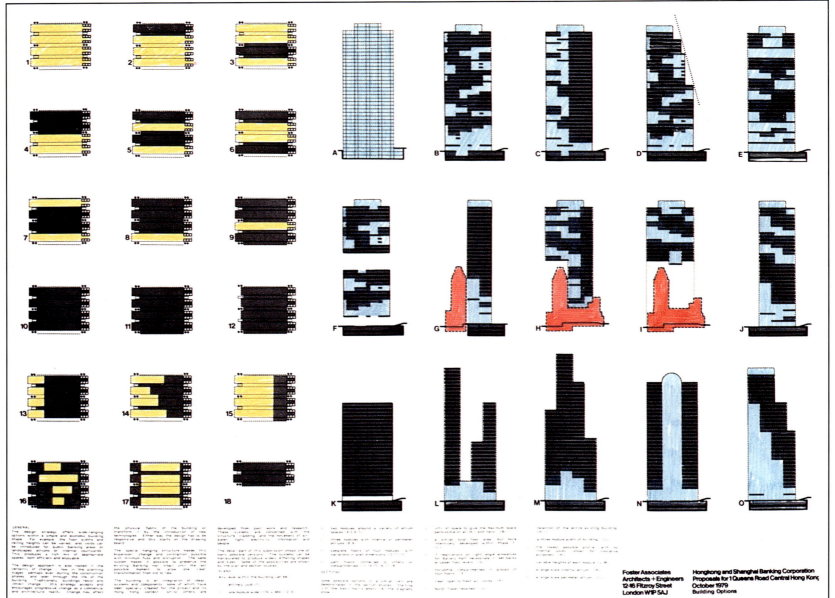

The phased regeneration principle is explained in this chart, entitled 'Building Options', that sums up the whole philosophy of the competition submission. Since the design team did not have the benefit of a dialogue with the client, they offered not a fixed proposal, but a framework or strategy that could lead to many different built outcomes. The diagrams show a few of the ways in which the basic, four-bay bridge structure could be interpreted in plan and section, adapting to accommodate all or part of the existing building, either permanently or temporarily.

146

A working model was made to demonstrate the principle of phased regeneration. It was damaged in transit but repaired overnight. Before being presented to the client it was tested on the balcony of Foster's hotel room, overlooking the existing 1935 building.

The main presentation model. In its final form the Competition scheme produced a rather squat, box-like building somewhat sober in character. At this stage, the scheme was based on a 14:1 plot ratio and was not influenced by light angles in the adjacent Bank Street, factors which were to be changed later.

structure. The final building was also to realise much more fully the potential of the laminated plan — four structural bays in the Competition scheme, three in the final building. Indeed the box-like, flat-topped form of the Competition scheme is rather surprising given that the structural system, with double trusses between each bay, clearly permits the bays to rise to different heights. However, it is important to remember that such things as plot ratios and overshadowing regulations were at this stage only vaguely defined.

Another surprise, coming to the Competition scheme with a knowledge of the final building, is that the revolutionary system of circulation by a combination of 'main-line' lifts and 'local' escalators has not yet been invented. Escalators do appear here and there in the plan in combination with atria, but they do not form an organised circulation system. And the lifts, unlike those in the final building, stop at every level. Clearly the circulation system, that some have seen as the most important innovation in the final building, was a development from, and a replacement of, the idea of 'flexibility in section'. There is a suggestion, in the Competition scheme, that the narrow strips of floor between the main bays should be made of glass so as to create a visual link, at least in the form of diffused light, between floors. In the final building this visual link has been replaced by an escalator link — offering a much more dynamic and satisfying spatial experience.

Whatever its merits as an actual building proposal, the Competition scheme certainly did its job more than adequately. Foster Associates was the only one of the seven competing practices to be invited to give a full verbal presentation. The scheme was a clear winner, and when Norman Foster returned to London in October 1979 he had the commission to design "the best bank in the world" safely in his pocket.

Colin Davies

The sudden appearance of a new idea: if the four bays of the building are structurally independent, why should they not rise to different heights to take full advantage of the maximum building envelope within the limits imposed by the overshadowing regulations? In the event, this idea was shelved while the implications of the Chevron scheme were worked through. It was to reappear, however, in the Final scheme and is fundamental to the character of the building as built.

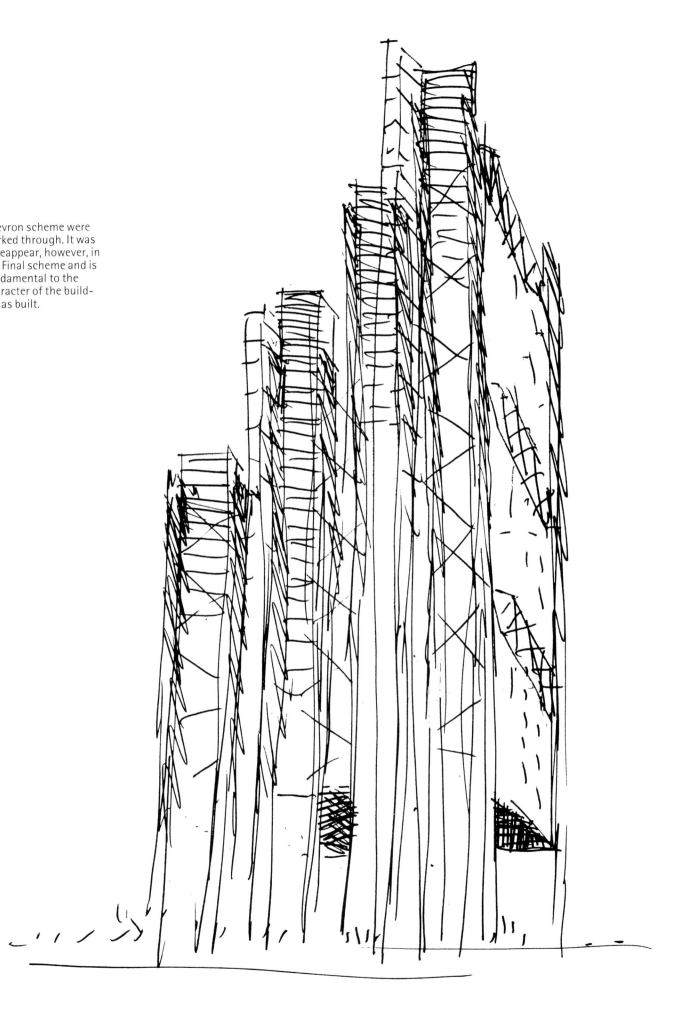

1980 Hongkong Bank
Chevron Scheme

For all the sophistication of the phased regeneration concept, one major problem would remain: retaining the original banking hall effectively precluded the use of deep basements. Aware of this shortcoming, the Bank decided to commission a totally new building, introducing a new sense of freedom to the scheme. Foster, however, was aware that many of the basic concepts of the original scheme remained valid. If anything, these ideas should be enriched rather than put to one side and, out of this process, the Chevron scheme emerged.

Having chosen Foster Associates, the client immediately decided to abandon the idea of retaining the old banking hall and north tower. Only the so-called annexe, a narrow six-storey block built on the west side of the site in the 1960s, was to be retained, and this was more out of a desire to preserve a symbolic presence on one of Hong Kong's most prestigious sites rather than out of practical necessity. It was to be an added complication to a brief whose full implications were to become clear to Foster Associates only now that the competition was won. By choosing Foster Associates, it was clear that the Bank was committed to their stated aim to build 'the best bank in the world', but this was not intended to be at the expense of time. Despite a still largely unspecified brief, and despite the problems of construction in a location with virtually no indigenous, heavy manufacturing facility, the new building had to be completed by the summer of 1985. Such problems, however, run as common themes in Foster's designs and, as we have seen, many of the elements of the Competition scheme had arisen from just such an awareness of the challenges that had to be addressed. It was, after all, an acknowledgment of these forces that had shaped the 'phased regeneration' concept. The decision to rebuild from scratch did not therefore necessarily imply a complete rethink. The bridge-like form, the laminated plan, the tension structure, flexibility in section and the clear differentiation of served and servant spaces all added up to a coherent design strategy which remained valid. The task now was to refine the design still further, taking into account the new factors of time, flexibility and the implied need for prefabrication. The result of this process came to be known as the Chevron scheme.

The essence of the Chevron scheme was to create a structural system that allowed almost unlimited spatial flexibility. The forces gathered together in the trusses at only three levels in the Competition scheme are now distributed evenly over the entire height of the building. By this homogeneity of structure, it now became

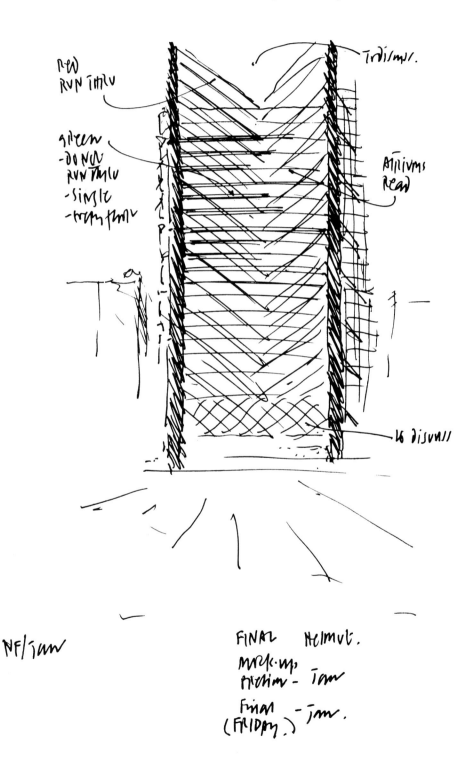

"As we spent more time in Hong Kong and did more research we became aware that the Chinese saw their grey stone building as a red building on bank-notes and advertising symbols, and we became aware of how important colour was symbolically. This led to much research into traditional Chinese architecture, its colour and form, in an attempt to understand the spirit behind the appearance."

Norman Foster, lecture at Centre Pompidou, February 1981

The use of red columns in traditional Chinese architecture, for important public buildings, was incorporated into the new Bank scheme.

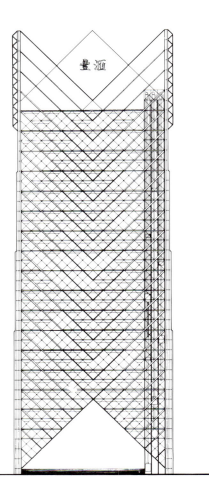

The Chevron scheme introduced two major new concepts: an all-steel structure and a system of continuous suspension members. These would allow greater flexibility and, more importantly, quicker construction through prefabrication.

Like bundles of bamboo poles, the masts were grouped steel tubes that reduced over the building's height in response to the decreasing loads.

An outrigged structure appears in this option, as a means of supporting service towers still positioned at the edge of the building.

possible to remove almost any section of a particular floor to allow an infinite variety of layered and interlocking spaces. Whereas the main elements of the Competition structure were few and massive — concrete towers and girder bridges — the main elements of the Chevron structure are many and delicate — slim tapering masts and a rapid rhythm of V-shaped tension members. The effect on the appearance of the building is dramatic. The sturdy, heavy engineering quality of the Competition scheme is dissolved into a filigree framework.

To Western eyes the Chevron scheme has a distinctly Oriental look about it, and this is not mere coincidence. At one stage it was proposed to paint the frame a typically Chinese red, an idea which was to persist through to the Final scheme. The main masts were to be clusters of slim columns bound together like bamboo poles. Where they emerged from the top of the building they were to support a huge sky-sign in the best Hong Kong tradition. But it would be a mistake to interpret all this as mere image making.

There were other reasons, both practical and philosophical, for this radical reinterpretation of the tension structure principle.

The first reason is that it permitted the use of steel, instead of concrete, for the main structural members. In-situ reinforced concrete is not one of Foster's favourite materials. It is a 'wet trade', site-labour intensive, relatively inaccurate and subject to movement as it cures. Foster prefers the 'kit-of-parts' approach to building construction, using dry, accurate, factory-made components which can be as-

As this model shows, with its filigree structure and bright red colouring, the Chevron scheme was a dramatic development from the Competition stage. In other respects, however, the overall diagram remained consistent, with service towers drawn to the side of open floors grouped in clear bays.

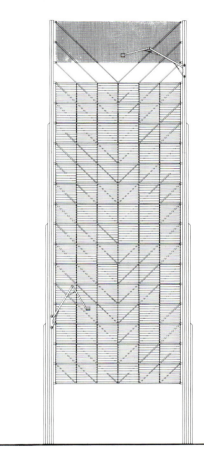

Should the ground floor plaza have a dramatic V-shaped or more formal horizontal soffit? This series of drawings explored a wide variety of options, including here maintenance cradles on arms that travel along the structural masts.

sembled speedily on site. Metal and glass, not concrete and masonry, are the characteristic materials of his architecture.

There is, however, a major obstacle to the use of structural steel in a multi-storey building: it must be protected from fire, or, more accurately, from intense heat that will quickly weaken it and render it unsafe. One way to fire-protect steelwork is to encase it in concrete but this, of course, negates most of its advantages. Another method is to keep it cool by wrapping it in some kind of incombustible insulation, but this destroys the hard visual quality of its surface and reduces its slenderness. The third method, rarely used, is water cooling. The main vertical and inclined members of the Chevron structure lent themselves well to water-filling and offered the real possibility of a steel-framed tower that showed off its steelwork, rather than hiding it away.

The second practical and philosophical advantage of the Chevron scheme is the thoroughgoing modular nature of its construction. Though a large and spatially complex building,

"To realise in excess of a million square feet in such a short time-scale informed the need for a high degree of prefabrication, extending to the use of factory-finished modules made to tolerances unusual for the construction industry."

Norman Foster, *L'Architecture d'Aujourd'hui*, February 1986

The success of the Chevron scheme depended, among other things, on the satisfactory resolution of a number of awkward 45-degree junctions between structural members. Various options were explored in sketches.

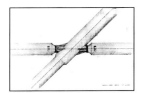
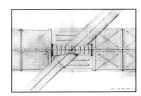

it is constructed from a kit-of-parts of very few standard types. Each mast is an assemblage of identical sub-components, more 'bamboo poles' being added to the cluster as the load increases towards the base of the building. The V-shaped tension members all carry the same load, equivalent to two complete floors, and are therefore identical. Each is a kind of chain with rod-like links diminishing in thickness — this being a tension member — from top to bottom. The majority of the horizontal structural members are again identical since they span the same distance and must be capable of carrying the same load. And that load takes the form of a section of floor of standard width and span.

Apart from the obvious conceptual elegance of all this, it has practical implications for the production process. What lies behind it is Foster's commitment to the inevitable reality that buildings, like most other artefacts of twentieth-century industrial culture, should be made in factories. It may not be feasible — or desirable — to mass-produce buildings like cars or washing machines, but that does not mean that building designers should ignore the advantages of a controlled production environment. The recent arrival of ever more sophisti-

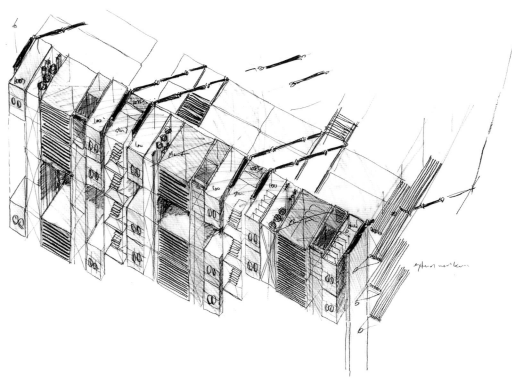

The service zones along the east and west sides of the building begin to be conceived as an assemblage of modular units. The pressures of a fast-track programme and need for future flexibility combined to impress on the design team the need to consider radically different forms of construction based on modularisation and prefabrication. These concepts are crucial to understanding the technical aspects of the Chevron scheme. The whole building is a kit-of-parts of remarkably few standard types.

Modularisation extends even to the floors, which are assembled from steel sections, prefabricated in a factory complete with service runs.

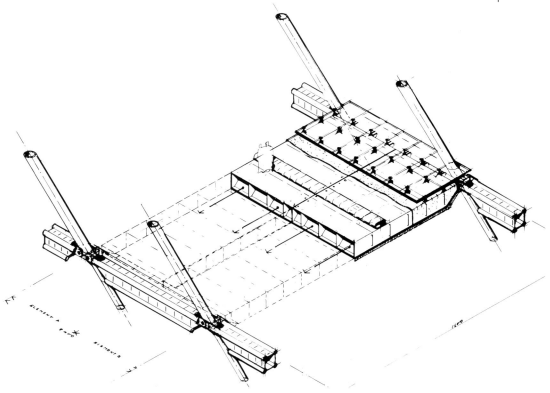

Early in the development of the Chevron design, the building lost one of its structural bays. From this point on the scheme was to remain a three-bay building.

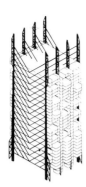

This development model was one of dozens made to explore the implications of this radically new concept. Still with four bays, it gives a good impression of the rich variety of internal spaces that could be achieved using the Chevron structure. It also indicates why the Bank considered the raking tension members intrusive: these occur not just on the facades but throughout the building. A full-size mock-up was constructed in Foster Associates' London office to gauge the effect of this on office layouts.

cated machines, computer controlled and capable of responding with ease to new procedures, makes this process even more inevitable. No longer is the old-fashioned concept of mass production by standardisation even relevant: the new technologies have been developed specifically to allow a high degree of customisation around a basic form, a method of production well suited to the manufacture of building components. If the building was to be completed in time, Foster was aware that such methods of production would be essential to its success.

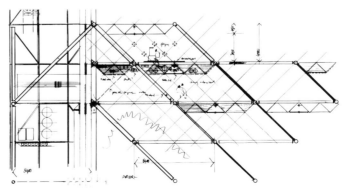

This detail of the elevation shows how the various structural elements might be standardised. The masts are made up of tubes of the same diameter, while the raking tension members form a kind of chain, with rod-like links diminishing in thickness from top to bottom.

153

From the earliest sketches, the view from the building had been treated as a key element. It reappears in this sketch which also questions the location of furniture.

Structure is always an integral part of a design by Foster Associates and never a means to an architectural end in isolation. The structural idea that is the essence of the Chevron scheme emerged from discussions within the Foster office but, to develop the idea, the architects needed the co-operation of a sympathetic team of engineers. This was provided by Ove Arup & Partners. In fact the structural realities of the Chevron scheme are much more complex than surface appearances would suggest. In the development drawings and models produced by Foster Associates and Arup's we can see evi-

A tentative exploration of the spatial possibilities for the main entrance and banking hall.

This 'slice' through the middle of the building seems to imply that it might be extended indefinitely up or down by the addition of more standard components. It is as much a system as a one-off building.

dence of the struggle to solve inherent problems, chiefly to do with lateral stability. What appears to be a suspension structure is more accurately described as a series of overlapping trusses, each six storeys high. The diagonal members which make the chevron pattern are the bracing members of these trusses and the edges of the floors, their tension and compression booms.

It is important to realise that the tension members of the structure occur at each bay, not just on the facades. This means that they

The spatial possibilities created by the 45-degree geometry of the structure at plaza level were explored in a variety of sketches. For the first time, lift-cars appear in glazed shafts, a feature that was to remain in the final solution.

154

"We became aware, through research in Hong Kong, that buildings are often decorated for festivals; either small scale in a village or even the main facade of the Bank itself."

Norman Foster, lecture at Centre Pompidou, February 1981

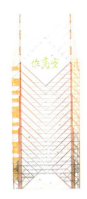

"The Bank questioned what it would be like to work inside a space suspended from inclined members. We mocked-up these ideas full-size in our own office, to learn for ourselves and to prove its feasibility."

Norman Foster, lecture at Centre Pompidou, Febuary 1981

slice across the space, like sloping columns, at 12 positions on each floor. Mock-ups of several of these diagonal members were constructed in Foster Associates' London office, at the correct spacings, and it convinced the designers that they would not be a serious planning obstacle.

To develop an innovative structure like this demands very close co-operation between architect and structural engineer. This is characteristic of the Foster design method, which is integrated and multi-disciplinary even at the early stages of a design. It is not only the structure, however, that is innovative in the scheme. The mechanical services are equally unconventional and equally well integrated into the design. Architecture, structure and services all come together in the modular concept.

In the design and construction of modern office buildings the integration of structure and services is often little more than a matter of allowing sufficient space, on plan and in section, for the installation of plant, trunking, pipework and cables. With the Hongkong Bank, the decision had already been made, in the interests of time and availability, to prefabricate as much of the building as possible. But if the whole building is conceived as a kit of prefabricated parts then it also makes sense for the main components of the services installation to be fitted in the factory rather than on site. This demands integration of a much higher order. In the Chevron scheme Foster Associates begin to explore some of the implications of this innovative idea.

The most obvious example of the modularisation of the services installation is to be seen in the 'servant zones' on the east and west sides of the building. The sketches and final drawings clearly indicate that these parts of the building are to be constructed not as monolithic tower structures, as in the Competition scheme, but as stacks of 'plug-in pods' containing lavatories, local air-conditioning plant and clusters of vertical ductwork and pipework. Even the lift shafts and escape stairs are broken down into transportable units. The idea is that these pods should be made on a production line, in controlled conditions, and delivered to the site complete down to the last valve, tap, wash-basin and lining panel. This concept was later to be realised in the final building. But the Chevron scheme goes even further by modularising the horizontal as well as the vertical services. The floor components too are conceived as complete, fully-fitted modules incorporating not just a service void, but the services themselves.

Despite all this technical sophistication, the spatial and contextual qualities of the building are not neglected. The idea of flexibility in section, first proposed in the Competition scheme, is developed to even more dramatic effect. In sketches of the early, four-bay version of the Chevron scheme we see how the atria can be combined to create an internal landscape of hills, valleys, cliffs, canyons and even lakes – the swimming pools. We can also see how the building might form a link, rather than a barrier, between Statue Square to the north and the steep bank of Battery Park to the south. One section shows a bridge over Queen's Road Central bringing the landscape of the park tumbling right down into the banking hall itself.

This last idea does not survive in the final presentation of the Chevron scheme. Nevertheless the banking hall becomes a very dramatic space indeed. Far more than just a foyer, it takes on an urban quality. It becomes an extension not of Battery Park but of Statue Square: the bustle of Hong Kong is brought into the heart of

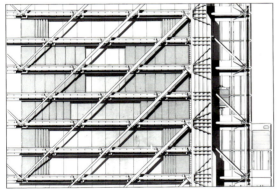

Jan Kaplicky's elegant presentation drawing brings the elevation to life. The modules are strongly articulated while steel binding clearly expresses the stresses acting within the masts. Sliding screens are also introduced to provide solar protection to the glazed facades.

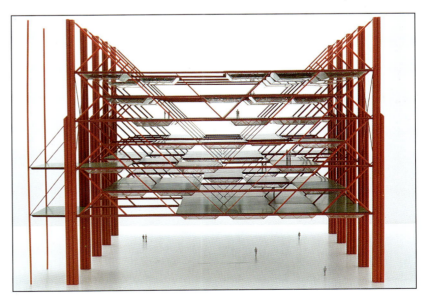

This early study model was made with movable floor panels – imitating the building itself – so that alternative layouts could be explored.

This early sketch expresses the dynamic internal spaces Norman Foster wished to create for the plaza entrance and banking hall atrium. A rich series of options was explored in a variety of drawings.

In one option, the plaza was stepped up and continued out on the south side of the building to form a bridge over Queen's Road Central, thereby allowing the landscaping of Battery Park, on the hillside opposite, to be brought into the scheme. The theme of hillside and valley persisted through several variations, even to the inclusion of miniature lakes.

the building. From now on the ground level will be referred to as the plaza; a large open space within and beneath the building, freely accessible to the public. From it, long escalators rise to the various levels of the banking hall — platforms literally hanging above the city.

This concept of a plaza was to be preserved throughout the subsequent development of the design, though for the Final scheme the volume above was simplified into a single, cathedral-like atrium.

Apart from the perspectives of the banking hall, the final presentation drawings show a simple, rational, even sober building, similar on plan and in section to the Competition scheme but with three bays instead of four and without set-backs. Many of the most exciting ideas that appear in the development drawings were understated or omitted altogether for fear of frightening an essentially conservative client. This caution turned out to be fully justified.

In May 1980, after almost eight months of development work on the Chevron scheme, disaster struck. A preliminary version of the scheme had been presented six weeks earlier to the chairman of the Bank who had received it well. But when the scheme was finally put

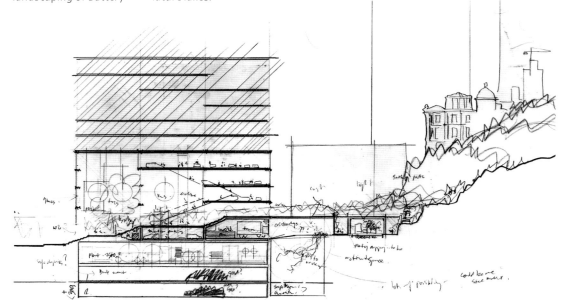

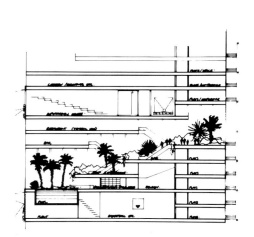

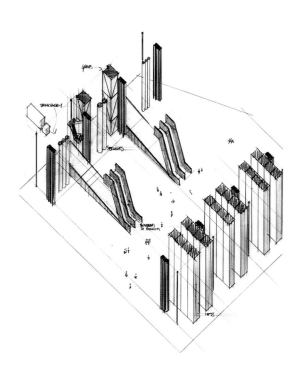

Deeper basements were introduced in the Chevron scheme. In this sketch, vehicular access is proposed from Bank Street — at one side of the building — down covered ramps positioned under strategically located escalators that help break up the space.

For the final presentation, Birkin Haward prepared a series of his inimitable perspectives. Here the view across the public plaza towards the lifts on the west side is shown. The idea of an atrium is maintained but in a very relaxed form that takes full advantage of the structural system to create a 'hanging gardens' effect in both the plaza and banking hall above. Richly populated, the drawing was intended to convey the excitement and vitality of the new scheme.

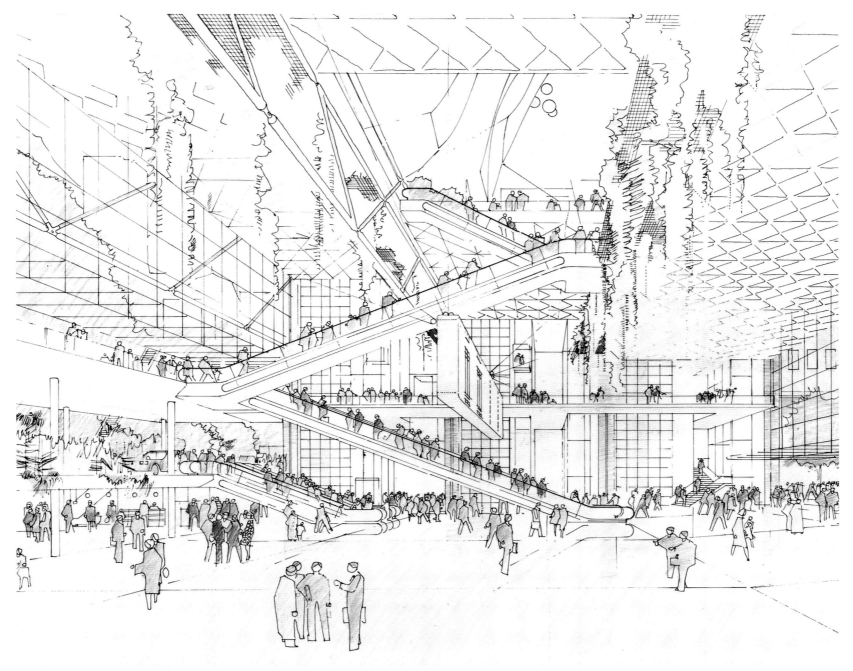

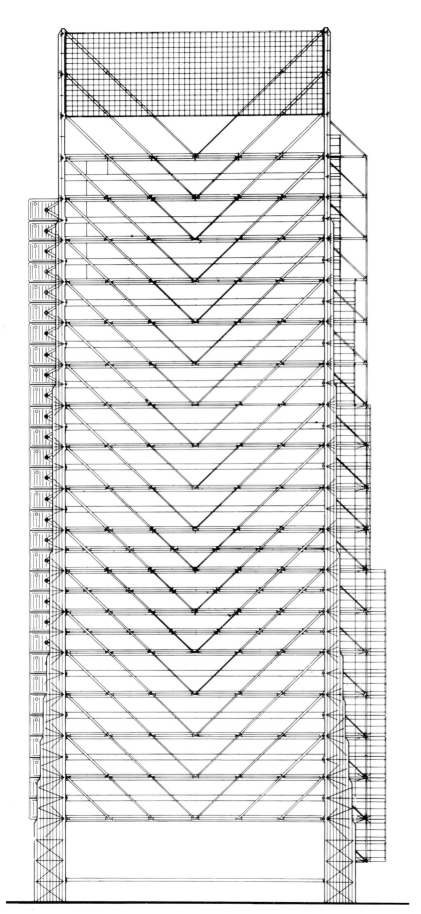

The first sketch elevation of the final scheme, with all the major elements clearly expressed. The service modules (on the left) are clamped to the building with short brackets, while the lift-shaft assembly (on the right) is suspended in a more formal frame. The lifts reduce in number over the height of the building but, curiously, are not shown reaching ground level.

In the final presentation drawing by Helmut Jacoby (left), the building towers over Statue Square like an ancient Chinese gateway. At night (right) the building takes on a dramatically different character, its open plan and full-height glazing creating a beacon of light in the heart of Hong Kong.

before the main board the reaction was at best mixed. Some members shared the chairman's enthusiasm, but it very soon became clear that there were fundamental objections and finally the scheme was rejected.

The real reasons for the board's dislike of the scheme are not entirely clear. Perhaps its members had expected a less radical reinterpretation of the Competition scheme. Perhaps they were worried by the intrusive diagonal structure. Or perhaps it was the external appearance of the building that disturbed them. Ironically, given the superficially Chinese aspect of the building, it was the Chinese members of the board who objected most strongly. And the reason they gave for their objection was that the downward-pointing chevrons would bring bad luck. To Western minds this is a baffling notion and in order to understand it, it is necessary to learn something about the Chinese philosophy of Fung Shui.

Colin Davies

A typical floor plan with one complete bay omitted. Alternative furniture layouts demonstrate that the raking tension members need not interfere with the plan.

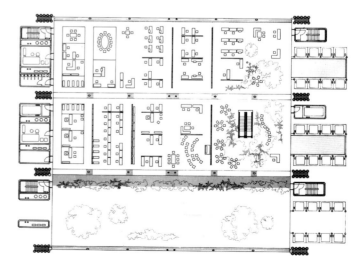

The basic simplicity of the concept is illustrated in this north/south presentation section. The spatial potential of the structural system is somewhat played down so as not to alarm but, even so, the Chevron scheme turned out to be too revolutionary for a basically conservative client.

As with the competition submission, a series of floor plans was prepared to show typical layouts in the new scheme. The reduction to three bays lessened the intrusion of raking structural members, leaving a clear floor area, further emphasised by removing all ancillary services to the sides of the building in clearly defined 'pods'. Vertical risers, lifts and stairs are continuous but other service modules are positioned to suit individual floor layouts. Below are shown a single-bay banking hall and a more typical office floor with central atrium.

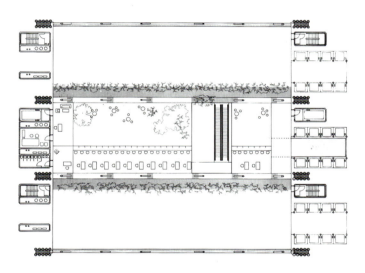

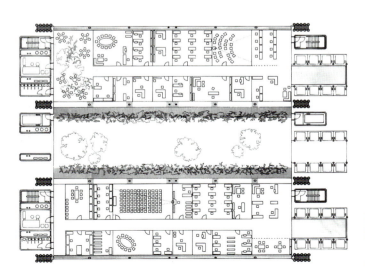

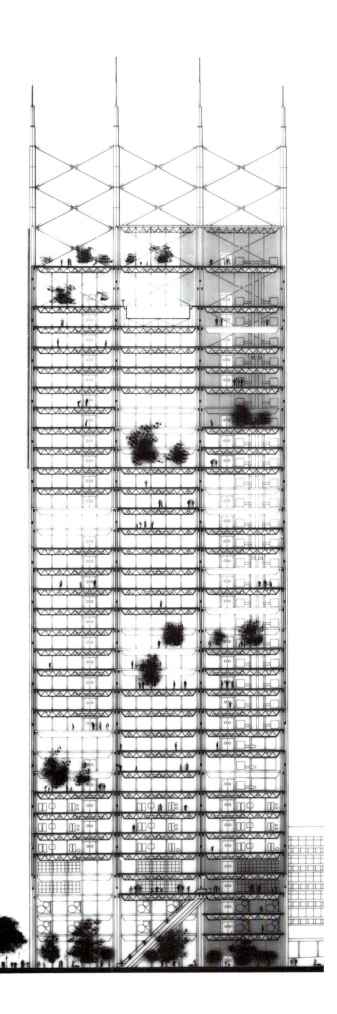

Hugh D. R. Baker is Reader in Modern Chinese at the University of London, where he teaches Mandarin, Cantonese and Chinese Social Institutions. He has carried out anthropological fieldwork in Hong Kong and China, and frequently visits both. Publications include: *A Chinese Lineage Village: Sheung Shui*, London and Stanford; *Chinese Family and Kinship*, London and New York; *Ancestral Images: a Hong Kong Album* (3 vols.), Hong Kong; *The Overseas Chinese*, London; and, with Y. L. Ng, *New Peace County: A Chinese Gazetteer of the Hong Kong Region*, Hong Kong.

Fung Shui
Applied Ecology Chinese Style

by Hugh D. R. Baker

The issue of the Japanese magazine, *Process Architecture — Foster Tower*, contains the following statement: "Foster's design for the Hongkong Bank building was influenced by a variety of sources outside the traditional building industry, from a Concorde design team to a Fung Shui expert." One wonders how many readers would have understood the reference to Fung Shui. What is it, and why should it influence an advanced design and engineering project?

Fung Shui is a Chinese term which translates literally as 'Wind and Water'. Nature is at the heart of Fung Shui, as the name implies, and its philosophical origins can be traced back to early Chinese ideas of the unity of man and nature. In the West there was the Pathetic Fallacy, where nature was invested with human emotions and was thought capable of reflecting man's moods; in China there was Fung Shui, where man did not influence but, rather, was influenced by nature. Fung Shui has been defined by J. J. M. de Groot as, "...a quasi-scientific system, supposed to teach men where and how to build graves, temples and dwellings, in order that the dead, the gods and the living may be located therein exclusively, or as far as possible, under the auspicious influences of Nature." It is not difficult to detect a note of scepticism in de Groot's writing, but other non-Chinese observers have been far more scathing. E. J. Eitel, writing in 1873, calls Fung Shui "a farrago of nonsense and childish absurdities".

Most Westerners, however sceptical, would probably agree that surroundings can have an influence on quality of life — a house at an airy location in a beautiful setting may be expected to have a happier resident than would a smoke-begrimed house next to a city cesspit. But Fung Shui goes much further. It says that a properly located house will not only make the residents happier, but that they will live longer, be healthier, have more sons, and get richer. It claims that the correct siting of a temple, a village, a government building, or an office can similarly affect those who worship, live or work there. And because Fung Shui is part of the Chinese religious system which includes ancestor worship, there is a great deal of emphasis on the correct siting of graves, so that ancestors and descendants alike can benefit from nature's good influence. No doubt it is this extension from the idyllic to the supernatural that makes Eitel describe Fung Shui as "the foolish daughter of a wise mother".

In theory all Fung Shui sites face south, and the direction in which a site faces is always thought of as south whatever the true direction may be. The back of the site, the north, is usually protected by a hill or grove of trees or even a high wall, all to keep the baleful north winds from sweeping over the site and dissipating the beneficial airs. The south is often called the Vermilion Bird, the north is the Black Tortoise, the west the White Tiger, and the east the Azure Dragon. A good site will take account of the position and comparative strengths of the physical landscape in each of these four directions. It is very necessary, for instance, to balance the White Tiger with a stronger Azure Dragon. This is because tigers are dangerous animals which are harmful unless under the control of dragons, the only beasts which can control them and turn their strength to good account. So if to the west there is a high hill, then it is necessary for there to be another hill at least as powerful-looking to the east.

Straight lines in the form of rivers or roads are much feared in Fung Shui because they are thought to be like arrows threatening the site, or else like drains running off all the beneficial influences. Perhaps even worse are those features of the landscape which cannot easily be seen by the untrained eye — they may all unsuspected be causing problems. Altogether Fung Shui is a very complicated business, much too complicated for the layman to comprehend and manipulate; and so there exists the need for the specialist to interpret, advise and locate. The specialist is called a Fung Shui Gentleman or, more correctly, a geomancer.

The geomancer needs little equipment other than a special compass set in the middle of a large number of concentric circles. Segments of the circles are marked off and identified by symbols, and he can interpret the significance of a site's alignment by reference to these. A client might be asking him to locate a new house in such a way that there will be sons born to the occupants, or perhaps that academic success will come to those who live there, and by choosing to face the house in a certain direction the geomancer will hope to maximise the required benefits.

Fung Shui is made more complicated by the fact that good sites are not easily found, and that when found they do not necessarily confer all-round benefits. A site might be good for creating wealth but poor at producing sons, or good for examination success but short on longevity. Moreover, the size of some sites is quite limited. Some excellent grave locations may only be able to take one or two sets of bones. Some building sites may only accommodate a small house, or perhaps a limited number of storeys. Even when a good site has been found, the slightest error in alignment can negate its beneficial effects — or even produce harmful ones — and later one of the surrounding features may change, thus destroying the good effects associated with it.

Fung Shui, then, is a belief that the environment can be tapped for the benefit of those who live, work or are buried in it. Because it is not easy to understand, it is necessary to have (paid) specialist help. Because the system is complex and fragile, it is easy to mismanage and constantly goes wrong. Because it affects everyone, it can be used not only to create good effects, but also to explain 'bad luck' or failure. Is your business going downhill? Blame it on grandfather's grave. Is your wife producing daughters instead of sons? It must be because the house has been built slightly out of line.

In one case in Hong Kong, a family were very distressed that a grave they had had expensively sited by a geomancer had failed to produce good effects. "Oh", said cynical friends, "you know geomancers: they only promise good effects after 70 or 80 years, by which time they have spent their fee and died!" A second opinion was sought. The second geomancer pronounced the site excellent, but said that the grave had been built six inches too low down the hillside, thus missing the vital spot where the benefits were located. In another case, two clans point proudly to the deserted ancestral hall of a third clan which has died out in the village: "We did

Before the lions were moved from their traditional place guarding the front of the 1935 headquarters, their temporary home in Statue Square was assessed by the geomancer, Koo Pak Ling, with the help of these cardboard representations.

On 1 June 1985, four years after their removal, the two bronze lions returned to the Queen's Road Central site. Koo Pak Ling was again present to ensure that the time of the move and their final position were the most propitious.

it by paying a geomancer to misalign a brick in the wall, and so we got rid of them!"

So Fung Shui can become a weapon in the hands of the aggressive or the ambitious. If your neighbour annoys you, you can go secretly to the graves of his ancestors and by cutting down a tree, or perhaps by diverting a stream, ruin his luck. If you want your business to succeed, ask a geomancer to site your office in such a way that it will give you an edge over your rivals. If you are jealous of your elder brother, get the geomancer to site your father's grave so that it benefits the number two son rather than number one, then you as second son will do better than he.

Fung Shui is not a moral system: it will work as well for the wicked as for the innocent. It could be called a philosophy of greed, for it plays a zero-sum game with the good in the landscape. That means that no-one can escape its influences, for there are bound to be evil people looking to monopolise good influences at the expense of others. And so there has to be defensive Fung Shui as well as offensive. Much activity is directed at making sure that other people are not scoring at your expense, and at warding off possible malign influences from inadvertent or unavoidable poor siting.

Many Chinese believe that the Fung Shui of Government House is what makes Hong Kong prosperous. Over a century ago Eitel reported: "Why, they say, there is Government House, occupying the very best spot on the northern side of the island, screened at the back by high trees and gently-shelving terraces, skirted right and left by roads with graceful curves, and the whole situation combining everything that Feng-shui (Fung Shui) would prescribe — how is it possible that foreigners pretend to know nothing of Feng-shui?" Governors of the territory do not comment, but their civil servants and their policies have been recognising the existence and power of Fung Shui for many years. When a new road is built in the rural areas, it is quite common for the government to pay large sums of money to local villagers as compensation for damage to Fung Shui. And when new government offices are built, it is not unknown for geomancers to be called in to help in planning the layout.

And so with the Hongkong Bank. A Fung Shui expert, Koo Pak Ling, was retained to advise on the plans long before they were implemented, and his specialist view was consulted at various stages of the project. He is not a designer or an architect, it was not his function to make the building 'look Chinese'. He was there to ensure that Fung Shui principles were not violated and that the siting, the construction, and the fitting out were as closely in harmony with the surroundings as possible. Norman Foster was so impressed by the importance placed on Koo Pak Ling's advice that he discussed the project with him during the design team's first visit to Hong Kong. Koo sketched his impression of the most favourable direction from which to enter the building — not directly from the front but angled to one side — advice that was followed through to the final design.

It was not his advice that caused the demise of the Chevron scheme, as the directors were sufficiently concerned by the symbolism of the downward pointing 'arrows' to raise their own objections, but he was on hand to oversee the positioning of the main escalators during their erection. Later, it was he who determined the position of the furniture in senior executive offices and who had potted trees and foliage strategically placed to hide areas of the interior which he found dangerous in Fung Shui terms. It was he who supervised the moving of the famous bronze lions from their place outside the main door of the old building to two carefully chosen temporary positions, and finally back to their posts in front of the completed tower. There they protect the fortunes of the Bank and, it is claimed, Hong Kong while bringing luck to any passer-by who touches them.

The site itself was not, of course, of his choosing, but it has proved itself (to the believer's eye at least) by the success of the Bank over so many years of operation from that same address. It stands in a direct line between Government House and the harbour, so it has a very powerful protective Black Tortoise composed of the Peak and the Governor. In front of it are the waters of the harbour, and water which cannot be seen to flow away is indicative of wealth in Fung Shui terms. Across the water are the Nine Dragon Hills of Kowloon, permanent markers of good fortune and a stately presence. To the east and to the west, White Tiger and Azure Dragon ridges sweep down to the harbour, cradling the Bank's site. No road points arrow-like at the building, for in front of it is Statue Square, and the main pedestrian way to the Bank runs alongside the Square and only then disgorges people at an angle towards the carefully aligned escalators.

All that sounds nonsensical to scientific ears, but there is an uncanny echo of much of it in that special issue of *Process Architecture* on the Bank project: "The strong influence of the surrounding topography in sheltering the site is apparent, particularly for winds from the south coming over the Peak. This is, of course, a direct reflection of the original reason for the founding of Hong Kong, whose sheltered harbour..." The geomancer and the research team of the Boundary Layer Wind Tunnel Laboratory of the University of Western Ontario seem to speak the same language, though perhaps one is a poet and the other has only plain speech.

Western interior designers go to great lengths to furnish space in ways which help relaxation or concentration, and they choose colours to harmonise with function. Chinese geomancers position desks, re-site doors and change colour schemes to harmonise with an overall view of man's place in his surroundings. The aim of both is similar: to tune the relationship between life and environment. The worker in the Bank where the office space has been passed as 'harmonious' by the geomancer feels better integrated with the company and its fortunes. Fung Shui may go beyond what Western rationalism can accept, but it is more than merely "a farrago of nonsense".

1980 Hongkong Bank
Transition

Eventually, the developing design was to return to a structural arrangement similar to that of the Competition scheme. Knowing this, it is hard to understand the turn that it took immediately after the rejection of the Chevron proposal. But if we reconstruct the state of play in mid-1980 we can perhaps begin to see why it was necessary to explore a completely new concept for the building.

The main purpose of the Competition had been to find the right architect, and the main purpose of Foster Associates' submission had been to secure the job. This done, the client had changed the brief, ruling out the possibility of retaining parts of the existing building — other than the annexe — and thereby negating the concept of 'phased regeneration' that had been central to the submission. Despite this, Foster had decided to retain the main features of his original design, in its 'final' form, believing that they remained valid. Pursuing the logic of the design, especially that of the tension structure, he had produced a scheme so revolutionary that it was almost a new kind of architecture. This had been rejected, probably because it was so revolutionary. But it was not just one scheme among many, it was the culmination of

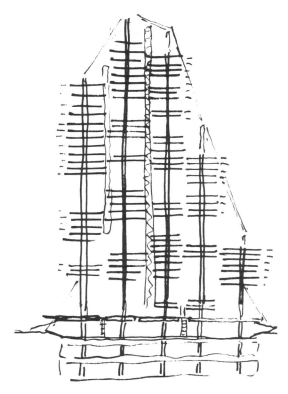

a long development process. That whole process had therefore been called into question. It was necessary to return to first principles and produce a radical alternative, if only to test the validity of the original strategy.

For the time being, everything had to go: bridge form, tension structure, laminated plan, open floors, served and servant zones, even the frontal relationship to Statue Square. The sketches from this time show a curious cluster of towers, relatively small on plan, rising to different heights. This came to be known as the Organ-pipe scheme. Each tower has a central column from which floors are cantilevered. The structural system has a parallel in the Renault Centre which was being designed in the Foster office at about the same time: the 'organ-pipes' are in many ways multi-storey versions of the structural 'umbrellas' proposed to support the roof of the Renault warehouse.

It might be argued that these towers are, in fact, 'kebab' structures, smaller versions of the kind of office block that the original design had implicitly criticised. But, whereas in a conventional office block the lifts and vertical services are enclosed by a concrete structural shaft, here they occupy the spaces between the towers. The concept therefore has a potential richness and complexity that the conventional office block lacks. Apart from a far more sculptural and picturesque external profile, the cluster form offers some exciting internal spatial possibilities. We can see how atria might be created by omitting floors and how these spaces might be juxtaposed in many different combinations: a new version of the idea of flexibility in section. But between this

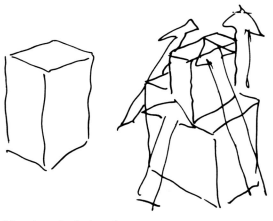

After the submission of the Competition scheme, Foster had introduced the idea of a stepped profile for the tower (page 148) but had not developed it. When the Chevron scheme was rejected by the client, he returned to the idea as a new starting point.

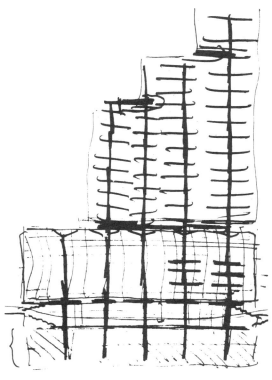

The Organ-pipe scheme proposes a cluster of 'kebab' towers. As these sketches demonstrate, it is additive and cellular rather than subtractive and linear, creating a building that can step back in any direction.

The structure of the Organ-pipe scheme is a multi-storey version of the centrally-supported 'umbrella' structure proposed for the Renault Distribution Centre in Swindon, which was being designed in the office at the same time.

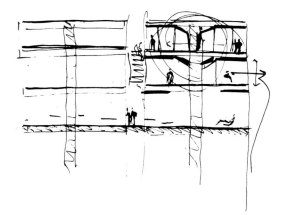

and either the Competition or Chevron schemes there are far more differences than similarities. It represents a complete change of direction.

What is it then that generates and justifies this curious form? For the answer it is necessary to go right back to the Competition submission. In that submission, the final building illustrated a simple box-like form. Its plan, however, with four structurally separate bays, had contained within it the possibility of a stepped profile, with each bay rising to a different height to maximise the potential of the site within the constraints of the planning regulations, particularly the shadow angles related to regulated light angles. From the earliest sketches of the Chevron scheme, it is apparent that Foster and his team were well aware of this possibility. In the event, however, it did not become a feature of the developed Chevron scheme. In fact, even the set-backs between the concrete towers on the east and west sides of the Competition proposals are precluded in the Chevron scheme by the stacks of service modules between the steel masts. Evidently it was assumed that it would

be possible to find a loophole in the letter of the planning regulations which, in any case, seemed to bear little relation to any real, visible effect that the building might have on daylight in the surrounding streets.

This then was a fundamental weakness of the Chevron scheme, and it was natural that Foster, clearing the decks on his return from Hong Kong after that disastrous board meeting, should make this the starting point for his re-think. The essentially linear nature of the design as developed so far meant that set-backs were always modifications to an essentially monolithic and complete form. They were, in short, a compromise, and Foster is a singularly uncompromising architect. The Organ-pipe scheme is his uncompromising answer to the set-back problem. Set-backs become the generator of the form, a form which is additive and cellular, rather than subtractive and linear; which

Open terraces at intervals in the height of the building had been a recurring idea throughout the development of the design. They appear in this sketch of the Organ-pipe scheme and were to be realised in the final design.

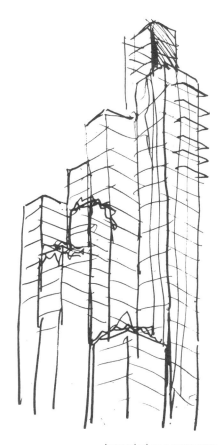

Intended as a response to planning regulations, the picturesque profile of the Organ-pipe scheme is not fundamental to its design, but is enjoyable nevertheless.

163

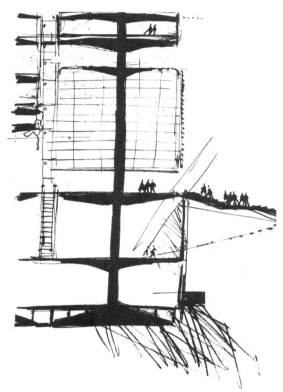

The scheme was never fully developed, but it is possible to see how atria might be created by omitting floors and how these spaces might be juxtaposed in different combinations. The structural system is carried through to the basements.

Organ-pipe scheme served to emphasise the positive qualities of the original strategy and to revive confidence in it.

But there was something else. The Organ-pipe scheme was not a dead-end, but an experiment which led to a positive result, for it unlocked a latent possibility in both the Competition and Chevron schemes: simply that the structural bays of the building might rise to different heights. When Foster begins once again to sketch a building similar to the Com-

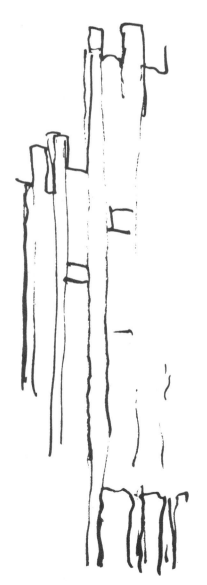

not only accommodates set-backs but would be meaningless without them. It was never fully developed, though models were made of it, including one representing it in context with the towers placed at an angle to the urban grain as if to emphasise its non-linear nature. In the event, though the scheme may have coped well with the set-back problem, in almost every other respect it had very serious drawbacks and was soon abandoned. (However, the principles of the Organ-pipe scheme were to be explored further in the much smaller Billingsgate redevelopment proposals which the office was to start only a few months later.)

It is no secret that the Organ-pipe scheme was unloved and much grumbled about by some of Foster's colleagues, who saw it as panic reaction and a complete loss of direction. To some extent this was valid, but it was also an important episode in the long saga, beginning with the Competition brief and ending with the final building. It was necessary to stand outside the main stream of the development process for a while in order to test it and confirm its validity. If nothing else, the negative aspects of the

As if to emphasise the cellular, as opposed to linear plan this model shows the towers placed at 45 degrees to the urban grid.

This sketch is faintly reminiscent of Sant' Elia's Citta Nuova project of 1914 — a powerful influence on architects of Norman Foster's generation.

164

The distinct modular form of the Organ-pipe scheme was taken up in the Billingsgate Market development, another office scheme that Foster Associates were working on at this time. There, the central support was omitted but the 'tartan grid' plan was retained, with the spaces between modules of floor being used as service and circulation zones. In this sketch of the Organ-pipe scheme, the elevations take on an almost conservative character, again a response to the client's rejection of the more dramatic Chevron scheme.

petition scheme, he draws not a stout box, but a slender stepped tower. At last the set-backs on the east and west sides of the Competition scheme have been combined with the north-south set-backs briefly explored, but not followed through, in the Chevron scheme. The missing link is now in place.

From this point on, the sketches begin to show what is obviously an early version of the Final scheme. All the strategic options have now been explored methodically in the approved Foster manner. One by one they have been set up and tested in a sort of theoretical version of the practical procedure that was later to be followed for the detailed design of the final building. Some, like the bridge form, the disposition of services, the suspension structure and the set-backs in both directions, have passed the test and survived. But there have been casualties. One of these has been the concept of flexibility in section: the idea that the building might be conceived as a set of adjustable shelves which can be shuffled around in random patterns creating a variety of spaces for a variety of activities. It was there in the Competition scheme and in the Chevron scheme, and even, in a sketchy form, in the Organ-pipe scheme. But it had to go.

Not that the building now emerging lacks spatial variety. It is still much more than just a stack of identical office floors. But atria and double-height spaces occur only at a few fixed positions, determined by the structural arrangement. The main trusses of the Competition scheme, which gathered the loads together at intervals in the height of the building, now reappear in a different form, no longer girder bridges but suspension bridges, or, as they came to be known in the Foster office, 'coat-hangers'. This has important structural advantages. Lateral stability in the north-south axis had been a major problem with the Chevron scheme, resolved only by continuous cross-bracing between the masts in that direction. But the new coat-hanger structure requires cross-bracing only in the main structural zones which, in effect, become rigid boxes. This allows greater scope for set-backs and greater freedom in the planning of the service zones. And, of course, the raking tension members now occur only within the few special structural zones, leaving the office floors less encumbered by structure.

Problems of construction would also be resolved by the new structure. The cantilevering nature of the trusses to east and west of the masts would allow the annexe to be retained, along the west edge of the site, until late in the construction programme. As the steelwork rose, the service modules, escape stairs and lift shafts could be suspended down over the roof of the annexe, only the lowest sections needing to be inserted, at a late stage, after the annexe's demolition. (In the event, the annexe was demolished before steelwork erection commenced to allow an earlier occupancy of the lower

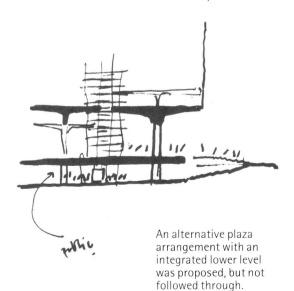

An alternative plaza arrangement with an integrated lower level was proposed, but not followed through.

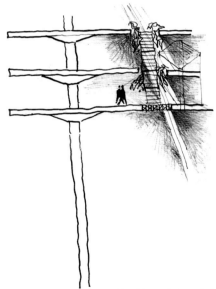

The idea of glazed floor zones between the main elements of the structure, first proposed in the Competition scheme, reappears in this sketch.

"Foster and his team were working on the other side of the world, in another culture with a simultaneously cosmopolitan and native face. In the end the building was not the creation of electronic international banking, nor a semi-colonial gift from an old power to a younger one; its design grew, more than anything else, from an unprecedented act of learning."

Martin Pawley, *Architectural Review*, April 1986

floors.) It was also becoming clear that the building would require a substantial basement zone — both for the Bank's main vaults and the extensive central services. Suspending the entire superstructure of the building from only eight masts would allow the main excavation work to be carried out after local excavation for the mast foundations had been completed. Erection of steelwork and basement construction could therefore be carried out simultaneously, allowing a significantly faster building programme.

Such benefits, however, form only part of the complex decision-making process of which particular proposal is better or worse. Such arguments were reassuring but it was the overall architectural quality of the project that was still the main concern of the design team.

From the point of view of spatial organisation, the important thing in the Final scheme is that whereas the 'bridges' had formerly been independent of the sectional arrangement of the floors, they now coincide with double-height spaces running right through the building. All

A return to the mainstream design development. This model of the so-called 'coat-hanger' scheme is seen in context, together with a proposal for a revised layout of Statue Square and the Star Ferry terminal.

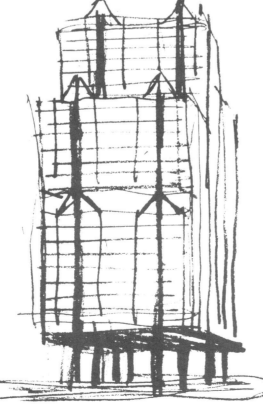

The Organ-pipe experiment has served its purpose. When Foster begins once again to sketch a building similar to the Competition scheme, he draws not a stout box but a slender stepped tower.

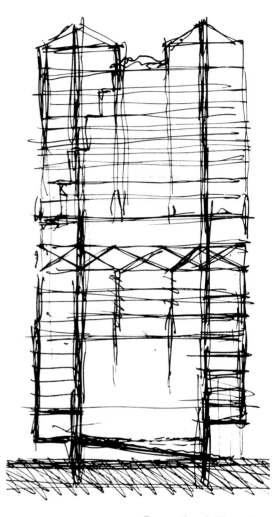

The sectional silhouette of the design begins to develop. The structure is confused but the central atrium is clear, with whatever it has lost in complexity and variety being gained in monumental scale and proportion. Set-backs also appear on the upper floors.

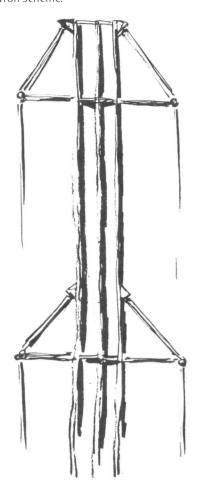

The structural form of the masts and coathangers was as yet largely undefined. This early sketch shows a distinct lineage from the Chevron scheme.

vertical zones which Foster will begin to think of as 'villages', each with its own social focus. Those first reactions to the multi-functional character of Hong Kong architecture have not been forgotten.

At the same time, the banking hall has also been simplified. The cathedral-like central space, created by simply omitting the lower floors in the middle structural bay, appears now for the first time. What it has lost in complexity and variety, it has gained in monumental scale and elegant proportion.

These are radical changes to the basic concept of the building, though they are easily overlooked because of their slight effect on its external appearance. The concept of a universal spatial system, capable of many different configurations in three dimensions, has given way to a single, specific arrangement. Space, form, structure and circulation are now locked into a fixed relationship. It only remains to feed the correct values into the equation.

other floors are single height. The reasons for this simplification are not entirely to do with the structure. The client had originally suggested that parts of the building might be let to other tenants. It was now becoming clear, however, that the Bank would be occupying the whole building. This put more emphasis on office space and reduced the need for the more simple single-storey varied spatial areas such as atria and mezzanine floors.

The double-height spaces will become the restaurants and recreation areas which Foster has regarded, ever since he designed the Willis Faber building in Ipswich, as essential to any civilised working environment. Later the social character of these spaces will be further enhanced when they become the interchange levels in a combined lift/escalator circulation system. The building is now divided into distinct

For the first time the sketches show a building that is unmistakably an early version of the Final scheme.

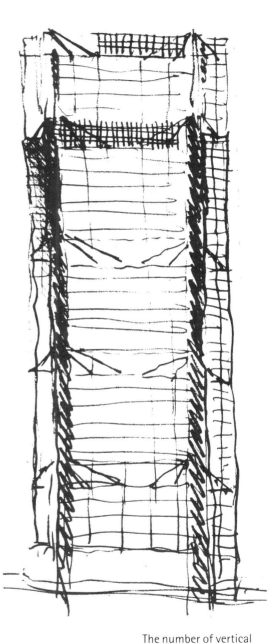

The number of vertical zones varies from sketch to sketch: here there are five zones, whereas in the sketch on the opposite page there are only three.

"The models show how such a building would look in the townscape, with large span spaces between towers of structure and movement, clusters of floors suspended from main beams, and the atria or gardens occurring in space up the building."

Norman Foster, lecture at Centre Pompidou, February 1981

In the first sketches of the new scheme the building had been divided into three vertical zones. Then two more were added so that the north, south and central bays of the plan now rise to four, three and five zones respectively. But there is still some way to go before the distribution of zones is finally fixed and one of the earliest montages, showing the building as seen from the harbour, indicates a four-zone tower. As usual, every possible option is being explored.

Meanwhile the structure is developing and changing as various ideas put forward by Foster Associates are analysed by Ove Arup & Partners. One visually subtle but structurally very important modification is the linking together of the twin coat-hangers from which the floors are suspended. This comes about because of the old problem of lateral stability. The separate coat-hangers are unable to resist 'racking' in an east-west direction. The problem is solved not by

This study model of the coat-hanger scheme assumes five equal vertical zones. Fine-tuning was still required to maximise usable floor area.

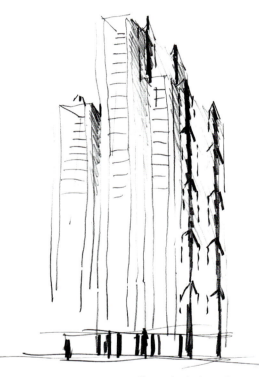

The articulation of service module and escape stair towers projecting between the set-back floors provided the opportunity to create a strongly sculptural effect on the east side of the building.

Faster than models, montages became a popular means of representing the various options that were now rapidly evolving as the Final scheme emerged. In this representation, the coat-hanger trusses remain but the Vierendeel mast structure appears, with the service and circulation towers suspended from the masts' sides.

168

"By working within the legislation of light angles it was possible to sculpt or articulate the form of the building and create a distinctive stepped profile of towers on the skyline. This was part of a conscious attempt to question the dumb-box of a typical high-rise monolith – visually as well as socially."

Norman Foster, *Process Architecture*, March 1986

The first representation of the final structural system, with the separate coat-hangers now meeting at the centre of the building to support a single vertical hanger. Without cladding, the steel frame seems almost too slender to support the 40-storey height of the building, now shown in four vertical zones. Module and lift-shaft towers also remain strongly articulated.

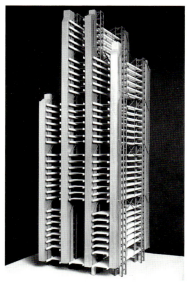

The first model of the scheme as built. The evolution from earliest sketch of the coat-hanger scheme to this stage was realised in less than four months of intensive collaborative effort by the whole design team.

providing cross-bracing between the coat-hangers, which would be visually and spatially disruptive, but by simply combining them to form something similar, in structural terms, to the straightforward trusses of the Competition scheme. In the execution of this solution, however, we are presented with a perfect example of the difference between an architect's and an engineer's view of structure. The extra horizontal member that forms the top, or compression boom, of the truss is hidden within the thickness of the floor and omitted on the column line exposed in elevation so as to maintain the appearance of a pure suspension structure.

It was now necessary to settle once and for all the relative heights of the three structural bays and the pattern of vertical division in the building in order to take full advantage of the allowable plot ratio within the limits imposed by the shadow regulations. Various alternative sections were measured and tested against the light angles. The breakthrough came with the realisation that it was not essential for all of the vertical zones to be equal. By varying the height of each stack of suspended floors the building could be taken right up to the limit. The north-south section was finally fixed at five zones, reducing from nine storeys at the bottom to five at the top. (One floor is omitted from the bottom section to create a double-height banking hall.) This progressive reduction from bottom to top also tends to enhance the effect of perspective, making the building look taller than it really is.

Shadow regulations are not exclusive to Hong Kong and there are many examples all over the world of buildings, on urban sites, which

A milestone in the development of the scheme. These drawings show the eventual solution to the vertical zones question. The breakthrough came with the realisation that the zones need not necessarily be of equal height. By reducing their height from eight storeys for the lowest zone to four storeys for the highest, the outline of the building could be extended right up to the limits allowed by the planning regulations.

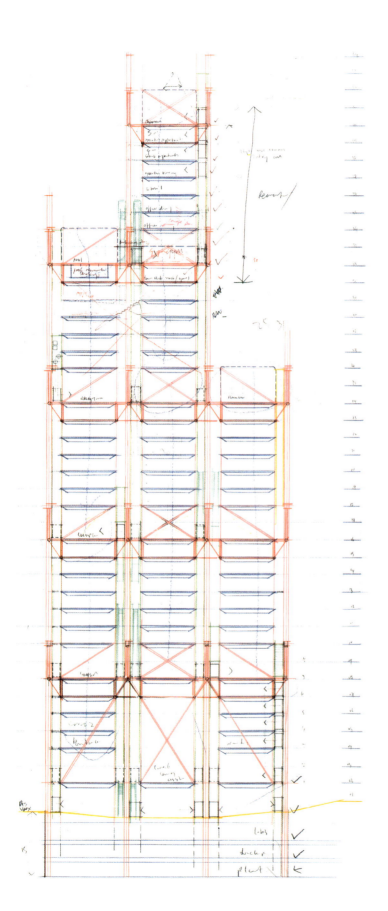

Five zones but of equal height, each being set at six storeys. While these studies progressed other issues were being resolved. A circulation zone for escalators appears between the floor bays. The central atrium had been determined for some time, but now a double-height banking hall is incorporated at its lowest level. At the top of the building, canopies are proposed where floor bays set back, with the higher of these enclosing a swimming pool.

One of the many studies made in resolving the problem of vertical zoning.

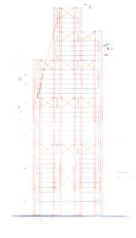

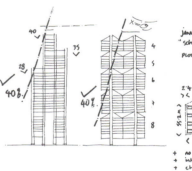

step back at their upper storeys. The Hongkong Bank, however, is rather different in that its complex silhouette arises as much from constructional and aesthetic considerations as from the necessity to conform to a set of arbitrary legislative requirements. The simple monolithic forms of the Competition and Chevron schemes have given way to a form which is essentially indeterminate. But this has become a positive architectural virtue rather than an ad-hoc accommodation.

A building that is conceived as an assemblage of prefabricated components implies the possibility that components might be added, or even subtracted, at some later date. It was always envisaged that, should the regulations

COMPETITION SCHEME TRIPLE CHEVRON MULTI CHEVRON COAT-HANGER FINAL SCHEME

The evolution of the structural system from Competition to Final scheme, but omitting the Organ-pipe detour.

The decision that the main masts of the building would be Vierendeel structures made up of four sub-columns — shown square in these early drawings — also resolved the precise location of the service towers. These could now be directly related to, and supported from, the main structure — access being possible through the masts. Rising services pass up the sides of the 'towers' on each side of the primary support structure, while on-floor services are supplied beneath a raised floor.

ever be relaxed, the set-backs between the masts on the east side, overlooking the narrow road known as Bank Street, might one day be filled in to provide valuable additional floor space. (An extra 15 per cent of office floor can, in fact, be added in this way.) After all, though the set-backs conform strictly to the letter of the planning law, their actual effect on the level of daylight in Bank Street is almost imperceptible. The complex, indeterminate form is therefore a clear architectural expression of the kit-of-parts concept and of the idea that a building should be capable of adapting itself to changing circumstances.

By now the concept of a column-free plaza at ground level is also firmly established. The logic of the bridge form of the building has been followed through to allow public space to flow under the bridge, uninterrupted by any entrance lobby or structural support. The building's 'footprint' has been reduced to the smallest possible area. Apart from its spatial and conceptual advantages, under Hong Kong's planning regulations — which have been specifically designed to encourage more public space — this had the effect of increasing the allowable plot ratio of the building from 15:1 to 18:1 — an increase guaranteed to put smiles on the faces of the client's property advisers.

As the Final scheme had developed, it had become apparent, from the structural engineers' analysis, that the eight masts which supported the whole building were going to be very massive indeed. Each, therefore, now becomes a composite element with four sub-columns — square in section at this stage — arranged in a square and linked together by rigid horizontal members at regular storey-height intervals. This is what engineers call a Vierendeel structure. Not only is this one of the most economic structural solutions, but it has definite benefits for the organisation of the plan since it is now possible to walk through the masts. Whereas in the Chevron scheme the service modules and escape stairs were placed between the masts — effectively precluding any set-backs on the east side — they can now be placed in line with the masts and still be accessible from the main floor area.

The basic elements of the plan are now fixed, with lift shafts and lobbies between the masts on the west side, and open areas of floor, set back where necessary, between the masts on the east side. Service modules alternate with escape stairs on each side of the building. This pattern was later to be altered, but from now on the module and stair service 'towers' are always in line with masts.

By the end of 1980 the development of the Final scheme had reached the point of no return. In the drawn record, free-hand sketches give way to careful explorations of the detailed technical consequences of strategic decisions. The structural frame, everywhere exposed to view, is steadily refined. Columns and tension members become round rather than square in section for this is steel and it must look like steel: a powerfully expressive, organic structure of steel

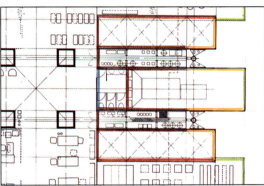

The arrangement of service tower and riser zones is now established, though the alternative stair/module pattern would be modified in the Final scheme. Lift shafts are no longer separate towers but are incorporated into the secondary floor structure on the building's west side.

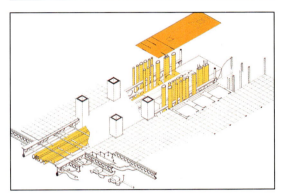

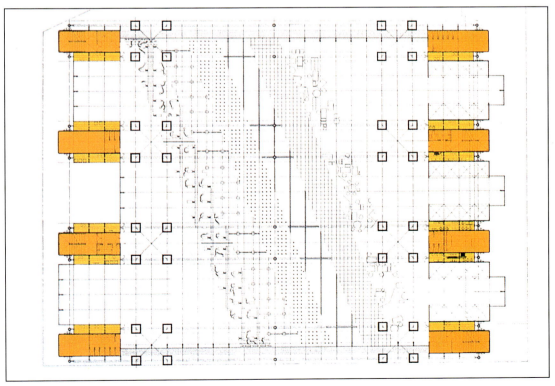

171

Vierendeel 'beams' connect the four columns that make up each mast at regular storey-height intervals. Their form and location were studied in a series of sketches, based on the assumption that the main service runs would pass through the masts tending to push the Vierendeels down into the office space. The characteristic 'bow-tie' silhouette evolved as a natural reflection of the forces acting within them.

Representations prepared to demonstrate the Final scheme to the Hongkong Bank board included this drawing (left) by Birkin Haward and a new model (right) set into the context of Statue Square, the Star Ferry terminal and harbour.

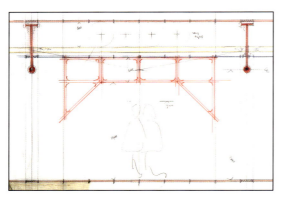

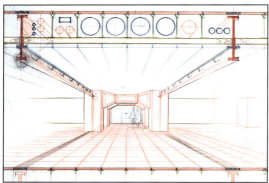

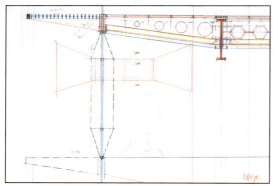

At the edge of the building, the soffit angles upwards to increase the area of glass and, consequently, daylight entering the building. A sunshade appears. The intrusion of the Vierendeel beams remains unresolved.

Jan Kaplicky's detail section assumes a highly expressive character for each element: even the now tubular structure changes size in response to the loads on it. External trusses are introduced to support the glazing and the service zone beneath a raised floor is further emphasised.

bones, muscles and tendons. The fireproofing problems have yet to be solved, but for the time being the steel is shown exposed — possibly water-filled, possibly sleeved in a thin layer of insulation that will not hide its characteristic profiles. External walling also begins to appear on the detailed sections and it is clearly going to be a complex assemblage of structural mullions like vertical trusses, perforated steel brackets, and louvres to filter the tropical sun.

Right from the start, the floors of the building had always been more than just flat surfaces on which to walk: they had also been part of the services distribution system. It was now time to make a realistic assessment of the space required for trunking, pipes, cables and light-fittings so that the floor-to-floor heights and the exact relationship of the floors to the Vierendeels could be fixed.

Over a period of several decades the typical office floor has gradually evolved into a multi-layered sandwich by the addition of more and more services above and below a basic structural slab. First there were light-fittings, followed by heating pipes, air-conditioning ducting, sprinkler systems, smoke detectors and so on, with a suspended ceiling to hide them all. For a long time the problem of wiring was effectively ignored by architects who happily sank the conduit into a cement screed on top of the slab and forgot about it. But then came the information technology explosion and wiring began to demand its own layer in the sandwich. Floors of removable panels raised off the structural slab to form a clear void for cables began to be used, not just for computer rooms but for whole floors. Foster and his in-house services expert Loren Butt were among the first to specify raised floors throughout a building — the headquarters for Willis Faber & Dumas in Ipswich — with dramatic effect on its efficiency as a flexible support system for the modern electronic office.

By the time the floors of the Hongkong Bank were being considered in detail, it seemed that the only layer in the sandwich that might possibly be dispensed with was the structural slab itself. In the detailed drawings from late 1980, it is clear that the design of the floor-as-duct is being considered afresh. Ideas which were tentatively suggested in the Competition and Chevron schemes are now being explored in earnest. It is no longer simply a question of leaving enough space for the services: mere co-ordination of structure and services — an essential task in the design of any highly-serviced modern building — has become true integration. Every factor affecting the design is taken into account, including flexibility, accessibility and the scope for factory production.

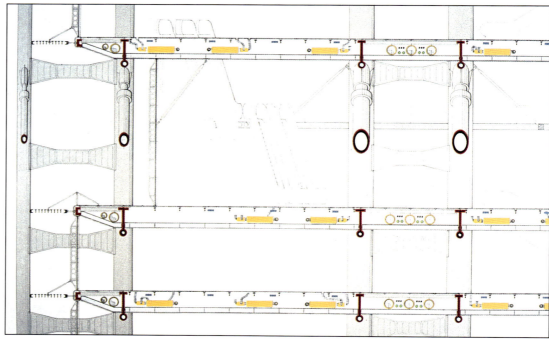

The basic idea is that all the services should be accommodated in a single, fully accessible void. Though the design was to change quite radically at a later stage, this basic idea survived.

All this development work was incorporated into a set of detailed presentation drawings. In them we can see some new features, such as elegant canopies over garden terraces at the set-backs, a helicopter landing-pad on the roof and, most important, a three-storey basement which houses a public banking hall, vaults and the main cooling plant.

Foster Associates had set up a Hong Kong office in January 1980 in order to work through the details of the brief with the client. In August 1980, the chairman of the Bank had seen a preliminary version of the Final scheme for the first time. The reaction had been positive and as the time approached when the finished scheme would be put before the main board the mood in the Foster office was one of quiet confidence. One reason for this was that, in pure real-estate terms, the building represented excellent value for money. The area of usable floor was the maximum that could possibly be accommodated on the site. Foster had beaten the property men at their own game and, in the process, had produced not a dull speculator's tower, but a revolutionary work of architecture.

Steel suspension structure, lift/escalator circulation system, plug-in pods, underfloor services, thoroughgoing prefabrication, ground-level public plaza: almost nothing in the design could be described as 'conventional' or 'tried and tested'. Bear in mind also that the building was to be built in a colony with no indigenous heavy industry so that everything would have to be shipped in; that Foster Associates had never worked outside the UK, let alone on the other side of the world; and that this was their first tall building. It was no doubt a great comfort to know that Ove Arup & Partners, one of the largest engineering practices in the world, was on the team. Nevertheless, it was a daring proposal and for many architects its realisation would have been a frightening prospect.

In January 1981 the scheme was presented to the board, which was suitably impressed and duly gave its approval. There was no going back now. It was going to be built.

Colin Davies

A full section of the Final scheme, as presented to the client in January 1981. Only one major modification has still to be made: the escalators are shown cutting diagonally across the main floor zones. In the final design they are in line with the masts.

"But now here we have Foster and his team producing an advanced technology building in which there is hardly a single component that has not been tailor-made for the job, and with machine-made precision. There is repetition, yes. But when you go to a manufacturer and tell him to make something for your building that he has never made before for any other building, and will probably never make quite the same way again, then you are not talking about standardisation. The only proper word to describe the sort of care and finesse involved in the making of purpose-made 'High-Tech' architecture such as this is craftsmanship."

Chris Abel, *Architectural Review*, April 1986

The top of the building in elevational silhouette and illustrating the transparency of space that the structural form achieves. The air-handling modules, with their own air intakes and extracts at the rear, are seen rising on the west side of the building. On the east, the structural frames of the escape stair towers are complete, with their raised lift-motor rooms in place. The independent floors, supported by the inverted truss atop the main masts, will contain VIP reception suites and ancillary plant.

"It is customary in Hong Kong to employ a local contractor using Chinese labour to carry out erection, and the British Steel/Dorman Long consortium saw no reason to do otherwise. Subcontractor Argos Engineering has an excellent workforce, especially welders. They have taken readily to producing site welds of an extent, size and quality never before attempted while working at dizzy heights above Hong Kong's streets."

Kenneth Brown, *Construction News*, October 1983

Notched and slotted plates provided a good 'first fit' for each mast section as it was lowered into position. Long bolts, through temporary plates, then formed a secure fixing of the section until it could be wedged and eased into its accurate location and welded up.

The last column sections of the main steel frame being lifted into place. These are intermediary sections of the highest suspension truss at level 41/42 and were the only column sections lifted during the day.

A section of mast being lowered into place at night.

"The job was probably the biggest in man-hours, if not in tonnage, since construction of the Sydney Harbour Bridge in 1924 — and that too was constructed by Dorman Long."

Kenneth Brown, *Construction News*, October 1983

For all the sophistication of the pin-joints, insertion of the pins themselves was achieved only with intense effort, a large block of wood and not a little brute force.

The masts arrived on site in 'quartered' sections with each column connected to its halves of Vierendeel beam. The sections, usually two storeys high, were known as 'Xmas trees'. For the greater accuracy required by the pin-joints at truss levels, those sections of mast with truss connection plates were lifted in individual short sections. The columns that make up the masts reduce in diameter over the height of the building, stepping down at level 4 and every suspension truss level.

At the base of the building, the columns are 1.4 metres in diameter with wall thicknesses of up to 100mm; the topmost sections have reduced to 800mm diameter with a 40mm wall. The main steel frame had to be positioned within plan tolerances of plus/minus 40mm. Erection of the entire structure was achieved with the top sections of each mast no more than 11mm out of position.

The site's central location and limited access restricted the arrival of large loads until after midnight. All major steelwork was consequently lifted in the early hours of the morning; eight 'Xmas trees' forming two complete mast sections being lifted on alternate nights, three times a week.

Intrepid 'top-men' eased the huge truss members into position by hand.

"The new Bank building was conceived as clusters of layered space, suspended bridge-like from vertical masts with service 'cores' on the outboard edges. These cores were built off-site in a factory by a labour force who were not normally associated with the construction industry. They were then shipped to the site and clipped on to the building as sealed modules, already fitted out down to the last detail of soap dispensers and taps. Quality had been controlled in factory conditions and, by being able to work simultaneously on and off site, the overall time-scale for the project was dramatically reduced."

Norman Foster, *Process Architecture*, March 1986

The east elevation with its deep cutbacks revealing the sequence of module/stair/stair/module 'towers' each flanked by their own service risers. Like the modules, these risers were prefabricated in Japan and installed as semi-complete units in three-storey high frames.

"To explain how an undertaking of such magnitude could be achieved within so short a time span is clearly beyond the scope of this article but four principles can be identified as fundamental to that achievement. First, the site would be more an assembly point than a building site in the traditional sense. Second, the building would be conceived and produced as prefabricated elements, manufactured around the world and then shipped or air-freighted to the assembly point. Third, if industries outside the traditional sphere of the construction industry could offer a better performance then we would attempt to harness their skills and energies. Finally, we would actively collaborate with industry, using mock-ups and testing prototypes to anticipate, as far as possible, the eventual realities on site."

Norman Foster, *Process Architecture*, March 1986

The atrium under construction. This view, looking west, shows the three-storey high cross-bracing in position, with the link bridges and support structure for the lift shafts beyond.

Bamboo groves are common all over Asia, with certain species growing up to 20 metres in height. Properly maintained and soaked regularly to stop them drying out, the cut poles can last for many years.

"I think the contrast of technology is interesting. The bamboo scaffolding for example: I don't think it would be possible to realise this building without that indigenous bamboo scaffolding – which erupts everywhere – any more than it would without the cranes by which it erects itself."

Norman Foster, lecture to Sainsbury's Executive Club, March 1984

Bamboo works in tension just as effectively as in compression, so hanging or cantilevered structures can be erected with ease. Here, framing is supplied to the steelwork to provide access for the final application of corrosion and fire protection.

Traditional raffia ties may have given way to nylon straps, but in all other respects the techniques of bamboo scaffolding have not changed for hundreds of years. It is a craft based on experience, handed down from generation to generation in close-knit family businesses.

The flexibility of bamboo allowed localised structures to be erected almost anywhere, cantilevering from the exterior of the building by up to two metres.

Tied securely to the building over its height, it is not uncommon, in Hong Kong, to see bamboo providing continuous scaffolding over 40 or 50 storeys.

"The scaffolding is traditional bamboo which is more efficient than any more recent scaffolding; it withstands hurricanes, it goes up faster and more cheaply. It is one of the few true vernaculars in Hong Kong."

Norman Foster, lecture at Centre Pompidou, February 1981

The special rigs used to install the cladding panels could not extend to the highest extremities of the building, so bamboo had to be used instead. Shown here is the top of the east-side mast and stair tower at level 41.

The final coat of paint was applied to the jib of the maintenance cranes, at the top of the building, on location. A free-standing bamboo structure was raised over 10 metres from the open terrace below to provide access.

A temporary steel 'floor' was installed at level 11 over the central atrium to provide a work platform during installation of the bank of mirrors that form the inner 'half' of the sun scoop. It also supported this impressive bamboo structure — which was only in place for a few weeks — used to fix the ceiling panels and beam casings that line the atrium's soffit.

"The means of production were already an integral part of the set of presentation drawings approved by the Bank in 1981, otherwise it would have been impossible to translate them into more than a million square feet of built space by 1985."

Norman Foster, *Process Architecture*, March 1986

"We placed 6 000 000 cubic centimetres of weld on site with our Chinese welders. We had 49 welders as against the 150 that British Steel wanted to use. We placed that under very difficult conditions, yet we achieved a failure rate of only 0.75% – as against 3% in factories in the UK. We were producing three times more weld per man per day for one quarter of the problems: it gives you some measure of what can be achieved in Hong Kong in terms of the rate of production for buildings."

Ray Guy, lecture at the Burrell Museum, January 1986

December 1983. Erection of steelwork had commenced 11 months earlier, on 3 January 1983, with the preparation of the completed foundation heads at the lowest basement level, 19 metres below ground. 10-metre diameter 'access' caissons allowed steelwork erection to commence while the basements were still being excavated. Requiring absolute accuracy in alignment and setting out, steelwork did not emerge from the access caissons until mid-April. The first truss level was completed in September. Three months later, erection of the second truss has just commenced.

February 1984. With the completion of each suspension truss level, secondary fit-out of the structural zone it supports would commence. The escape stairs and modules arrived as completed elements, capable of spanning between the main masts and outer hangers, and were installed in parallel with the application to the steelwork of corrosion and fire protection. Cladding followed with the first panels being fitted to the building on 23 January 1984.

April 1984. The third suspension truss level is complete and steelwork is now advancing rapidly. Positioning of modules and escape stairs is completed at the second structural zone and cladding erection is settling into its steady routine of one complete floor a week. Inside the building, the first of the 50 escalators to be installed within the superstructure has been lifted into place and preparation is under way for the setting-out of the subfloor services.

June 1984. Apart from positioning of the outer hangers and erection of the special structure that tops the building out, primary steelwork is now complete. Over the 20 months of steel erection, some 27 000 tonnes of structural steelwork were lifted and positioned, requiring at the peak of construction the delivery of 300 tonnes of steel to site every day. The largest individual element weighed 46 tonnes.

Silhouetted against the evening sky and lights and hills of Kowloon, the topmost, pin-jointed suspension truss is seen here complete. Though rarely used on buildings, pin-joints were favoured for this project as the size of the loads – as much as 2000 tonnes in some members – made bolted connections impractical, being far slower to complete and creating a much bulkier joint profile. This, however, required extraordinary tolerances to be achieved during the manufacture of individual elements with the radial spherical plane bearings, that form the pin-joints, being positioned to within plus/minus 6mm. The pins themselves have a tolerance of +0 −0.25mm to ensure a glove-tight fit.

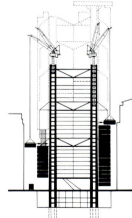

A diagram explaining how cranes attached to the main masts allowed the building to erect itself.

23 June 1984. The structure and cranes are silhouetted against the early morning mist. With the topmost outer hangers now in place, the main structure of the building is complete and the first of the six cranes is being dismantled. (This can be seen second from the left without its jib.) The cranes themselves had been purpose-built to a very compact design that ensured that each could work quite independently of its neighbour. The cranes were supported inside the mast as it grew. Once the mast was complete, the crane's central support was replaced by a special frame attached only to the top of the mast, allowing work on the steel structure to be completed.

"I think there are a lot of misunderstandings about the use of industrial processes related to architecture. Once upon a time it did lead to standardisation because that was the only way in which you could harness industry on any scale. I think the breakthrough came with the introduction of computer-controlled robotic tools that give the scope to customise individual projects to an extraordinary degree of richness very economically."

Norman Foster, lecture at Aspen Design Conference, June 1986

August 1984. Work on site is now at its peak with over 4500 people on site. Steelwork is still being erected at the top of the building while at the lower levels subfloor services are in place and the raised floor panels are being positioned. Installation of the suspended ceiling will commence in a few weeks. Basement construction was completed in April, and assembly of the main services in those areas is now well advanced, as is fitting out of the vaults. Installation of the main vault door is under way as it had to be lowered into place before construction of the plaza level had been completed.

October 1984. The last service module had been lifted into place at the top of the building on 14 September. Four days later, the main plaza escalators were positioned at the building's base. Practical completion of the steelwork has been achieved and erection of the cladding continues smoothly. In all, around 3500 tonnes of aluminium were to be used in the production of the cladding which covers a total of 93 000 square metres of structural steel, modules, risers and lift shafts. A further 32 000 square metres of glass was required to complete the weather-tight skin.

January 1985. The external hoists are being dismantled to allow completion of the cladding at the lower levels of the building where fit-out is now well advanced. The first of 23 passenger liftcars will not be installed until March, but all will be in place by the end of June in time for the Bank to take possession of the first phase. This includes the main banking hall and offices surrounding the atrium, and the planthalls, vaults and public reception areas in the basement. All these open to the public on 30 July. Official handover of the completed building will be celebrated in November with the official opening following five months later, on 7 April 1986.

The completed building photographed, at dawn, from the Star Ferry terminal at the end of Statue Square.

"By breaking up the building into distinct spatial units, Foster sought not only to avoid the monotony of looking up at nothing but identical storeys, but also – more importantly – to introduce a sense of identity to the main operational functions of the Bank. The vertical breakdown into blocks of floors, or villages as Foster likes to call them, therefore lends a spatial focus to the principal organisational divisions within the headquarters: local main branch operations down near street level; electronic data processing further up; then international operations and senior executive offices; and finally special services and the chairman's apartment on the uppermost floors. A smaller, streamlined block of VIP dining rooms with a helicopter pad on the roof tops the building out.
 In between these units, the upper three double-height zones accommodate the larger communal facilities, such as staff dining and conference rooms. Setbacks at each of these levels have the effect of emphasising the breakdown on the outside of the building, as well as serving as refuge terraces in the event of fire."

Chris Abel, *Architectural Review*, April 1986

1980 Hongkong Bank
Final Scheme

Structure: eight massive masts, supporting trusses like suspension bridges at five levels, from which the floors are suspended.

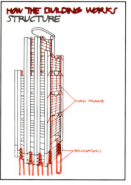

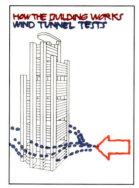

Staff movement: a combination of mainline lifts to the double-height floor levels and local escalators to the floors in between.

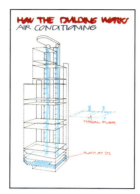

Air-conditioning: localised air-handling plant in container-size modules at each level serves the occupied space via ducts in the floor.

Wind tunnel tests: an essential precaution in typhoon-prone Hong Kong. Special provision must be made to shelter the public plaza at ground floor level.

Customers: the banking hall is a high central atrium accessible from the public plaza via a pair of escalators.

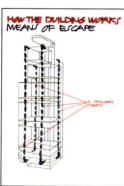

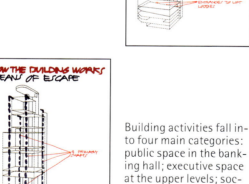

Building activities fall into four main categories: public space in the banking hall; executive space at the upper levels; social spaces in the double-height zones; and general office space on the floors in between.

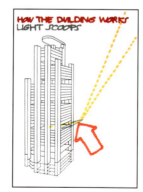

Light scoops: daylight and sunshine brought into the central atrium and public plaza by a computer-controlled periscope arrangement.

Means of escape: four fire escape staircases with 'refuge floor' terraces at the double-height floors to comply with local regulations.

Client approval for the Final scheme was given at the beginning of 1981, and, immediately, the 18-month investment in methodical trial and error began to pay dividends. Within a few months the design team, working smoothly and efficiently on the development of a basic concept no longer subject to possible fundamental re-thinks, had produced a set of drawings showing a complete and clear representation of the building as built. Every option had been explored and tested so that detail design decisions could be taken rapidly and with complete confidence. It had become clear, for example, that water cooling of the steel structure would not be accepted as a practical proposition by Hong Kong's Building Ordinance Office. The steelwork would have to be insulated against fire by some other means and then clad, preferably in a closely-tailored aluminium 'glove'.

Meanwhile final adjustments were also being made to the plan. When the Bank was first completed many architects and critics saw the system of circulation by combination of lift and escalator as its most important innovation. Foster, they said, had re-invented the office block, not just technically but spatially. And yet, as the history of the development of the design shows, the circulation system was slow to reach its final logical form. Even in the drawings presented to the client in January 1981 (see page 173), the escalators are shown cutting diagonally across the main floor zones. In the final design they occupy the intermediate zones, in line with the masts. This final adjustment is one of those design ploys which looks obvious only with the benefit of hindsight.

Everything has now fallen into place. Space, function, structure and circulation coincide to form a single, coherent pattern. The intermediate zones, originally introduced for reasons to do with structure and services distribution, take on a new function as circulation routes, not just on plan but also in section. The double-height spaces, the gathering points of the tension structure, are now gathering points in a more literal sense: they function as interchanges between mainline lifts and local escalators; as social and recreational spaces quite different in character from the working office floors between; and as fire-escape 'refuge floors'. Hong Kong regulations require tall buildings to be provided with protected areas

Whether in the Eiffel Tower or the Bradbury building in Los Angeles, early 'elevators' delighted in expressing their movement with exposed machinery and open views. Norman Foster proposed that the Hongkong Bank enjoy the same drama, with glazed lift-cars in glass-sided shafts.

at intervals in their height to allow people escaping from the building to rest in their long descent and, if necessary, change to an alternative staircase. In the Bank, the double-height zones are provided with automatic two-hour fire-resistant shutters on the glazing line and at the escalators, so as to seal off the external refuge areas and compartmentalise — because of the continuous escalators — an otherwise single-volume building. These various functions of the double-height spaces reinforce each other in a way that transforms the character of the building. It is indeed a new kind of office block.

The lift/escalator system offers some quantifiable benefits; it halves the number of lifts required and produces a marginal increase in usable floor area. But its main benefits are spatial and social. The conventional multi-storey office block is spatially monotonous, repetitive and fragmented. The fourth floor is

The overall form of the building is clearly established in this section which includes an option for the top of the building. The escalators now align with the masts, but are shown in an early arrangement which assumed the lift arrival point at each double-height space would be at a mezzanine level. Except for the special condition at the top of the atrium (level 12), this was not carried through.

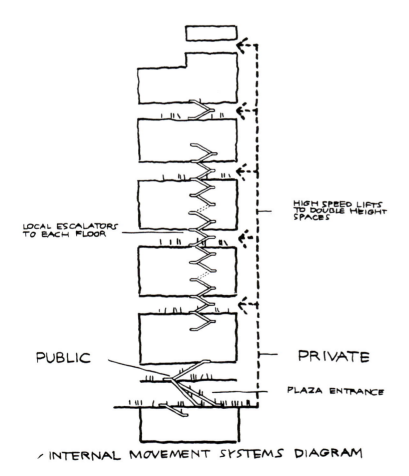

INTERNAL MOVEMENT SYSTEMS DIAGRAM

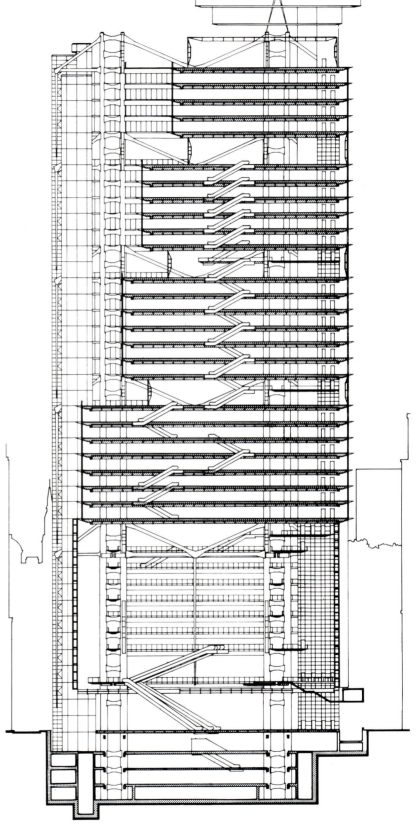

The transparency of the building – and an alternative escalator layout – is illustrated in this 1:200 scale model.

Towards the end of 1982, as the final details of the design were being resolved, the decision was taken to assemble a detailed 1:100 scale model. Primarily a study exercise for design team and client alike, the model was later exhibited at MOMA in New York.

April 1981. By the standards of later models this 1:500 version is merely a sketch. Finishes are approximate and there is no colour.

The first detailed model was completed in August 1981 at 1:200 scale. Unlike the earlier model, the structural frame was now clad and coloured to startling effect, but as yet there was no top to the building.

April 1982 and this second 1:200 scale model includes a slightly uncomfortable-looking circular helicopter pad and viewing gallery. Chinese red is still being considered, but for mullions rather than structure, and mirror glass is shown.

Models were an essential tool in the design development process, helping the architects to understand fully the implications of their design decisions and then to explain these decisions to the client and consultants. Over the 15 months of refinement carried out on the Final scheme, five models of the whole building were made, four of which are shown here.

much the same as the 40th and the journey from one to the other is not a journey at all, but simply a period of time spent in a windowless cubicle. Right from the start Foster had wished to break out of this spatial strait-jacket. At first it seemed that the atrium might be the answer. By the early 1980s the atrium had become the standard architectural device for the unification of internal space in multi-storey buildings. Foster himself had made an important contribution to the development of the form in the Willis Faber & Dumas building with its top-lit central space and cascading escalators. In the Competition and Chevron schemes there are explorations of the idea with smaller atria distributed throughout the height of the building. In the final design the atrium form is used only once, in the dramatic 13-storey cathedral-like space of the banking hall.

The Willis Faber building provided the precedent but it was its escalators rather than its atrium that suggested the solution. By dispensing with dispersed atria and simply weaving escalators up through the office floors, making them a part of the everyday circulation system

Outdoor photography required the strategic location of steadying hands to ensure valuable models were not inadvertently knocked or blown over.

"When a model of the Hongkong Bank appeared in an exhibition of skyscrapers at New York's Museum of Modern Art earlier this year, its poised elegance wiped the floor with all-comers. Not surprising, therefore, to find that Michael Graves, currently the darling of the East Coast avant-garde and author of a bizarre series of wilfully eclectic fantasies, should feel the need to counter-attack with a claim that he would rather practise law than have to design architecture like Foster's."

Deyan Sudjic, *The Sunday Times*, June 1983

Practically as built, the 1:100 scale model from November 1982.

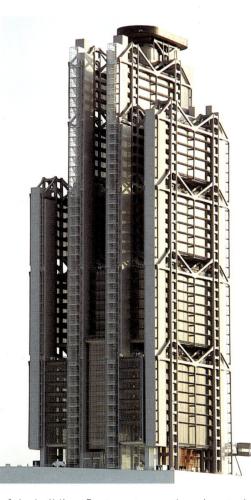

Far from being a mere showpiece, a detailed model provides an excellent focus, forcing the design team to really understand the inherent three-dimensional complexities of a design, often so easy to underestimate in drawings alone. Even the act of briefing a model-maker throws up areas of difficulty that then require a solution. The process, however, demands a high level of detail. The design of the 1:100 model was a project in itself, relying on close collaboration with a talented team of model-makers to find ways of achieving the most realistic results.

of the building, Foster sets an otherwise static space in motion. And in so doing he introduces a social dimension by making possible the chance encounter, not in the lift (that most unconvivial of all spaces where eye contact is practically forbidden), but on the open floors where there is space to pause and acknowledge. Occupants of nearby floors become neighbours and each stack of floors, between the double-height spaces, becomes, as the current cliché has it, 'a village in the sky'.

 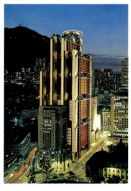 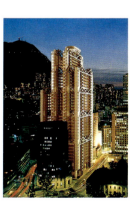

For an early presentation to the Bank, a montage was prepared showing the first 1:500 model 'stripped' into a real photograph of Hong Kong. It proved so successful that subsequent models underwent the same treatment.

The design of the top of the building presented the designers with a conundrum: how to terminate an essentially indeterminate form? The decision to combine a helicopter pad with a viewing gallery/reception suite provided the focus for a series of studies.

This early study model is little more than a massing diagram but proves the validity of the reversed truss structural form which was developed for the final building.

Norman Foster's sketch for the canopy shows a structure quite different in character from the 'skeletal' main building.

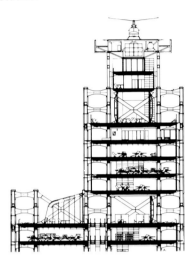

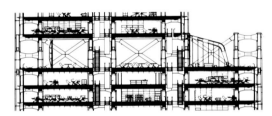

How to design the top of a tower block is an architectural problem that is rarely solved in a convincing manner. The pre-war American skyscraper tradition required some kind of decorative flourish, whether Gothic, Art Deco or Classical (think of the Chicago Tribune building, the Chrysler building or, more recently, Philip Johnson's AT&T headquarters). Decoration for its own sake, however, is definitely not Norman Foster's style. On the other hand the post-war Modernist, or Miesian solution — simply to slice off the extruded shaft — seems less like a solution than an admission of defeat.

Characteristically, Foster sought his solution in the deployment of functional elements. The nature of the structural frame suggested that its main components — the masts and raking tension members — should simply extend above the mass of the building like suspension bridges. This, however, is not quite as straightforward as it looks, because in strictly engineering terms these elements had been conceived not as suspension bridges, but as trusses. Lower down the building the extra horizontal compression members are concealed. In the event, the engineers at Ove Arup & Partners were persuaded to make the necessary adjustments and design out the extra members where they would otherwise be exposed to view. Sometimes, even in a Foster building, aesthetics must take priority over rational structure.

The exposed suspension bridges were a natural and, one might even say, decorative way to finish off the three slices of the tower. And yet, perhaps because the same form appeared at intervals in the height of the building, they also seemed not quite convincing as final statements. They seemed to imply that at some future date further stacks of floors and suspension bridges might be added. This of course was entirely consistent with the indeterminate aesthetic of the building, which was by now well developed, but still some kind of formal gesture of termination seemed to be called for. Another functional element had to be deployed.

This element was the helicopter pad. The development sketches show how various versions were drawn and examined from the aesthetic as well as the structural point of view. The final version takes the form of a straight sided oval deck, propped and strutted off the main structure exactly as if this were an enormous offshore oil rig. The superstructure also

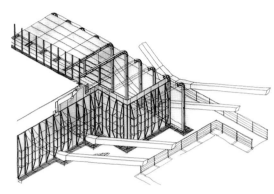

The final solution for the canopies, with their panels and smooth-skinned form, is curiously reminiscent of the Sainsbury Centre. The half-portal structure is supported off a compression boom required at that location to brace the top level of the main suspension truss.

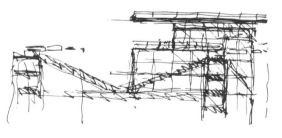

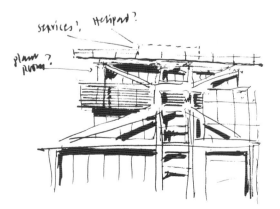

accommodates a suite of directors' reception and dining rooms. A programmable moving illuminated sign, which was to have been wrapped around the deck, fell victim to client cuts. In its place there is a simple metal skirt displaying the Bank's red and white logo.

It might be argued that the helicopter pad is mainly a formal gesture and only incidentally a helicopter pad, but nevertheless as a formal gesture it is completely convincing. In the final building the masts are equipped with additional terminating devices, equally effective aesthetically but this time more essential in their function: large telescopic cranes from which the maintenance cradles are suspended. But devices such as this, which enhance what has been described as the building's 'techno-romantic' image, should not be allowed to distract attention from more essential qualities of the architecture. While the design of the helicopter pad was being finalised, work was continuing on the development of the social spaces.

To take up the village analogy once again, the double-height spaces are equivalent to high streets, or perhaps community halls, though their architecture could hardly be more different. Development studies show the range of

The double-height zones were intended as social centres separating the blocks of office floors. The uppermost, at level 35, is given over to a conference suite and the boardroom, while that at level 28 is a restaurant area for senior staff. The lowest and largest of these areas, at level 20, was originally designated as a combined training centre and staff club – a place for relaxed lunches or evening entertainment as well as instruction. These sketches show proposals for a demountable auditorium.

In the evenings, the double-height areas could transform into social centres; suitable for parties and table-tennis tournaments as well as official gatherings.

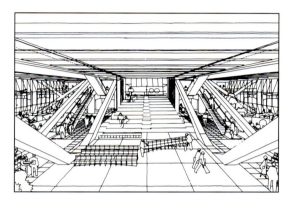

possible activities: relaxing, eating, games playing, parties, meetings, conferences, film shows, seminars, concerts and so on. The extra height permits small auditoria to be created with demountable partitions and bleacher seating. All these activities take place between the raking structural members which, despite their size and intrusiveness, give the spaces a relaxed, ad hoc quality. It is as if they have been colonised in the way that a market or a travelling theatre might colonise a town square.

There is a certain creative tension between, as it were, the 'official' function of these spaces – as necessary components in the structural system, as lift arrival points and as fire-escape refuge floors – and their 'unofficial' use for Christmas parties or table tennis tournaments. One thinks of the social function of fire-escapes in New York tenements, or of office workers sunbathing on flat roofs in London, or, most obviously, of the amazing functional richness of those older buildings in Hong Kong that had so impressed Foster on his first visit.

There are gardens too, on the roof terraces created by the set-backs in both directions; or, at least, that was the original intention. The Bank's director responsible for the project was enthusiastic about the 'hanging gardens' and even passed the idea on to the architect of the neighbouring Hong Kong Club building, but, in the event, he was overruled by the company's property department responsible for running the new building, who were worried about the maintenance implications. This has been a great disappointment to Foster who reckons that soft landscaping would have cost no more, would have been easy to maintain and would have improved the insulation value of the structure. Indeed the potential of the double-height spaces in general has not been fully realised. Perhaps the quasi-unofficial use of space is a difficult concept for an institution like the Bank to grasp. Nevertheless, the roof terraces add yet another new spatial event to an already rich repertoire. It is not just that they afford spectacular views of the harbour, city and Peak: to be able to walk out into the fresh air 35 storeys above the ground completely transforms the user's experience of the whole building.

The main terraces, at levels 35 and 28 where the north and south bays of the tower terminate, are provided with lightweight enclosures known as 'canopies'. If the terraces are village greens, then these are marquees or pavilions. They are permanent enclosures but quite different in character from the main building – smooth, rounded skins rather than exoskeletal structures. Among the Foster precedents they owe more to the Sainsbury Centre than to the Renault building. Again they have that unofficial quality and again one is reminded of Hong Kong's pre-war multi-storey buildings with their ad hoc balconies, screens and awnings, themselves recurring images in any talk Foster gives on the building.

This model of the level 20 double-height floor shows how the massive raking members of the structure interrupt but also give character to the space. The open terraces at this and other double-height levels were originally to have been landscaped gardens but the client was unwilling to invest in soft landscaping and the necessary maintenance.

The banking hall – the building's main public space – was the subject of exhaustive studies in the development of the Final scheme but, as this drawing from the original competition entry shows, a single central atrium was always an option.

Solar furnaces employ vast banks of mirrors, carefully controlled to focus the sun's heat on a single point. Norman Foster knew that the technology for his much simpler 'sun scoop' should be readily available.

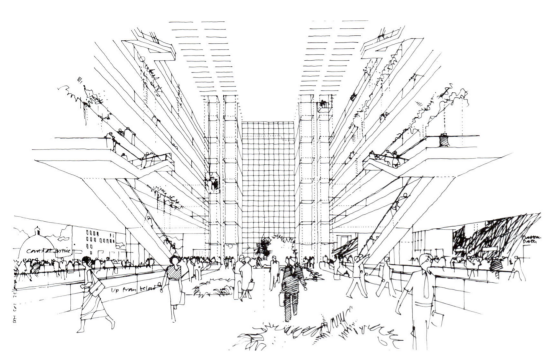

The first ideas are often the best. This scribbled sketch of the sun scoop principle is contemporary with the first competition design.

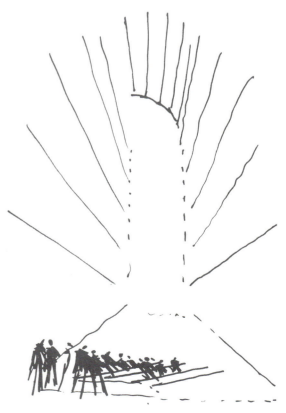

trian route from Statue Square to Battery Park, also dates back to the Competition scheme.

Plaza and atrium might quite easily have been separated by the floor of the banking hall. The plaza would then simply have been an open ground floor, not so different from countless others except that, because of the tension structure, it would have been uninterrupted by columns. The banking hall would have been a conventional atrium, but without the benefit of the usual glazed roof. A version of this solution was proposed in the Competition scheme. But how much more exciting, thought Foster, to make the two spaces into one, so that pedestrians on the plaza could look right up into the atrium, and the Bank's customers on the galleries of the atrium could look down on the public space. But there was an obvious problem, expressed in a simple question: where does the outside space end and the inside space begin?

The resolution of this conflict was to produce one of the most breathtakingly elegant features of the final building, but not before all the possible options had been considered. One option was to incorporate the plaza into the

If commerce is the religion of the modern age, then banks are its churches and banking halls the architectural settings for its public rituals: the cathedrals of commerce. One of the most impressive features of the original 1935 building had been the banking hall with its glorious Italian mosaic ceiling. The original intention had been to preserve this space in the new building but, in the end, this had proved impracticable. The new banking hall, therefore, had to match the scale and grandeur of the old.

Since Foster's design method is one of trial and error – a systematic, experimental process by which every option is explored and tested – it is not surprising that the banking hall should have undergone many transformations as the building developed. But design is as much a matter of creative instinct as of rigorous method, and frequently the first ideas turn out to be the best. In Foster's earliest Hong Kong sketches, the idea that the banking hall might take the form of a high central atrium had been explored. There is even a sketch from 1979 indicating how sunlight might be brought into such a space by means of a system of reflectors – a 'sun scoop'. The idea of a plaza beneath the building, providing a public pedes-

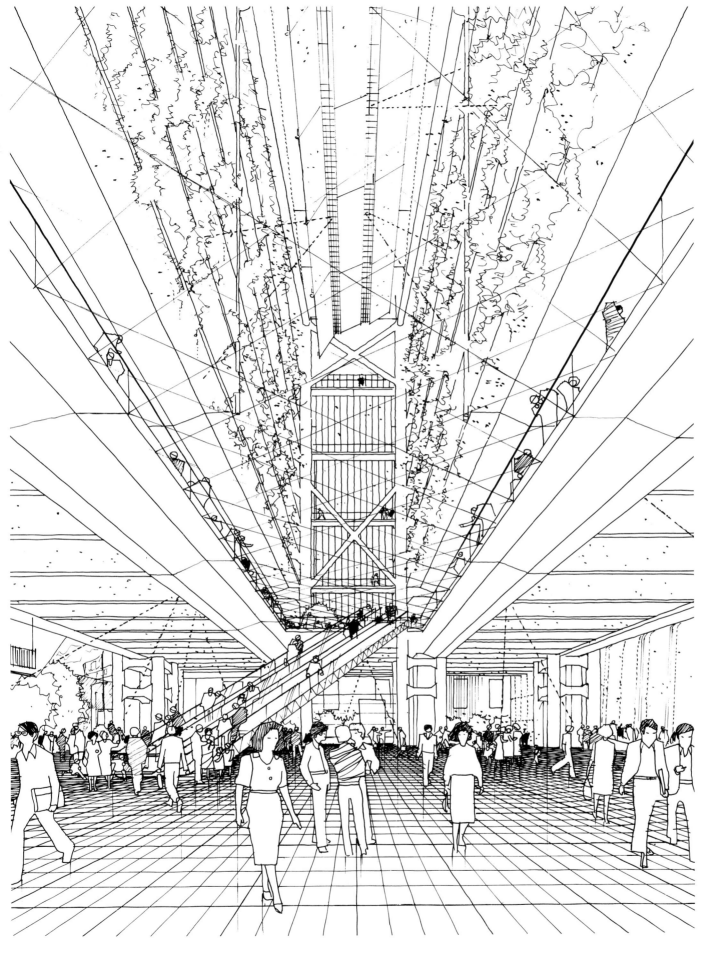

From the earliest competition drawings the possibility that the public plaza at ground level and the banking hall atrium above might be conceived as a single space had been explored in sketches. Through these, the internal component of the sun scoop became not only a device to introduce sunlight but also a satisfactory formal termination of the space. As the Final scheme developed, realistic drawings began to give form to the earlier ideas. Here planting is shown lining the atrium, but the problem of separating atrium from plaza is evaded, with only the vaguest indication of some form of horizontal barrier indicated.

"Given the power of the present set-up, it is hard to imagine what the reaction would have been if Foster had been permitted to carry out his intention of putting a glazed floor into the plaza, so that atrium, plaza and lower banking floor at basement level could be experienced as one continuous vertical space. The sensation of walking across such a space, especially at night, with the plaza floor illuminated from below, regrettably has to go down as one of the great might-have-beens of architecture."

Chris Abel, *Architectural Review*, April 1986

Just as for the overall building, models formed an important design tool in the development of the atrium. This early 1:200 model is little more than a diagram but already the vitality and drama of the space is beginning to express itself.

atrium by closing it off from the streets on the north and south sides of the building with glass walls and lobbies. But this would certainly have deterred pedestrians from using the plaza, which would have become not a public space, but merely a large private foyer. Another possibility was to incorporate the atrium into the plaza, making the atrium effectively an outdoor space. But this would have meant glazing in the galleries overlooking the atrium.

There was a third possibility, and a very unusual one. What if the plaza could be enclosed not by glass walls but by air curtains?

This white study model could be readily disassembled so that options and variations could be interpreted almost immediately in three dimensions. The glazed plaza floor appears, glowing from within, and, like the first model, three escalators are shown rising from the plaza itself.

As the design was finalised, so the models could become more detailed. This 1:100 model was prepared for a major presentation to the Bank. The full sun-shades lining the edge of each floor were an early proposal to support plants.

The necessary mechanical equipment might have been incorporated in the so-called 'typhoon screens' – steel-framed glass skirts designed to modify the air flow at plaza level. Research revealed, however, that in order to do the job effectively, the air curtains needed to be so powerful that they would have deterred pedestrians just as surely as any glass wall.

Only one possibility remained: to construct some kind of transparent horizontal barrier between atrium and plaza. Whatever form this barrier might take, it would have to span the 21-metre width of the atrium. Rule of thumb calculations indicated beams more than a metre deep: a clumsy structure, sure to obscure the upward view. Other alternatives were considered, including space-frames, tension structures and arches, until eventually the rigid catenary form was hit upon and instantly recognised as the perfect solution.

A catenary structure works on the rope bridge principle: a rigid catenary is a rope bridge that can resist lifting wind loads. The final version of the horizontal barrier hangs beneath the atrium like a transparent hammock. Toughened glass

As the public face of the Bank, the atrium was in many respects the most sensitive of the design issues. A magnificent 1:50 scale model was built in Hong Kong, allowing the client to understand the space completely before it was constructed.

"Hong Kong is special in its mix of culture, climate and urban pace. The design is an attempt to respond to these special qualities – for example the way in which the ground level is open to the public; sunlight being pulled into the heart of the building; gardens and terraces in the sky; grillages to break down the scale into something more human; colour accents informed by the traditional Chinese context; or simultaneous translucency rather than transparency. The list is a long one."

Norman Foster, *Building*, June 1983

NASA's vertical assembly building is 160 metres high and requires air-conditioning to avoid clouds forming inside. At 50 metres the Hongkong Bank's atrium cannot compete. In height and width, however, its dimensions almost exactly match the nave of Cologne cathedral.

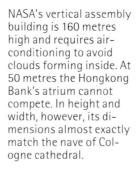

One alternative to the installation of an 'underbelly' separating plaza and atrium was to glaze the internal walls of the atrium instead. Options were modelled as much, perhaps, to prove the idea undesirable, as to explore its possibilities.

A development of the earlier white study model, this more detailed model was also made in sections that allowed parts to be changed at will. The glazed pavilions between the service towers on the east side of the plaza are seen here: that at the centre houses a vehicular hoist, while the outer two form protected entrances to the secondary banking hall located in the basement area below the plaza.

A space combining the scale and complexity of the atrium created exceptional lighting possibilities – especially when the glass floor was included in the mix. A large-scale study model was prepared in which a wide variety of options could be tested.

197

Below: Concerts had been held with great success in the banking hall of the 1935 headquarters. With an extended bridge installed at the west end of the atrium, Foster proposed they continue this practice in the new building.

panels are supported by slender curved-steel members only 260mm deep. Fresh air has been separated from conditioned air, the view up into the atrium remains unobstructed and the building has acquired its famous glass underbelly.

The main public entrance to the banking hall takes the form of a pair of long escalators linking the plaza to a projecting platform at the east end of the atrium. Main entrances have a spiritual significance in Chinese culture and the angles of these escalators were therefore fixed only after due consultation with the Fung Shui advisor. Development studies show three escalators, the third intended to serve as a stand-by during busy periods or in case of breakdown. In the event, however, only two were installed in order to leave space for a second pair rising from the 'landing' platform at the main banking hall, level 3, to a secondary banking hall above at level 5. Back up is provided by the lifts and by

additional escalators rising from a separate entrance lobby on the south-west corner of the building.

Beneath the plaza, at the first basement level, lies another public banking hall. Foster's dislike of basements, both from the technical and spatial points of view, is well known: a more exciting proposition was required. Foster's idea was to dispel the gloom by roofing the basement banking hall totally in glass, creating a plaza with the qualities of a luminous and rip-

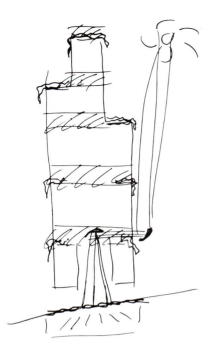

It was Norman Foster's intention, by paving the plaza in glass, to allow light from the sun scoop to enter the basement banking hall. In the event the idea had to be abandoned.

The internal part of the sun scoop is a static bank of reflectors. The external mirrors, however, are motorised and controlled by a simple computer program to track the path of the sun.

The reality of the atrium space. The public plaza beneath the building is clearly visible from the galleries of the atrium through the glass underbelly that gently arcs across the atrium. High above, the internal part of the sun scoop is suspended in the space like an aeroplane in a museum, reflecting gentle sunlight on to the massive structure.

The external element of the sun scoop. Twenty 'racks' are positioned on an exact north-south axis, each containing 24 mirrors that adjust to ensure sunlight enters the building at a constant angle.

pling sea. The design was developed, successfully, in collaboration with a single specialist subcontractor. The client, however, insisted on competitive bidding and there was no time to go through the design development process with other firms. Without this, technical performance could not be guaranteed and the client would have been at risk in the event of a failure. Consequently, the proposal was defeated on a procedural technicality and stone substituted for the glass panels.

It is all the more surprising, therefore, that an even bolder idea – the sun scoop – should have been realised. In principle the sun scoop is a simple optical device, a kind of huge periscope that projects sunlight into the atrium and through the underbelly to the plaza pavement below. It has two main components: a bank of movable flat mirrors attached to the south side of the building at level 12, and a curved canopy of convex mirrors suspended inside the building at the same level, over the atrium. This configuration was arrived at after considerable testing and analysis. Lighting Sciences, of Arizona, were called in as specialist consultants and, using computer models, they arrived at a concept that could be realised using relatively simple existing technology.

In its final form, the effect of the reflected sunlight is subtle rather than spectacular, and in winter rather fleeting. Nevertheless it creates an illusion so convincing as to puzzle passers-by on the plaza and it adds an extra element of mystery to a unique spatial experience.

Many of Foster's ideas for the atrium were not realised, including an extendable platform at level 3, suitable for concerts and other after-hours events, and continuous planting at the edges of every floor. In the event, planting was limited to the bridges at the east and west ends and even this was not installed until after the building was handed over – the Fung Shui advisor, on seeing the completed atrium, considered it to be essential to the spiritual harmony of the space and he insisted that temporary plants be brought in to guard the fortunes of the building and its users in the interim.

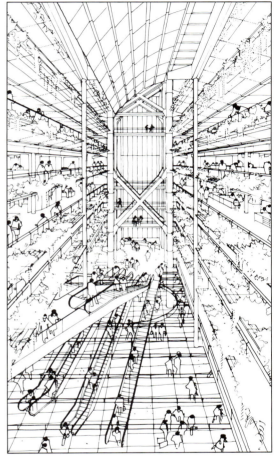

This perspective shows three escalators from plaza to atrium, emerging through a circular hole in a flat underbelly. In the final building there are only two escalators and the openings are much smaller, closed off by motorised shutters.

199

After three years of development, the design is now finalised. This section shows the building's relationship to Battery Park, rising on the hillside behind the building, Statue Square and the Star Ferry terminal. The long tunnel between the harbour and building is used to convey sea water. This is used as a cooling medium for the air-conditioning — a system common in Hong Kong — and also provides flushing water for lavatories. The basement now has four floors and the mast foundations can be seen extending into bedrock, where they are 'belled' out to resist the uplift that can occur under typhoon wind-load conditions. The sea water tunnel was also sunk and driven through bedrock as, in the high water-table conditions, this was easier than placing a shaft through the poor fill areas above. The two small tunnels passing adjacent to the building's perimeter diaphragm wall are part of Hong Kong's Mass Transit Railway system. The Bank paid for the rails to be rubber mounted so that vibration from the trains would not be transmitted to the steel structure.

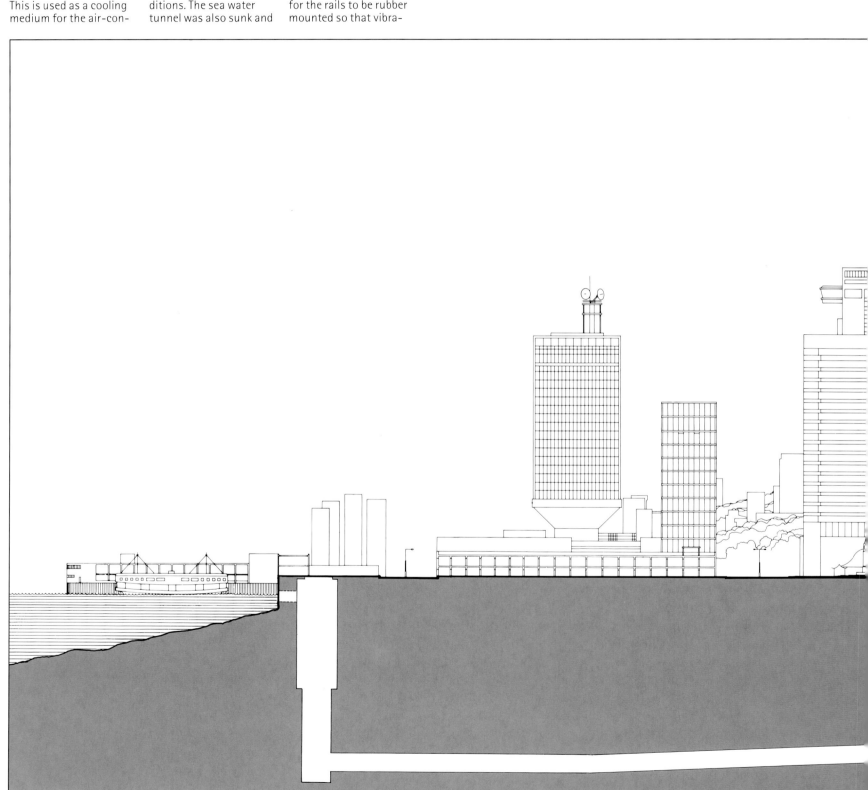

"The sea water tunnel basically pays for itself within 10 years, because we have saved something like 25 000 square feet of space within the building that would have been lost to machinery had we gone for conventional air cooling."

Ray Guy, lecture at the Burrell Museum, January 1986

"We use approximately 1000 litres of sea water per second in the building. We were a little concerned over the ecological breakdown that might happen within the harbour and so we commissioned the British Hydraulics Research Institute to carry out a series of tests for us. They modelled the harbour and came up with a solution where we direct our out-pour under the Star Ferry. There is a ferry leaving every eight minutes, so we achieve a total dissemination of water right the way through the harbour at no cost to us at all."

Ray Guy, lecture at the Burrell Museum, January 1986

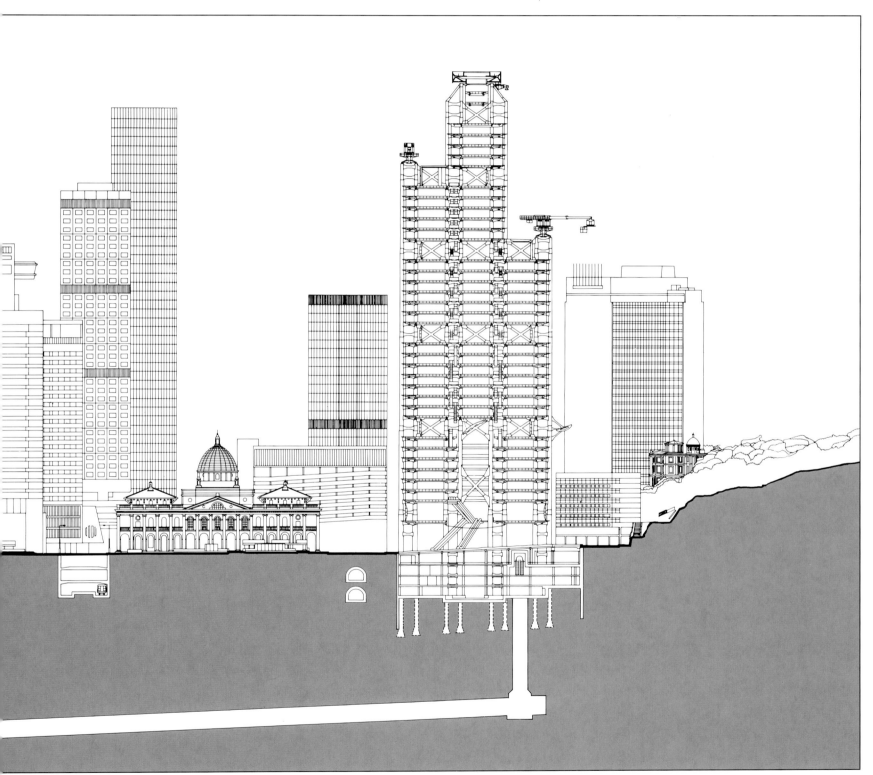

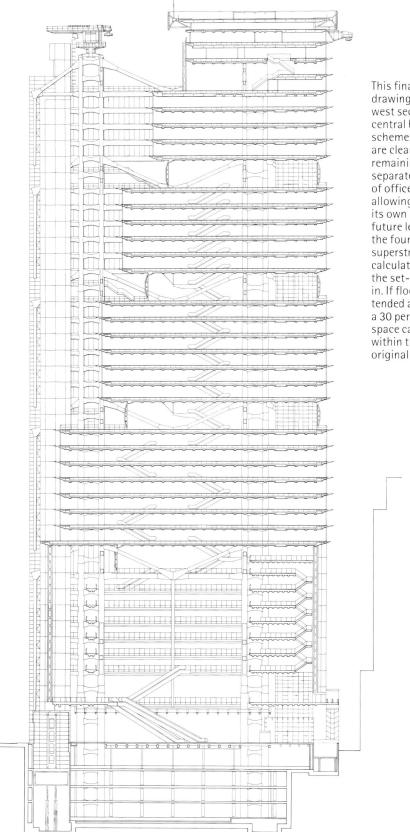

"The Hongkong Bank strives to produce a sequence and progression of architectural spaces from the public plaza at the base, to the double-height reception areas located at intervals up the building, through to the workplace — a combination of vertical and diagonal movement through the structure by high-speed lift and escalator."

Norman Foster, *L'Architecture d'Aujourd'hui*, February 1986

This final presentation drawing shows an east/west section through the central bay of the Final scheme. The set-backs are clearly expressed, remaining constant over separate vertical zones of office floors, thereby allowing each to adopt its own identity. Should future legislation permit, the foundations and superstructure have been calculated to allow for the set-backs to be filled in. If floors were also extended across the atrium, a 30 per cent increase in space can be achieved within the building's original planning outline.

By January 1983 the overall design was complete. Considerable development work still remained to be done on the various components, but all the basic decisions had been made. The members of the design team knew the size of the major elements and where they were located, even if they did not yet know who would manufacture them and precisely how they would be fixed.

The building is a three-dimensional composition which does not lend itself readily to representation in conventional plans and sections. Perhaps this is the reason for Foster's use of models, not just as presentation media but as development tools. Features like the suspension structure, the main entrance, escalators and the set-backs at the upper levels look almost wilful on plan, though in three dimensions they make perfect sense. The plans and sections are merely an abstract record of a design visualised in the mind in three dimensions, with occasional help from models.

The plans also reveal Foster's attitude to space. Space in a Foster building is not finite, nor static, nor sequential. It is neither moulded nor carved-out. It is, rather, constantly on the move, flowing from inside to outside, from atrium to plaza, from one level to another. This is why the drawings have a curiously abstract and scaleless quality, more like sections through a piece of mechanical equipment than the plans of a building. What is depicted is mainly structure — from main masts to curtain wall mullions — rather than space enclosure. There are no room names on the plans because there are no rooms as such. This is not a collection of spaces but a structure through which space flows.

Even in the basement, where space is carved out more literally, there is no deliberate manipulation of scale or sequence. This is hardly surprising in the levels that house mechanical plant or rows of deposit boxes, but even the public basement banking hall is a single, undifferentiated area. In its initial form, this would also have been a continuation of the plaza and atrium above — in spirit if not in reality — by use of the translucent glazed plaza floor, but, unfortunately, this is one idea that was never to be implemented.

Colin Davies

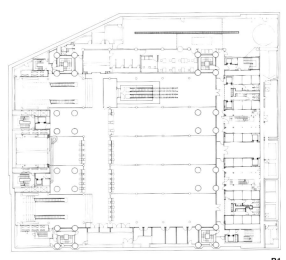

The secondary banking hall at basement level B1. Public access to the safe deposit vault below, on level B2m, is by escalators protected behind their own imposing circular vault door.

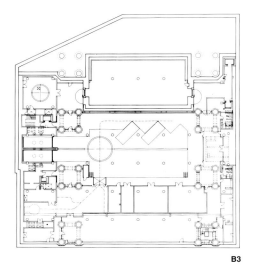

The lowest basement level, B3, is the building's service yard: vehicles arrive by hoist from an entrance on Bank Street. Ancillary services at this level include the main fire pumps and a special document shredder and compactor which is fed by a chute rising the full height of the building.

On the south side of level B2 are the Bank's main vaults, access to which is by secure lift from a protected delivery bay at level B1. Most of the remaining area is given over to the complex pumping gear which services the main chilling plant above, on level B2m.

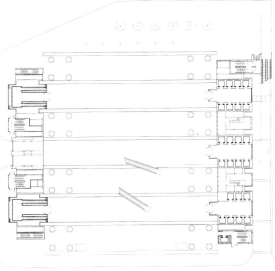

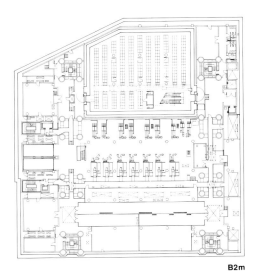

The main plant hall is located across the centre of level B2m. Five centrifugal water chillers — connected to titanium plate heat exchangers — supply chilled water to the air-handling plant modules above. The building's high-voltage switch-gear, back-up battery supply and telephone exchange are also located at this level.

The main street level plaza is interrupted only by two escalators, the angle of which was determined after discussions with the Fung Shui advisor. The building's main lift-lobby entrances are contained by glazed pavilions situated between the service towers on the west side of the plaza. Similar pavilions on the east give access to the secondary banking hall at level B1.

203

"The building is really a series of towers, either side of a structure. Towers which are to do with escape, with movement, with services and the things that drive the building, creating a very strong emphasis on flexibility."

Norman Foster, lecture to Sainsbury's Executive Club, March 1984

A secondary banking floor is located at level 5, access being provided by escalators that rise at an angle across the atrium from the reception bridge at level 3.

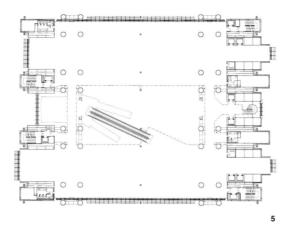

5

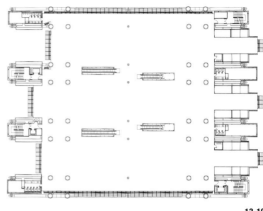

13-19

The four double-height areas that occur over the building's height — together with the fifth roof-top terrace — form the main punctuation points in the vocabulary of the building, visually and socially creating distinct breaks between the more constant groups of office floors. At these levels, the glass is set back to create open terraces (shown here shaded grey) which provide enjoyment for the building's users, while also forming the refuge terraces required by Hong Kong regulations. Two-hour fire shutters on the glazing line close to create protected areas, allowing escapees to rest or change stairs during their descent from the building during an emergency.

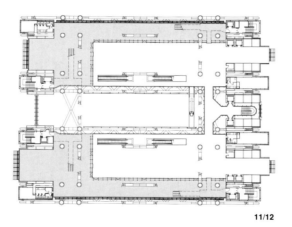

11/12

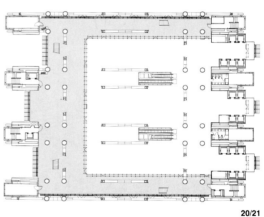

20/21

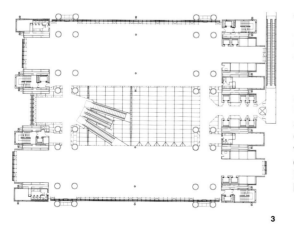

The public banking hall at level 3. The main entrance escalators rise through the glazed underbelly from the plaza below, arriving at a reception bridge that links the two sides of the atrium. Secondary access is provided at the west end by lift or secondary escalators installed in place of a planned high-level walkway.

3

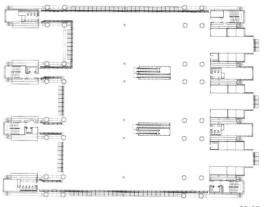

22-27

"The design does not preconceive whether layouts are open plan or cellular or generated by corridors. All such possibilities can be achieved."

Norman Foster, client presentation, March 1982

"To the surprise of the Bank's own specialist consultants, the current scheme is calculated at 73.5% gross to nett and 80% plus for certain individual floors. A pleasant surprise, I hasten to add, especially as it provides an extra 90 000 square feet of usable space in the building if compared with the percentages achieved by most office layouts."

Norman Foster, Flexibility in Design lecture, Brighton, April 1981

Above level 30, the separate up and down escalator circulation of the lower floors has to be combined at the centre of the two-bay floors. Escalator circulation to the single-bay floors of levels 37 to 40 was not possible; access to these areas is provided by lift only.

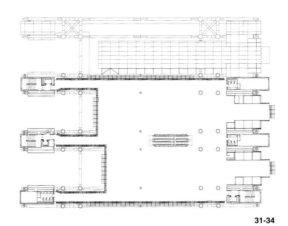

31-34

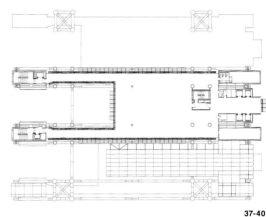

37-40

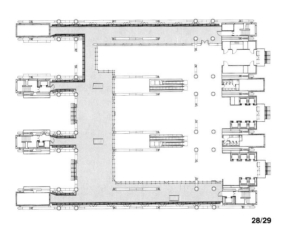

28/29

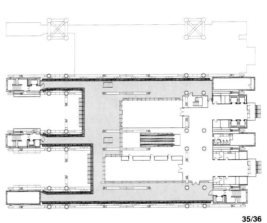

35/36

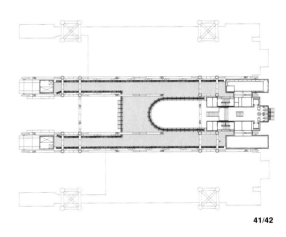

41/42

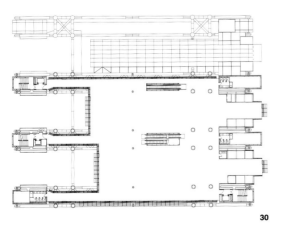

30

The special structure raised above the topmost suspension truss of level 41/42 houses an executive reception suite which includes private dining rooms at level 43 and a viewing gallery at level 44. A planned rooftop helideck has not been installed as current regulations would not allow its use.

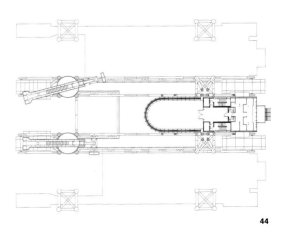

44

205

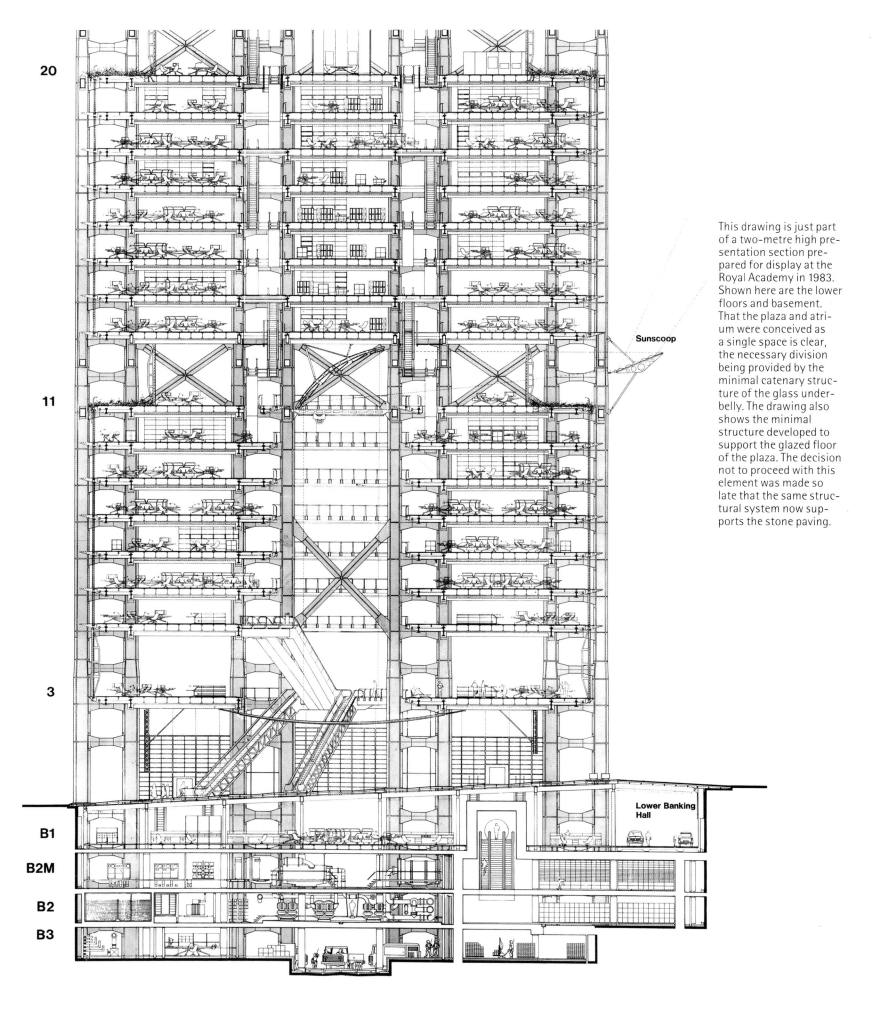

This drawing is just part of a two-metre high presentation section prepared for display at the Royal Academy in 1983. Shown here are the lower floors and basement. That the plaza and atrium were conceived as a single space is clear, the necessary division being provided by the minimal catenary structure of the glass underbelly. The drawing also shows the minimal structure developed to support the glazed floor of the plaza. The decision not to proceed with this element was made so late that the same structural system now supports the stone paving.

"The bank is very fluid in its staff movements. The design had to reflect that and it also had to reflect the changes which are coming into banking. We were the first electronic bank in the Far East and the rest of the world has now caught up; now we are taking a 10-year step and the building has had to reflect that. It has also had to confront everyday changes within the building because we move approximately 50 per cent of this building every year in terms of office accommodation, so flexibility had to be built into the building."

Ray Guy, lecture at the Burrell Museum, January 1986

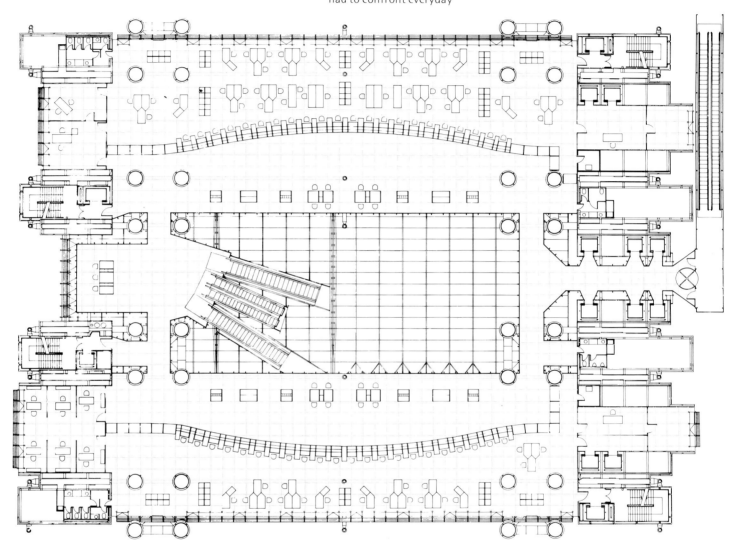

The main banking hall at level 3 takes the form of galleries overlooking the atrium and public plaza below. The building's 'front door' is a pair of horizontal shutters closing off the openings in the underbelly through which the escalators pass. Visitors arrive at one end of the 10 storey atrium, beneath the 'cathedral wall'. In the final design, the long continuous counters are gently curved, echoing the curve of the underbelly and of the sun scoop high above. Staff, who do not need to pass through the banking hall, can bypass the main escalators by using the lift lobbies on the west side of the plaza. Note how the external walls of the building pass through the masts so that the muscular structure becomes the main feature of the elevations.

A Project Diary
by Patrick Hannay

Patrick Hannay is buildings editor of *The Architects' Journal*. Over the last 10 years he has interwoven periods of research and journalism with design practice in Marseilles and Paris, and in London with DEGW. He qualified as an architect and urban designer at the School of Architecture, Planning and Urban Design, Oxford.

Edmund Sixsmith entered the portals of the Royal Institute of British Architects, at 66 Portland Place, in April 1979. The subject on his mind was competitions; the man he wanted to see, now nearing the end of his term as RIBA president, was Gordon Graham. Sixsmith was sent by Roy Munden who, as assistant general manager, management services of The Hongkong and Shanghai Banking Corporation, had been delegated by its chairman, Michael Sandberg, to procure a new headquarters on its existing site at 1 Queen's Road Central. In Hong Kong alone, the Hongkong Bank's existing 195 branches were projected to become 280 by 1980. Even greater percentage growth rates were planned for overseas branches, making colossal demands on many of the headquarters' departments.

Sixsmith and his colleague John Scott from PA Management Consultants were hired by Munden to assemble a team of local consultants for a feasibility study. They began work in January 1979. The London and Hong Kong offices of PA had been working on personnel policies for the Bank. Sixsmith and Scott, from PA's London-based 'projects office', had civil engineering and project management backgrounds; both were Cambridge men.

Module assembly proceeds at the specially-rented plant in Ako, Japan; a facility more commonly used for the manufacture of huge electrical generators.

Palmer and Turner (P+T), the Hong Kong architects of the existing 1935 headquarters building, joined the PA feasibility team along with Ove Arup & Partners, J. Roger Preston & Partners the service engineers, quantity surveyors Levett & Bailey, and property agents Jones Lang Wootton. The report completed in March 1979 put forward two preferred physical and organisational strategies for phased re-

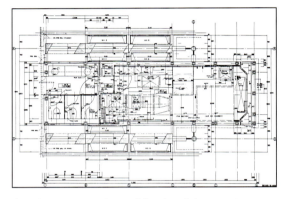

A co-ordination drawing, establishing critical setting-out dimensions for fixing points between risers, modules, steelwork and cladding.

development and a multitude of data on town planning, building, property and organisational constraints.

PA was charged to assemble a short international list of architects for Munden to approach. The grapevine news was that the selection process for the Lloyd's project, then under way in London, had been a success. Gordon Graham was seen as its author and was naturally one source of advice for the shortlist; hence Sixsmith's visit. Graham requested direct talks with the Bank; Munden came to Portland Place and also met Courtenay Blackmore, his equivalent in the Lloyd's hierarchy.

By June 1979 PA's feasibility study had become the base for a 20-page 'Request for proposals' (with 50 pages of appendices). Graham was sent a copy for comment in London. The two preferred strategies were spelt out plus all the data, but the Bank "had not closed its mind to other solutions". Predictions were made on how much of the new building was to be sublet. Like Lloyd's, the Bank intended to seek an architect, not a fixed solution.

Sixsmith mentioned Foster's name to Munden. Graham agreed on the inclusion, but alongside the track records for multi-storey

A full working prototype module was built by HMT Consort which allowed all details to be tested and agreed before production began.

Below: Manufacture of the steel 'Xmas trees' that make up the main masts in progress at British Steel's plant in Middlesbrough.

headquarters for corporate clients of the other shortlisted practices (Harry Seidler, SOM, Yuncken Freeman, Hugh Stubbins, P+T and YRM) Foster was recognised by Graham, Sixsmith and Munden as the wild card in the pack. The 'Request for proposals' document suggested that the quantity surveyor, structural engineer, and mechanical and electrical consultants of the feasibility study were to join the winning architect. Alternative proposals could be made by competitors "with reasons".

Munden nominated Graham as architectural adviser for the selection process with a local architect, David Thornburrow, assisting.

The six shortlisted practices arrived in Hong Kong on 11 July for a preliminary day's briefing, meeting with John Boyer (the deputy chairman), Munden, Graham, Thornburrow, Scott and Sixsmith. Foster's request to tape the proceedings was granted. Some practices left

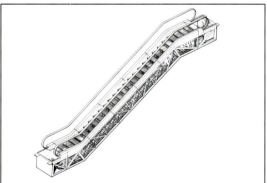

The escalators used in the building are refined versions of a standard type, adapted to accept glass sides. A prototype was prepared to help resolve design details and check production techniques.

with the impression that they would get a second and separate interview. The 'Request for proposals' document only says "may". The visiting practices flew home after a few days. Foster's three-person team stayed three weeks, paying frequent visits to Munden and other departments of the Bank.

Scott had strongly advised Munden — now elevated to the position of general manager, planning (group head office) — to visit all the shortlisted architects in their offices and to see examples of their work. The advice was eventually taken. Munden went alone. Lasting impressions were formed on this trip.

The written and drawn submissions arrived by 6 October. Graham flew to Hong Kong. Consultants from the feasibility report team were now in some cases consultants to the competitors. So an in-house team of architect, surveyor, a banker and an administrative manager carried out a comparative analysis on the submissions. Munden, Graham, Thornburrow and PA worked in parallel. One submission stood head and shoulders above the rest — Foster's. There was no need for second interviews.

Munden phoned Graham late one evening at his hotel. Graham agreed. Sandberg was holidaying in southern France. Munden phoned his recommendation through. It was accepted. PA was told the next morning. A paper was circulated to board members with the recommendation — a rare occurrence in board proceedings. Foster gave a slide and model presentation of his proposals to the board on 13 November. It was rumoured to be the longest board meeting in the Bank's history. Chairman Sandberg was a banker. Several of the strongest board members were property magnates. The debate was tough. The chairman eventually achieved a unanimous decision. "Welcome aboard", said Sandberg.

The two alternative strategies of PA's feasibility study were not recommended by the Foster team. Foster proposed a third — a radical and dramatic reassessment of the Bank's options based on phased regeneration of the site which allowed the banking hall to be operational throughout construction. The suspended bridge-like structural concept, the deep largely column-free floors — with dramatic open views along the total width of north and south elevations and with 'in board' cellular offices if necessary — the east and west perimeter service and vertical circulation zones, the open ground-level plaza given over to improving circulation across the city, the multi-level banking hall raised off the ground and accessed by escalators, the raised floor, the arguments for prefabrication, flexibility, steel structure, energy savings, cost in use — all major elements of the final building are present in the first Foster submission.

The submission strongly recommends that internal layout, colours, finishes and furniture should be an integral part of the total design. It also makes recommendations for the project management. "Past experience has shown the value of direct and personal contact through key individuals between client and design team. It is then possible for a small but powerful client-based committee to make financial and planning decisions and get on with the job…", and again, "the project management structure should ensure maximum interaction between the Bank and design team — hopefully direct and personal." Through this process key decisions will have been well programmed and the status of the project subjected to continuous review.

Once Foster was appointed, Sixsmith and Scott's contract with the Bank was not renewed. PA had no further involvement with the project. With Graham no longer RIBA president, Munden

asked him to become the Bank's paid architectural adviser. Graham accepted.

1980

The month is January. The Foster Associates' team is back in London hard at work. The Ove Arup structural team is in its office next door. The quantity surveyors, Levett & Bailey, have

A full-size mock-up of a section of typical office floor was installed in Foster Associates' own workshop. This included an accurate representation of the structural soffit at the edge of the building, on which alternative ceiling systems could be tested.

Lighting in the atrium was tested under an artificial sky, a dome of lights individually computer-controlled to recreate any variety of daylight conditions for any location in the world.

a UK London association with Northcroft Neighbour & Nicholson. Spencer de Grey and Graham Phillips establish a Foster Associates office in Hong Kong, working on the phased regeneration of the site. Ove Arup & Partners is considered for the mechanical and electrical side. The final services consultant appointment, J. Roger Preston & Partners, is not to be formally confirmed by the Bank's board until February 1981. The design work is co-ordinated through its larger London office.

Chris Seddon joins Foster Associates' Hong Kong office in February 1980. He later becomes the chief client liaison member of the Foster team when de Grey returns to London in February 1981.

With the prospect of elements being fabricated all round the world and with critical design, development and production periods required to meet the November 1985 completion date, there are intense discussions in London and Hong Kong about co-ordination. Foster, Jack Zunz of Ove Arup & Partners, Graham and Munden are the key participants.

Munden proposes to the board a London-based Ove Arup project co-ordination team led by Peter Bolingbroke. The board rejects the proposal and recommends the Bank should hire its own project co-ordination staff.

Munden seeks advice from R. J. Mead, project director for Hong Kong's largest ever civil engineering project, the Mass Transit Railway.

A shortlist is reduced to three. Graham Phillips, later to become director in charge of construction in Foster Associates' Hong Kong office, and Spencer de Grey interview them separately from Munden in April 1980. They agree with Munden's recommendations. Mead does not agree. Ray Guy with a wide experience in building site and construction management is formally appointed in June 1980 as technical manager. He is attached to 'property', a section of Munden's central services department. His salary is paid by property manager Doug Brown, but he reports directly to Munden.

Spencer de Grey of Foster Associates is living in Hong Kong during 1980, trying to firm up the schedule of accommodation. Group Methods Research (GMR) under Frank Reid, is the point of contact at the Hongkong Bank. George Tally, an analyst of organisation and method (O & M), is hired by Reid on a fixed term contract to gather data on departmental needs. No firm data are forthcoming.

Munden is in England in August and early September, at his second home in Sussex. Foster, de Grey and Graham are working closely with Munden. Ray Guy and Doug Brown are making periodical visits to London. John Lok/Wimpey,

As design work proceeded, the mock-up was developed to include trial sections of underfloor services, parts of the real cladding system and a working prototype of the gull-wing ceiling.

A working prototype of the glazed floor panels intended for the Bank's plaza, set up in Foster Associates' workshop.

the management contractor, is awarded an interim agreement in October by Munden.

In November 1980, Munden reorganises the former property section (with its fast growing property portfolio worldwide) as an independent property company and sets up Hongkong and Shanghai Property Management (HSPM), which he runs. He wants Foster's claims for cost-in-use benefits of the design audited. Foster and Graham recommend Dieter Jaeger of the German Quickborner office space planning team.

Munden hires Jaeger who assesses and confirms to Munden the efficiency claims of the project's net to gross, the raised floor services flexibility and the double-height 'village'-reception/lift-escalator transfer concept. These findings are presented by Foster and Jaeger to the board in a major slide presentation of the preliminary design in January 1981. There is still no agreed stacking plan or schedule of accommodation, nor agreement as to how much sublet space there will be in the building. George Tally and de Grey are making slow progress.

1981

Just before the January 1981 board presentation, Foster asks Graham to join the firm as a consultant. The proposal is put to Munden and

Based on drawings of an existing lift-car, Foster Associates developed an alternative design, producing this mock-up (left) as an aid to discussion with the manufacturer. The manufacturer, in turn, produced his own prototype (below) that allowed all parties – including the client – to assess the design's viability.

"Somebody once told me there are two kinds of pilot: those who take off and are surprised if their engines fail, and those who are surprised if they actually keep going. I would like to think that, as architects, we fit into the latter category – we always expect things to fail and try and work forward from that. As far as possible we try not to use the site as a testing ground just to find out whether something does or does not work."

Norman Foster, lecture to Sainsbury's Executive Club, March 1984

Sandberg. They both agree and Graham is no longer the paid architectural adviser to the Bank. Ian Davidson and Alex Lifschutz, who become two other key actors in the fit-out/user liaison side of the project, join the Foster office in London. Munden sets up a 1 Queen's Road Central steering committee. De Grey moves from Hong Kong and now stays in London with the rest of the team, travelling out monthly until January 1983.

By May 1981 Sandberg has proposed to the board that Munden is made executive director, services, the number three position in the Bank's executive hierarchy in Hong Kong, with a place on the board. (Non-executives are always in the majority on the board.)

A month later, on 26 June, the 1935 Bank headquarters at 1 Queen's Road Central is closed for the last time. Group Methods Research is relocated in Quarry Bay, which through daytime congested traffic is a 90 minute drive from Hong Kong Central. The former headquarters' departments are spread out all over Hong Kong. HSPM is in a distant location while group head office stays in the Central district. Munden signs the formal agreement with John Lok/Wimpey in July. Demolition begins.

Reid of GMR is replaced by Clint Marshall in August. Munden spends the late summer again in London with several meetings with Foster and Graham. Ray Guy is coming back and forth also to Foster Associates' London office and visiting the main subcontractors' works with members of the design and management contract team. By November 1981 Munden is back in London. He has signed the formal agreement with Cupples Products and British Steel Corporation/Dorman Long JV. A month later the formal agreement with HMT Consort for the services modules is also signed. Seventy per cent of the budget is committed. Munden checks with Foster Associates on their preparations for the January 1982 final design slide and model presentation to the board. Before the board meeting, there is a crisis over accommodation information for the basement. Minimising below ground accommodation is critical. The Jolyon Drury Consultancy is working alongside Ove Arup & Partners and Foster Associates in London trying to pin down exact needs for the basement loading bay options. There is still no concise data coming from GMR or the steering committee or HSPM on the stacking plans. Foster urgently asks Munden to appoint someone

independent of the Bank with the skills and clout to clarify the accommodation needs. Jaeger's name is discussed. Marshall of GMR sets up a 1 Queen's Road Central planning department.

Jaeger cannot be persuaded to work full-time in Hong Kong. An advertisement goes in the national press worldwide. Peter Herring, an O & M consultant with space planning experience, working for W. H. Smith, applies and is interviewed by a member of the steering committee, John Strickland. He is hired in January 1982 and attached to GMR, but given an office in Central district.

1982

In early Spring, Munden becomes concerned by the lack of exact and agreed costing figures for the steelwork. By late July/August, with steel fabrication begun in April at Glasgow, Teesside and Manchester, alarm bells start ringing. Munden holds a crunch meeting with all consultants and John Lok/Wimpey in London. Wimpey is directed to do an audit on the steel. This indicates by September a possible $50-million cost overrun. Meanwhile, Munden has appointed a new manager for HSPM, John Breen from the colony's largest property company, Hongkong Land.

Margaret Thatcher arrives in Hong Kong in September and the political reverberations of her statements on the 1997 handover of the colony to China send shockwaves through the Hong Kong economy. The three years of property boom in Hong Kong begins to turn into a dramatic slump. Land prices fall by as much as 80 per cent. In November, Munden demands that all consultants transfer offices to Hong Kong before Christmas, four months ahead of their scheduled move.

The Bank's board responds dramatically to news of the steel cost overrun. Trevor Bedford, Hongkong Land's managing director, and a non-executive board member of the Bank, is one of four non-executive directors appointed by the board in November 1982 to a newly-formed Project Policy Control Committee (PPCC). The board asks Graham to become its adviser again. Ron Mead, the former Mass Transit project manager, is hired as PPCC's executive project management arm to reassess and control all budgets and ensure the project meets its November 1985 completion date. Mead's former boss, Norman Thompson, is a PPCC member along with two Chinese property tycoons, Li Ka Shing and Hui Sai Fun. Munden is to be the new committee's

Smoke tests being carried out to assess the effectiveness of floor-based air-conditioning outlets.

Foster Associates were responsible for office planning in the new building. Here departmental zoning is under analysis.

A 'sawn-off' Corsair fighter plane and a grid of sprinklers combine to recreate typhoon conditions. Prototypes of each element of the cladding were tested and refined using this procedure.

secretary. A further total project audit is commissioned from Pell Frischmann. Morale in the consultants' teams is at an all-time low.

Every order and subcontract from now on must be ratified by four persons on the PPCC. The Jolyon Drury Consultancy is hired by the Bank to check all subcontractors' clauses for agreements on spares supply. Not all those already committed have the appropriate clauses. Negotiations begin to secure them and set up a major inventory of parts and the means for storing them. By December 1982, John Breen, manager of HSPM, has hired Dick Watts, a

former public works lift inspector to be the new building manager. Watts, with Marshall, Herring and other representatives from GMR, HSPM and the Bank's two main user departments, make up a new 'users' committee, the Building User Research Group (BURG).

1983

BURG meets for the first time in February 1983 with Strickland, manager of technical services, as chair. It has no executive power. Its role is to bring forward design proposals for the remainder of the project. Mead will be the single link from BURG to the PPCC. All design development and research work is to end. There will be no specially-designed general office furniture by Foster Associates.

The Bank will take over the total control of fitting-out. Products must be off-the-shelf. Chris Seddon, Ian Davidson and later Rodney Uren of Foster Associates can attend – in an advisory capacity only – GMR working parties chaired by Marshall. All slide presentations are to cease. Only written papers on design proposals can be submitted from the working party to BURG conforming to a strict Bank discipline instigated by Strickland. Fact, function, implication, cost is the format. Preferably, submissions to BURG should not be longer than one side of an A4 sheet of paper.

The May 1983 paper to BURG summarising the design team's assessment of the Bank's existing furniture and conclusions from a worldwide survey of furniture suppliers, is thrown out. GMR will do its own surveys, taking advice from Foster Associates where necessary. GMR, months later, confirms the Foster team's conclusions. They need new furniture. There is still no agreed stacking plan, no agreement on how much of the building is to be sublet.

Sample surveys on projected staffing requirements by Herring are found to be based on various managers' assessments of their own staffing, whose salary budgets had not been agreed by senior management. The surveying of staff requirements has to begin again.

Managers start to become agitated over what appears to be endless rounds of surveys. News of having enclosed offices 'in board' for a select few managers only makes survey work more awkward. Using Quickborner techniques, much of the work to establish job function, workplace types, furniture requirements and inter-departmental working relationships, is initially done twice over, by GMR and Foster

Right and above: Part of Cupples Products' production facilities at its main aluminium panel and extrusion plant in St Louis, USA.

Associates, one checking the other; then later, in parallel, and finally, after many months, together in unison.

Clint Marshall and Eddie Wang of GMR are the men who really start to pull the users' side together. Jennifer Tsui, a Chinese employee in Foster Associates' Hong Kong office working alongside Davidson, Uren and others, becomes an invaluable link with the Chinese workforce of the Bank.

Together, broken bridges are slowly rebuilt. The design work on special furniture items, mostly led by Alex Lifschutz, also assists in this rebuilding of confidence. He works directly with the foreign exchange and banking hall managerial staff. Gordon Graham is now back with Foster Associates as a director in the Hong Kong office. In July, Munden resigns from being secretary to PPCC and takes over the chairing of BURG.

1984

By the January 1984 board meeting, the rationalisation of all the Bank's furniture requirements down to 26 job functions and 18 workplace types with the 'mix and match' furniture selection policy is agreed by PPCC. The steelwork is now up to the 21st floor. Fees for fitting-out are re-negotiated. PPCC recommends to the board to bring forward completion of the basement and the first 11 floors to July 1985. The furniture orders are placed in May but there is still no final agreed stacking plan. Peter Herring leaves the project in June 1984.

Detailed furniture layouts are begun in July. Chris Seddon presses the Bank to set up a CAD agency agreement between Foster Asso-

"But what about the reactions of the industrial companies that do come face-to-face with the collaborative approach of Foster Associates. Some of them are completely thrown and find it very difficult to stop worrying about what we are after. When this happens, we are done for. If the industrial side of the design and development process is worrying about what they should be doing to please the architect, rather than being able to talk objectively about the facilities, possibilities and potential they are able to offer, then that potential is already being clouded by preconceptions."

Norman Foster, *Building*, May 1982

ciates, J. Roger Preston & Partners, the services engineers, and the Bank, to handle co-ordination of furniture and services planning. The Bank would prefer to create its own system in-house.

By August, at last there is an agreed stacking plan. There will be no sublet space. The CAD agency agreement is signed in October and final layouts and detailed negotiations with departmental managers through GMR and the relocation committee — BURG under a new name, with some new members — begin. There is practical completion on the steelwork by October. The last service module is installed. With the fit of department needs to furniture and space available established as workable, a planning guideline report is submitted in November 1984. In essence this had been a foregone conclusion since 1981 ... but it is only now, eight months before moving in, that there is a design team certainty that everything will fit.

Work on site is now at a fever pitch to ensure meeting the completion dates of the following year. Documentation and agreement procedures for inevitable changes and late additions, however, are causing delays. At a quarterly review meeting in November, Foster Asso-

Extruded aluminium mullions hanging on racks prior to painting.

Unimate robotic welding machines being used to produce the truss mullions that support the glazed curtain walling at double-height areas.

ciates propose the setting up of an on-site 'task force', headed out by Ken Shuttleworth and David Nelson of Foster Associates but including members of the entire consultant team. The task force is to have executive authority to make immediate decisions on site. The proposal is accepted and offices are created on nearly completed floors of the new building.

1985

Three thousand workplaces over 38 floors are planned, negotiated and agreed with users in six months. Eighteen-hour working days are commonplace. The furniture begins to arrive in May 1985. Apart from the chairman's apartment — fitted out by the chairman's wife — all other areas have been dealt with through the process of the design teams advising the GMR working party who pass these to BURG and then to PPCC. The July 1985 partial completion date is met.

The November total completion date is met. Munden retires from the Bank on 30 November. By the official opening in April 1986, the double-height levels 20/21, planned for the staff restaurant, have already become offices for the import and export department. The CAD space-planning, furniture and services inventory system is not updated.

1986

Even while the Bank is moving in after total completion, changes continue to be made to floor layouts. Foster Associates' office in Hong Kong is dramatically reduced, but maintains a small presence through to the end of 1986. Part of their work involves creating an Internal Planning Manual. By October, there have been 30 departmental moves on 24 levels and cellularisation has increased by 10 per cent.

The Bank sells one of the buildings it was temporarily housed in for $15-million. In December, Michael Sandberg retires to be succeeded as chairman by William Purves. The Bank has been in its new home for one year.

"Note that the most highly industrialised objects – whether on wheels, in flight or fixed to the ground – are those most subject to renewal, constantly being improved in quality, even in terms of price. Building is the only industry that does not advance."

Jean Prouvé, *The Organisation of Building Construction*, 1971

Running against the sentiments expressed in Jean Prouvé's observation of 1971, virtually every element used in the construction of the Hongkong Bank was specially manufactured for the project, often in quite different parts of the world. Total control of the co-ordination process was essential to ensure everything would fit when it arrived on site. Responsibility for this fell to every member of the design team. During the later stages of the project, a 'task-force' was established to drive through last minute decisions and revisions, executive decisions often being made on site to ensure the building was completed on time. Ken Shuttleworth and David Nelson of Foster Associates headed the team and this is one of Shuttleworth's own co-ordination drawings prepared at that time.

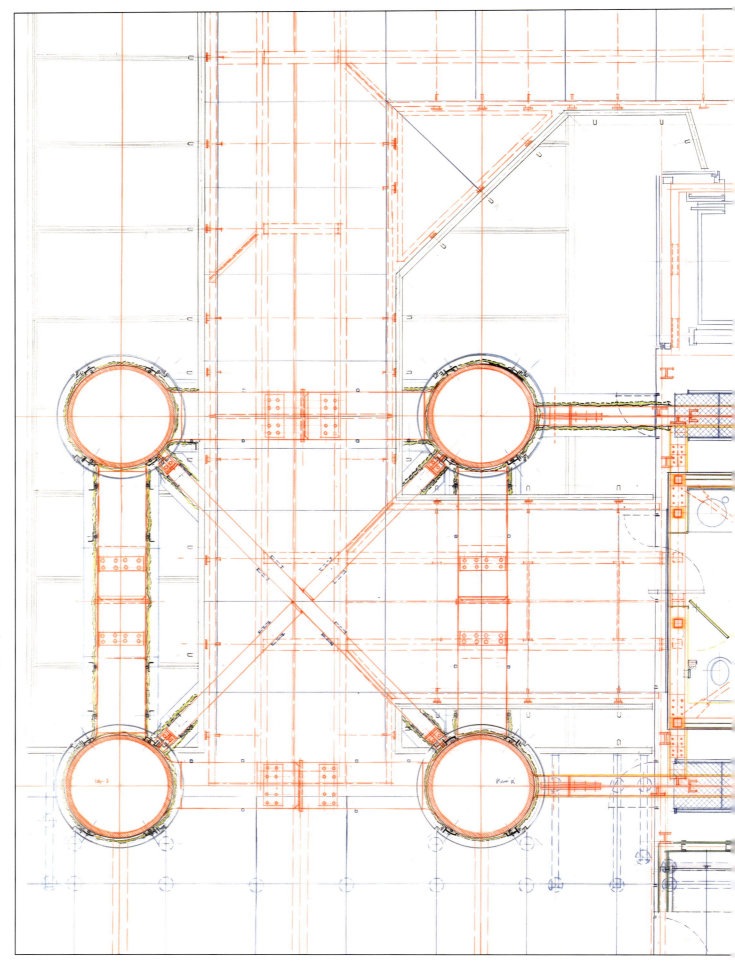

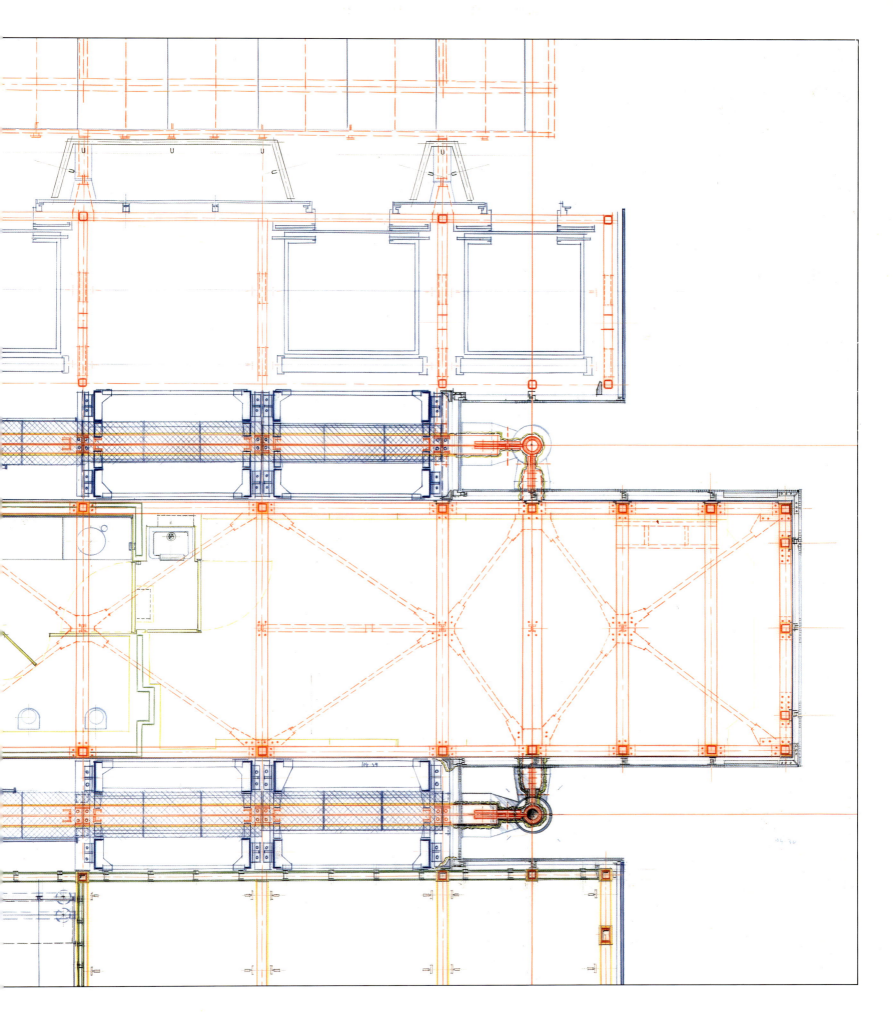

Hongkong Bank
Structure

"The wind studies identified that we would have problems in terms of wind acceleration, or enhancement, through the plaza. We spent HK$ 6 000 000 on these studies but saved something like seven times that amount in terms of steel economies alone — 700 tons of steel was removed because the building was too stiff."

Ray Guy, lecture at the Burrell Museum, January 1986

The Hongkong Bank has a structure more like that of a bridge than of an office building. The fabrication and erection of its steel frame was never going to be a routine matter. When Ove Arup & Partners had finalised their conceptual design, there was still a great deal of development work to be done on the various elements of the structure, and for this it was necessary to involve the steelwork manufacturer, making use of his technical expertise and testing facilities. A design development element was therefore included in the contract. Tenders were invited from 16 contractors from all over the world, but the job was won by a British consortium of the British Steel Corporation and Redpath Dorman Long.

There were a number of special problems, the solutions to which required great ingenuity and inventiveness. In most cases the standard solutions simply did not apply. First there was the problem of tolerances, and the related problems of differential loading and movement. In steelwork design, tolerances are rarely crucial in purely structural terms. A frame can be inaccurate to a degree and still be a perfectly safe structure, but the so-called following trades — in this case the frame cladding, the external walling, the floors, the service modules and so on — have much more demanding standards of accuracy. When each element is a separate production package involving a high degree of prefabrication, tolerances become critical. There was precious little room, or time, to make adjustments during construction. When the components arrived on site they had to fit perfectly.

Because the building was unevenly loaded, with large areas of floor omitted at the upper levels on the east side, it was subject to unusual deflections. This meant that it had to be constructed with a built-in bias. The frame actually leans several centimetres to the west. And there was another complication: the structure was subject to much more movement than would be normal in a building of this kind. To study these movements, special wind-tunnel tests were carried out at the University of Western Ontario. With typical thoroughness a complete reassessment of the wind climate of the Central district

With its eight massive masts taking all vertical loads, the Bank has a structure more like that of a bridge than of an office building. One by-product of this elaborate suspension structure is the column-free plaza created at ground level.

The masts are Vierendeel structures consisting of four circular columns connected by haunched rectangular beams at storey-height intervals. Each two-storey section was prefabricated in four parts as shown in this diagram. The first of these individual parts arrived in Hong Kong just before Christmas 1982, and for the rest of the project they were referred to as 'Xmas trees'.

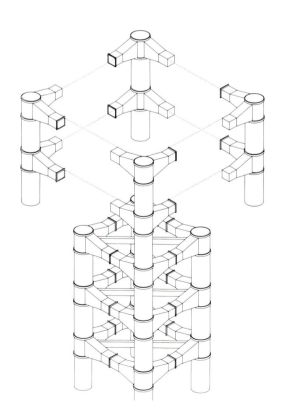

"This is no ordinary model. It has some 500 tap-off points connected by a spaghetti-like network of plastic pipes metering air pressures. Linked to a data processor they give valuable information on wind contouring, which has informed the design of the cladding and achieved economies both in that element and for the structure. It has also informed what kind of movements in typhoon conditions might be acceptable, as well as obviously proving what is safe for the building's occupants."

Norman Foster, client presentation of March 1982, describing the model shown below.

Left and bottom A detailed model of a large section of Hong Kong was tested in the wind tunnel. It proved the site was well sheltered by the surrounding topography – an unsurprising result since its safe harbour was the original reason for the founding of Hong Kong.

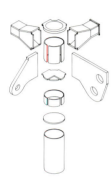
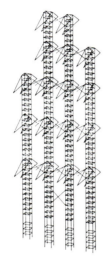
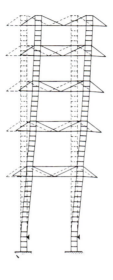
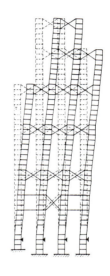

Structural engineers Ove Arup & Partners prepared their own drawings to explain the different components that make up sections of mast. They also used analytical computer models to demonstrate deflection profiles to the main structure under wind loading.

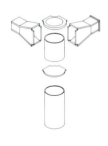
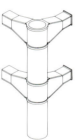

was carried out using a 1:2500 topographical model. The resulting wind profiles were then simulated on a 1:500 'proximity model', including all buildings and other features within a 600-metre radius of the site. Instrumented models of the building itself were tested in the proximity model to estimate external pressures and natural periods of vibration.

Accuracy was a general problem calling for constant monitoring throughout the fabrication and erection sequence. But there were more specific aspects of the design that benefited greatly from the design development process. A good example of this is the design of the connections between the vertical, horizontal and raking members of the two-storey high trusses. The original design, as sent out for tender, envisaged bolted connections with large flat plates to disperse the loads – a relatively clumsy solution relying more on brute strength than engineering subtlety. Ove Arup & Partners would have preferred simpler, smaller pin connections but these demanded an impossibly high degree of accuracy to function satisfactorily. The dynamic nature of the structure meant that loads could not be relied upon

217

"It takes us 23 minutes to get everybody out of the building. Margaret Law from Arup's did a fire study for us which showed that, even if our fire protection systems fail and the fire services cannot get there, the maximum length of time a fire can burn unattended is 70 minutes. More importantly, it wouldn't generate heat greater than about 325°C and we have two hours of fire protection against 600°C."

Ray Guy, lecture at the Burrell Museum, January 1986

A central 'butterfly' connection of the lower boom of one of the main suspension trusses. Here loads from the vertical hanger are transferred to the boom and the inclined truss members (not yet in place).

Mast components being fabricated in British Steel's Middlesbrough works. A design development element was included in the contract so as to take full advantage of the contractor's expertise and testing facilities.

These pictures begin to give some idea of the scale of the main elements of structure.

to act only in one direction. Unless the pins fitted their sleeves perfectly, they would be liable to shift from one position to another as the loads reversed, which might produce unacceptable deformations — quite apart from making worrying noises in windy conditions. This came to be known as the 'clunk-click' problem.

The solution that eventually emerged was a typical example of technology transfer in the form of a component normally used in large-scale machinery and known as a spherical plane bearing. This standard off-the-peg device, made on a production line and costing just two or three hundred pounds, solved the problem by compensating for a degree of misalignment of the pin while still ensuring a tight fit. More than 650 of these bearings were used in the final structure, varying in diameter from 150mm to 600mm. Ironically, this elegant detail is invisible in the final building because it is hidden away in the structure's cladding.

Another important element of the structure that is hidden from view is the corrosion protection system. This too emerged from the design development discussions between Redpath Dorman Long and Ove Arup & Partners. One might assume that, since the steelwork is everywhere cased in aluminium, corrosion would not be a big problem. However, the cladding actually increases the danger because, in Hong Kong's hot and humid climate, the air in the cavity between aluminium and steel is especially corrosive. If the steel were exposed to the weather then it would at least have a chance to dry out, but behind its aluminium skin it is likely to remain constantly damp. And, of course, clad steelwork is impossible to inspect. The corrosion protection system therefore had to be doubly effective and completely reliable.

Several options were considered, including air-conditioning the cavity. In this case an ordinary paint system would have been sufficient. Air-conditioning was rejected, however, as too complicated and too expensive. The next option was to encase the steel in concrete. Concrete corrosion protection works not as a simple barrier, like paint, but by increasing the alkalinity of the steel's immediate environment and thereby inhibiting rusting. Standard practice called for a minimum 50mm thickness of concrete, but this would have greatly increased the heaviness of the structure, in both visual and

The steel frame is protected from corrosion by a thin cementitious coating developed specially for the project. This works both by forming an impervious seal and also by increasing the alkalinity of the steel's immediate environment, thereby further inhibiting rust.

This computer-generated isometric drawing shows the main elements of primary structure for one of the outer line of masts. The upper compression boom that should span between masts at the top level of each suspension truss is omitted at the top and external edge of the building, as it was felt that a clear expression of the suspended nature of the structure was more important than a pure structural analysis. As loadings at these points tended to be less, alternative methods of internal strengthening were sufficient.

structural terms. Also, there would have been problems in the application of concrete to such complex profiles. What was needed, therefore, was a new kind of concrete, or cement-based coating, that could be much thinner and lighter than normal and yet perform equally well. The answer was a completely new process called cementitious barrier coating, or CBC. By adding special ingredients to a cement mixture, it was found that the required thickness of the coating could be reduced from 50mm to 12mm. And this solution had another advantage: the high humidity in the cavity, instead of causing corrosion, actually increased the chemical effectiveness of the protection.

The steel frame of the Hongkong Bank is therefore innovative in all respects, from conceptual design to corrosion protection. Like every other major element of the building it is the result of an intensive research, development and testing programme carried out by designers and manufacturers working together. While this may be normal for most industries, the adoption of this approach for use in building construction has been revolutionary.

Colin Davies

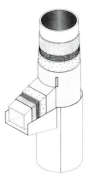

Fire protection takes the form of a ceramic-fibre blanket fixed to a stainless-steel mesh wrapped around the steel member. A reinforced aluminium foil then provides on-site protection and, later, prevents fibre break-off, necessary as the space between steel and cladding forms part of the air-conditioning system.

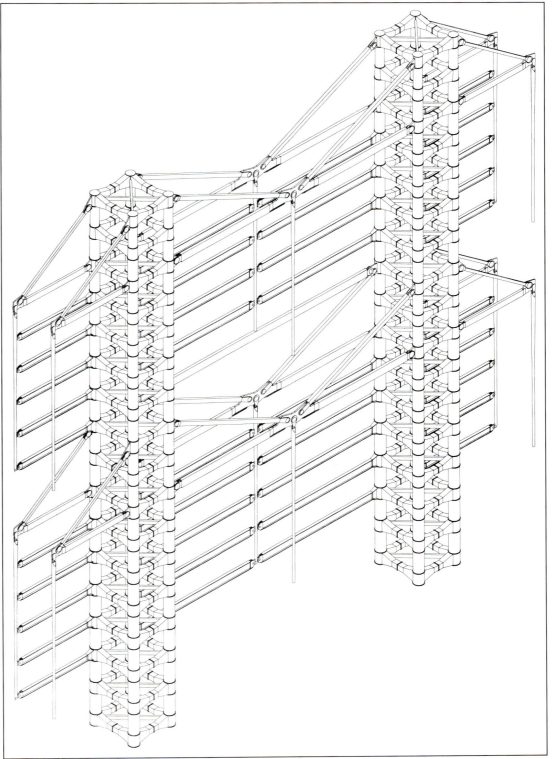

Hongkong Bank
Cladding

One of the largest individual sections of cladding protects the connection between cantilever truss and outer hanger. Setting this in place and ensuring a perfect seal at all the joints was a complex operation.

Stair towers and masts. The cladding to the stair towers, known as 'grid wall', has glass infill panels glued into the frame with structural silicon mastic. No mechanical restraint is required.

This isometric drawing shows the three main types of cladding: the aluminium structure cladding which is used both internally and externally; the glazed curtain walling; and the 'grid wall' used on service modules and stair towers.

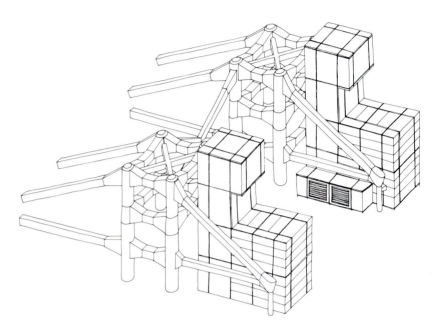

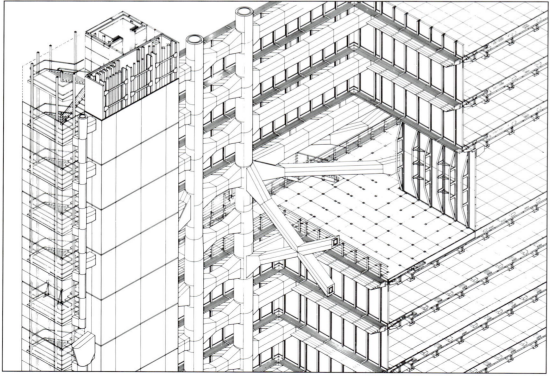

In conceptual terms the design of the Hongkong Bank – its plan, section, structure, servicing strategy, circulation system and so on – is simple; ingenious and innovative but essentially simple. The final, three-dimensional form of the building, however, is extremely complex. Cladding this form, keeping out the wind and rain, and protecting its various components was never going to be a straightforward business. There are various levels of complexity. First there is the 'laminated' and stepped form of the whole building, with its three slices rising to different heights, and the set-backs in between the service towers on the east and west sides. Then there are the service towers themselves – lifts, escape stairs, service modules and risers, all with different cladding requirements. And then there is the exposed structural frame, requiring its own separate cladding system. Finally there are all the special assemblies such as the so-called 'cathedral walls' at either end of the atrium, the superstructure supporting the helicopter pad, and the external part of the sun scoop.

Clearly this is not the sort of building that can simply be sheathed in standard curtain walling. There are, however, even more compli-

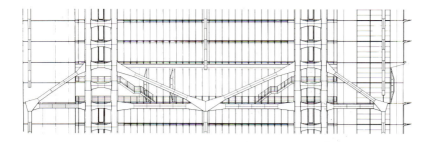

The 'flared' components of the structure cladding express the tensile stresses of the steel within.

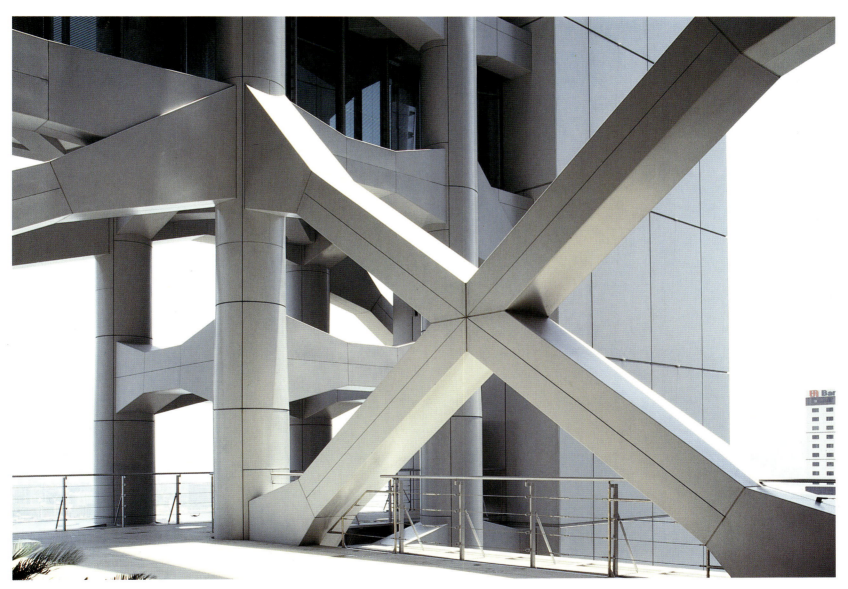

Two features of the structure cladding are immediately apparent: first, the great variety of shapes and sizes of panel and, second, the faultless finish which results from using 5mm thick aluminium sheet for the panels and computer-controlled welding machinery. All exposed areas of the cladding are finished with a fluoropolymer coating applied electrostatically and cured at 450°F producing a surface almost impervious to fading, weathering or chemical attack.

cations. Two basic design decisions introduced a new order of complexity to the cladding problem: the decision to expose parts of the structural frame on the outside of the building, and the decision — essential to the design strategy from the start — that the floors should hang from, rather than stand on, the primary supports. The first means that the walling somehow has to accept beams and struts penetrating the glass in thousands of places. In most cases the wall passes neither inside nor outside the composite Vierendeel masts, with their horizontal beams and cross-bracing, but right through the middle. And all of these junctions have to resist water penetration during the extreme conditions created by typhoons.

The problem is made even more intractable by the effects of the second decision. The tension structure is much more mobile than its conventional compression counterpart. In theory there can be anything up to 50mm differential deflection between floors. This somehow has to be accommodated in the curtain

"Prefabrication no longer means repetition and standardisation; it can mean total customisation, economic customisation, which opens up a whole new rich world of possibilities."

Norman Foster, Eric Lyons Memorial lecture, November 1986

The structure cladding prototype undergoing extreme weather testing at Cupples' plant in St Louis. Wind speeds of over 200 mph could be simulated by the retired US Navy fighter.

walling and in all those innumerable penetrations of the structure. Given this degree of complexity it is easy to see why the painstaking process of design development and prototype testing was not just a theoretically desirable procedure but an absolute practical necessity.

Most of the cladding was fabricated and erected by Cupples Products, the St Louis-based cladding subsidiary of H. H. Robertson & Company. Cupples was appointed at an early stage, following a worldwide survey of possible contractors, and was closely involved with the conceptual as well as the detailed design. It was the only firm to demonstrate the necessary commitment to quality and innovation, and a positive attitude to the concept of design development in collaboration with the architects. It was a collaboration which was eventually to produce a mountain of design information to be checked and double-checked on both sides of the Atlantic.

Cladding contractors usually have well established design offices to develop their standard systems and adapt them for specific applications. This, however, was a development programme of quite a different kind. All the systems were designed from scratch; they had to be able to cope with the unique performance requirements and the ruthless rigour of the Foster design ethos. More than 2500 sketch assembly drawings were prepared by the Foster Associates design team and these called forth no less than 10000 shop drawings from Cupples. Cupples' designers made frequent extended visits to London to advise on detailed design and a team of architects was stationed in St Louis to oversee the design, testing and manufacturing operation. Prototypes were made of all major joints and junctions and tested for watertightness under typhoon conditions simulated by an old Second World War Corsair aeroplane and a grid of sprinklers.

There are three main types of cladding: that for the structure, the curtain walling, and what was referred to as the 'grid wall' for service modules and stair towers. The first is not really cladding in the normal sense, but a form of steelwork protection. The steel is protected against corrosion with a cementitious coating and fireproofed with a fibrous ceramic blanket. This means that in order to preserve the smooth, metallic finish which is essential to the building's aesthetic, every column, beam, brace and strut, whether inside or outside the building,

As the design developed, large-scale models were prepared on which the implications of the joint and setting-out geometries could be accurately tested. At all times visual considerations had to be balanced with an understanding of production and erection procedures.

The first of the structure cladding panels under erection. Using purpose-built 'brake press' machines and robot welders, individual panels were manufactured to tolerances of ± 0.5mm.

Close design development with the full support of an expert manufacturer was essential. A survey of leading companies identified Cupples Products as by far the most experienced and, with the Bank's agreement, they were directly appointed as early as May 1981. Phil Bonzon, the company's senior designer, led a team from Cupples who were to work closely with Foster Associates over the next three years. As these free-hand drawings of his demonstrate, his unique understanding of the aesthetic as well as the technical considerations was to play an important part in the successful design and manufacture of the cladding.

Only plastic and wood, this first mock-up of the curtain walling, complete with sunshades and access walkways, was erected in the Great Portland Street office.

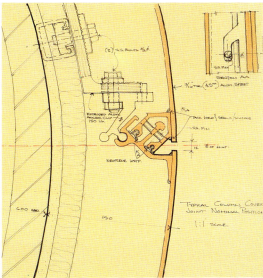

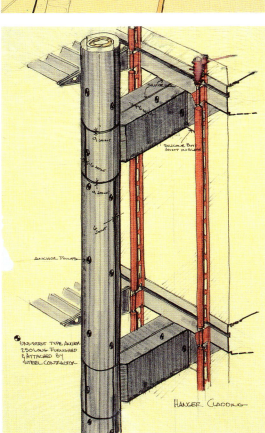

has to be encased in aluminium. Outside the building the aluminium protects the fireproofing from the weather, but inside it has another function to perform: the gap between the steel and its casing is part of the air distribution system. The aluminium panels, with extruded edge sections for added stiffness, are fixed to the steel with a subframe of 'Unistrut' channel sections, and jointed on the butt-strap principle, with 9mm flash gaps. The bare description, however, does little to explain the refinement of the finished product.

Two features are immediately striking. First, the great variety of shapes and sizes of panel, some of which are more than three metres long. Every steel member is clad in a closely tailored glove so that its form and structural function remain clear. The most complicated components, such as joint extrusions, are standardised and there is a degree of repetition of panel types, but no mass-produced, off-the-peg system could possibly have coped with all the combinations of rectangular, tapering, cylindrical or conical shapes.

The second striking feature is the faultless finish. Standard steelwork fireproofing and cladding systems often have an outer layer of aluminium less than 1mm thick. This usually becomes buckled and distorted at seams and fixings. The thickness of the Bank's aluminium structure cladding is 5mm. This, however, only partly explains the complete absence of any blemishes. The real secret is a new generation of computerised machinery which can be programmed to produce perfect, distortion-free welds. The machinery was installed by Cupples Products for this project, but it is capable of adapting to any job on a one-off basis, coping easily with geometrical profiles that would require months of drawing-board work and repeated re-jigging on conventional machines.

The concealed fixing system for these panels is even more complex than the visible surface of the aluminium. One reason for this is the differential tolerance between the cladding — plus or minus 3mm — and the steelwork — in theory plus or minus 40mm, but in practice anything up to three times that over the whole height of the building.

The same degree of precision and quality of finish is apparent in the aluminium curtain walling components. The standard mullions are

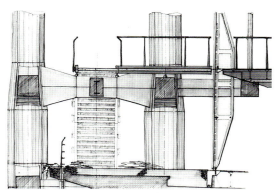

Detail design had to respond to production requirements. As this study model demonstrates, the curtain walling was fully resolved long before the joint geometry of the structure cladding.

The structure/curtain wall relationship was explored in a variety of sketches and models. The curtain walling has to accept beams and struts penetrating the glass in thousands of places, and yet accommodate extensive structural movement without leaking in high winds.

The extruded blades of the sunshades are angled so as to keep out the sub-tropical sun without obstructing the downward view from inside the building.

Shown here awaiting their coating of 'paint', the tapering, cantilevered brackets of the walkway/sunshades, perforated with round holes, are somewhat reminiscent of Foster's earlier designs for furniture.

In this development sketch by Phil Bonzon, the tubular mullion support is also shown inside the building. It was a relatively late change that moved it outside.

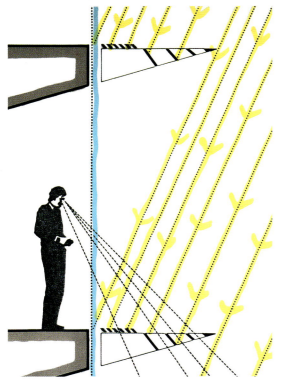

very large extrusions: effectively vertical beams with circular section outer flanges and perforated webs. At the double-height floors they become fully-fledged trusses. Originally these mullions were to be internal, but as the design developed it became clear that the exterior scale of the building could be broken down further and several awkward interior junctions could be resolved if the whole assembly were turned inside out. Like so many elements of the building, the curtain walling is, of necessity, an assemblage constructed of moving parts. In order to accommodate the floor-to-floor differential deflection, each storey-height wall is suspended from the floor above, sliding up and down in a slot weather-sealed by neoprene 'wiper-blades' at its base.

Wind-tunnel testing was an important part of the design development process for the curtain walling as well as for the structure of the building. It was necessary to understand the microclimate around the building in detail so that cladding fixings and joints could be designed to resist water penetration under the most extreme conditions. The comfort of passing pedestrians was another important consideration. It was as a result of model studies

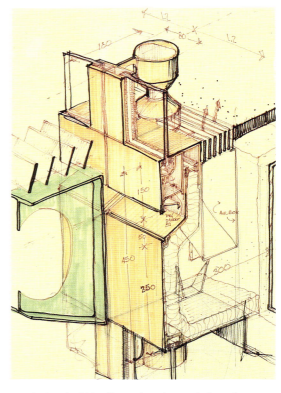

The relationship between structure and cladding was complex. For example, horizontal cross-bracing within the mast at each Vierendeel level, required an accurate positioning of the cladding line to ensure a regular spacing of mullions.

Every major option was modelled before a final decision was made.

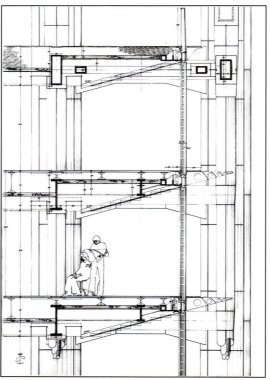

carried out at the Boundary Layer Laboratory, at the University of Western Ontario, that the glazed 'skirts' at plaza level were developed. These effectively cancel out the 'wind-tunnel' effect that is such a common nuisance in the vicinity of tall buildings.

Keeping out the wind and rain, however, is only part of the problem. The glazed curtain walls also have to be shaded from the sun to reduce heat gain and air-conditioning loads. This is done by means of external horizontal projections at every floor, with louvres angled so as not to obstruct the view downwards from inside the building. These projections also double as access walkways for window cleaning and routine maintenance. It is for this reason they have been installed over the whole of the north elevation, facing the harbour, even though this side of the building receives direct sunlight for only a few months of the year. Needless to say, the walkway/sunshades are finely engineered pieces of metalwork, as precise as anything you will find in an aerospace factory. The vacuum die-cast cantilevered brackets, perforated with

The sunshades at work, here on the east elevation set-back at the top of the building.

round holes, are particularly elegant and somewhat reminiscent of Foster's furniture designs.

Other elements of the external enclosure were designed with an equal thoroughness and determination not to let the complexity of the building defeat ingenuity. Service towers are clad in a 'grid wall' system supporting infill panels either of glass, for the lift-shafts and escape stairs, or aluminium honeycomb, for the service modules and risers. This latter is a favourite technology transfer material from the aeroplane manufacturing industry. Thin gauge metal sheets are laminated to an aluminium-foil 'honeycomb' core to produce a light, strong and perfectly flat panel. The stacks of modules, rising to the full height of the building, look almost as if they have been extruded from solid metal. The glass walls are also flat and true, with no projecting mullions, transoms or glazing beads because the glass is literally glued into the frame and requires no mechanical restraint. What would be a daring innovation in most European buildings, in this building seems almost run-of-the-mill.

Colin Davies

"The sheer visual delight of the cladding details on the Bank could not have happened without a shared endeavour, enthusiasm and dedication which extended from a factory in Missouri, through to a Chinese workforce on site, and a highly mobile design team who were as much at home on the shop-floor as on the drawing-board. It is as much about aesthetics as water penetration and tolerances, but it is not about the architect as a remote aesthete removed from the production process."

Norman Foster, *L'Architecture d'Aujourd'hui*, February 1986

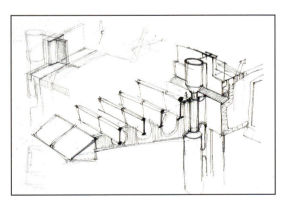

At a technical level, moving the mullion support to the building's exterior also solved the problem of how to support the sunshades, a detail omitted in the earlier sketch.

An arrangement of lateral, horizontal and vertical slotted joints is accommodated behind the curtain wall to ensure perfect alignment.

The rich filigree and fine detailing of the elements that make up the curtain walling effectively break down the exterior scale of the building. Evacuated die-casting was used to achieve the superb quality of the sunshade brackets, and the sunshades themselves have proved very successful in reducing the amount of solar radiation entering the building. On the building's north elevation, which receives sun at only a steep angle for a few months of the year, it has been possible to eliminate the back-up wall entirely.

Hongkong Bank
Modules

The idea of plug-in service modules is not a new one. As long ago as 1937, the great American architect/technologist Richard Buckminster Fuller designed a steel prefabricated and mass produced 'Dymaxion bathroom'. More recently the container revolution, the offshore oil industry, the theoretical projects of the Archigram group and the buildings of the Japanese Metabolists have all made contributions to the development of the concept. There are two basic approaches to the use of modules in building. The first is to take a fixed infrastructure of services and attach the modules to it in the form of 'living pods'. Peter Cook's Plug-in City project of 1964 is an exploration of the application of this idea on an urban scale, and Kisho Kurokawa's Nagakin Capsule Tower of 1972 is the best known built example. The second approach is to regard the occupied space of the building as the fixed element and put the services into the plug-in modules. The Hongkong Bank adopts this latter approach.

There are 139 service modules, made on a production line and shipped to the site fully fitted out, commissioned and tested, and then suspended in towers on the east and west sides of the building. The modules each contain lavatories and local air-handling plant — or secondary plant such as generators, boilers or electrical substations — and they are linked together by risers which were also prefabricated in two- and three-storey high steel frames. Flexibility, demountability, renewability and mass production are all ideas implicit in the module concept. The implication is that the plug-in modules can be unplugged and replaced by new modules when they wear out, or perhaps that they might be moved to another location in response to some alteration in the use of the building.

What, however, are the real practical advantages of the modular approach to services? There are three main ones: speed, quality and compactness. The modules are made on a production line in a factory. This takes them out of the on-site construction programme and allows their production to proceed in parallel with the building of the main structure. It saves time and it saves valuable working and storage space on site. A traditional on-site fit-out would have been out of the question given the short space of time available for design and construction. Since the modules are made in a clean, controlled environment, the quality of the finishes and the precision of the services installation are

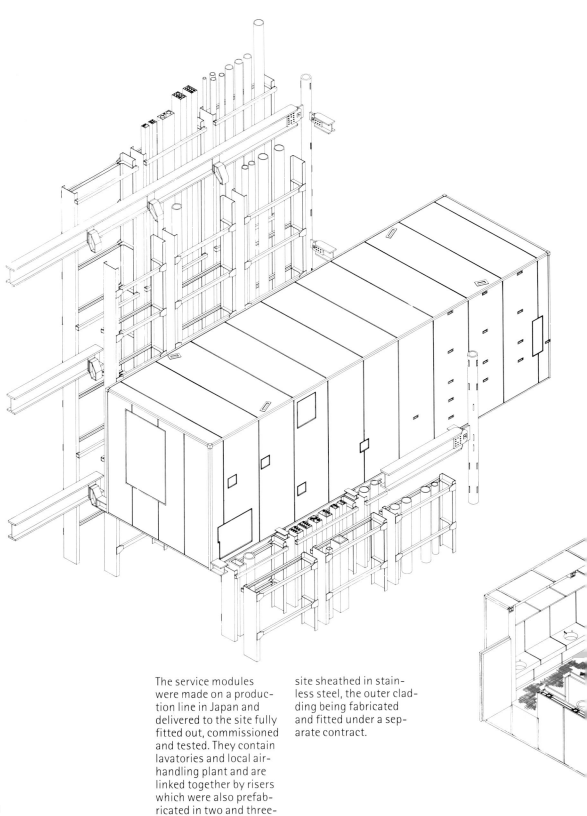

The service modules were made on a production line in Japan and delivered to the site fully fitted out, commissioned and tested. They contain lavatories and local air-handling plant and are linked together by risers which were also prefabricated in two and three-storey high steel frames. The modules arrived on site sheathed in stainless steel, the outer cladding being fabricated and fitted under a separate contract.

"This process of modelling from small scale through to full size can be seen in the development of the service module. It was originally simulated in wood and plastic in a model less than a metre in length. It was then made, in those same materials, as a full-size working mock-up. This was built in Tokyo and formed the basis of a pre-production prototype, which was assembled in south-west Japan to test out the final steel and aluminium components as well as the engineering systems that it contained."

Norman Foster, Royal Gold Medal speech at RIBA, June 1983.

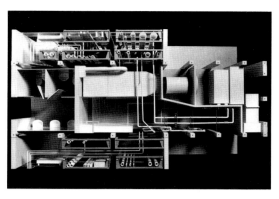

Model of a service module viewed from above and the side to show its relationship to the prefabricated risers. In Japan prefabrication of pipe- and ductwork is more common than in Europe or America.

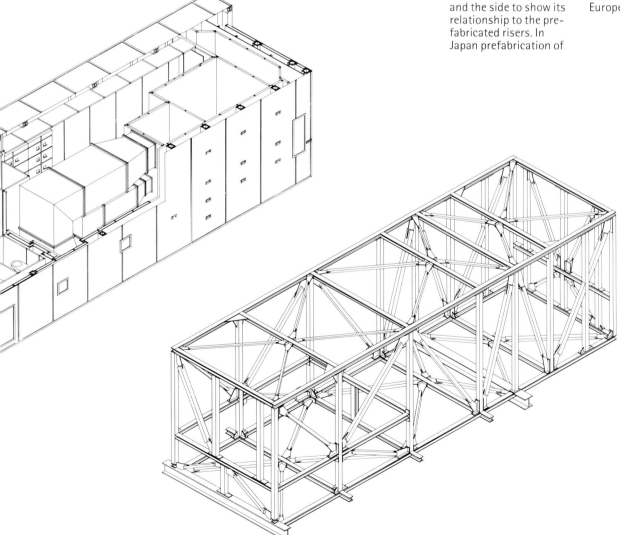

Foster Associates' outline design of the container-size enclosures was left open for suggestion by the tendering contractors. Sophisticated monocoque and plate structures were finally rejected in favour of a simple steel frame combined with a reinforced concrete floor that provided the necessary fire separation.

"What I found particularly enjoyable, again in terms of quality control or attitude of mind, was the fact that the prototype was handled as if it were a revered traditional inn or temple. When we inspected it and made all the various development changes we were all in stockinged feet. Shoes were left outside. It is this degree of reverence and care, I would submit, which is central to any quest for quality, whatever the stage of a project."

Norman Foster, lecture to Sainsbury's Executive Club, March 1984

Studies being carried out in HMT Consort's first prototype module. On his visits to Japan, Norman Foster found that ideas put forward in design sessions one day would appear in the prototype on the next.

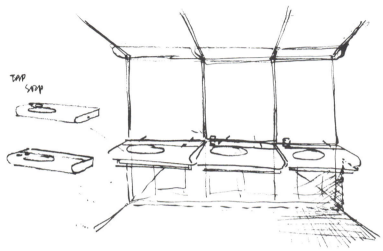

Norman Foster's sketch explores wash-basin options. No less attention was paid to taps and soap dishes than to any other detail of the building.

much higher than they would be on a chaotic and dirty building site. Finally, since the production line allows access to the module on all sides at ground level, mechanical plant, pipework and ductwork can be arranged much more compactly. In an owner-occupied building the extra usable floor space that this creates is a definite bonus.

Accessibility is usually the governing factor in the planning of plant rooms and mechanical services layouts. Often the space allocation is over-generous because of the difficulty of visualising complex assemblies in three dimensions. But when the services are modular and factory-produced it is much easier to build

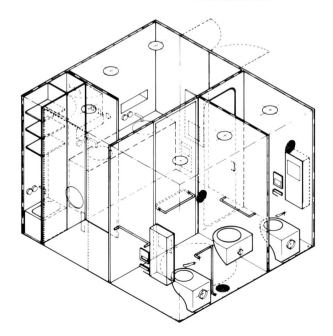

A variety of lavatory types and sizes was required for male and female staff depending on staff seniority and location. In these early drawings, the possibility of windows had not yet been ruled out.

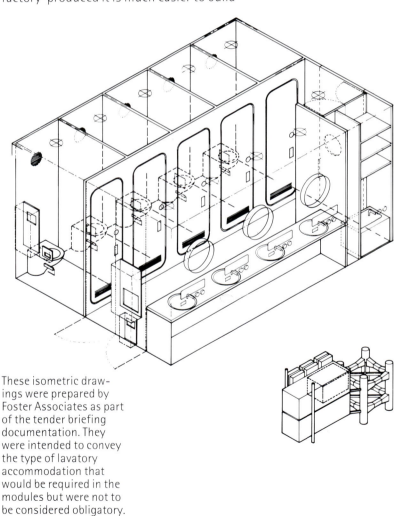

These isometric drawings were prepared by Foster Associates as part of the tender briefing documentation. They were intended to convey the type of lavatory accommodation that would be required in the modules but were not to be considered obligatory. Each manufacturer would be allowed to put forward his own proposals.

HMT Consort prepared this full-size mock-up to coincide with the design team's first visit to Japan. In principle, the design of the module was already realised. Only detail changes were required before production began.

As when visiting a Japanese temple, shoes had to be left outside during inspections of the module prototype.

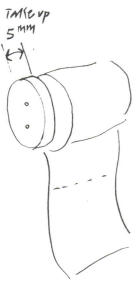

Norman Foster's sketches for toilet-roll holders and ashtrays. No detail is left unexplored.

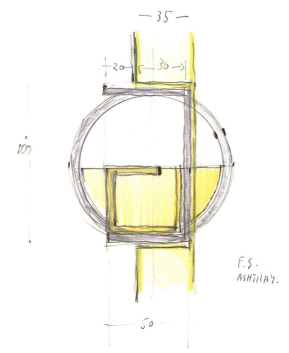

mock-ups and prototypes to make sure that every valve, switch, motor or filter is accessible for maintenance.

These, then, are the basic principles behind the modular services concept. The problem for the Foster design team, working with services engineers J. Roger Preston & Partners, was to find a manufacturer for the modules. Five contractors – from Western Europe, Britain and Japan – were invited to tender on the basis of an outline design and a performance specification. As with the other major elements of the building, the detailed design would be a collaboration between architect, consultant and manufacturer. It was no surprise to anyone that the job went to Japan, because there the prefabrication of pipe- and ductwork is much more common than it is in Europe and indeed for certain building types it is almost the norm. Even for the Japanese, however, this was a highly unusual project requiring the establishment of a powerful consortium which brought together the skills of Hitachi, Mitsubishi and Toshiba. The tender submission by HMT Consort – as the consortium was known – displayed a firm grasp of the principles involved and provided an impressive set of pre-contract documents.

Critical dimensions, loads, internal finishes for the lavatories and performance criteria for the mechanical plant were all spelt out by the architects and engineers, but the design of the container-size enclosures was left open for suggestions by the tendering contractors. Several solutions were proposed, including sophisticated monocoque and plate structures, but the winning Japanese design was, in comparison, plain and simple: a straightforward steel-framed box with, rather surprisingly, a concrete floor. This was necessary for interfloor fire protection while the extra weight also helped to reduce vibrations.

It is important to realise that the design development procedure did not extend to the mechanical plant itself. There was no attempt to re-invent the technology of air-conditioning, drainage, or electrical distribution. Engineering components, though the latest and best of their kind, were standard items such as might

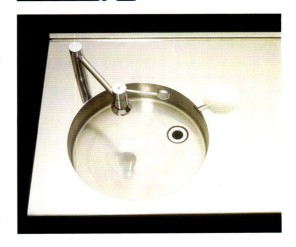

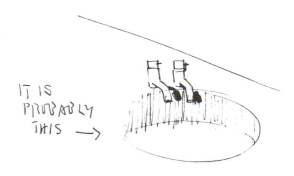

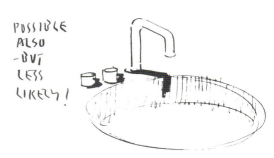

Norman Foster proposed a circular wash-basin formed as a continuous element within a stainless-steel work-top. A prototype, simple and elegant, was produced in London. Tap options were also proposed.

The container-like modules arrived from Japan by ship. Unloaded on to barges in Hong Kong's harbour they were placed in storage and moved to site only when required.

As with the steelwork, the modules were delivered to site and lifted into place during the early hours of the morning. Arriving from their storage point by low loader, their exceptional size required a special route where road and overhanging display signs had been removed.

Interior of the mechanical plant compartment of a typical module. One important aspect of off-site production was that ground-level access to all sides allowed plant, pipework and ductwork to be arranged much more compactly.

This view down the completed module tower on the south-east corner of the building shows the riser frames in position, attached to both sides of the outer primary beams that span between mast and outer hanger.

Lifting was restricted by the erection procedure of the steelwork to limited 'windows' in the overall programme, requiring all the modules of one zone to be positioned within a three week period. On alternate nights, two modules were lifted between the hours of midnight and 6 am.

be found in any highly-serviced, modern building. What was new was the organisation of the production process and the method of assembly. As if to emphasise that this was a practical strategy, not an architectural conceit, the modules were clad under a separate contract by Cupples Products after they had been installed on site. The expression is that of clusters of towers, some for services and others for vertical movement. Separate cladding meant that the walls of the modules as produced in the factory were merely internal linings. They were covered, nevertheless, in stainless steel to protect them until the cladding arrived.

The original intention was that the modules should be standardised so that they could be mass produced like cars and, to a certain degree, this was achieved. As design development proceeded, however, necessary special adaptations began to multiply. There are seven different types of lavatory and many more different plant installations, all with connections in different positions, so that in the final building no two modules are identical in every detail.

To cope with the massive design workload that this imposed, HMT Consort and its design consultants, Takanaka Komuten, sent a staff of 50 to work in Foster Associates' London office for three months in early 1982. In April of that year several mock-ups were produced, mainly to test accessibility, and in June a production prototype was ready for testing. By October fabrication was under way in a specially rented electrical engineering workshop in Ako, Japan, usually used for manufacturing huge turbine generators. Not only did this location provide sufficient space with the correct facilities, it

The first module (shown here) was positioned on 12 November 1983. Exactly 10 months later, the 139th and last was lifted into place.

"The only thing we had to do, literally, with the modules was to connect them to the vertical services, put in toilet paper, soap and towels and we were in business."

Ray Guy, lecture at the Burrell Museum, January 1986

had its own dockyard from which the finished modules could be shipped directly to Hong Kong. Meanwhile, on site, the building had yet to rise out of the ground. A curious situation therefore arose whereby very minor components like soap dishes and toilet-roll holders — having been subjected, of course, to the usual rigorous option-testing procedure — were being installed in the lavatories before structural steelwork design had been finalised. Co-ordination problems were formidable. Cladding fixings, for example, had to be precisely positioned in the Ako workshop, while the panels they were designed to hold were being made thousands of miles away in St Louis, Missouri. Similarly, structural fixing points had to be co-ordinated with steelwork under manufacture in the UK.

Once the modules had been designed and fabricated, their delivery and installation was a quick and relatively painless operation. They were carried by container ship from Japan to a storage facility in Hong Kong at Junk Bay, and from there to the site by a combination of barge and low-loader. To avoid congestion, the final stage of this journey had to be made in the early hours of the morning. Once at the site, it was a relatively simple and quick operation to hoist the individual modules into their final allocated position using the building's tower cranes. To have fitted all the plant, risers, internal fittings and finishes in the conventional way would have been impossible without disrupting other trades on this cramped urban site. Months would certainly have been added to the overall programme, quality would have suffered and space would have been wasted. This is not quite the fully demountable assemblage of mass-produced modules envisaged by Archigram and the Metabolists in the 1960s, but in the end the strategy has been fully justified on purely practical grounds and the modular services concept has been taken several stages further.

Colin Davies

The modules are in place and fixed securely to the steelwork. Fire protection of the steel proceeds just ahead of the cladding. The fixing points for cladding support rails, which had to be accurately positioned during manufacture of the modules in Japan, are clearly visible.

A typical lavatory interior. The predominant material is stainless steel, the effect austere and functional rather than lavish. Everything has its place and no detail is unconsidered. Access to service plant is made through the door containing the towel dispenser.

Hongkong Bank
Services

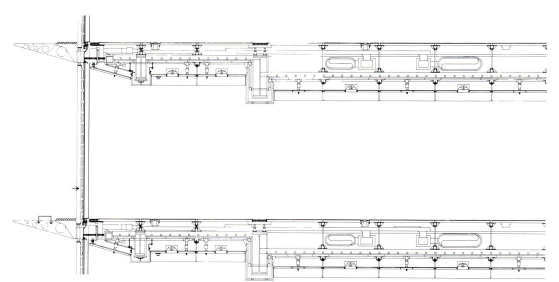

Foster Associates pioneered the technique of distribution of services in floor voids, a strategy which is now increasingly common in highly-serviced buildings. The idea was first proposed in a project for IBM as long ago as 1970, and was put into practice, in a simplified form, in the Willis Faber building completed in 1975. A far more complex version was proposed for the unbuilt Hammersmith project, but the Hongkong Bank was the practice's first opportunity to apply the concept in full and on a large scale.

Lift up the 1200 x 1200mm floor panels and a 600mm deep void is revealed, criss-

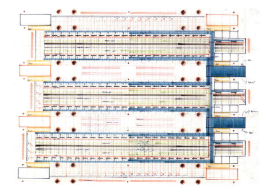

A section through the edge of the building. Each floor's main service requirements are located at floor level, with only an electrical supply for the luminaires and smoke detection system being provided within the suspended ceiling. Sprinkler outlets are supplied from pipework in the floor above.

Sketches were used to study alternative distribution patterns from the main air-handling modules on the west side of the building.

crossed by a dense network of air ducts and electrical trunking. Ideas about the possible modularisation of the horizontal services, explored in the Chevron scheme and in the early development stages of the Final scheme, were, in the end, abandoned in favour of a simple, continuous void above a conventional concrete slab. The slab acts as a structural diaphragm and provides the necessary fire protection between floors. It is also an ideal flat working surface on which to install services. To combine ducts, trunking and floor structure in an integrated factory-assembled component was an

A comprehensive grid of service distribution points – for electrical supply, telephone and computer links, and air-conditioning – is positioned beneath the raised floor system and connected to outlets in the individual floor panels as required. As this detailed isometric drawing illustrates, accurate setting out of the services was essential to ensure the regular grid of raised floor supports was never obstructed.

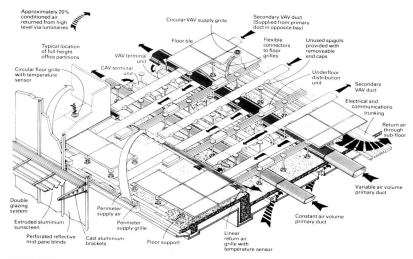

HongkongBank Headquarters Building — Isometric view of modular sub-floor services layout

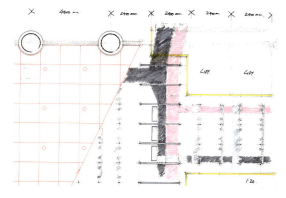

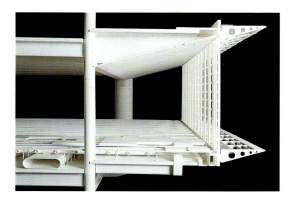

An early model explores the relationship of the services and raised floor system to structure. At this stage a straightforward sloping soffit was proposed for the edge of the building, strikingly similar to the solution used at Willis Faber & Dumas.

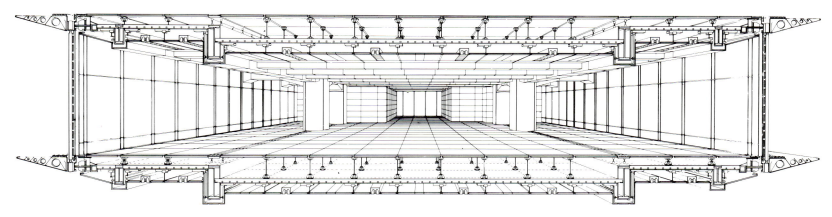

This late presentation drawing shows the final arrangement of raised floor and suspended ceiling systems as applied to a single-bay floor near the top of the building. The concrete diaphragm slab steps up at the edge of the building, while the ceiling system at this point now clearly expresses the structure.

Floor panels of 600 x 600mm, supported on rails, are shown in this early study model, but the two-level service distribution system is already accurately resolved.

idea in tune with Foster's view of the building as a kit of prefabricated parts, but it would have introduced many unnecessary complications. The basic structural configuration of the building dictated that secondary floor beams run north/south while air ducts had to run east/west. It proved impossible to overcome this conflict in any reasonably economical way without separating the structure and services distribution zones.

The air-conditioning system works mainly on the variable volume/constant temperature principle, augmented by a secondary constant temperature/variable volume system at the perimeter to counteract solar heat gain. Primary air-supply ducts running east/west feed secondary ducts above them running north/south. These, in turn, feed special circular floor grilles via flexible hose connections. Eighty per cent of the air is returned directly into the floor void, which acts as a plenum, via linear grilles; the remaining 20 per cent finds its way through the light fittings into the ceiling void, from whence it returns to the floor via the space between the internal main masts and their outer aluminium cladding. Electrical and electronic services follow a similar primary and secondary distribution pattern to the air-supply ducts, and are also linked by flexible hoses to special outlets set into the floor panels.

It is worth looking in detail at the design of the floor panels for they are an excellent example of the design development process in action. There are a number of standard raised-floor systems on the market from which Foster Associates might have chosen, but none

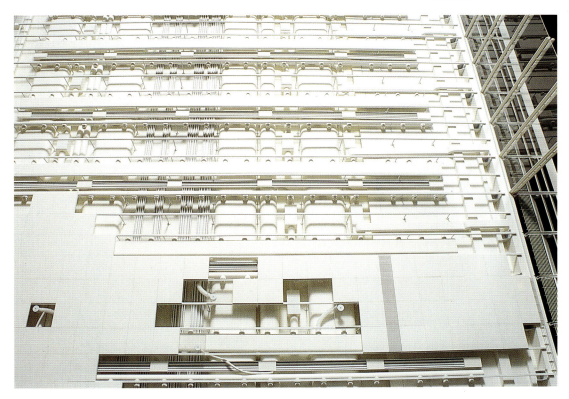

The subfloor services installation on the main banking hall level complete and awaiting final inspection. The increased ducting on the right is part of the special provisions required for the atrium.

The Japanese subcontractor for the internal partition and ceiling systems was so impressed by the raised floor at the Bank that it now produces its own system for the Japanese market.

Below: Prior to tender, a subfloor services prototype was installed in Foster Associates' typical office floor mock-up to help assess the possibilities of prefabrication.

seemed to meet their special requirements and standards of quality. They therefore set about designing a new system in collaboration with the manufacturers.

The first requirement was flexibility, but all 'flexible' plans have rules of some kind and in practice that usually means a grid. The standard grid for off-the-peg systems is 600 x 600mm and, for a time, the possibility of using die-cast aluminium panels of this size was considered. Another strong contender was an extruded panel 1200 x 600mm, but in the end 1200 x 1200mm was settled upon. It allowed sufficient flexibility in the layout of partitions; it reduced the number of joints and more than halved the number of support pedestals; it facilitated access to the mass of trunking and ductwork below and, perhaps most important, it created a refined and elegant floorscape.

However, it also meant that panels of standard construction would either not be strong enough to span between the supports, or would be too heavy to lift. The solution was again laminated aluminium honeycomb, a light, but strong, material most commonly used in the construction of aircraft. H. H. Robertson, the selected contractors and parent company of

Cupples Products, was familiar with its use in cladding panels but had not before considered using it for flooring.

Although a fine enough grid for the partition planning, 1200 x 1200mm was too coarse for electrical, communications and air-conditioning outlets. The solution was simplicity itself. The purpose-made, circular die-cast aluminium outlets are positioned not in the centre of the panel but in the centre of one of its quarters. Thus, by simply rotating the panel, they can be placed anywhere on a 600 x 600mm grid. This was the first ever use of floor-level air

The raised floor system. The basic panel is machine-made to minimal tolerances and is capable of accepting a variety of floor finishes. Holes for the service outlets were simply drilled through the finished panel. Like the panels, the pedestals were specially manufactured for the project. The heads can adjust vertically and laterally, and are provided with rubber covers to avoid the 'drumming' effect experienced in some raised floors.

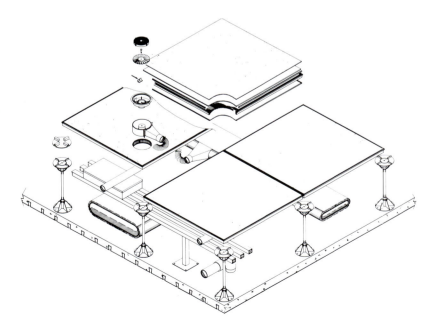

Following early scepticism that air-conditioning could be achieved satisfactorily with outlets only at floor level, the final system has proved so successful that Trox now produces outlet grilles as a standard item.

The 'Marilyn Monroe' factor. When floor outlets were first proposed, there was some concern expressed about the effects of up-draughts. While not strong enough to raise skirts, their design was nevertheless carefully controlled to avoid any possible discomfort.

supply and it was therefore necessary for the manufacturer of the air outlets, Trox, to carry out original research. One particular problem came to be known as the 'Marilyn Monroe factor' – the effect of strong up-draughts on women's skirts. Output from the Bank's grilles was never

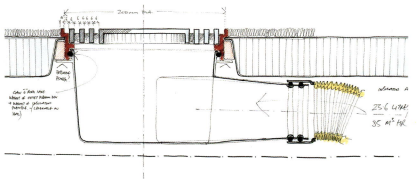

going to be strong enough for that to be a problem, but undue draughts were a concern. Extensive aerodynamic tests successfully solved the problem by the introduction of spiral grilles designed to project the air high into the space at relatively low velocity. So successful has the system proved that the outlet is now a standard Trox product. Electrical and communications outlets match the air outlets visually, but internally are more complex. The circular top plate, with a trap-door through which cables emerge, conceals a segmented junction box with ample spare capacity to cater for the inevitable increase in the use of electronic equipment.

The floor panels have other functions to perform. They must be airtight, acoustically sealed and they must accommodate higher than normal structural movement. To cope with all this they are provided with rubber 'wiper-blade' seals at all edges. Finally, they must be able to accept a variety of floor finishes from carpet to marble. As ever, prototypes were rigorously tested in conjunction with the manufacturer, various edge-bead profiles and materials being matched with a variety of floor finishes. The result was aluminium for carpet and stainless steel for marble.

In this way a completely new flooring system has been developed with the benefit of the Foster Associates design ethos: no conventional wisdom was accepted and no option was left unexplored.

Colin Davies

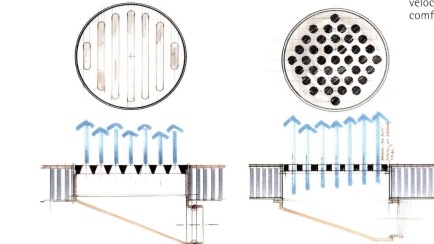

These early sketches concentrate as much on the visual impact of the floor outlet grilles as on their construction, but the basic principles of the subfloor pressure box and flexible connections are well explained. In reality considerable research was required to resolve the problem of how air could be projected high into the space at velocities within normal comfort criteria.

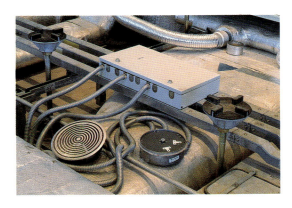

The cover plate for the electrical outlet (left) matches the final design of the floor outlet grilles of the air-conditioning system (far left above). Both outlets are supplied by flexible connections, allowing them to be repositioned to suit changing office layouts quickly and with ease.

Hongkong Bank
Interior Systems

A sketch section through a typical office floor showing an early proposal for the partition system and the 'gull-wing' ceiling. This device alternated curved near-perfect reflectors with flat perforated panels – backed with sound absorption material – to form a ceiling that was its own light source, evenly reflecting the light of a single fluorescent tube over an area of 2400 x 1200mm.

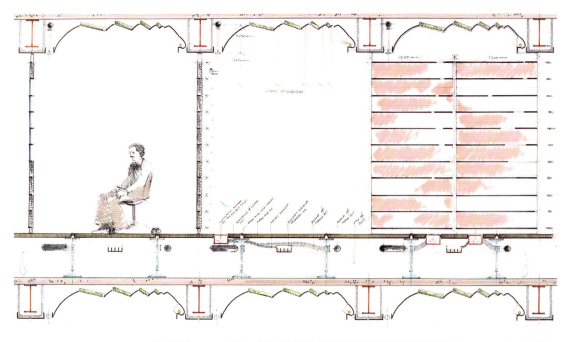

The gull-wing ceiling would have been a dominant element in the interior fit-out. Sketches explored its impact on a typical office floor.

A working prototype of the gull-wing ceiling was installed in the typical office floor mock-up. The regular holes along one side were to house sprinkler outlets, smoke detectors and supplementary task-lights.

Partitions and suspended ceilings are possibly the most conventional of the major elements of the building, at least in appearance. The interior might, however, have looked very different if the so-called gull-wing ceiling had progressed beyond the development stage. The ceiling evolved from an idea by lighting consultants Bartenbach Wagner. Most standard fluorescent-strip light fittings are very inefficient, losing 20 per cent or more of the light's energy in the fitting. The Bartenbach Wagner idea was that the whole ceiling could become a light source, using a careful geometric alignment of near-perfect reflectors to harness the total light output of the fluorescent tubes with the minimum of glare. The relatively low level of illumination would be supplemented by task lighting at desk level.

The system that was developed consisted of 2400 x 1200mm units, incorporating sound absorption panels and provision for additional downlighters, sprinklers and smoke detectors. Accurate models were made and tested under Bartenbach Wagner's artificial sky in Innsbruck and full-size mock-ups were constructed by Foster Associates in London. Eventually, however, the gull-wing ceiling had to be abandoned because of changes in the partition planning grid. The client insisted on a 1200 x 1200mm grid and the gull-wing ceiling could not be adapted in time.

Three basic principles were adopted in the planning of the office floors. First, that the transparency and fluidity of the space should be preserved: to have closed off the escalators from the spaces they served, treating them as mere vertical corridors, would have made a nonsense of the whole circulation philosophy. Second, that as many occupants as possible should have the benefit of the spectacular views out to north and south. To achieve this

Traditional Japanese architecture – with its movable screens given order by the fixed module of *tatami* mats – was one source quoted by Norman Foster as an influence in the design of the Bank's interior systems.

Frank Lloyd Wright's translucent screens for the Johnson Wax building use glass tubes of varying diameters. The Bank's partitions are simpler, but translucency is retained using *shoji* glass – a material that sandwiches glass-fibre, made to resemble Japanese paper, between two sheets of glass.

The quality of lighting within the building was tested using working models at Bartenbach Wagner's artificial sky in Innsbruck. Here, typical daylight conditions for Hong Kong could be accurately reproduced.

most of the cellular offices were placed at the centre of the building with fully-glazed partitions facing the external walls. The third principle was concerned not with visibility, but with containment. The Bank was very much in favour of open planning for the majority of office areas, while Foster Associates were concerned to maintain a more even balance. As a general rule, therefore, it was agreed that the view from any particular desk should never be less than a third of the width of the building and never more than half.

There were some special problems to be solved in the design of the demountable partitions themselves, mainly caused by the movement characteristics of the suspension structure. No proprietary partitioning system could have coped with a maximum floor deflection of 50mm without drastic modification, so the system had to be purpose designed. Foster Associates quickly concluded that the only satisfactory way to allow for the deflection was to hang the partitions from the ceiling and provide a slip-joint at skirting level. But the movement characteristics were more complicated than that. There was also what came to be known as the 'washing line' effect. As well as moving up and down, panels had to be free to move from side to side. This meant more slip-joints at all the vertical junctions. And the problems did not end there. There were the doors to be considered: 50mm gaps under doors could not be tolerated, so the doors and their frames had to stand on the floor and slide up and down

One disadvantage of the gull-wing ceiling was the fitting of partitions. In this proposal sheets of glass rise from the top of floor-supported partitions into slots within the ceiling.

Photographed against a backdrop of a view of Hong Kong at night, a working model of the gull-wing ceiling simulates a typical office area. Later, scale partitions and furniture would be added.

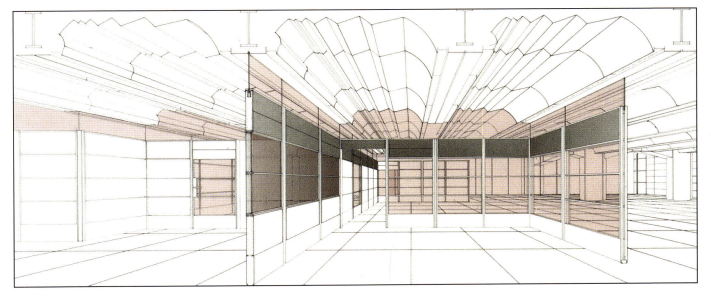

"It is not exceptional for the Bank to incur an annual expenditure of HK$300 million in covering the work on new layouts required by departmental changes. If the inherent flexibility of the systems in the new building makes this work easier and quicker by a factor of five – and I believe that that might well be the right sort of figure – the Bank will save roughly HK$240 million every year."

Norman Foster, *L'Architecture d'Aujourd'hui*, February 1986

An early mock-up of the partition system – seen here with the gull-wing ceiling – but with its basic characteristics already resolved.

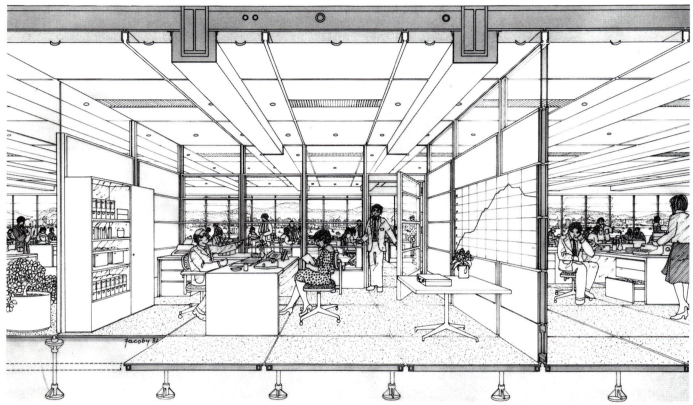

The partitions are made up using a series of standardised components added to a finely proportioned frame to create walls that can be clear-glazed, translucent, solid or, indeed, any combination of these.

Helmut Jacoby's perspective of June 1983 shows the final partition and ceiling systems in their integrated form. The partitions now hang from the top, connecting into a frame that also supports the suspended ceiling. The same subcontractor was used to supply both elements.

in relation to the panels. The whole partition system was therefore designed as an assemblage of moving parts but with every joint sealed to prevent the transmission of sound.

All visible parts of the system, including doors, are of either metal or glass. Mullions and transoms are of extruded aluminium and blank panels are of galvanised steel sheet lined with gypsum board. Doors are also steel, with special recessed hinges. The surface finish is acrylic paint. Demountability is catered for in two ways: the whole partition can be removed and re-erected, mullions and all, or the mullions can be left in place while the glass and metal panels are rearranged to suit particular requirements.

The design of partitioning cannot be separated from the design of ceilings. It was sensible, therefore, to employ the same contractor, Naka of Japan, for both. In the event, after the gull-wing proposal had been abandoned, a fairly conventional ceiling design was adopted: ordinary perforated metal panels and fluorescent light-fittings, but with a special fixing that combined ceiling and partition suspension points in one component. Partitions stop at

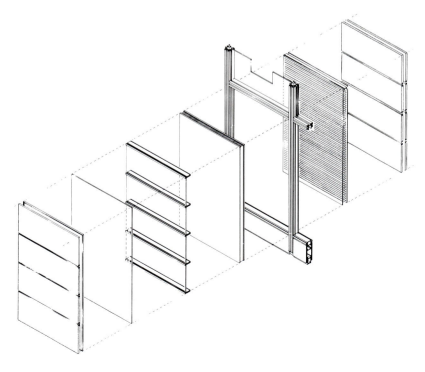

The glass sheet forming the top light of the partition slots directly into the ceiling support rail, with no need for any extra frame.

An early sketch by Norman Foster proposed the use of venetian blinds to provide extra light control at the edge of the building.

ceiling level, so panels have to prevent the transmission of sound between offices. They are therefore lined with plasterboard. The module of the soffit structure was used to humanise the scale of the spaces. Secondary beams, again clad by Naka, are consequently expressed in acrylic-painted steel casings which match, almost perfectly, the Cupples aluminium structure cladding.

One more element of the interior deserves comment, though technically it is a part of the external curtain walling. This is the so-called back-up wall provided to the glass areas on

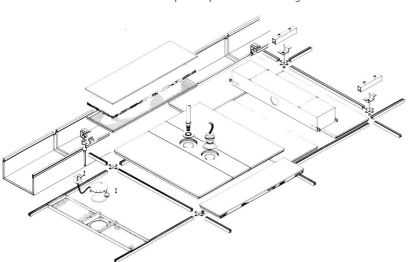

The ceiling system is formed in flat perforated-metal panels backed with acoustic material to avoid the necessity for partition extensions between ceiling and structural soffit. Changeable centre panels in each 1200 x 1200mm module house recessed spotlights, smoke detectors and sprinkler outlets, or luminaires.

three sides of the building, and which gives secondary defence against solar radiation with the use of venetian blinds. The latter are perforated and metallic silver in colour. Blinds can be very untidy and unsightly things, however, easily damaged or disarranged. To preserve some kind of order, therefore, they are kept behind an easily opened panel of slightly tinted glass. Control levers are neatly tucked into recesses in the backs of the mullions with the option of only two blade positions, open or closed. The north elevation has no back-up wall because the external shading devices are more than adequate to cope with the occasional direct sunlight on this side of the building.

Installing blinds in the irregular, L-shaped panels where the structure penetrates the wall was just one of the hundreds of intricate design problems which consumed hours of trial and error and earnest discussion.

Colin Davies

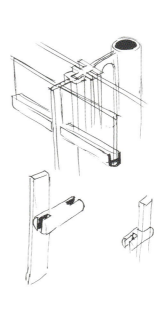
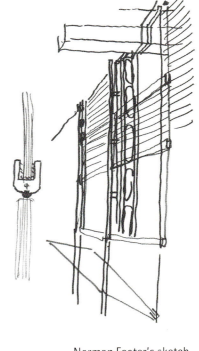

Norman Foster's sketches explore variations for a back-up wall (shown completed above) that sets venetian blinds behind a secondary layer of glass supported off extensions to the curtain wall mullions.

Handrails and Bicycles
by Norman Foster

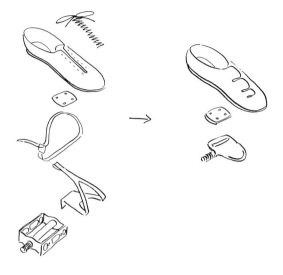

Pedal bindings old and new. Norman Foster's sketch compares the traditional system with its modern counterpart, demonstrating the greater simplicity of the latter.

Earlier this year, I was cycling with my eldest son in France and talking to him about this article. I explained how designing a handrail might be likened to designing a building; it was important in its own right even though it was only one of many thousands of components which must come together to complete the whole building. Looking back through my own sketchbooks shows how design is a continuous process in which individual elements evolve through constant reworking, even while the building itself is under way. It is an approach that requires concern for the smallest elements; no detail should be considered too small. Also, a handrail, like furniture, is subject to constant physical touch by the users of a building and, as such, it might be seen to demonstrate by its quality — or lack of it — an attitude of mind.

I am fascinated by this man-machine relationship and the racing cycle seemed particularly relevant to the conversation. Here too is a design that has evolved gradually over time. For example, the junctions between the tubes that make up a frame have been constantly refined and are now very beautifully resolved.

Thinking back to my teenage obsessions with racing cycles, the frames have, in relative terms, remained almost static compared to the development of add-on accessories — does this have a familiar echo in terms of buildings? However, new developments with streamlined carbon-fibre and composite frames seem to offer exciting new directions. Consider, for instance, the linkage between the foot and the pedal. Up to quite recently it would be normal to bolt a toe-clip on to the pedal, add a grooved plate to the sole of the cycling shoe, slip one into the other and tighten it all up with a leather strap — a loose and clumsy conversion job on the original concept of a pedal. Compare it to the snap-on device which is now becoming commonplace. By a process of integration, the number of components has been halved, enabling a block on the underside of the shoe to engage on to a minimal clip which pivots at the end of the traditional crank. This man-machine link is easily made by literally stepping on to the

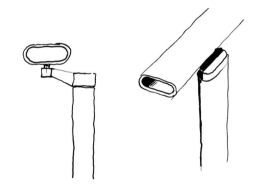

bike. Conversely, by twisting the foot the mechanism releases itself. It is an immensely satisfying combination, both physically to use and aesthetically to contemplate. I can sense similar satisfaction in the process of architectural design; when, for instance, the old order of separate systems to hold up a building and to make it thermally comfortable is superseded by one system of more eloquent simplicity.

Our conversation continued, branching out in a multitude of directions. One thought linked the evolution of these bindings to competitive cycle racing, rather in the way that motor racing has extended the frontiers of aerodynamics, braking systems, or electronic monitoring of the engine; all of which, in turn, have been fed back into the family car. Another thought concerned the question of technology transfer. Surely the initiative for these bindings had come out of the ski equipment industry? Had this been initiated by sports racing with its links to the commercial competition of the open market? Then there was the game of styling and the dangers of muddling true innovation with pastiche. Wasn't the 'go faster' image of tack-on car spoilers like the worst excesses of so-called architectural 'High-Tech' — both equally gratuitous?

Another thought concerned the funding of research and development programmes which are commonplace in industry. We already take for granted the many down-to-earth 'spin-offs' from the space race. Unlike the world of industrial production, however, architectural innovation has to be dependent on one individual project, often conceived in competitive circumstances, to generate new ideas. Such special projects become the architectural equivalent of commercial research and development programmes: if they are sometimes individually expensive, surely they should be measured in the context of the wider total market?

Although I referred earlier to the design of handrails being like a building in miniature, the difference of scale can affect the means of realisation. For the larger-scale structure of a building, the architect is largely dependent on the engineer for modelling, calculations and eventual sizing of its members. A handrail, like furniture, can with advantage lend itself to more empirical methods. I recall on the Willis Faber building our vision of the balustrades around the central escalator-well being a minimal vertical cantilever of toughened glass. The

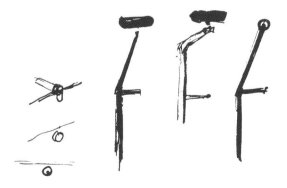

Norman Foster's sketches explored a wide variety of handrail options.

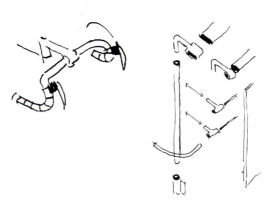

Bicycle handlebars. The way in which interchangeable components can be easily attached to a basic frame was one analogy Foster drew upon in developing his ideas for the handrails.

concept was proved by suspending, pendulum-like, a bag of sand equivalent to the weight of a large adult alongside a mock-up of the proposed balustrade. This was then swung violently to collide with the glass sheet which, despite extreme distortion, withstood the most frenzied attacks by the sandbag. It was dramatic proof to the client, building inspector and ourselves that the idea was sound. The final touch was to add a handrail as protection to the exposed glass edge which, if hit by a sharp object, might have fractured. This handrail was designed to relate to that on the moving part of the escalator

see that harmony between the riders and their machines. This is more than just a physical synergy; there are also visual links between the clothes, equipment and trim. Together, they have the same kind of sparse beauty that I find so moving in the best aircraft.

The start of the race is a flurry of excitement as the competitors commence the first of five circuits, following the motorcycle that will clear the path ahead of them. At the end of the first circuit the leaders speed through the square, a tight group of eight or nine. By the second circuit a clear leader has emerged breaking ahead of the field. As the race progresses his lead increases by seconds, but remarkably he makes it all look so easy; dancing up the hills while the rest seem to strain. It reminds me of those professionals, as diverse as pilots, athletes or even designers, who are so accomplished that they actually make their task look simple — like these new pedal bindings, which look so obvious and direct you wonder why it took so long for them to evolve. But then such simplicity is really quite deceptive.

Aluminium extrusions and castings are combined in the final design to produce a handrail of the utmost simplicity. A threaded connection provides tolerance in the positioning of the handrail itself, though in this photograph — taken during construction — the locking ring has yet to be tightened.

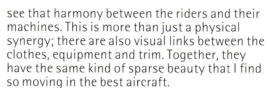

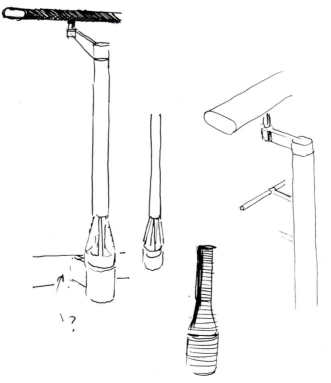

and was slightly soft and generous, encouraging people to lean with their arms on the rail at the edge of the atrium.

I am reminded of Paul MacCready's description of how his man-powered aircraft was designed. Successive versions of this craft were built, each being progressively strengthened where the earlier version had failed under flight testing. Only when a version withstood its required loading was the structure considered correct — any more would have been excessive; anything less, a failure.

The cycle ride meandered in the same way as this conversation until we stopped for a drink in the square of Valbonne. Normally quiet out of the holiday season, the town was alive with the noisy activity of a local cycle race. We had now become spectators, removed from the direct experience of cycling and able to actually

The main banking hall at level 3. The banking counter shown here sweeps across the southern half of the banking hall which is bathed in spring sunshine filtering through the perforated louvres lining the double-height glazing at the edge of the building. Security is assured by the very openness of the space, backed up by discreet closed-circuit television monitoring. The design of the deep counter prevents a clear sight of the cash drawers which are positioned well beyond the reach of the public. For finishes, the simplest palette of materials is used, with only clear, tinted or translucent glass, and polished marble complementing the grey cladding of the structure and wall panels. A lightly-veined grey marble is used for the floor panels, while a flawless black marble is used to form the banking counters, courtesy desks and seats provided for use by the public. The escalators which rise across the atrium to the secondary banking hall at level 5 can be seen at the left of this photograph.

"The normal assumption that a bank be akin to a vault, an impenetrable massive block, is nowhere to be seen. Indeed, the openness seems contradictory to the very idea of security. But safety is inherent in a building in which you can be seen as easily as you can see. In my innocent attempts to photograph the interior, I was stopped before I could even focus the camera. The security of the place is firmly stressed, yet the feeling is not one of Orwellian control."

Maya Lin, *The New Republic*, December 1985

"A more inviting building to the public; those customers who will use it; who will bank there; who will move in, through, up and around it; and those people who will spend their working life there."

Norman Foster, client presentation, March 1984

"That philosophy, that difference if you like, is perhaps best summed up by the fact that it is a building which does not have, in modern terms, an inside and an outside. I don't quite know how best to explain that other than by saying that, perhaps as with certain buildings in the past — whether the cathedrals of the Middle Ages, the temples of China or later developments in Japan — the inside and the outside are at one. You can perceive the one from the other so that you know where you are; you have a sense of orientation."

Norman Foster, client presentation, March 1984

"It is perhaps when one is in motion, when one becomes a part of the ongoing pageant, that one appreciates Hong Kong best. In that sense, Foster – with his vertical circulation systems and his atrium over a plaza that affords a view of the passing populace – has captured the spirit of the city."

Hiroshi Watanabe, *Architecture*, September 1985

Basement level B1, the area just below the plaza, is in effect another banking hall. This handles the larger commercial and cash transactions, where more solid forms of security are preferable, and forms the reception to the safe deposit vault located on the level below. To retain continuity with the main banking hall at level 3, the same materials are used for the flooring and counters while a special metal cladding encases the steel columns and reinforced-concrete structure supporting the plaza. Entrance to the safe deposit vault itself is made through a circular doorway sealed by an impressive steel-cased door, successfully combining the 'moon door' of Chinese tradition with a recognisable symbol of security.

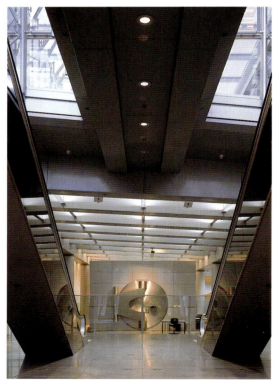

Access to the level B1 banking hall is by escalators that descend from plaza level under glazed lobbies located between the service towers on the east side of the building. Positioned symmetrically to emphasise its symbolic importance, the vault door is over one metre thick and weighs nearly 50 tons, but it has been so balanced that it can be moved with one finger.

This view across the atrium demonstrates the clear open span of the floors. The two banking hall floors, at levels 3 and 5, are clearly identifiable with their curved banking counters. Supporting office accommodation is located on the levels above.

Following considerable research of the furniture systems available, a 'mix and match' method of selection, with elements from different sources, was chosen to meet the Bank's requirements. Standard ranges were used throughout, the only special feature included was the adaptation of desks and chairs to Oriental ergonomic standards. A fixed colour range of black, white or grey was specified as a co-ordinating device.

Using Quickborner Bürolandschaft techniques, research of the Bank's needs had identified 18 standard workstations. The various components of the final system can easily be rearranged to produce dozens of possible variations on each of these basic types which, combined with flexibility of positioning floor outlets, enable the Bank to maximise the efficiency of the overall plan.

"Standing at a point midway up the atrium, one looks from corner to corner through a whole stack of transparent floors, with apparently precious little to hold them all up, apart from some slender 'skyhooks' hanging down in the middle. This 'look no hands' effect is only slightly mitigated by the sight of the mammoth masts and cross-bracing at each end of the atrium, and the trusses overhead."

Chris Abel, *Architectural Review*, April 1986

Chinese attitudes to money and banks are quite different from those of the West, consequently the Hongkong Bank had to fulfil expectations and criteria not usually expected of such projects. At one level, the Bank is an important symbol of Hong Kong's well-being. The demolition of the old headquarters and construction of the new held with it the whole prosperity of the Colony. That the dramatic fall in the economy, that came about with the start of the 1997 negotiations, should coincide with the destruction of the old headquarters was seen by many as inevitable. Fortunately, Hong Kong's fortunes have recovered fully with the completion of the new building.

At a more practical level, for the local account holder, the headquarters has always been the prime symbol of security. Local branches are convenient, but great store is set in having one's account based at the head office. Nearly 80 per cent of all personal accounts are consequently held at 1 Queen's Road Central; accounts which still rely to a large extent on transactions in cash. At peak periods the main banking hall has to be able to accommodate several hundred customers. This photograph was taken a few days before Chinese New Year, always the busiest time of all.

"Not since Frank Lloyd Wright's Larkin building with its use of an interior atrium, has there been a conscious effort on the part of the architect to create a more socially responsive workplace."

Maya Lin, *The New Republic*, December 1985

"We have the capacity for 81 teller positions within the banking hall — which is approximately an acre in area if you count the void space in the centre of the building — and we have the capacity to handle anywhere between 8000 and 10 000 transactions a day. If you talk to the majority of banks in the UK they might do that in a year."

Ray Guy, lecture at the Burrell Museum, January 1986

"The building was an opportunity to totally re-evaluate the nature of high-rise buildings; in humanistic as well as in urban terms, in terms of its performance and in terms of the quality of life that it might offer its occupants."

Norman Foster, lecture at Aspen Design Conference, June 1986

"From day one the Bank's traditional headquarters, with its bosses in offices on the perimeter at the windows and the minions in the corridor, was going to be overturned by Foster's designs. Everyone was to share in the same quality of space; those less well paid were certainly going to get the compensation of the fabulous view. There certainly wasn't a vote for such a strategy and there was inevitably much resistance to it by certain levels of management."

Patrick Hannay, *Architects' Journal*, October 1986

The escalator system was, in part, a response to the Bank's requirement for simple inter-departmental communication between floors.

Though a double-height space, level 11, adjacent the top of the atrium, is laid out as a typical open-plan office floor.

Subfloor services have been planned assuming all work stations will eventually include a vdu linked directly to the Bank's main computer.

One of the building's few executive offices. Wall partitions are lined in Thai silk or translucent *shoji* glass.

The chairman and directors' reception area runs across the centre of level 34, surrounded on all sides by the executive offices. *Shoji* glass partitions combine privacy with the transmission of daylight. Specially-built display cabinets contain items from the Bank's private collection.

Three basic principles were adopted in designing the final layout of each floor: to preserve the transparency and fluidity of the space and avoid corridors and enclosed areas; to allow the maximum number of occupants the benefit of the spectacular views; and to use what cellular offices were required to screen and control points of arrival and passage. In general this was achieved by placing cellular offices at the centre of the building around the escalators, leaving the outer third of each floor open, partitioned only by low screens or large storage units. Internal cellular offices are also usually glazed on their north and south sides, allowing most points on any floor a clear view to the outside and a sense of daylight.

Where partitions are required for security reasons, these are usually glazed so that views are retained from the centre of each floor. Venetian blinds provide privacy as and when necessary.

Formal reception and waiting areas are positioned throughout the office areas, facing the arriving escalators. Low red partitions are used to identify these locations, while planting provides a screen to the more open-plan areas beyond.

249

The 'dining room' at the double-height level 28 provides the building with both its canteen and main reception area. Serving regular meals for senior staff during the day, its size and direct access by lift also make it a practical and generous location for evening functions. All meals are prepared in the main kitchens one floor below, delivery being by a dedicated lift which runs in one of the main liftshafts. This also services the executive reception and dining areas at the top of the building. A bar (seen on the left of this photograph in the distance) is provided in the floor's most southerly bay, under the canopy which marks the setback in the main structure at this level.

"With a quite extraordinarily bold vision Foster redrew much of the vocabulary for movement around and up through a high-rise building. He dismantled the negative sense of segregation created by monofunctional buildings, minimal entrance lobbies and enclosed lifts, and redefined it by overlapping many boundaries between public, semi-public and various hierarchical thresholds of private territories."

Patrick Hannay, *Architects' Journal*, October 1986

"Communication again; the building is the village, the office group is the community, the escalator is a lane. In Foster's imagery, you could call them that."

Stephen Gardiner, *The Listener*, February 1983

"The Hongkong Bank brings architectural structure into line with civil and aeronautical engineering: its family resemblance to suspension bridges and rocket-launching installations is immediately apparent, but it is its extraordinarily spacious interiors and roof-top gardens that may prove to be of even greater interest."

Arthur Drexler, *Three New Skyscrapers*, MOMA exhibition catalogue, January 1983

Hongkong Bank
Conclusion

by Colin Davies

Colin Davies is an architect with 10 years experience in private practice. He now works as a journalist and regularly contributes to a number of British and European architectural journals. He was International Building Press Journalist of the Year and Architectural Journalist of the Year in 1985. He has taught at the Bartlett and Canterbury schools of architecture and frequently lectures on architectural theory and the history of modern architecture. His book *High-Tech Architecture* was published by Editions Hatje and Thames and Hudson in 1988. In July 1989 he takes over the editorship of *The Architects' Journal*.

There is already a place reserved for the Hongkong Bank in every future history of modern architecture. Its stature must be acknowledged, whatever one's critical position. And it will continue to be acknowledged for decades to come.

It could so easily have been just another big commercial building, but for Norman Foster no commission is ever routine. Every new job is an opportunity to innovate. Critics writing at the time of the Bank's completion naturally tended to concentrate on its innovations: its suspension structure, its circulation system, its sun scoop, its extraordinary main entrance, its social spaces, its flexibility, its servicing system, the organisation of its production. But ultimately it will be judged for the contribution it has made to the development of that difficult-to-define discipline that we call architecture.

Any discussion about the Hongkong Bank as architecture must centre on the attitude it

This outlet of the air-conditioning system — here set into one of the marble-faced floor panels of the banking hall levels — stands as a typical example of the high standard of detailing and craftsmanship found throughout the whole building.

takes to technology. In his book *Theory and Design in the First Machine Age,* Reyner Banham suggests that in the twentieth century an unbridgeable gap may have opened up between architecture and technology: "What we have hitherto understood as architecture, and what we are beginning to understand of technology may be incompatible disciplines." Martin Pawley takes up this theme in an article entitled 'Technology Transfer' in *The Architectural Review* of September 1987. Pawley argues that the history of modern architecture is the story of a failed attempt to assimilate technology. Despite the heroic efforts of the pre-war pioneers, technology moved too fast and architecture could not keep up. Many architects are now content to give up the struggle, to separate out the purely artistic element of building and call it architecture. Very few take the opposite approach, denying the validity of any architectural tradition. The history of architecture then becomes the history of 'technology transfer'. As Martin Pawley puts it: "Not only must the trappings of 'artistic assimilation' be abandoned, but even the idea that the process of building design is 'creative', in the fine art as opposed to the engineering sense. In reality, because it is a theory of architecture as economic, multi-sourced element combination, it belongs to a different and more appropriate value system alongside production engineering, automobile, marine and aerospace design."

Is this, then, how we must see the Hongkong Bank — as an exercise in economic, multi-sourced element combination? At first it seems that we must. Most buildings are either crafted from natural materials or — more commonly now — assembled from a limited range of standard manufactured components. But the components of the Hongkong Bank were designed and developed from scratch in laboratories, workshops and factories all over the world. In this respect it is more like a car or an airliner than a building. The search for materials and techniques ranged far beyond the traditional building sources. And can we really describe the rigorous option-testing process as creative in the artistic sense? Surely this kind of methodical research is more akin to engineering than architecture. Norman Foster's personal enthusiasms are well known — the extraordinary beauty of the machinery of man-powered flight, for example. Surely this is the quality he wishes to capture in his designs, not the traditional architectural virtues of monumentality, solidity, permanence and repose.

But there is a flaw in this argument. Lurking behind it is the idea that there is an optimum solution to every building problem and that, once found, it will inevitably look right. It will have its own natural beauty, like Paul MacCready's Gossamer Albatross, the first man-powered aircraft to cross the English Channel, or its successor, Daedalus, that flew the 74 miles from Herakleion to Santorini, in Greece, on 23 April 1988. But this idea — we might call it 'vulgar functionalism' — is mistaken, as Norman

"The phrase 'made in Hong Kong' has not always implied the very best that money can buy. But buildings of this quality do not just happen anywhere, at any time. They happen because a rare combination of circumstances leads them to happen. That does not just mean that an innovative, perfectionist architect was lucky enough to have an innovative, perfectionist client who wanted the best and had enough ready cash to be able to afford it. Nor was the Hongkong Bank merely maintaining a well-established tradition and standard when it once again demanded to have 'the best bank in the world'. With 1997 closing in, and the 'Sleeping Dragon' next door waking up at last to claim its rightful place in the world, and with it the territory of Hong Kong, the whole project was a calculated gesture of self-confidence designed to steady the nerves of Hongkongers for the changes ahead."

Chris Abel, *Architectural Review*, April 1986

Foster himself knows very well. A detailed analysis of the Hongkong Bank reveals that many aspects of the design are far from being optimum solutions in the purely technical or economical sense. Engineers have argued that the structure might have been more efficient as a compression rather than a tension frame. Many difficult constructional details might have been solved at a stroke by simply bringing the structure inside the cladding rather than exposing it on the facade. The chief justification for the tension structure — the retention of the old banking hall — was removed early in the development of the design, and yet the tension structure remained: an elegant solution to a non-existent problem. These are only the most obvious examples of Foster's stubborn refusal to be a slave to the optimum solution. It is as if he is insisting that this is not just engineering; it is architecture.

The differences between architecture and engineering are highlighted when we look at the professional relationship between architects and engineers. A building is a far more complex artefact than a bridge or an electricity pylon or a man-powered aircraft. Spatial, social and contextual considerations usually take priority over structure and this is as true of the Hongkong Bank as of any other building. The engineer cannot begin to make an input to the design until the architect has made some indication, however vague, of the form that the building might take. Some architects are content to make a complete design for a building and then hand it over to be 'engineered'. The result is frequently a structure that, though perfectly reasonable as engineering, is clumsy and incoherent by the standards of architecture. This is of no consequence if the structure has been excluded from the architecture, hidden away behind false facades. But this is not Foster's way. For him structure and form must be integrated. This is not to say that the architecture has become engineering. Rather the engineering has become architecture and is therefore to be judged by architectural criteria.

The same can be said, of course, about mechanical and electrical services. In the Hongkong Bank they are not merely accommodated in the design, but profoundly affect the form of the building. Here again it is not that the building has become a huge piece of mechanical equipment, but that the services installation

The public escalators arriving at the secondary banking hall on level 5. Throughout the design, opposing scales had to be brought together and resolved; the finest details often rubbing shoulders with massive structural elements.

has become architecture. There are many purely functional justifications for the service modules, but it is doubtful if they can be regarded as an optimum solution in purely engineering terms. The module idea is an architectural idea.

It is the fully integrated nature of the Hongkong Bank design — the degree to which it has assimilated technology — that gives it its stature as architecture. Nothing has escaped the architect's control, from the steel frame to the raised floor panels, from the prefabricated service modules to the handrails. This hegemony extends far beyond the drawing-board and the building site into the factories, laboratories and testing stations.

But is 'assimilation' the right word? In the Hongkong Bank, engineering has not merely been assimilated into the discipline of architecture; rather its own architectural potential has been realised. The building demonstrates that the distinction between artistic creativity and engineered creativity is a false one. There is no such thing as an optimum solution; there is always a choice, always another option, and that choice will ultimately be made on architectural grounds. Once we abolish the engineering/architecture distinction we realise that there is just as much architecture in a man-powered flying machine as there is in a Classical temple. Regularity, symmetry, articulation, proportion: these are essentially architectural qualities, but they are not to be found only in buildings.

The conventional view of Norman Foster's architecture, and that of a handful of — mainly British — kindred spirits, is that it borrows imagery from modern engineering. This would seem to relegate architecture to a secondary, parasitical role, dependent upon the creativity of other disciplines. But the reality is that it borrows that imagery only in so far as it is already architectural. Architecture does not have to assimilate technology; it is already inevitably present in technology. Attempts to separate building design from technology in the name of the 'restoration' of architecture — to borrow Martin Pawley's phrase — devalue the currency of architecture. This Foster refuses to do. The Hongkong Bank is neither a retreat from technology into architecture, nor from architecture into an "economic, multi-sourced element combination". Rather it is a reaffirmation of the fundamental human values that architecture represents, and an extension of those values into the world of technology. This is its most important innovation.

"Whenever you finish a project you always want a second bite at it, without exception. But you also know within yourself whether you took advantage of the opportunity, or just let it slip through your fingers. In the case of the Bank I can honestly say that we did take the opportunity and we did not lose the overall expression of an organisational and structural order that we started out with. Yes, it is tragic that the four huge terraces were not turned into gardens. And the reason they weren't was not cost but maintenance — they will probably end up with plants in tubs instead of the full landscaping that we wanted. Yes, it is tragic too that the prefabricated cast-glass floor was lost, with the possibility of flooding a basement with natural sunlight. But what is left is not arbitrary, nor is it mechanistic. It has logic and it has the social idealism that was — in our terms — manifest in our approach from the outset. I am suspicious of an architecture where you say: 'It's like that because it satisfies this checklist of 10 items.' There is always a subjective element in the decision-making process. You get that

with lighting, where it is not solely a question of the quantity of light but of the quality of light; the fact that the needle on a meter flicks over at a certain point is only the beginning of it, not the end.

But despite the things that had to be left out, the building as a whole did come through the programming uncertainties more or less intact. For me one of the most enjoyable things was the number of people, who have been involved with the job over here or were bankers who had seen earlier presentations, who finally saw the real thing and said: 'Look, it's just like the photograph of the model. It's just like you said it would be'."

Norman Foster, *Architectural Review*, April 1986

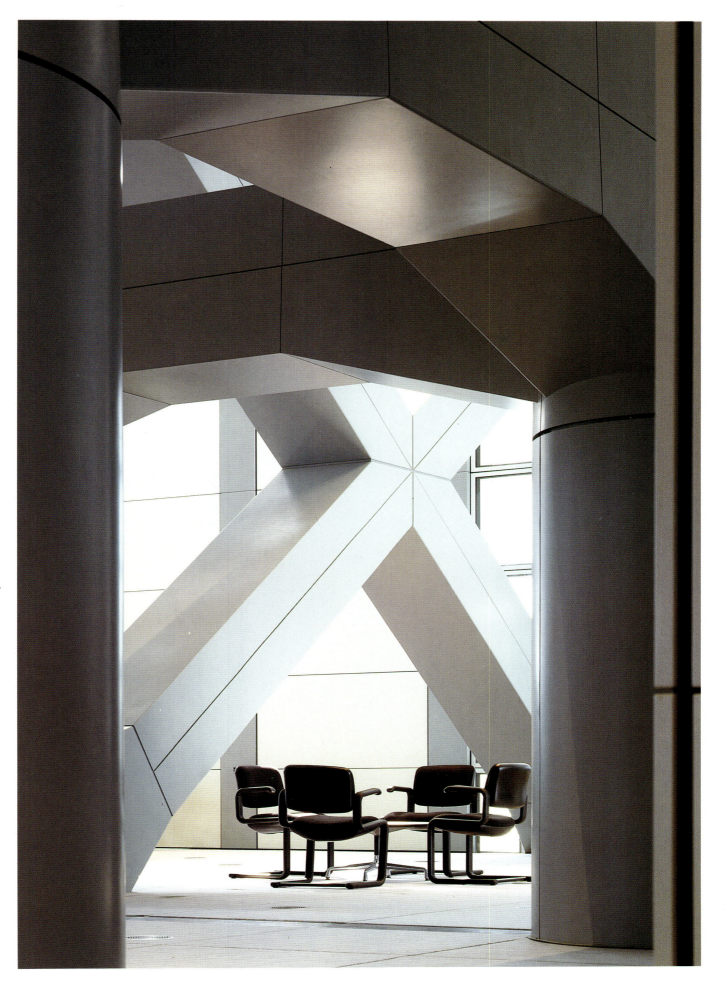

1978–1985 Foster Associates

The years covered in this book mark a time of dramatic change and growth for Foster Associates. This was inevitable given the scale of the Hongkong Bank project alone, but there were a number of other schemes during the latter part of this period which, for various reasons, have not been included in this volume. These projects will appear in Volume 4 which covers the years 1982 to 1989.

By 1981, after 10 years in the Fitzroy Street offices, larger premises had become essential and the move was made to Great Portland Street nearby. The photograph on this page was taken outside the Fitzroy Street offices shortly before they were vacated.

For reasons of organisation, the list given here includes all who were employed by Foster Associates during the years 1978 to 1985, regardless of which projects they worked on or for how long they were part of the office. Clarification may be found in the project profiles on the following pages.

Foster Associates

Directors

Loren Butt
Chubby Chhabra
Spencer de Grey
Norman Foster
Wendy Foster
Martin Francis
Gordon Graham
David Morley
David Nelson
Graham Phillips
Ken Shuttleworth
Mark Sutcliffe

Associates

Roy Fleetwood
Birkin Haward
Mickey Kuch
James Meller
Frank Peacock
Mark Robertson

The Team

Ram Ahronov
Sue Allen
Lucy Annan
Ken Armstrong
Nic Bailey
Gerry Baker
Ralph Ball
Julia Barfield
Vicky Bartlett
Peter Benison
Caroline Benson-Hall
Charlotte Best
Andrew Birds
Michael Borinski
Giuseppe Boscherini
Arthur Branthwaite
David Brindle
Peter Busby
John Calvert
Shireen Carlsen
Colin Catchpole
David Chipperfield
Sarah Christodolo
Geoffrey Clark
Chris Clarke
Simon Colebrook
Michael Conroy
Diane Copeland
Jane Cunningham
Neena Davé
Ian Davidson
Carol Davis
Kim Davis
Rudi de Boer
Craig Downie
Alex Duckworth
Hugh Dutton
Helen Eastwick
Brian Edes
Nick Eldridge
Mike Elkan
Georgina Fenton
Trish Flood
Mimi Francis
Fiona Franek
Garnet Geissler
Howard Gilby
Margot Griffin
Keith Griffiths
Anthony Hackett
Vakis Hadji-Kyriakou
Pauline Hanna
Katy Harris
Bernard Harte
Richard Hawkins
Chris Hennessey
Paul Heritage
Lorraine Hill
Eric Holt
Neil Holt
Richard Horden
Edward Hutcheson
Syd Jeffers
Paul Jones
Paul Kalkoven
Jan Kaplicky
Ben Kern
Angela Ketley
Lisette Khalastchi
Melissa Koch
Nicola Kutapan
Simon Lambert
Valerie Lark
Kamil Latiff
Annette Le Cuyer
Alex Lifschutz
Huat Lim
Steve Martin
Naonori Matsuda
Paul Matthews
Will Matthysen
Michael McColl
Liz McCubbins
Graham MacDougall
Clair Medhurst
Bobbie Michael
Andrew Miller
Nick Morgan
Colin Muir
Max Neal
Anna O'Carroll
Robin Partington
Norman Partridge
Gregoris Patsalosavvis
Richard Paul
Robert Peebles
Tom Politowicz
Janet Procter
Alex Reed
Lois Reich
Rosemary Ringrose
Mark Rock
Sam Rosling
Jane Ross
Fiona Scott-Maxwell
Winston Shu
Alexander Sien
John Silver
Ian Simpson
John Small
Mark Smith
Tony Smith
Mike Stacey
Howard Stephens
Kenji Sugimura
Carolyn Sullivan
Peter Terbüchte
Mary Thum
Rodney Uren
Kathy Ward
Martin Webler
Melior Whitear
Julie Wilkins
Chris Windsor
Arek Wozniak
Angela Young
Ric Zito

As part of the celebrations to mark the official opening of the Hongkong Bank in April 1986, a children's drawing competition was held. This drawing by prize-winner Law Kin Wai, aged 6, later became a Christmas card for Foster Associates' Hong Kong office.

A small liaison office was established in Hong Kong as early as January 1980. Spencer de Grey and Graham Phillips, from the London office, were appointed as resident directors and they were soon joined by locally-based architect Chris Seddon.

During the early part of the project, the main design team was based in London and the Hong Kong office remained few in number. This situation was to change rapidly after the design team moved to Hong Kong in January 1983, shortly after construction had begun on site. Over the next two years the office was to grow to well over 100 with many local staff.

The photograph shown here was taken shortly after handover of the completed building in November 1985, when the office was already decreasing in numbers. The office was closed in December 1986.

Foster Associates Hong Kong

Directors

Spencer de Grey
Roy Fleetwood
Norman Foster
Gordon Graham
David Nelson
Graham Phillips
Chris Seddon
Ken Shuttleworth

The Team

Lucy Annan
Joanlin Au
Peter Basmajian
Fannie Bau
Arthur Branthwaite
Peter Busby
Charles But
Agnes Chan
Alan Chan
C. F. Chan
Jacky Chan
Joshua Chan
Peter Chan
Pusey Chan
Ricky Chan
Silvia Chan
Tony Chan
C. K. Chau
Cecer Cheng

Suzanne Dewar
John Dryden
Timothy Gale
Howard Gilby
Mary Gilby
Ann Greenway
Keith Griffiths
Anthony Hackett
Pauline Hanna
Lau Kwan Hing
Andy Ho
L. K. Ho
Jim Hughes
James Hui
Simon Koon
Peter Kou
Peter Kwan
W. C. Kwan
Kelly Lai
Sheric Lai
Vato Lam

Steven Lee
Edwin Leung
Jeff Leung
Lorena Leung
Thomas Leung
Ivan Li
Alex Lifschutz
Huat Lim
William Lo
Kent Lui
Jenny Ma
Andy Mak
Ricky Mak
K. Y. Man
Kim Man
Naonori Matsuda
Will Matthysen
Andy Miller
Arthur Mok
Judianna Mok
K. K. Mok

Bernard Suen
Kenji Sugimura
Billy Sze
Cydia Tang
S. C. Tang
Simon Tang
Michelle To
Mirenda Tsang
Jennifer Tsui
Sam Tze
Rodney Uren
Winnie Wan
Elizabeth Wang
Fanny Wat
Annie Wong
Arthur Wong
Carrie Wong
David Wong
Edward Wong
Ricky Wu
Alan Yeung

Charles Cheung
Lily Cheung
Mabel Cheung
Maylie Cheung
Samuel Chiu
Ming Lai Chong
Stephen Chou
Clement Chu
Geoffrey Clark
Chris Clarke
Peter Clash
Ian Davidson

Ian Lambot
Hing Lau
Peter Lau
Tony Lau
Bensen Lee
Charles Lee
Hollman Lee
Monita Lee
Peter Lee
Royee Lee

Flora Moon
Carrell Murphy
Anthony Ng
William Ng
Caeser Ngai
Jose Ngo
Richard Paul
Lalitha Rathnayake
David Richards
Sue Robertson
Anthony Robinson
Ellen Sin
David Smith
Danny So

Thomson Yiu
Angela Young
Ali Yu
Cecilia Yu
Charles Yu
P. P. Yu
Ray Yu
Vincent Yu
Andrew Yue

Great Portland Street Office

Client
Foster Associates

Project Team
Chubby Chhabra, Norman Foster, Wendy Foster, Jan Kaplicky, James Meller

Consultants
Mechanical and Electrical Engineer: Foster Associates

Furniture Systems

Client
Foster Associates

Project Team
Ralph Ball, Norman Foster, Paul Heritage, Jan Kaplicky, Arek Wozniak

Nomos Furniture System

Client
Tecno spa

Project Team
Clifford Denn, Norman Foster, Wendy Foster, Martin Francis, Gordon Graham, Janet Procter, John Small, Tony Smith, Arek Wozniak

Consultants
Office Planning: Dieter Jaeger/Quickborner Team

Principal Awards
1987 Premio Compasso d'Oro Award
1987 Design Center Stuttgart Award
1988 Dining table chosen for design collection of the Museum of Modern Art, New York

 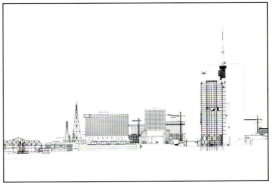 

Whitney Development
with Derek Walker & Associates

Client
Sviluppo Tecnica and SGI/Sogene

Project Team
Norman Foster, Birkin Haward, Neil Holt, David Reddick, Derek Walker

Consultants
Structural Engineer: Felix J. Samuely & Partners
Mechanical and Electrical Engineer: Foster Associates
Real Estate Advisors: Stanley Thea Associates

Humana Competition

Client
Humana Inc

Project Team
Loren Butt, David Chipperfield, Roy Fleetwood, Norman Foster, Wendy Foster, Vakis Hadjikyriakou, Birkin Haward, Neil Holt, Richard Horden, Jan Kaplicky, Annette le Cuyer, Nick Morgan, Winston Shu, Chris Windsor

Consultants
Structural Engineer: Ove Arup & Partners
Mechanical and Electrical Engineer: Foster Associates
Quantity Surveyor: Monk Dunstone Associates

Students' Union

Client
University of London

Project Team
Norman Foster, Birkin Haward, Neil Holt, Chris Windsor

 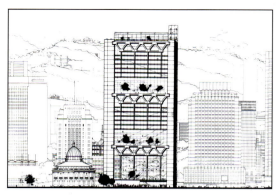 

Billingsgate Market

Client
Furness Withy Ltd

Project Team
Spencer de Grey, Norman Foster, Birkin Haward, Neil Holt, Chris Windsor

Consultants
Structural Engineer: Ove Arup & Partners
Quantity Surveyor: Northcroft Neighbour & Nicholson
Property: Jones Lang Wootton

The Hongkong Bank — Competition Scheme

Client
The Hongkong and Shanghai Banking Corporation

Project Team
Sue Allen, Peter Busby, Loren Butt, John Calvert, Chubby Chhabra, Spencer de Grey, Ian Dowsett, Roy Fleetwood, Norman Foster, Wendy Foster, Birkin Haward, Neil Holt, Richard Horden, Jan Kaplicky, Paul Matthews, David Morley, David Nelson, Graham Phillips, Ken Shuttleworth, Chris Windsor

Consultants
Structural Engineer: Ove Arup & Partners
Mechanical and Electrical Engineer: J. Roger Preston & Partners
Quantity Surveyor: Davis Belfield & Everest/Levett & Bailey/Northcroft Neighbour & Nicholson
Acoustics: Tim Smith Acoustics
Financial Planning: Coopers & Lybrand
Corrosion Protection: Cranfield Institute of Technology

The Hongkong Bank — Chevron Scheme

Project Team
Sue Allen, Loren Butt, Chubby Chhabra, Spencer de Grey, Norman Foster, Wendy Foster, Birkin Haward, Neil Holt, Jan Kaplicky, Paul Matthews, David Nelson, Graham Phillips, Ken Shuttleworth, Chris Windsor

Consultants
Structural Engineer: Ove Arup & Partners
Mechanical and Electrical Engineer: J. Roger Preston & Partners
Quantity Surveyor: Levitt & Bailey/Northcroft Neighbour & Nicholson
Lighting: Bartenbach Wagner Lichttechnische Planung GmbH
Acoustics: Tim Smith Acoustics
Landscaping: Urbis Ltd
Corrosion Protection: Cranfield Institute of Technology
Planning: Dieter Jaeger/Quickborner Team
Wind Engineering: Boundary Layer Wind Tunnel Laboratory, University of Western Ontario
Vibration: Mass Transit Railway
Local Culture: Fitch & Chung
Chinese Culture: Professor Eric Lye
Management Contractor: John Lok/Wimpey Joint Venture

The Hongkong Bank — Final Scheme
1 Queen's Road Central
Hong Kong

Project Team
Lucy Annan, Joanlin Au, Peter Basmajian, Arthur Branthwaite, Loren Butt, Tony Chan, C K Chau, Lily Cheung, Chubby Chhabra, Geoffrey Clark, Chris Clarke, Ian Davidson, Spencer de Grey, Suzanne Dewar, Roy Fleetwood, Norman Foster, Wendy Foster, Timothy Gale, Howard Gilby, Mary Gilby, Gordon Graham, Ann Greenway, Keith Griffiths, Anthony Hackett, Pauline Hanna, Katy Harris, L K Ho, Neil Holt, Jim Hughes, Peter Kou, Peter Kwan, Tony Lau, Charles Lee, Edwin Leung, Thomas Leung, Ivan Li, Alex Lifschutz, Kent Lui, Noa Matsuda, Paul Matthews, Will Matthysen, Andrew Miller, K K Mok, Arthur Mok, Judianna Mok, Nick Morgan, David Nelson, Richard Paul, Graham Phillips, Lalitha Rathnayake, David Richards, Sue Robertson, Anthony Robinson, Christopher Seddon, Ken Shuttleworth, Ellen Sin, David Smith, Kenji Sugimura, Michelle To, Jennifer Tsui, Rodney Uren, Elizabeth Wang, Fanny Wat, Chris Windsor

Consultants
Structural Engineer: Ove Arup & Partners
Mechanical and Electrical Engineer: J. Roger Preston & Partners
Project Co-ordinator: R.J. Mead & Company
Quantity Surveyor: Levett & Bailey/Northcroft Neighbour & Nicholson
Lighting: Claude R. Engle/Bartenbach Wagner Lichttechnische Planung GmbH
Acoustics: Tim Smith Acoustics/Arup Acoustics
Landscaping: Technical Landscapes Ltd
Programming: Project Planning Group
Movement Systems: Jolyon Drury Consultancy
Catering: Cini-Little Associates
Office Planning: Dieter Jaeger/Quickborner Team
Maintenance Systems: Humberside Technical Services
Glazing: Corning Glass
Management Contractor: John Lok/Wimpey Joint Venture

Principal Awards
1986 Structural Steel Award
1986 Marble Architectural Awards, East Asia — Special Mention
1986 R.S. Reynolds Memorial Award
1988 PA Innovations Award (Overseas)

Bibliography

Banham, Reyner, ed., *Design by Choice*, Academy Editions 1982
Benedetti, Aldo, *Norman Foster*, Zanichelli Editore Bologna 1987
Chaslin, François, *Norman Foster*, Electa Moniteur 1986
Foster Associates, eds., *Foster Associates*, RIBA Publications 1979
Foster Associates, eds., *Selected Works 1962-1984*, Whitworth Art Gallery 1984
Foster Associates, eds., *Six Architectural Projects 1975-1985*, Sainsbury Centre for Visual Arts 1985
Foster Associates, eds., *Tre Temi Sei Progetti*, Electa Firenze 1988
Jencks, Charles, *Current Architecture*, Academy Editions 1982
Lambot, Ian, *The New Headquarters for the Hongkong and Shanghai Banking Corporation*, Ian Lambot 1986
Lasdun, Denys, ed., *Architecture in an Age of Scepticism*, Heinemann 1984
Nakamura, Toshio, ed., *Norman Foster*, A&U Special Publication 1988
Suckle, A., ed., *By Their Own Design*, Whitney 1980
Sudjic, Deyan, *New Architecture: Foster Rogers Stirling*, Thames & Hudson 1986

General Interest
Architects' Journal, 21 April 1982, *Fast Track Response* by Birkin Haward and Loren Butt
Architects' Journal, 30 March 1983, *Gold Standard* by John McKean
Architectural Record, mid-August 1979, *Industrial Materials and Techniques become Art at Foster Associates*
Architectural Record, August 1985, *The Metal Skin in Technology of Foster Associates* by Darl Rastorfer
Architecture and Urbanism, September 1975 Special Issue
Architecture and Urbanism, February 1981 Special Issue
L'Architecture d'Aujourd'hui, November/December 1973, *Foster et Associés*
L'Architecture d'Aujourd'hui, February 1986, *Norman Foster* by Marc Emery
Beaux Arts, February 1986, *Norman Foster* by Martin Meade
Blueprint, May 1984, *Norman Foster* by Martin Pawley
Building, 18 March 1983, *Glass by Foster* by Robert Matthews
Building Design, 3 February 1978, *Powerhouse* by Stephanie Williams
Casabella, No. 375 1978, *Assembly without Composition*
Connaissance des Arts, November 1983, *Technologie de Pointe pour une Architecture Optimiste* by Philip Jodidio
The Face, February 1983
Interiors, May 1984, *British Technique* by Jose Manser
Nas-Dom, April 1983 Special Issue
New Society, 9 November 1972, *LL/LF/LE/v. Foster* by Reyner Banham
Progressive Architecture, February 1979, *Modernism Reconstituted*
RIBA Journal, June 1970, *Exploring the Client's Range of Options* by Norman Foster
RIBA Journal, January 1978, *Designing the Means to Social Ends* by Barbara Goldstein
Space Design, No. 3 1982 Special Issue
Wonen Tabk, November 1982, *Appropriate Technology, Variaties op de Services Shed, Een Geloofwaardige Rol voor de Architect* by Jan Dirk, Peereboom Volker and Frank Wintermans

Great Portland Street Office
Interiors (USA), May 1984

The Tecno System
L'Arca, January/February 1987, *A New Line of Office Furniture* by Anty Pansera
Architectural Review, February 1987, *Design Review* by Penny McGuire
L'Architecture d'Aujourd'hui, February 1986

Blueprint, February 1987, *Nomos Reinvents the Office* by Deyan Sudjic
Designers' Journal, January 1987, *Nomos – Three Points of View* by Lance Knobel, Rodney Cooper and Michael Glickman
Domos, January 1987

Whitney Museum
Architectural Record, mid-August 1979, *Interchangeable Panels: A Foster Motif*
Architecture and Urbanism, October 1980
Building Design, 27 July 1979, *British Teamwork Wins Out* by Deyan Sudjic
International Architect, No.2 1979

Humana Competition
Architectural Design, August 1982, *British Architects*
Building Design, 18 June 1982, *A Human Face for the High Rise* by Linda Relph-Knight
Techniques et Architecture, August/September 1984, *La réponse de Norman Foster* by Alain Pelissier

Billingsgate Market
L'Architecture d'Aujourd'hui, February 1986

The Hongkong Bank
Abitare, April 1986, *Grattcielli a Hong Kong* by Fulvio Irace
Actuel, No.73 November 1985
L'Arca, January/February 1987, *Foretaste of the future* by Olivier Boissière
Arch+, May 1987
Architects' Journal, 22 October 1986, *Lloyd's and the Bank* by Patrick Hannay
Architects' Journal, 29 October 1986, *A Tale of Two Architectures* by Patrick Hannay
Architects' Journal, 18 November 1987, *Design for Asset Management* by Derek Allcard and Jolyon Drury
Architectural Design, March/April 1981
Architectural Review, May 1981, *Hongkong Bank* by Jonathan Glancey
Architectural Review, April 1986 Special Issue
Architecture, September 1985, *Steel Corseted Bank Tower gives the City a Needed Landmark* by Hiroshi Watanabe
L'Architecture d'Aujourd'hui, October 1982
L'Architecture d'Aujourd'hui, October 1986
Architecture Intérieure/Créé, April/May 1986
Architecture and Urbanism, October 1983, *Hongkong Bank* by Kenji Sugimura
Architecture and Urbanism, June 1986, Special Issue
Arup Journal, Winter 1985, Special Issue
Blueprint, November 1985, *Re-inventing the Skyscraper* by Deyan Sudjic
Building, 17 June 1983, *Foster's Hongkong Bank* by Brian Waters
Building, 16 September 1983, *Like a Rocket to the Moon* by Brian Waters
Building, 16 December 1983, *Summing up the Hongkong Bank* by Stephanie Williams
Building, 6 July 1984, *Teamwork Pays Dividends* by Brian Waters
Building, 6 September 1985, *Final Account* by Brian Waters
Building Design, 13 February 1981, *Money in the Bank*
Building Design, 11 February 1983, *The Six Billion Dollar Bank*
Building Technology & Management, March 1985, *Fast Track* by P.J. Wright
Construction Today, July 1985, *Hongkong Bank Finishes in Credit*
El Croquis, November/January 1986/1987
Detail, July/August 1986
Deutsche Bauzeitschrift, September 1986
Deutsche Bauzeitung, May 1986
Discovery (Hong Kong), July 1985, *Building for the Future* by Gillian Chambers
Domus, July/August 1986
GA Document, 16 November 1986, Special Issue
Industria delle Costruzioni, October 1985
L'Information Immobilière, No.34 Autumn 1987, *Hong Kong: the Bank* by Melinda Gee
Lichtbericht, No.24 1986
Mimar Architecture in Development, March 1988
MOMA Catalogue, January 1983, *Three New Skyscrapers*
Le Moniteur, 21 September 1984, *Hong Kong: La Tour du Futur*
New Civil Engineer, 18 March 1982, *Founding the World's Most Exciting Building* by Hugh Ferguson
Nikkei Architecture, 7 May 1984
Nikkei Architecture, 24 February 1986
Process Architecture, 15 September 1986, Special Issue
Progressive Architecture, March 1986, Special Issue
RIBA Journal, June 1984, *Foster in Hong Kong* by Brian Waters
Techniques et Architecture, November 1983
Techniques et Architecture, June/July 1987, *Foster à Hong Kong* by Alain Pelissier
Vision, January 1983, *Hongkong Bank Headquarters* by Suresh Shamah
Vision, July 1985, Special Issue

Credits

The editor extends his thanks to all those who helped in compiling and preparing the material used in this volume: the clients, consultants, contractors and members of Foster Associates past and present who gave freely of their time and knowledge, and the commissioned writers who shaped and gave meaning to the considerable amount of information that was gathered in the process.

Special mention must also be made of those whose contribution to the production of this book has proved equally invaluable. At Foster Associates, Katy Harris for all her help in sourcing and giving order to the drawings and photographs, ably assisted by Gillian Charman, Sheila Jack and Victoria Reis. Jennifer Riedel patiently typed the captions which, together with all the main texts, were exhaustively sub-edited and proof-read by Julia Beever and Lesley Chisholm. In Hong Kong, production management was supervised by Alice Ng of Watermark Studio.

My thanks to one and all.

Drawings and Photographs

As far as possible, only contemporary material has been used in preparing the layouts for this volume. On the rare occasions that original drawings were found to be unsuitable for publication, these were redrawn in the original style by Huw Thomas.

For the sake of simplicity the drawings and photographs have not been individually credited; on those pages where the work of more than one draftsman or photographer is shown, the number in brackets indicates only how many pictures on that page can be assigned to each contributor. All attempts have been made to credit each image correctly. Where this has proved impossible, credit has been given under the more general name of Foster Associates, from whose extensive library the majority of this material was selected.

Drawings

Otl Aicher 53(1)
Ove Arup & Partners 66 79 217(1)
Nic Bailey 65(2)
Phil Bonzon 223(2) 224(1)
Bundesanstalt für Flugsicherung 96(1)
Central Office of Historic Monuments Norway 63(1) 64
David Chipperfield 88/89 259(1)
Roy Fleetwood 142/143 260
Foster Associates 13 14 15(1) 36 37 40 41 52 67 102(1) 104/105 109 110(1) 145(5) 153(1) 158(1) 159(2) 171(1) 183 192(2) 219(1) 224(2)
Foster Associates Hong Kong 202 203 204 205 207 220(1) 226/227 232(1) 233 234 238(1) 239(1)
Norman Foster 12 30 32 33 34 38 39 42 43 44 45 46 47 53(2) 56 60 61 68 69(2) 72(1) 73 74 75 76 77 80 81 82 83(1) 84 85 86 87 93 102(1) 103(2) 106(1) 128 129 130 131 132 133 134 135 136 137 138 139 140 141 148 149 154(2) 156(1) 162 163 164 165 166 167 168(1) 192(3) 194(2) 199(1) 228(1) 229 239(3) 240 241
Michael Goodman/Scientific American 62 63(2)
Anthony Hackett 172(1) 173 206 220(1) 225
Vakis Hadjikyriakou 88/89 92 111 259(1)
Birkin Haward 69(2) 72(1) 100 101(1) 106(1) 107 108 110(1) 130/131 157 159(1) 168(1) 172(1) 188 193(2) 194(1) 195 198 199(1) 236(1)
HMT Consort (HK) Ltd 208
Richard Horden 88/89 90 91 142/143 144 159(1) 189(1) 260
Helmut Jacoby 70 158(1) 193(1) 238(1) 259(1)
Jeppesen & Co GmbH 94 95 96(1)
Jan Kaplicky 83(1) 150 151 152(3) 155(1) 158(1) 169
Ben Kern 200/201
Koo Pak Ling 145(1)
Ian Lambot 189(1) 221 228(2)
Law Kin Wai 257
Library of Congress of USA 63(2)
Kent Lui 199(1)
Naonori Matsuda 237
David Morley 156(1)
David Nelson 232(2) 235 236(1)
Richard Paul 223(1)
J. Roger Preston & Partners 232(1)
Tony Pritchard 15(1)
Dave Reddick 71(5)
Ken Shuttleworth 146 152(1) 153(1) 154(2) 155(1) 156(2) 170 171(3) 172(3) 214/215
John Small 48 49
Kenji Sugimura 209
Tecno spa 55 58
Huw Thomas 65(2) 71(2) 97 99 101(3) 103(1) 130/131 216 217(1) 219(1)

Photographs

Architectural Association/Parsons 14
Architectural Press/Jules Schick 17
Ove Arup & Partners 67(1)
Richard Bryant/Arcaid 41(1) 241 253 255
Trustees of the Chatsworth Settlement 64(2)
Cupples Products 18(1) 212(2) 213(1)
Daily Telegraph/Mike Dobel 18(1)
Daily Telegraph/Adam Woolfitt 13(1)
Richard Davies 8 15 19(1) 20(8) 22(6) 23(12) 24(6) 25(8) 26 27 29(3) 30 31 35(4) 36(5) 37(1) 39 40 41(3) 46(1) 48(1) 49 50 51(5) 53(1) 55 59(1) 66 67(1) 72 73 86 93 98 99 106 107 113(1) 142 144 147(1) 151 153 155(1) 169 173 190 191 192 193 196 197(7) 209(2) 210 211(2) 212(2) 216 218(3) 222(2) 223 224(1) 225(1) 227 229(1) 233 234(1) 236 237(2) 256 258(1) 259 260
Design Council/Gestetner 11(1)
John Donat 13(1) 164 166 168
Richard Einzig/Arcaid 12(1)
Roy Fleetwood 213(1) 224(1) 228 229(1)
Foster Associates 11(1) 12(1) 16 28 29(2) 36(1) 37(1) 44 47(1) 52 53(1) 67(1) 78 79 146 150 194 197(1) 211(1) 234(1) 235(2) 238
Norman Foster 35(1) 147(2) 189 209(1) 229(2) 237(2)
General Panel Systems 11(1)
Lee Hall 63 64(1)
Birkin Haward 155(1)
HMT Consort (HK) Ltd 208
Alastair Hunter 248(1) 249(1)
Ken Kirkwood 20(2) 21 22(1) 23(1) 24(5) 25(2) 41(1) 65 258(1)
Ian Lambot 22(2) 25(1) 38 114/115 116/117 118/119 120 121 122/123 124 125 126/127 128 174/175 176(5) 177(1) 178 179 180 181(3) 183 184 186/187 197(1) 198 199 218(1) 219 220 221 222(1) 225(1) 230(5) 231(2) 234(1) 235(2) 239 242/243 244 245 246/247 248(3) 249(2) 250/251 252 254 261
Malcolm Last 225(1)
Bruce Nicoll/Blueprint 51(1)
John Nye 113(6) 161 176(3) 177(6) 181(1) 182 185 230(1) 231(1) 237(1) 257
John Small 54
Brian Brace Taylor 62
Tecno spa 19(1) 43 48(1) 53(1) 56 57 58 59(1) 258(1)
University of Western Ontario 217
Arek Wozniak 46(3) 47(2)